Ladino on the Internet

Ladino on the Internet constitutes the first critical and systematic account written in English on the online revitalisation of Ladino.

This book conclusively demonstrates that nowadays the global Ladino-speaking community connects first and foremost online, which calls for a full, comprehensive examination of the web-based development of the Sephardic diaspora (including that of Ladino) as a qualitatively different stage, termed 'Sepharad 4' in this monograph.

Drawing upon the methodological framework of Revivalistics and including a comparative analysis with similar initiatives apropos Yiddish, this volume analyses case studies including YouTube digital archives, social media platforms, language learning apps, online schools, and Ladino on Netflix, plus on Web 3.0 platforms.

This monograph will appeal to scholars and postgraduate students seeking to familiarise themselves with the use of technological tools to further the revitalisation of endangered languages such as Ladino.

Carlos Yebra López (PhD from New York University) is an Assistant Professor in Spanish Linguistics at California State University, Fullerton. He has worked as a Ladino instructor at the Oxford School of Rare Jewish Languages, and as a CEO of Ladino 21 Community Interest Company, a public outreach initiative and digital archive devoted to the grassroots documentation of Ladino.

Routledge Studies in Jewish Languages
Series Editors: Lily Kahn *(UCL)* and Aaron D. Rubin *(University of Georgia)*

About the Series

Routledge Studies in Jewish Languages is dedicated to scholarly research into the multiplicity of languages that have been spoken and written by Jews worldwide throughout history. Jewish languages are a record of the rich, enduring history of the Jewish people over the last three thousand years and are attested in the ancient Mediterranean world, medieval western Europe, the Middle East and North Africa, Central Asia, Eastern Europe, the Ottoman Empire, and beyond. From a linguistic perspective, Jewish languages provide an unparalleled opportunity to explore the effects of language contact. Nearly all Diaspora Jewish languages reflect an ongoing relationship between Hebrew and a co-territorial non-Jewish vernacular. They can also explain the development of non-Jewish sister languages, such as medieval French and German. From a cultural perspective, Jewish languages offer unique insights into Jewish life. Today, Jewish languages can serve as instructive case studies of language endangerment, language shift, and revitalisation, as the Internet and technologies open new avenues for minority languages to flourish among heritage speakers. Routledge's Studies in Jewish Languages is the first book series focused entirely on the scholarly examination of this vibrant linguistic activity.

Ladino on the Internet
Sepharad 4
Carlos Yebra López

Find out more about the series here: https://www.routledge.com/Routledge-Studies-in-Jewish-Languages/book-series/RSJL

Ladino on the Internet

Sepharad 4

Carlos Yebra López

Routledge
Taylor & Francis Group
LONDON AND NEW YORK

First published 2025
by Routledge
4 Park Square, Milton Park, Abingdon, Oxon, OX14 4RN

and by Routledge
605 Third Avenue, New York, NY 10158

Routledge is an imprint of the Taylor & Francis Group, an informa business

This work was supported by the UKRI [grant number EP/X024652/1] as part of the project *Digital Jewish Revivalistics: The Case of Ladino (Ladino Revival).*

British Library Cataloguing-in-Publication Data
A catalogue record for this book is available from the British Library

ISBN: 978-1-032-75365-2 (hbk)
ISBN: 978-1-032-75368-3 (pbk)
ISBN: 978-1-003-47366-4 (ebk)

DOI: 10.4324/9781003473664

Typeset in Times New Roman
by codeMantra

To the migrants who have made language(s) their homeland(s)

Contents

Acknowledgements

Although I am listed as the sole author of this book, this volume is in fact the result of prolonged and effective teamwork. I owe a debt of gratitude to many individuals who contributed to its creation.

1 Rachel Bortnick, who accepted me into *Ladinokomunita*. Benni Aguado, whose life story provided me with the inspiration to perfect my Ladino, learn Solitreo and start *Ladino 21*. Alejandro Acero Ayuda, for his friendship and support since the early days, particularly as the co-founder and co-director of *Ladino 21*. Finally, all the participants and collaborators of *Ladino 21*, particularly Malka Fradkin, Aldo Sevi, Eliezer Papo, Zeljko Jovanovic, Karen Gerson Şarhon, Roz Kohen, Nissim Ashkenazi, Albert Israel, Yvette Bürki, Kent Fredholm, and Joël-Esther Verard.
2 Alex Rawlings, who introduced me to Ghil'ad Zuckermann's *Revivalistics* within the context of a conference organised by Richard Simcott (The Language Event, held at Edinburgh in 2020), for whose support I am also deeply grateful.
3 Ghil'ad Zuckermann himself, for our friendship and intellectual dialogue.
4 Julian Weiss, who was kind enough to introduce me to Lily Kahn.
5 The UCL Hebrew and Jewish Studies Department. I am most indebted to Lily Kahn, for her supervision. I am also grateful to Seth Anziska, Sonya Yampolskaya, and Sonia Gollance for helping me settle in London in the early days of this project. Likewise, I am appreciative of Sima Beeri and Beruriah Wiegand (Oxford) for teaching me Yiddish, and would like to thank my department colleagues Francois Guesnet and Shirli Gilbert for the research dissemination opportunities. Finally, I am very grateful to Michael Berkowitz for his indefatigable friendship, support, and guidance.
6 Everybody I interviewed as part of this manuscript, i.e., Aldo Sevi, Ethan Marcus, Richard Howeson, Leah Mundy, Liliana Benveniste, Judith Olszowy-Schlanger, Julio Alejandro, İzzet Bana, and Shmuel Refael, as well as the participants of my online survey on Ladino on Netflix.
7 My UCL Ladino students, Joël, Haoran, Albert, Yuanpin, Kelly and Rose, for giving me the opportunity to teach Ladino in person for the first time, as well as all my UCL Ladino and Haketia Summer School students.

8 The Oxford School of Rare Jewish Languages, particularly its director, Judith Olszowy-Schlanger, the staff (Celeste, Madeleine, Priscilla), and all the students from my Ladino and Haketia courses there.
9 Yordanka Dimcheva, for motivating me to write this and many more books, and having as much faith in me and my work as I do.
10 My family, for I know they will still be there when the dust settles.

This work was supported by the UKRI [grant number EP/X024652/1] as part of the project *Digital Jewish Revivalistics: The Case of Ladino (Ladino Revival)*.

Introduction

Theoretical Framework, Scope, Methodology, and Chapters

Theoretical Framework and Scope

In a globalised world where approximately 96% of the population speaks 4% of the total number of languages, digital revitalisation is becoming increasingly urgent to prevent heritage loss and foster worldwide diversity and inclusivity.

Ladino, i.e., the language spoken by the Jews that were expelled from the Iberian Peninsula in 1492, constitutes a case in point. The fact that this language is currently classified by UNESCO as "severely endangered" (see UNESCO 2003), featuring a few thousands of speakers (51,000 – Ethnologue 2024) and minimal intergenerational transmission, makes its digital revitalisation particularly urgent.

Ladino on the Internet: Sepharad 4 constitutes the first critical and systematic account written in English on the online revitalisation of Ladino.

It challenges the academic and popular assumption that (i) in the 21st century, Ladino continues to be spoken and written fundamentally offline, and that (ii) the online realm is supposedly a more or less passive receptacle of offline linguistic activities, or else a (mostly anecdotal) supplement to them. For example, in his survey chapter on Ladino (Bunis 2017, 2018), David Bunis, arguably the most competent Ladino linguist alive, devotes just two paragraphs and one page, respectively, to online resources in this language and the role of the Internet in its documentation and revitalisation, not covering any Ladino-speaking platforms created since the 2010s (see below).

By contrast, this volume conclusively demonstrates that nowadays the global Ladino-speaking community connects first and foremost online, which is where the bulk of the linguistic interaction of its members takes place, thus constantly reshaping language and community in dialogical fashion. This trend, which remains vastly underexamined and is likely to experience an exponential growth in the years to come, calls for a full, comprehensive examination of the online development of the Sephardic diaspora (including that of Ladino) as a qualitatively different stage.

Drawing upon his own breakdown of the history of Ashkenaz and Yiddish in 1973 (2008, 124–74), Max Weinreich subdivided the history of the Sephardic diaspora into three stages (Sepharad 1–3). This breakdown has been generously adopted in the subsequent scholarly literature apropos Sepharad (Hassán 1995; Hernández

DOI: 10.4324/9781003473664-1

González 2001; Šmid 2002; Álvarez López 2017). For the purpose of this book, I have adopted the above distinction while also expanding on it to encompass the Internet, thus summarising the history of the Sephardic diaspora (including its continuous, reciprocal interaction and exchange with Ladino) into four stages: three offline ones (Sepharad 1–3), plus an online one, which I call 'Sepharad 4.'

Sepharad 1 designates the period of Jewish settlement in the Iberian Peninsula (Sepharad), from the 1st century CE until 1492. This stage encompasses the early emergence of proto-Ladino as a co-territorial dialectical variety (resulting from the interaction of Jewish immigrants that had just arrived in Romanised Iberia and non-Jewish Romance speakers) (Bunis 2019), as well as the subsequent development of Ladino as a word-for-word calque for liturgical purposes since the 13th century (Sephiha 1977).

Sepharad 2 covers the period from 1492 to the mid-20th century and refers to the Sephardic diaspora in the Mediterranean basin. During this stage Ladino emerged as a koine (i.e., developed organically from the interaction between two or more closely related linguistic forms) around the Mediterranean basin (Papo 2020b; Yebra López 2021c, 96–7), crystallising into a co-territorial diasporic vernacular. Here we can distinguish between two types of vernaculars, i.e., Haketia (Western, focused on North Morocco) and Judezmo (also known as '*djudyó*' and '*djidyó*') (Eastern, in the lands of the Ottoman Empire, particularly current Turkey and Greece). For formal purposes, the speakers of each of these vernaculars deployed a common, mutually intelligible written register (Judeo-Spanish) (Bentolila 2008) (see Chapter 1).

Sepharad 3 designates the global diaspora of Sephardim since around the 1950s, particularly into Israel and the Americas, and as motivated by the Holocaust (Europe), the Turkish wealth tax (1940s), the foundation of the State of Israel (1948), and the Istanbul pogroms (1955) (see Chapter 5). This stage witnessed the evolution of Ladino into a post-co-territorial diasporic vernacular, geolectal boundaries beginning to blur, thus heralding the digital acceleration of this process as part of Sepharad 4.

Sepharad 4 refers to the online articulation of the Sephardic diaspora, and it is also characterised by the emergence and evolution of Ladino as a cyber-(post)vernacular. This period started in the 21st century with the implementation of Ladino on the Internet, and can be divided according to the latter's web versions, namely: 1.0, 2.0, and 3.0. Web 1.0 is the mostly read web stage (1990s to present). Web 2.0, which is the current hegemonic version, designates the participative, multisemiotic (vernacular/postvernacular)[1] and multimodal social web (including the linguistic, visual, aural, gestural, and spatial modalities) (2000s to present). Lastly, Web 3.0, which still finds itself at an embryonic stage, is premised on decentralisation, blockchain technologies, and token-based economics (2010s to present).

Committed to bringing their cultural and linguistic struggle into the online sphere, a handful of Ladino activists from both within and outside the Ladino-speaking community have launched various innovative projects. These include language revitalisation efforts such as online repositories of Sephardic culture, email lists, social media groups, WhatsApp communities, Ladino learning apps, Zoom classes, and even YouTube channels featuring feminist rock and hip-hop songs in this language.

By contrast, in the current scholarly literature the revitalisation of Ladino on the Internet has only been addressed in the form of book chapters and journal articles (rather than a comprehensive book). Out of these sources, only two journal articles (Held 2010; Yebra López 2021c) and a book chapter (Bürki 2021) have discussed the conceptualisation of Ladino interactions on the Internet as a potentially new stage in the sociolinguistic development of Ladino.

Held (2010) was the first to theorise Ladino virtual communities, which she defined as "a territory where a culture may be revitalized after having faced a state of severe decline" (84). Held further underscored the significance of Ladino as the primary agent of assemblage within a context characterised by worldwide migration and dispersion (Yebra López 2021c), facilitating the cohesion of its global speaker community:

> The new Sephardi courtyard forming on the Internet is based primarily upon the ethnic language: the vehicle for the recreation of a fragmented offline personal and collective Sephardi identity. Thus, a replacement for the Sephardi homeland (or rather the system of homelands that Sephardi Jews yearn back to, such as Eretz Israel and Jerusalem, Spain, the Ottoman Empire, the State of Israel–to name just a few) is being constructed.
>
> (83–4)

To conceptualise this innovation, Held introduced the notion of 'Digital Home-Land (DH-L),' insisting in its characterisation as an online surrogate compensating for the imminent loss of traditional Sephardic physical homelands while also acknowledging its uniqueness:

> Digital Home-Land (DH-L): a virtual territory in which long-lost offline communities, such as the Sephardi one in our case, are reconstructed online … a virtual replacement for the actual Sephardi 'place' leading to the creation of a contemporary reconstructed Sephardi personal and collective memory that could not have existed otherwise or anywhere else.
>
> (91/3

The inclusion of a hyphen in 'Home-Land' introduced a sense of contingency into the presumed continuity between the *home* and the *land*, rightly implying that members of this community no longer necessitated a shared physical territory delimited by political boundaries (the State) to foster a collective national identity (cf. Anderson 1983).

Notwithstanding its pioneering merit, Held's article was published before the development of either Web 2.0 or Web 3.0 platforms in Ladino (to which the bulk of my volume is devoted). Consequently, it only included as case studies platforms that are characteristic of the Web 1.0., i.e., email lists, notably *Ladinokomunita* (see Chapter 1).

The remaining book chapters (Bunis 2017, 2018; Schwarzwald 2019) and journal articles (Brink-Danan 2011; Bunis 2016; Pons 2018), plus some online talks, magazine articles, and news, have only dealt with specific platforms (rather than a holistic conceptualisation of Ladino on the Internet), mostly *Ladinokomunita* (Carrión 2012; Santacruz 2019). Web 2.0 platforms have received much less attention: Yvette Bürki discussed Facebook groups in Ladino (Bürki 2021) and has recently mentioned further Facebook groups, Twitter accounts, YouTube channels, and the uTalk course (2024); Kenan Cruz Çilli (2021) and Paula Jacobs devoted a few paragraphs to Ladino on Zoom. Lastly, Web 3.0 platforms are virtually absent.

By contrast and for the first time in the scholarly literature, in my 2021 article, I outlined the main Ladino-speaking online platforms over the 1999-to-2020 period, including *Ladino 21* (Chapter 2), *Los Ladinadores* (Chapter 3), and *Enkontros de Alhad* (Chapter 4), noting the significance of these recent developments. Furthermore, I argued that the proliferation of Sephardic online communities in the second decade of the 21st century had made necessary for us to distinguish between basic Ladino-speaking online groups, on the one hand, and genuine Ladino-speaking genuine communities, on the other, restricting the use of the term 'Digital Home-Land' to the latter. Unlike the former, the latter are premised on a process of linguistic ethnicisation (Linke 2004; Eisenlohr 2006) and a sense of home, which in turn necessitates four aspects: (i) adopting a Ladino-mostly or Ladino-only policy, (ii) giving voice to Sephardim in decision-making processes, (iii) transcending a one-to-many interaction paradigm, and (iv) including name-and-place signatures (Yebra López 2021c, 110–1).

Indeed, the key insight that the online realm constitutes the primary arena for the revitalisation of Ladino has not only inspired my intellectual endeavours, but also my activist work since I first encountered this language in 2014. It happened in Jerusalem, Israel, as I was presenting my edited volume *Shoah and the Ethics of Citizenship* (2014) in Yad Vashem, The World Holocaust Remembrance Centre. As part of the program of events, I was invited to a concert by Sephardic singer Yasmin Levy. As an L1 Spanish speaker (born and raised in Zaragoza, Spain), when Levy began to intone *Adio' Kerida* ['Goodbye, Dear Love'] (see Chapter 5), I quickly detected a number of inconsistencies vis-à-vis 'modern' Spanish. After inquiring about aspects such as the absence of 's' in *Adio*' (as opposed to the Spanish *Adios*) and the conjugation of the second person singular of the past tense ('*amargates*,' as opposed to the Spanish '*amargaste*'), somebody in the audience informed me that this language was actually not Spanish, but Ladino.

Upon my return to Spain, I conducted preliminary research on this linguistic variety, which led me to discover the *Ladinokomunita* email list (Chapter 1). After a brief period of careful observation and modest participation, I reached New York City in the Fall of 2015 to start my PhD studies at New York University. Mindful that there was a sizeable community of speakers in town, I sent an email to *Ladinokomunita*, asking whether anybody would be interested to meet in person to *echar lashon* ['to talk' – in Ladino]. L1 speaker Benni Aguado graciously accepted my invitation. It became apparent to me during our interaction that Aguado felt deeply honoured that I was expressing an interest in acquiring proficiency in 'his' language, as he fervently sought to safeguard its legacy. After discussing this experience with my hometown and alma mater friend and colleague Alejandro Acero Ayuda, we concluded that establishing a YouTube channel dedicated to showcasing Ladino-language content could serve as an auspicious inaugural step towards the preservation and dissemination of Ladino culture and language on the Internet.

As a result, in 2017 we co-founded *Ladino 21*, a digital archive devoted to grassroots documentation of the contemporary Sephardic diaspora through interviews (folk)stories, jokes, readings, and songs produced in the 21st century (see Chapter 2). Two years later, I co-translated the corpus of a Ladino course for the language learning platform uTalk (see Chapter 3). Then in 2020 I co-founded and became the CEO of the non-profit *Ladino 21 Community Interest Company* (non-executive director: Alejandro Acero; external advisor: Dr. Aldo Sevi), a public outreach initiative devoted to the creation and dissemination of digital solutions (archives, apps, courses, workshops) to further the preservation of Ladino in the 21st century. Lastly, since 2021 I have been teaching Ladino remotely at Oxford University (see Chapter 4), and since September 2022 I have been working as a UKRI Postdoctoral research fellow at UCL on the project *Digital Jewish Revivalistics: The Case of Ladino* (under the supervision of Prof. Lily Kahn), whose main outcome is precisely this book.

At this juncture, it is necessary to acknowledge a few important caveats. First, while I have used the glottonym 'Ladino' as part of the title, the present volume does not actually cover the online revitalisation of Ladino in all of its varieties (i.e., proto-Ladino, calque, Haketia, Judezmo, Judeo-Spanish – see above). Rather, it focuses largely on the most relevant one for contemporary purposes, i.e., Judezmo (*djudyó*/*djidyó*) understood as a (cyber)-(post)vernacular, with only occasional references to Judeo-Spanish (e.g., Chapter 4) and even more sporadic ones to Haketia (e.g., Chapter 2). Second, at least in its initial edition, this volume encompasses solely online Ladino-speaking initiatives established by June 1, 2024.

Methodology

My methodological framework in this volume revolves around Revivalistics, which I will complement with extensive literature review, private interviews, surveys, computer-assisted quantitative methods, and Critical Discourse Analysis.

In his seminal work *Revivalistics: From the Genesis of Israeli to Language Reclamation in* Australia and Beyond (2020),[2] Ghil'ad Zuckermann defines Revivalistics as follows:

> Revivalistics is a new trans-disciplinary field of enquiry studying comparatively and systematically the *universal* constraints and global mechanisms on the one hand (…) and *particularistic* peculiarities and cultural relativistic idiosyncrasies on the other, apparent in linguistic reclamation, revitalization, and reinvigoration attempts across various sociological backgrounds, all over the globe (…)
>
> (2020, 199; emphasis in the original)

In his volume, Zuckermann stresses the increasing importance of digital (and in particular, online) tools in language revival efforts. As per the above quote, he classifies these endeavours into reclamation (i.e., the revival of a no longer spoken language, such as Hebrew in the 20th century), reinvigoration (i.e., the revival of a language that has a high percentage of speakers but is still endangered, such as Yiddish), and revitalisation (i.e., the revival of a severely endangered language with minimal intergenerational transmission, such as Ladino).

From Zuckermann's discussion, I have derived several key insights for this book, incorporating them as part of my critical discussion of the revitalisation of Ladino on the Internet.

Transdisciplinarity

Drawing upon the characterisation of Revivalistics as a transdisciplinary field of inquiry, I will be combining insights from Jewish Linguistics, Digital Humanities, Critical Theory, Cultural History, and Diaspora Studies. Additionally, I will also incorporate observations from language revitalisation beyond Revivalistics (Ferguson 1959; Fishman 1967; Eisenlohr 2004; Austin and Sallabank 2011; Nathan and Austin 2014; Hinton et al. 2018; Olko and Sallabank 2021; Yebra López 2021c). Likewise, I will draw on critical linguistics (Del Valle 2011; García and Wei 2014; Lippi-Green 1994; Shandler 2004, 2005; Makoni and Pennycook 2007; Otheguy et al. 2015; Yebra López 2023b), archive ethnography, information science, machine learning, and human–computer interaction (Noble 2018; Ball 2022; Srinivasan 2022). All of these supplement and/or problematise specific tenets from Revivalistics.

Comparative Analysis vis-à-vis further Jewish Languages

This book is influenced by the Revivalistics insight that it is crucial to offer clear, direct, practical, and comparative insights into revivalist movements worldwide without delay, as well as the contention that there is a distinct and discrete group of languages that are best characterised as Jewish (e.g., sharing by the use of Hebrew scripts and the incorporation of Hebrew and Aramaic words to convey distinctively Jewish concepts) (Weinreich 1967; Wexler 1981; Szulmajster-Celnikier and Varol 1994; see also Chapter 4). Drawing upon both ideas, I will critically examine the extent to which reinvigoration concepts and initiatives apropos Yiddish (e.g., Shandler's concept of "postvernacularity," Master-Apprentice programs, documenting LGBTQIA+ voices, emphasis on written literature, Netflix subtitles in the target language), and to a lesser extent, reclamation efforts concerning Hebrew (e.g., Ulpan programmes) can be utilised in the case of Ladino (or else this application could be counterproductive based on the respective idiosyncrasies of each language). And vice versa: I will analyse if and how online revitalisation initiatives that have been more successfully in the case of Ladino than apropos Yiddish and/or Hebrew (e.g., language learning apps) could and/or should be realistically applied to these languages.

Prioritising Community Engagement over Language Reification

Revivalistics transcends documentary linguistics, focusing on speakers and community field activism over language objectification and armchair linguistics. Lest linguists lose touch with the very people that make their efforts worthwhile and relevant (Zuckermann 2020, 208).

Consequently, Zuckermann departs from the traditional ontological framework of languages which conceptualises the latter as discrete, self-contained, and reified autonomous identities, instead redefining them as named languages (thus emphasising their socioculturally constructed nature, rather than assuming they are pre-existing entities in the world out there) (Heller and Martin-Jones 2007). From this perspective, languages are a collection of lects, i.e., "an abstract ensemble of (…) (idiolects, sociolects, dialects, and other lects)" (2020, xxvi). Accordingly, and in further alignment with proponents of translanguaging (Otheguy et al. 2015) and my own research (Yebra López 2023b), in this book I will be conceptualising Ladino as a named language and in particular, a cultural-linguistic ensemble of idiolects and translanguaging practices deemed valuable by the members of the global Sephardic community. Consequently, my focus will be on their linguistic activity (languaging), rather than on Ladino as an essentialised, prescriptivised artefact.

Provincialising Prescriptivism

The ability of community field linguists to engage with real-life languaging (in our case, that of Ladino speakers) further entails provincialising prescriptivism, critically interrogating (self)ascriptions of authority over the language, as well as various practices of authentication, standardisation and gatekeeping.

By contrast, Revivalistics embraces the fact that as famously put by Zuckermann "shift happens": "Revivalistics discards any imprisoning purism prism and makes the community members realize that shift happens. And there is nothing wrong with shift happening. Hybridization results in new diversity, which is beautiful" (2020, 209).

In alignment with this understanding, in the present volume I will be rejecting pervasive myths about the supposed purity of Ladino (Chapter 1) and the alleged convenience of keeping traditional geolects separate (Chapter 3), instead accepting the inevitable influence of the revivalist's first language (L1) (in our case, Spanish, English, Turkish, Hebrew), embracing, and celebrating inevitable hybridisation.

In this sense, I will discuss the vigorous advocacy for the cyber-standardisation of Ladino as a symptom of (rather than a solution to) the anxiety triggered by the emergence of a new, geographically de-localised, online-native sociolinguistic phase in the evolution of Ladino as part of Sepharad 4.

On the other hand, and nuancing Zuckermann's enthusiasm, I will argue that some degree of prescriptivism might be necessary, even beneficial, to revive Ladino in the 21st century.

For example, as identified by Bunis, at times of socio-technological change, a number of concerns recur about Ladino which have been debated since at least the 1880s, namely: the glottonym, the transcription system, and the linguistic (i.e., orthographical and lexical) items that are legitimate in Ladino and/or integral to it (cit. in Brink-Danan 2011, 110). Regardless of how descriptivist or anti-prescriptivist we might wish to be *qua* critical linguists, I will argue that apropos these and further issues, it is simply not possible to not make decisions. In turn, this predicament leads to various forms of what I will call 'implicit prescriptivism,' i.e., prescriptivism which while unstated in the rules and content pertaining to a specific Ladino-speaking online platform, is *de facto* reproduced through most of its content, affecting all the above-mentioned aspects, plus key geolectal, sociolectal, and even genderlectal varieties of Ladino.

Additionally, I will observe that while emphasising diversity over standardisation is commendably inclusive, it might not always be the most effective solution for revitalisation purposes. Instead, I will show that in most Ladino-speaking online communities some form of balance between standardisation and hybridity needs to be sought to preserve the linguistic diversity of Ladino while also ensuring effective communication and language vitality.

Lastly, while rejecting prescriptivism, Revivalistics uncritically reproduces several language ideologies[3] which are deeply intertwined with it, including the distinctions between 'native' and 'non-native speakers,' the notion of a 'mother tongue,' and the idea of linguistic ownership. All of them will be problematised in this volume from the perspective of critical linguistics.

The Centrality of Language to Nationhood

The Internet exacerbates a tendency identified by Shmuel Refael as intrinsic to the (pre-Internet) Sephardic diaspora, namely: extra-territoriality, i.e., the enduring cultural, spiritual and, most importantly, linguistic sovereignty the Sephardic community has maintained throughout history, irrespective of geographical boundaries and external influences. As observed by Refael,

> Sephardim preferred to maintain their extra-territorialism, and every time, in keeping with their psychological need, they chose another territory with which to identify. In the meantime, Ladino served as a liaison between the various geographies and territories in which the Sephardim lived.
>
> (2012, 323)

Drawing upon the above insight and Zuckermann's discussion of the centrality of Israeli (i.e., the hybrid reclaimed language resulting from cross-fertilisation between Hebrew and the languages of its revivalists) to the State of Israel, I will discuss the extent to which the use of Ladino as a vehicular language brings together and strengthens the global Sephardic community via language ethnicisation. Ultimately, this dynamic crystallises into a sense of national belongingness as part of which fellow members come to share a common code and norm, thus catalysing the articulation of certain virtual platforms into Digital Home-Lands (i.e., genuinely cohesive communities), even network states (see below).

In alignment with the above understanding, a further limitation of this volume is that rather than aiming to cover every single Ladino-speaking or Ladino-related online platform, I will be focusing on Ladino-speaking Digital Home-Lands. I understand the latter to be online groups where the use of Ladino as a vehicular language leads to and is reinforced by the growth of an associated community of Ladino speakers (i.e., the users, the audience) that can interact on that platform (a)synchronously. Therefore, otherwise commendable and remarkable initiatives such as the Sephardic Studies Digital Collection (University of Washington), Documenting Judeo-Spanish, *El Kantoniko de Ladino*, plus the digitisation of the newspaper *El Amaneser* and the magasine *Aki Yerushalayim*, all fall outside of the scope of the present volume.

The Talknological Revolution

According to Zuckermann, there have been four linguistic revolutions in History: speaking (over 70,000 years ago), writing (approximately 5,200 years ago), type-printing (1041–8/1450), and what he dubs 'talknology' (a portmanteau of 'talk' and 'technology'), i.e., digital mass media and social media (Facebook, X), leading to 'big data' (since the 20th century) (2020, xxiv). The talknological era, Zuckermann adds, would have inaugurated a shift from things to ideas, leading to a renewed interest in heritage, culture, and language (xxiv). From this perspective, the main Ladino-speaking online platforms I will be discussing in the present volume, such as *Ladinokomunita* (Chapter 1), *Ladino 21* (Chapter 2), *Los Ladinadores* (Chapter 3), *Enkontros de Alhad* (Chapter 4), the Ladino courses at the Oxford School of Rare Jewish Languages (Chapter 4), Ladino-speaking Netflix series (Chapter 5), and the eventual Sephardic metaverse and network state (Chapter 6), are best understood as milestones within the Ladino talknological revolution.

Transvaluation

Drawing upon Patrick Eisenlohr's discussion of the electronically mediated change of ideological valuations of lesser-used languages (2004), my own coinage of the collocation 'Ladino 21' (2017 – see above), and Zuckermann's discussion of transvaluation (2020 xxvii, 127–43), in this volume I will argue that the flourishing and thriving of Ladino on the Internet have resulted in an undeniable amelioration of its ideological valuation. To the extent to which Ladino is consistently and widely featured across the main Web 1.0 and 2.0 platforms, this language is increasingly perceived as belonging indeed in the 21st century, thus dismantling traditional prejudices against it as an archaic variety whose disappearance is imminent and unavoidable (Harris 1994, 2011; Armistead 1995; Nieto 2003; Rouy 2021).

Ethical and Utilitarian Reasons to Revive Endangered Languages

Revivalistics allows us to identify and discuss several deontological and utilitarian reasons to engage in the online revitalisation of Ladino, with a focus on its importance for cultural autonomy and well-being.

Concerning deontological reasons, which are paramount to inspire present and prospective activists, I will draw upon Revivalistics to contend that reviving Ladino is "simply the *right* thing to do" (Zuckermann 2020, xxiii), as it implies "righting the wrong of the past" (xxiii), including in the case at hand, the Decree of Alhambra, the Holocaust, the stigmatisation of Ladino as a supposedly lesser form of Spanish, and its marginalisation in Israel.

As regards utilitarian reasons, awareness apropos of which is necessary to positively influence policy making, I will concur with Zuckermann that language revival will become increasingly pertinent as individuals strive to reclaim their cultural autonomy, enhance their spiritual and intellectual independence, and improve their overall well-being. Consequently, I anticipate that the online revitalisation of Ladino will continue to result in a protracted process of individual and collective healing, and I very much hope this book can contribute to this commendable effort.

Chapter Division

The structure of this volume is chapters is based on the division of the evolution of Ladino online as part of Sepharad 4 into the three web versions 1.0, 2.0, and 3.0, each of which corresponds to the book's three primary sections. Within each of them, chapters follow a chronological order based on the emergence of the main Ladino-speaking community/content in the platform in question (rather than the platform itself).[4]

Web 1.0

Beginning in the early 1990s, it is characterised by static web pages, read-only content, and limited user interaction, functioning primarily as an information repository.

Chapter 1: Correspondence Circles (1999-): Ladinokomunita, Ladino Culture Forum, and SefaradiMuestro

This chapter explores the emergence and development of Ladino-speaking Digital Home-Lands during the Web 1.0 era, with a particular focus on the pioneering email list *Ladinokomunita* as a pivotal platform in the revitalisation of Ladino on the Internet whose interactive affordances heralded the Web 2.0 stage. Through an examination of *Ladinokomunita*'s inception, methodologies, and influence, it demonstrates how the widespread integration of the Internet empowered members of the Sephardic diaspora to take charge of the future of their language, fostering active engagement and intergenerational transmission, broadening Ladino's domains of use, and adapting the language to contemporary contexts. While recognising *Ladinokomunita*'s merit in standardising Ladino as a cyber-vernacular, the chapter critically evaluates the ideological ramifications of this process, particularly concerning diversity and inclusivity within the wider framework of postcolonial linguistics. In particular, this chapter underscores the tensions between preserving [illegible]cultural identity and perpetuating language ideologies, with specific atten-[illegible] to the impact of *Ladinokomunita*'s policies on Ladino's prescriptivism, or-[illegible]graphy, pedagogy, and revitalisation. Lastly, by juxtaposing *Ladinokomunita* with other Ladino email lists (*SefaradiMuestro*) and Yiddish email lists (*Mendele*) as well as online forums (*Kave Shtiebel*), the chapter elucidates the intricacies of cyber-standardisation, cyber-(post)vernacularity, and the subtleties of language ideologies in shaping the online revitalisation of Ladino during the Web 1.0 era.

Web 2.0

Emerging in the mid-2000s, it introduced dynamic, multimodal, and user-generated content, fostering greater interactivity, social networking, and collaboration through platforms such as blogs, wikis, and social media.

Chapter 2. Digital Archives on YouTube (2011-): Autoridad Nasionala del Ladino i su Kultura, eSefarad CCSefarad, Wikitongues, Ladino 21, and VLACH

This chapter examines Ladino-speaking digital archives hosted on YouTube. Drawing upon Revivalistics' proposed shift from documentary linguistics to community field linguistics, the chapter provides a critical analysis of several YouTube-hosted Ladino digital archives, including the *Autoridad Nasionala del Ladino i su Kultura* (2011–16), *eSefarad CCSefarad* (2013 to present), select Ladino videos from the 'Jewish Languages' playlist of Wikitongues (2016–21), *Ladino 21* (2017 to present), the 'Judeo-Spanish Collection' of Vanishing Languages and Cultural Heritage (VLACH, 2019–20), and the 'Ladino (Judeo-Spanish)' playlist of the Endangered Language Alliance (2020). The chapter's analysis centres on four primary themes: (i) revitalisation, (ii) the tension between descriptivism and prescriptivism, (iii) multimodality, postvernacularity and transvaluation, and (iv) pedagogics and awareness-raising opportunities. This investigation is complemented by an ethnographic perspective that attends to the broader power dynamics shaping the creation and multimodal, multisemiotic functioning of Ladino digital archives in the 21st century. Additionally, the chapter includes a comparative analysis with two prominent Yiddish counterparts, namely: the *Yiddish Book Center* (2008 to the present) and *Forverts* (2008 to the present), as well as the postvernacular content of JEWBELLish (2013).

Chapter 3: Social Media and Language Learning Apps (2017-): Facebook, X, WhatsApp, TikTok, Duolingo, and uTalk

This chapter investigates the online revitalisation of Ladino through social networking platforms facilitating real-time interaction, such as Facebook (2004), X (formerly Twitter; 2006), WhatsApp (2009), Instagram (2010), and TikTok (2017), as well as language learning platforms employing gamification techniques, including Duolingo (2011) and uTalk (2016). It assesses the extent to which these endeavours embody and/or challenge two central tenets of Revivalistics, i.e., the 'talknological revolution,' and the appreciation of linguistic hybridity/diversity (or lack thereof), particularly in the face of standardisation. Drawing upon original interviews with their managers, the chapter examines the case studies of *Los Ladinadores* (2020; overseen by Ladino linguist Aldo Sevi) and uTalk's Ladino course (2019), with the former focusing on reading and writing skills and the latter emphasising speaking and listening proficiency. Additionally, the chapter juxtaposes *Los Ladinadores* with the Yiddish Facebook group Learning Yiddish (2017), among others, and compares uTalk's Ladino course with its Hasidic Yiddish counterpart (2024) and Duolingo's Yiddish course for English speakers (2021).

Chapter 4: Zoom Boom (2020–2): The Sephardic Digital Academy, Enkontros de Alhad, the Oxford School of Rare Jewish Languages

This chapter investigates the transformative impact of the videotelephony software Zoom during the COVID-19 pandemic (2020–23), which led to a significant phenomenon termed the 'Ladino Zoom Boom,' as part of the 'talknological revolution.' It posits that this phenomenon encompassed the following key developments: (i) the consolidation of Ladino as a prominent cyber-(post)vernacular of the 21st century, (ii) the predominant use of the Internet as the primary platform for communication among the global Ladino diaspora, and (iii) the widespread adoption of online platforms for Ladino teaching and learning. To explore these aspects, the chapter engages in original interviews with the leaders of three notable initiatives central to the 'Ladino Zoom Boom,' namely: the Sephardic Digital Academy, *Enkontros de Alhad*, and the Oxford School of Rare Jewish Languages. Furthermore, the chapter compares these initiatives with analogous endeavours in the realm of Yiddish, where a comparable 'Zoom Boom' has not been observed. It concludes that the 'Ladino Zoom Boom' represents a pivotal shift in the status of Ladino within Sepharad 4, strongly suggesting the need for a reassessment of Ladino's degree of endangerment with regard to critical factors outlined in UNESCO's assessment of language vitality (2003), particularly intergenerational transmission and adaptation to new domains and media.

Chapter 5: Video-On-Demand and Streaming Services (2021): The Netflix Shows Kulüp and The Beauty Queen of Jerusalem

This chapter addresses two principal inquiries: (i) how is Ladino used on Netflix *qua* major platform within the Video-on-Demand (VOD)/streaming communication landscape? and (ii) how may this utilisation contribute to enhancing awareness of Ladino, fostering its revitalisation, and facilitating its acquisition in Sepharad 4? To this end, the chapter conducts a comparative analysis of the inaugural seasons of *Kulüp* (2021) and *The Beauty Queen of Jerusalem* (2021). Each television series is subjected to an individualised examination structured into three segments: an introductory overview, a quantitative and qualitative assessment of Ladino usage therein, and an in-depth discussion of these findings with respect to key aspects of Revivalistics (i.e., community engagement and postvernacularity), as well as policies governing dubbing and subtitling. Then drawing upon these insights and private interviews with the principal Ladino advisors of *Kulüp* and *The Beauty Queen of Jerusalem*, plus an original survey administered to the respective audiences of these series, the chapter evaluates the perceived impact on awareness-raising, revitalisation efforts, and educational potential engendered by these productions. Finally, this analysis is supplemented by a brief examination of Yiddish usage in Shtisel (2018) and Unorthodox (2020) which provides a contrasting perspective, as well as a blueprint for the improvement of Ladino on Netflix.

Web 3.0

The current and emerging phase of the Internet (and by extension, of Sepharad 4), the Web 3.0, aims to create a more intelligent and autonomous web by leveraging technologies like artificial intelligence, machine learning, and decentralised blockchain systems, thereby enhancing personalised user experiences and fostering greater data interoperability and security.

Chapter 6. Sepharad 5? (2022-): The Metaverse and the Network State

This chapter examines the sociolinguistic evolution of Ladino within the context of the transition from Web 2.0 to Web 3.0, with a specific focus on two hypothetical use cases: the Metaverse and the network state. It begins by discussing the potential and current phase of Web 3.0 concerning the preservation of endangered languages and cultural heritage. Then it explores the Metaverse as an emerging interconnected system of virtual environments, discussing its capacity to empower Ladino speakers and collaborators as users and developers, thereby enhancing national consciousness and fostering closer community ties. Third, it analyses the conceptualisation of Sepharad as a network state (SNS), discussing how its eventual implementation would introduce novel forms of citizenship and governance for the global Ladino-speaking community, potentially marking the advent of Sepharad 5 – a distinct new phase in the evolution of Sepharad (and Ladino), with far-reaching implications. Finally, the chapter examines Yiddish and Hebrew initiatives as potential models for integrating elderly Ladino speakers into Web 3.0, facilitating a unique form of intergenerational transmission and even partially reversing the Sephardic diaspora.

Notes

1 The concept of "postvernacularity" was coined by Jeffrey Shandler, who explored it apropos Yiddish (2004, 2005). It describes a phase where a language is no longer used for daily communication (vernacularity) but holds cultural and symbolic significance. This shift emphasises heritage value over practical use, with the language preserved through cultural practices, education, and art. It highlights the transition from functional usage to a focus on identity and collective memory, maintaining cultural relevance despite diminished everyday use. In this volume, I will show that this phase is significantly more advanced in Judezmo (and even more so in Haketia) than in Yiddish.

2 Henceforth capitalised in this volume capitalised to refer to the field of study ('Revivalistics'), plus italicised ('*Revivalistics*') only when referring to the homonymous book.
3 Here I understand language ideologies as the "sets of beliefs about language articulated by users as a rationalisation or justification of perceived language structure and use" (Silverstein 1979, 193) (see Chapter 2).
4 For instance, Facebook (2004) was created before YouTube (2005), but the first major Ladino channel on YouTube (i.e., that of the National Authority for Ladino and its Culture) was created in 2011, whereas the first popular Ladino-speaking page on Facebook (*Ladino 21*) appeared in 2017. Consequently, even though Facebook was founded before YouTube, the chapter on YouTube archives (Chapter 2) comes before the one featuring Facebook (Chapter 3).

Part 1

Web 1.0

The Mostly-Read Stage (1990s-)

1 Correspondence Circles (1999-)

Ladinokomunita, Ladino Culture Forum, and *SefaradiMuestro*

Introduction

This chapter discusses the first generation of Ladino-speaking online communities, i.e., Web 1.0 correspondence circles (popular email lists and fora), which rely almost exclusively upon the written word (as opposed to the more contemporary audio-visual format). In particular, it focuses on the foremost exponent of this digital affordance, namely: the email list *Ladinokomunita*, created by Rachel Bortnick in 1999 [hereafter interchangeably called *Ladinokomunita* or *LK* for short (*Ladinokomunita* 1999)], which pioneered the creation and maintenance of Sephardic Digital Home-Lands (2021) understood as successful online communities devoted to the revitalisation of Ladino in the 21st century in Ladino (see Introduction).

On the one hand, I will argue that *LK* constitutes a remarkable and inspirational example of how to use the global reach of the Internet to bring together thousands of members scattered in diaspora, empowering Sephardim to control the fate of their own language, getting members to actively participate in the preservation of the unique ethnolinguistic identity of their speakers via functional differentiation (Ferguson 1959; Fishman 1967), promoting intergenerational transmission, expanding Ladino's domains of use (Brink-Danan 2011; Pons 2018), and adapting this endangered linguistic variety to the realities of the 21st century (Eisenlohr 2004; Yebra López 2021c). Additionally, *LK*'s pioneering journey demonstrates that the Internet is more than a passive repository of information, instead actively shaping the fate of endangered languages like Ladino and ultimately contributing to its cyber-koinesation (i.e., the creation of a new koine or common language arising from the interaction of different linguistic groups on the Internet) and its eventual cyber-standardisation (through both explicit and implicit prescriptivism).

On the other hand, I will argue that this cyber-standardisation is also a symptom of the postcolonial tendency to revitalise diasporic endangered languages by taking advantage of the global reach of the Internet to bring vernaculars into standardised languages reconstructed in the image of European "modern" (i.e., colonial) languages (in our case, Spanish/French) (Pons 2018). This dynamic reinforces the Standard Language Ideology (Lippi-Green 1994, 166; Walsh 2021) that led to the subalternisation of these linguistic varieties and their speakers (in our case, Ladino and Sephardim, respectively) in the first place (Stroud 2018).[1]

DOI: 10.4324/9781003473664-3

Additionally, *LK* incurs multiple forms of hitherto unacknowledged implicit prescriptivism, including the privileging of a specific geolect, sociolect, and genderlect, reducing the complexity of Ladino to its vernacular aspect (for a discussion of implicit prescriptivism apropos *Ladino 21*, *Los Ladinadores*, and *Enkontros de Alhad*, see Chapters 2, 3, and 4, respectively).

Lastly, I will juxtapose *LK* to further Ladino email lists/forum (Ladino Culture Forum 2002; SefaradiMuestro 2008) and Yiddish email lists/forum (Mendele 1991; Kave Shtiebel 2012), respectively. This will allow us to better understand the relevance of implicit prescriptivism (even over its explicit counterpart) for the purpose of cyber-standardisation, as well as the functionality of (non)nativespeakerism as a language ideology through which Ladino continues to be performed nowadays as a real imaginary space.

Ladinokomunita

The Emergence of Ladino as a Cyber-vernacular

In 1999, the mass adoption of mainstream social networks was still a far-fetched proposition. Instead, the vast majority of the users, and certainly the elderly (which continues to be the primary demographic of Ladino speakers), were still relying on text-based forms of communication and were rather amazed by the novelty of innovations such as email and real-time news retrieval. Notwithstanding the embryonic stage of these features, it is not unreasonable to hypothesise that the following question must have crossed the minds of many a language activist at that time: how can we leverage the World Wide Web, its global reach, and its innovative features to foster the preservation of diasporic, endangered languages? Or in current lingo, what digital affordances of the Web 1.0 could possibly lead to the revitalisation of these linguistic varieties?

It is within this context that we ought to understand the felicitous idea suggested by Turkish-born Israeli journalist Moshe Shaul (1929–2023), L1 Ladino speaker and vice president of the National Authority for Ladino and its Culture (NALC). On the occasion of NALC's 1999 conference, devoted to Ladino orthography, Shaul proposed founding an online discussion group in the form of a listserv and website by the name of '*Ladinokomunita*' for the purpose of "perpetuating the language" (Bortnick 2004, 3) by using the orthography of *Aki Yerushalayim* (henceforth interchangeably referred to as 'French-Ottoman Romanisation' – see below for a justification). Shortly after Shaul's suggestion, in November 1999, Rachel Amado Bortnick, who had also attended the conference, implemented this initiative. In a 2022 interview for the Ladino-only weekly meeting *Enkontros de Alhad* (see Chapter 4), Bortnick recalls those early days, emphasising the pioneering nature of this initiative:

> After having voted by a large margin that we want to adopt the orthography that the magazine *Aki Yerushalayim* had stipulated (…) Moshe Shaul (…) told us that given that we accepted that this will be (…) the best way of writing Judeo-Spanish with Latin letters, we can, now that we have the Internet,

> and many of us have computers at home (mine was new, it was my first computer), we can create a correspondence circle to practice and promote this writing. It seemed to me a very good idea, as I said, I had a new computer. I came home, I asked somebody 'How do you create a correspondence group? Teach me' and [they] told me that there was … it was before Yahoo Groups, there was another site … go there and say 'start a group' and I opened … I opened it … but before this I asked a bunch of friends, I said 'look, I learned how to open … like this, a group … but you need to register yourselves. If you agree, I will open it. Otherwise, I will not open it.' They told me 'yes, yes, good idea, good idea.' We started with four or five people. And all of the sudden, how it expanded … it was a miracle, because we didn't … even … even write articles, not did we do any ads … word of mouth…
>
> (my translation)[2]

Since then, *LK* has been operating as an email distribution list for the specific purpose of promoting the use of Ladino (and in particular, Ladino standardised via French-Ottoman Romanisation – more on this below) as the cyber-vernacular in which to discuss the language, culture (e.g., music, films, theatre), history, and traditions (e.g., religious practices, but also recipes) of Sephardic Jews, plus any other topic of interest to them, such as private issues, trending topics, and the latest news.[3]

LK's Self-Fulfilling Prophecy

In a 2012 interview with Israeli journalist and Judeo-Spanish specialist Zelda Ovadia, Shaul recalls the answer he had given about 50 years before (thus, around 1962) to the question of whether Ladino would eventually disappear, stressing the performative nature of language, i.e., its ability to generate that which it says (Austin 1962),

> (…) when we are asked such questions, we must answer optimistically, because there are many who say 'yes, the language is agonising, nobody else speaks it anymore, after one or two generations it is going to disappear…" I say, 'these are prophecies that become true if you say them for a long time. If you believe that the language will not be spoken, then five years later nobody will speak it anymore. If I [on the other hand] say 'no, the language will survive (…) it is a language that can continue to exist as a language of culture.'
>
> (my translation)[4]

It is perhaps in this vein that we ought to understand an early *LK* message from Bortnick, where she claimed that Ladino was still alive, only to then encourage others to participate, thereby reinforcing its aliveness: "Ladino (Judeo-Espanyol) is NOT a language that Sephardim USED TO speak! It is alive and well, and if you don't believe me, subscribe to the LK list" (my translation). And so began the story of this pioneering Ladino-only virtual community, still among the most influential to date.

Initially hosted by an unknown platform (see above), then by Yahoo! for most of its existence, and since 2019, by Groups.io (Santacruz 2019), *LK* features over 71,000 messages and over 1,500 members from more than 50 countries. Historically, *LK* experienced a steady growth between 1999 and 2003, followed by a consolidation period over the following two years, and a renewed rise between 2006 and 2014. Whereupon *LK* started a decline that lasted until the 2020 COVID-19 pandemic and its lockdown, the latter predicably resulting in an increased activity in Ladino, not just on *LK* but also on many other virtual communities (see Chapters 3 and 4). Consequently, participation on *LK* increased during the 2021–22 period, only to decrease thereafter, perhaps in favour of Web 2.0 platforms such as *Los Ladinadores*, thus suggesting a critical mass adoption of and transition into Web 2.0 platforms among Ladino speakers.

The Inception of Ladino as a Cyber-vernacular: From Koineisation to Standardisation

In a 2018 interview for *Ladino 21* (see Chapter 2), Bortnick acknowledged that, as illustrated by the above-referred trajectory, the expansion of *LK* as a correspondence circle owes much of its success to the digital affordances of the Internet:

> The Internet is very, very important. The proof is *Ladinokomunita*. It was with great pleasure that I was delighted to see that [it] became big so fast (…) and without any publicity, only from people searching on the Internet things about Ladino, Judeo-Spanish or Sephardic [stuff] (…) and day after day there are more and more things (…) the Internet is the way of expanding it [Ladino] nowadays, because those like us, who know the language from … from birth are already passing away, we will not be here and thanks to the Internet (…) we are being heard, and we hope that a lot of people in the upcoming years will continue to hear us and to have a bit of … fondness for this language, and the Internet is the way to do this.
>
> (my translation)[5]

Ladinokomunita constitutes a remarkable and inspirational example of how to use the global reach of the Internet to bring together thousands of members scattered in diaspora enroute to the crystallisation of a (Sephardic) Digital Home-Land as originally characterised by Held in 2010 and rearticulated in my 2021 article, namely: a virtual territory capable of facilitating an ethnolinguistic re-assemblage and generating a feeling of belonging conducive to the development of a Ladino-speaking national community (Held 2010; Yebra López 2021c, 109; see Introduction). As I have written elsewhere, "with the benefit of hindsight ten years later [i.e., ten years after Held's article], it is fair to conclude that *Ladinokomunita* has been the pioneering and most iconic Sephardic Digital Home-Land to date" (2021, 102; my italics). So far, only *Los Ladinadores* (see Chapter 2) has achieved a comparable degree of success, though it remains to be seen whether this group will also be able to sustain it over two decades (see Conclusion).

LK's successful leveraging of the digital affordances of Web 1.0 to articulate a process of linguistic ethnicisation and a sense of home is arguably premised on at least two successful practices, namely: encouraging the participative online use of Ladino as a vernacular (i.e., as a medium for daily communication), and placing Sephardic voices at the heart of decision-making processes.

Employing Ladino as a Cyber-vernacular

Over a long-enough period, exhorting members to participate online by using (only) Ladino as a medium for daily communication leads to several innovative disruptions.

First, it extricates Ladino from traditionally dominant languages, such as Israeli Hebrew, Spanish, Portuguese, and more recently, English, redistributing hegemonic flows of linguistic and cultural influence over the language and its global community of speakers (Yebra López 2021c, 110).

Second, by allowing fellow members to share a common code and norm, it fosters a sense of national belonging (Yebra López 2021c, 110.

For instance, in a 2018 message written upon the passing away of Selim Amado (Bortnick's brother), *LK* moderator Guler Orgün expressed her condolences as follows: "It is with great regret that we learned about the loss of Selim Amado, Rachel's dear brother, a person of great value to our community and culture/ May his soul rest in Heaven. / Guler from Istanbul" (my translation).[6]

Third, *LK* effectively counters language attrition by targeting its two main causes as identified by Joshua Fishman (1991): intergenerational transmission (bringing the elderly into a technological field that is still dominated by the youth, thus reducing the digital gap) and functional differentiation (as it creates a space where only Ladino is used) (see also Ferguson 1959; Fishman 1967).

Fourth, the adoption of a many-to-many interaction (i.e., every member can interact with any other member) allows participants to express themselves and share their real-life experiences and viewpoints regarding Sephardic culture and language, while also openly acknowledging their own positionality when speaking, writing, and sharing documents. The latter is emphasised by the (compulsory) inclusion of name-and-place signatures at the end of each email (Yebra López 2021c, 111), which offers concrete proof of the proverbial Sephardic extra-territoriality. In so doing, it reinforces a sense of "diasporic intimacy" (Boym 1998) and "diasporic citizenship" (Weheliye 2005, 145–97), where "the national and the transnational are quasi-dialectical partners in the movement of globalization" (149), the Derridean iteration (i.e., repetition and difference) of name-and-place signatures reproducing in a game-of-mirrors-like fashion the experiential hermeneutics and affect of the global Sephardic home (Yebra López 2021c, 111).

For example, Orgün's message (see above) sent from Istanbul, was answered by several members, including Moshico Cohen from Israel, who wrote the following:

> With great pity I learned about the loss of Selim Amado/A very unique person whom I had the pleasure to know/ A person of great value to the Ladino world/

> A person we will miss a lot./ To his family I want to say "No more deaths [Sephardic expression],/ May Blessed God [Sephardic expression] give you Patience"/May your soul rest in Heaven, dear Friend Selim/ "*Menuchatcha Eden*"/ Moshico Cohen – israel [sic].
>
> (my translation)[7]

Moreover, to the extent to which *LK*'s *modus operandi* and goal is for members to read in Ladino, but also and to a large extent, to write in this language, we would be justified to think more accurately of *LK* as a Web 1.5 platform (rather than 1.0 one, which is characterised by a one-to-many, mostly-read model – see Introduction). In fact, in *LK* both aspects are mutually necessary, because without members writing, there would be nothing to read, other than the occasional messages from the moderators (see Chapter 3 for Aldo Sevi's acknowledgement of a similar fact apropos *Los Ladinadores*). At the very least, we should acknowledge that *LK* foreshadows many of the participative aspects that we are currently enjoying in the online revitalisation of Ladino within Web 2.0, which also helps account for its durability into today's Web 2.0-dominated Internet.

Fifth, by incentivising users to adapt Ladino to the realities of the 21st century, *LK* has contributed to expanding its domains of use, e.g., incorporating English loanwords to discuss technological advances. For example, following a 2022 trip to Vegas, *LK* member Jake Kohenak wrote the following message, which Bortnick helped contextualise underneath:

> Dear Carlos, /Did you lose your shirt or win enough [money] in the game tables (21/Blackjack, craps, roulette, poker, etc.) or in the 'slots' [slot machines] (that take and give money) in cryptocurrency to fill your wardrobe with new clothes?!/ Jake/ Rachel: Carlos went to Vegas.
>
> (my translation)[8]

Sixth, *LK* offers conclusive evidence that the Internet is not just a passive repository of offline Ladino, but instead it encompasses a rich arsenal of digital affordances that actively and inexorably shape the very name, vocabulary, grammar, community, and domains of use of Ladino in the 21st century (see Introduction).

Finally, *LK* has been pivotal to the turn-of-the-century ideological transvaluation of Ladino from a supposedly "archaic" and "dying" "dialect" to a language that belongs in our time (see Introduction). In the words of Eisenlohr:

> A central concern of the use of lesser-used languages in electronic mediation is not only encouraging language maintenance and revitalization by providing speakers with opportunities to hear and maintain skills in the language, but also is achieving a transformation of ideological valuations of the language so that the lesser-used language is viewed as part of the contemporary world and as relevant for the future of a particular group.
>
> (2004, 24; cit. in Yebra López 2021c, 106)

Empowering Sephardic Voices within Decision-Making Processes

The decolonial empowerment of the Sephardic nation by digital means is partially predicated on the ability of Ladino-speaking members of the global Sephardic diaspora to make key decisions related to how they would like to produce, store, and share their online interaction. While non-Sephardic members, activists, and experts (i.e., "allies") can and do provide invaluable assistance, they should by no means override or replace the voice of Sephardim themselves with their own representation of it.[9] Lest they end up reproducing all-too-familiar forms of benevolent (neo)-colonialism in the name of humanitarian protection (Spivak 1988; Morton 2003).

Critiquing LK's Standardisation

For all its commendable and inspirational efforts over the years, *LK*'s successful revitalisation of Ladino in the 21st century is not entirely unproblematic, and it behoves critical linguists to analyse its ideological roots and implications. Paramount among *LK*'s shortcomings is its persistent push for standardisation around the French-Ottoman Romanisation of Ladino. I would like to contend that this policy is the name of a viable solution to the problem of how best to revitalise Ladino online (see Chapter 3) as much as it is a symptom of the more general postcolonial tendency to revitalise diasporic endangered languages by taking advantage of the global reach of the Internet to bring vernaculars into standardised languages. As stressed above, this reconstruction takes place in the image of European "modern" (i.e., colonial) languages (Pons 2018), reinforcing the Standard Language Ideology (Lippi-Green 1994, 166; Walsh 2021; see above) that led to the subordination of these linguistic varieties and their speakers (in our case, Ladino and Sephardim, respectively) in the first place (Stroud 2018). Ultimately, this process undermines many of the above-discussed advances towards the online and decolonial furthering of Ladino in the 21st century.

LK's stated goals are the "maintenance, revitalization and standardization of Ladino" (cit. in Brink-Danan 2011, 108). The welcome message featured on the Groups.io *LK* website (which is entirely in English) states that its goals are in this very order, the following: furthering the use of Ladino, disseminating its standardisation in the Latin alphabet (by using the *Aki Yerushalayim* orthography, which follows French-Ottoman Romanisation – see below), and promoting knowledge about the history and culture of Sephardim, as well as further topics:

> The purpose of the Ladinokomunita is to:
>
> 1 promote the use of Ladino;
> 2 spread the use of a standardized method for spelling Ladino with Roman characters, according to the rules established by the journal "Aki Yerushalayim."
> 3 promote knowledge of Sephardic History and culture.

Additionally, *LK* abides by a small but rigid set of rules that are periodically posted by the moderators as a special message in the email list entitled (in English) "group guidelines." These rules are accompanied by a table summarising the Ladino orthography according to *Aki Yerushalayim* (also included on the website).

I will now break down the prescriptivist and orthographical aspects of it, followed by the pedagogical element and the implication of these three aspects for revitalisation purposes.

Prescriptivism

Whereas the existing scholarly literature on *LK* (Brink-Danan 2011; Bunis 2016; Pons 2018) has focused exclusively on explicit prescriptivism, it is my contention that *LK*'s implicit prescriptivism, i.e., one that while unstated in the group rules and mail list messages, is *de facto* reproduced through most of its messages, deserves much attention too. Discussing the latter serves to shed light on key geolectal, sociolectal, and even genderlectal aspects of Ladino, as well as to delve into its postvernacularity, i.e., its ability to symbolise cultural commonality over its utility as a means of communication [which Jeffrey Shandler originally explored apropos Yiddish (Shandler 2004, 2005); see Introduction].

First and foremost, *LK* is explicitly prescriptivist. This aspect can be readily surmised from both its website and the first commands issued as part of the group rules to the effect that all messages be written in Ladino, as well as in accordance with the orthographical rules of *Aki Yerushalayim* (see also below).

Thus, the moderators claim the following to begin with:

> We ask you all to please follow these rules:
> - Writing in Judeo-Spanish/Ladino.
> - Writing as per the *Aki Yerushalayim* orthography rules.
>
> (my translation)[10]

Additionally, the moderators effectively normalise their own prescriptivism by presenting it not just as unproblematic (this aspect arguably testifying to their lack of critical awareness), but also as a solution. Thus, later on in the message, it is stated that the moderators "correct mistakes" ["*los moderadores tambien korijan yerros*"], which entails both that there are mistakes based on the *Aki Yerushalayim* rules (prescriptivism), and that the moderators are capable of and willing to correct them (authority self-ascription).

Furthermore, *LK* is implicitly prescriptivist in three respects: first, even though most of its messages follow a specific geolect, sociolect, and arguably even a genderlect, respectively, these aspects go largely unacknowledged (e.g., they are nowhere to be found within the group rules); second, by its very activity, *LK* implicitly reduces the complexity of Ladino languaging[11] to its vernacular aspect; third, even members who explicitly oppose standardisation, welcome clear guidelines concerning how to write Ladino.

The privileged geolect is that of Istanbul, Turkey. This is perhaps unsurprising, given that the mastermind (Shaul), the founder (Bortnick), and four out of the five moderators (Bortnick herself, Gormez, Orgün, and Sevi) are *turkanos* (i.e., Ladino speakers born and/or raised in Turkey). Although due to socio-historical factors, Turkey in general and Istanbul in particular currently feature a significantly larger community of Ladino speakers than other traditionally major speech centres in the Balkans, such as Salonika or Sarajevo, *turkanos* do not really amount to 90% of the total global population of Ladino speakers. This means that the place of origin and geolect of *LK*'s board members is overrepresented, thus constituting a form of (unacknowledged) bias.

Concerning sociolect and genderlect biases, Bosnian rabbi Eliezer Papo has argued that the current standardised variety of Ladino, which relies heavily on Spanish (Castilian) vocabulary at the expense of Turkish and Hebrew words and is closer to the contemporary vernacular (rather than the more formal rabbinical register), is mostly based on the female genderlect. This genderlect would have been transmitted intergenerationally at home by Sephardic women as part of their children's educational upbringing:

> it ought to be understood that since he got up, a man (…) spent the day in the market with other men; and the woman, at home and in the courtyard with other women. Hence why there were entire male genderlects (…) which is everything that has to do with finances (…) politics (…) government (…) men spoke a very Turkish-inflected Judeo-Spanish (…) and on the other hand, the second men begin to speak about law, they switch to Hebrew.
>
> (2021; my translation)[12]

From this perspective, even Gormez and Sevi, both *turkanos* that self-identify as males, can be said to reproduce Ladino's female genderlect, to the extent to which they learned Ladino at home, from their mothers, and in a predominantly secular context.

Additionally, and as remarked by Marcy Brink-Danan (2011, 109), *LK*'s reduction of the Ladino languaging to its vernacular aspect (i.e., as a means of communication) creates a false equivalence between Ladino vernacularity on the one hand, and Sephardic identity, on the other. In turn, this conflation obfuscates an additional dimension of Ladino, i.e., its postvernacularity.

Moreover, even some of the *LK* members who explicitly oppose standardisation on the grounds that it reduces Ladino's complexity, appreciate clear rules and guidelines concerning how to write Ladino. On the one hand, reducing the complexity of Ladino's heteroglossic reality (i.e., the coexistence of multiple dialects, geolects, sociolects, and genderlects within the global Ladino-speaking community) makes it less difficult to learn (and teach) the language. It suffices to memorise only specific dialectal variations, spellings, and constructions, namely, those that abide by the group rules (explicit prescriptivism) and/or else are overrepresented in the messages (implicit prescriptivism). On the other hand, the subsequent creation of breakaway Ladino forums and email lists (see below) would seem to lend further credence to the perceived desire to use Ladino's full range.

Lastly, given that strict prescriptivism permeates much of *LK*'s discourse, it is perhaps unsurprising to find that its content revolves around language, particularly what counts as a "legitimate," "authentic" glottonym (i.e., language designation), speaker/speech community, and (loan)word, respectively (see Brink-Danan 2011; Bunis 2016; Pons 2018). In turn, these are always predicated on and negotiated through processes of legitimation and authentication (Yebra López 2023b, 94).

First, and concerning the glottonym,[13] as observed by David Bunis, *LK* features *ladino* as the preferred language designation (incidentally foreshadowing Web 2.0 platforms such as *Ladino 21* and *Los Ladinadores* – see Chapters 2 and 3, respectively). It does so on the grounds of negative as well as positive reasons. The negative reasons, or arguments not to choose alternative designations, are framed by Bortnick in post-ideological, descriptive terms: *espanyol* [Spanish] would also include "those from Spain and the Americas" (2013, cit. in Bunis 2016, 328), *djudió* [Jewish] only makes reference to Jews, *djudezmo* [Judezmo] (also) means Judaism, and *djudeoespanyol* [Judeo-Spanish] also designates Haketia (the North African variety of Ladino, as opposed to an Eastern Mediterranean one). Conversely, the positive reasons are that the glottonym *ladino* coincides with the name the wider public uses for the language, and it is the prevailing language designation in Israel, where most speakers of the language live nowadays (Bunis 2016).

While partially true, these reasons can and should be problematised, not least because by being couched in descriptive terms, they effectively erase the ideological contours that inform the choice to use *ladino* over any alternative designation. In reality, *espanyol* has often been favoured by Sephardim as a language designation (sometimes adding the possessive *muestro* before it to disambiguate it from Peninsular Spanish and its counterparts in the Americas, Africa, and Asia). The same goes for *djudió*, which is not particularly inaccurate given the strong ethnolinguistic homogeneity of the global Ladino-speaking community (i.e., the fact that the overwhelming majority of speakers self-identify as Sephardic Jews). Similarly, the glottonym *djudezmo* emphasises a (factual, for the most part) affiliation with the (Sephardic) Jewish community and reflects the popular use of the term in the Sephardic community since at least 1824, as well as its use by many scholars since the 20th century (Pressman 2013). Finally, whether Haketia is a variety of *djudeoespanyol* or a language of its own is by no means a settled debate, so that *djudeoespanyol* does not necessarily include (or exclude) *Haketia* (strictly speaking, though, both Haketia and Judezmo are vernaculars whose respective speakers wrote in Judeo-Spanish as a common written register – see Introduction).

Moreover, since *LK* was founded, alternative glottonyms have been used consistently. A case in point was Haim Sephiha's (and his disciples') ongoing insistence that what is written on this email list is Judeo-Spanish and not Ladino. According to them, the latter should be reserved for the calque variety of the language used in literal translation of the sacred text in Hebrew or Aramaic (even though Sephiha's mentor, Israel S. Revah, did acknowledge that originally 'ladino' referred to all varieties of the language – Bunis 2016, 327). Occasionally, this line of thought has led to accusations of "ladinolatry" (a neologism meaning idolatry for Ladino as a language designation) directed at anyone who uses the glottonym *ladino* to speak of the current vernacular variety, including myself.

In her above-mentioned article, Brink-Danan observes that in 2001, *LK* moderators conducted an online survey about the members' preferred glottonym, yielding 52% of votes for *ladino*, 20% for *djudeo-espanyol*, and no votes for *djudezmo*.

Ultimately, though, attempting to find a conclusive answer to the glottonym debate is futile, since this is not only a matter of linguistics, but also of extralinguistic considerations, which means its resolution is not entirely incumbent upon linguists *qua* linguists. Instead, I agree with Brink-Danan (and to a lesser extent, Pons) that since "the negotiation for the right to name languages highlights the question of what the community sees as its essential characteristics" (2011, 111), struggles about the best glottonym should be treated as symptoms of what the language represents to its community of speakers (i.e., indexes, through a relationship of iconicity – Gal and Irvine 1995). In our case, the question would then be as follows: what does the preferred glottonym of *LK* members tell us when it comes to understanding how this subset of the global community of Ladino speakers perceives the language and its speakers? The clear preference for *ladino* over *djudeo-espanyol* and *djudezmo*, on the one hand, and for *djudeo-espanyol* over *djudezmo*, on the other hand, would seem to suggest the privileging of Romanisation (and, to a lesser extent, Spanishness) over Jewishness.

Second, with regards to the discursive articulation of the Ladino speech community on *LK*, drawing upon Held (2010) and Brink-Danan (2011), we can argue that the perceived difference between mere participants and authentic/legitimate members is predicated on a mixture of the following: competence/proficiency, (non) nativespeakerism, ability and/or willingness to standardise, and alignment with the moderator's view on Ladino maintenance as based on its constant use as a Romanised vernacular. According to these criteria, the most legitimate speech member would be an L1 ("native") speaker with the ability and willingness to standardise the language around the French-Ottoman Romanisation system advocated by the moderators (see below), and to constantly use that variety with the utmost degree of proficiency. To the extent to which members are able and/or willing to fulfil the above requirements, they are considered one of *los muestros* ["ours"] speaking *muestra lingua* ["our language"]. Conversely, anybody who does not fulfil all of the above, can and will be gatekept by other members, particularly if the latter are perceived (by themselves and/or others) as more authentic or legitimate members of the community. Thus, in a 2019 email to *LK*, Sephardic author Benni Aguado argued that mere language proficiency in Ladino should not allow people to talk about Ladino as "their" language." He tried to justify this viewpoint by drawing parallels with Spanish speakers from Puerto Rico and Catalonia:

> I firmly believe that knowing how to speak a language that is not yours does not mean that you belong to the nation of that language. For example, a few years ago, I knew how to speak Spanish with the accent of the island of Puerto Rico in the Caribbean, and I knew it so well that many Puerto Ricans called me 'Boricua,' which means Puerto Rican. Now, did knowing the language like them made me Puerto Rican? Surely not! I am Sephardic, of soul and heart! I really like the culture and the way of being of the Catalans of

> Spain, and no matter how much admiration and affection I have for them, and even if I succeed at learning Catalan, I will never be able to be one of them, because I am just not Catalan. For me, the Sephardim are the descendants of the Jews expelled from the Iberian Peninsula in 1492.
>
> (my translation)[14]

Once again, here one should be less interested in finding out which members fit the above description of "authentic Ladino speaker" than in the rationale behind the above-mentioned criteria as the preferred indicators according to which to judge genuine belongingness to the community of Ladino speakers. First, the question of proficiency/competence can be (and it is in fact) judged in terms of mastery of the "correct" or "authentic" Ladino, which is intrinsically controversial. In the case of *LK*, it would seem to correspond to the language heard at home (whence it follows the assumption that being raised at home in Ladino is a necessary condition for proficiency), as per Bortnick's admission: "There is no doubt that it seems to every one of us that the language we heard in our houses is the correct one" (2011, cit. in Bunis 2016, 346). Moreover, as acknowledged by Bunis, even the concept of "family dialect" is problematic, given that numerous *LK* members have parents that spoke different regional variations (e.g., Benni Aguado, whose parents are from Çanakkale, Turkey, and Kavala, Greece, respectively) (Bunis 2016, 341) (see also Chapter 3 for a similar discussion apropos *Los Ladinadores*).

Second, (non)nativespeakerism runs rampant on *LK* (anticipating a similar behaviour in iconic Web 2.0 platforms such as *Los Ladinadores* – see Chapter 3). This language ideology is premised on a twofold assumption, namely: (a) that "native speakers" and "non-native speakers" exist *qua* empirical, objective realities, as determined by a combination of birth and upbringing manifested into the learning of the language in question since early childhood, and (b) that the competence of "native speakers" in that language is necessarily higher than that of "non-native speakers" (Flores 2013; Chow 2014; Aneja 2016; Holliday 2018; Yebra López 2021b). The pervasiveness of this ideology transcends *LK*, and permeates the scholarly discussion of this email list, as in Bunis' observation (implicitly accepting the label "native speaker" at face value and reproducing it as unproblematic) that "the great majority of Ladinokomunita members seem to favour the use [of] in site communications of the variety of language that members heard naturally among native speakers" (2016, 346).

However, as I have noticed elsewhere (Yebra López 2023b), the staunch defence of Ladino-speaking "nativeness" as a (supposed) proof of authenticity, legitimacy, and/or proficiency (and thus, representativity) *qua* Ladino speaker, is contradicted by two fundamental aspects. To begin with, by the realisation that authenticity (whether couched in nativeness, heritage, and/or ethnicity terms) does not have an intrinsic, self-evident meaning, but is instead the result of a process of authentication that is socially negotiated and defined. Consequently,

> rather than asking what is authentic, we should ask what it means to be authentic in a particular setting, according to what norms, and what are the authenticating practices by which it [authenticity] is conferred or denied.

> should pay attention to how speakers use the notion of authenticity, to at ideological ends, through which authenticating practices.
>
> (Creese et al. 2014, 939)

Additionally, even if we were to agree on nativeness, ethnicity, and/or heritage as proofs of legitimacy, the available statistics tell a different story: as cited in Brink-Danan (2011, 113), responding to an online survey from 2001 that asked participants whether they spoke Judeo-Spanish as their "*lingua maternal,*" ["mother tongue"][15] only 11% answered in the positive. Moreover, as admitted by Bortnick in an interview, beginning around 2009 (i.e., ten years after the creation of *Ladinokomunita*), non-Sephardim started to join the email list:

> The first ten years or so almost everyone was a Sefardi [sic] from a Ladino-speaking background. Then, slowly others, Ashkenazim, Spaniards, people claiming or suspecting *anusim* background and academics of all backgrounds, such as linguistics, Spanish, Jewish studies, began to join. Now, a sizable number are non-native speakers of the language, or new learners.
>
> (Santacruz 2019)

These findings are consistent with the idea that the authenticity of Ladino (and ultimately, that of the speech community itself) cannot so much be described in accurate terms as performed in idealised fashion by resorting to ethnic and linguistic stereotypes conducive to the suppression of an otherwise *de facto* heteroglossic reality (see above). As observed by Brink-Danan, this manoeuvre reveals an underlying anxiety: "by delimiting the possible topics for discussion, as well as the language to be used online, *LK*'s members do boundary work that otherwise would leave blurred edges and an undefined community, or, alternatively, a group of post-vernacular Ladino aficionados" (2011, 113).

Furthermore, with regards to the members' ability and/or willingness to standardise the language and align with the moderator's view on Ladino maintenance as predicated on its constant use as a Romanised vernacular, two mechanisms are implemented for optimisation. The first one is prescriptivist and revolves around corrections, which are made by moderators to "help" members write "properly." The second one is censorial and ultimately exclusionary, as it entails not publishing messages that do not abide by the proposed Romanised standardisation. Eventually, this may lead (and has led) to excluding participants from partaking in the email list. Drawing upon Gal and Irvine (1995), Brink-Danan (2011) has rightly characterised this twofold process as one of ideological erasure, understood as "the process in which ideology, in simplifying the field of linguistic practices, renders some persons or activities or sociolinguistic phenomena invisible. Facts that are inconsistent with the ideological scheme may go unnoticed or get explained away" (Gal and Irvine 1995, 974).

In turn, such exclusion has historically resulted in some of the ex-members creating alternative, more heteroglossic (though significantly less popular) correspondence circles (see below).

Third, the lexicon is by far the element that has received the most attention, though there are other linguistic aspects discussed on *LK* (e.g., phonology [including accent], morphology, verbal system, pronouns and forms of address, and word formation – see Bunis 2016, 333–5). The lexical choices of *LK* members are heavily regulated, particularly around the erasure of "foreign" elements whose conceptualisation is defined by opposition to "authentic" (i.e., authenticated – see above) lexico-structural aspects. This characteristic further exemplifies the puristic drive that informs the negotiated discursive articulation of Ladino on *LK*. This linguistic purism is best understood in light of Ranko Bugarski's definition of it as "(…) a common sentiment that (…) the standard language must be preserved at all costs in a maximally pure form, which frequently means protecting it from change and, in particular, from the pernicious influence of other languages" (cit. in Pons 2018, 261).[16]

Rather than discussing what languages are "foreign" to Ladino (which is a question that cannot be settled in exclusively linguistic terms), we should be interested in elucidating what the prevailing conceptualisation of certain languages as "foreign" to Ladino on *LK* tells us about its members' predominant understanding of this linguistic variety. Indeed, as argued by Pons, *LK*'s strand of linguistic purism cannot be understood outside the Eurocentric lenses of post-18th-century Standard Language Ideology (Lippi-Green 1994, 166; Walsh 2021; see above), which is closely related to the alleged defence of the "language" from "foreign" influences (loanwords):

> (…) linguistic purism cannot be interpreted outside the framework of linguistic prescriptivism ideology and the cultural modern of standard language that since the 18th century have functioned in a great deal of the Eurocentric world as the main framework of reference to understand the role of language in society (…) language standard ideology and the ideology of nationalism (…) are based on the romantic idea that a language is the expression of the collective being of an ethnic community, so that 'defending the common language against foreign influences (loanwords, essentially) means also defending people's cultural identity'.
>
> (my translation from the Spanish original in Pons 2018, 261, 263)

As further summarised by Pons (2018, 278), there are three main forms of lexical purism on *LK*.

First, the school of thought that Spanish and English (Brink-Danan 2011, 116) are alien to Ladino, the authenticity of the latter residing in the language spoken by the parents and grandparents of the members that articulate this viewpoint.

Both forms of opposition would seem to reflect the perception that Ladino is an endangered language mostly menaced by the "foreign" and "modern" influence of Spanish (particularly since the 19th century and up to date) and English (more recently, especially in the technology domain) as prestiged varieties (as opposed to inherently prestigious ones). This threat would have been exacerbated in Sepharad 4 by the implementation of the Internet as a global technology and the concomitant contact of Ladino with non-co-territorial languages (Pons 2018, 276; see Introduction). Additionally, and as remarked by Pons in light of Peter Hohenhaus' as well as James Milroy and Lesley Milroy's work, the conceptualisation of Ladino as a language in decline implies the purist myth of a supposed Golden Age by opposition to which Ladino would be nowadays in a state of deterioration (2018, 267). This myth is consistent with the authentication of words (whether historically or from the members' childhoods) from Hebrew, Turkish, and French as either words that are supposedly intrinsic to Ladino or else legitimate loanwords that belong in it. At any rate, this Golden Age narrative is of course an idealisation, since as demonstrated by Aldina Quintana, all linguistic varieties, but particularly diasporic ones, such as Ladino, are contact languages. This circumstance is compounded by the fact that Ladino is a pluricentric linguistic variety, i.e., it features a complex diasystem or system of dialects developed around the various centres of economic, cultural, and political activity of modern Sephardim, such as Thessaloniki, Istanbul, Safed, Vienna, and Belgrade (Quintana 2010, 42).

Second, there is a Romance strand of purism according to which Ladino has to be purged of Turkisms (which is to say, of key elements introduced into Ladino during its formation stage in the Ottoman Empire – Minervini 2013). Taking this line of thought to its logical conclusion, there should be a return to pre-expulsion Ladino, which nonetheless is so similar to Iberromance that many scholars have questioned its very existence as a distinct language variety (Minervini 2006, 2013; Pons 2018; Papo 2020b). Nevertheless, given *LK*'s above-discussed geolectal bias, which privileges the Istanbul standard over other traditionally major speech centres in the Balkans (e.g., Salonika, Sarajevo) and beyond (e.g., Israel), attempts to fight Turkisms away from Ladino are bound to be short-lived.

Unsurprisingly, as well, there is also among these proponents a clear preference for Spanish-sounding loanwords and adaptations (particularly vis-à-vis equivalent words in English). This inclination is consistent with both their perception of modern Spanish as an element of cohesion around which to assemble an otherwise scattered global community of Ladino speakers and conversely, with their understanding of regional contact languages (Greek, Hebrew, Turkey) as obstacles against this amalgamation. For instance, in a 2010 message, *LK* moderator Yehuda Hatsvi (precisely the only one who is not a *turkano*) gave an example of how it would be preferable for Ladino neologisms to be based on Spanish words, rather than English ones:

> From the verb "*enlasar*" in Judeo-Spanish it occurs to me to use the word "*enlase*" ["link"]. One of the meanings of this verb (…) is: unite, put in relation. So, I'd like "*enlase*" more than "link" from English (which, actually, is a foreign plant in our garden).
>
> (cit. in Bunis 2016, 338)

More generally, this position is reflected in a survey conducted by Pons, where she asked *LK* members from which language should loanwords be introduced: 62.5%

chose Spanish, 15% answered that it did not matter, 7.5% picked French, and only a negligible percentage selected other option (2018, 275).

As noted by Bunis, though, even among this second group (i.e., those preferring Hispanic loanwords over local borrowings), elements of Hebrew-Aramaic origin are welcome, since their inclusion is perceived to reflect the pivotal importance of Judaism to the group's ethnolinguistic identity (2016, 349).

More generally, and as further observed by Pons, the tension between the first and the second group seems to be reflective of a broader concern. The challenge is to strike the right balance between preserving the ethnolinguistic distinctiveness of Ladino, on the one hand, and adapting the language to the needs of modern urban life, on the other hand (Pons 2018, 272). This is particularly acute for a lexicon that "shows trends towards convergence with Spanish while maintaining certain lexical elements that iconize Judeo-Spanish as an ethnic Sephardic language" (Bürki 2021, 271).

Third, in alignment with Revivalistics (see Introduction), a syncretic line of thought on *LK* embraces language change as a necessary part of the development of a language. Accordingly, it posits that the authenticity of Ladino is reflected in the combined use of the many languages that influenced its development, or in Ghil'ad Zuckermann's felicitous expression, in the realisation that "shift happens."[17] In fact, participant Cobert Rohen argued in a rare message on *LK* that were it not for these changes, Ladino would already be dead:

> A living language is perpetually changing; words are lost, others appear. To want to speak a pure Ladino of the fifteenth century is to erase five centuries of the life of our ancestors. It is to kill the dead of Salonika [who were murdered in the Holocaust] once again. What need do we have of Iberian purity? To rebuild the language of the Inquisitors? A language that no one speaks anymore? (…) We can say "*Ke tal?*" or "*Ke haber?*" ['What's doing?'; Sp. *¿Que [sic] tal*? and Tk. *Ne haber*?]; we don't have to choose one or the other – both are fine. French words entered the language? Where's the harm in this? It's a Romance language too. Even English words will enter? (e.g., I've already seen "*un lider politiko*" 'a political leader'). How nice! Only dead languages don't have this problem.
>
> (cit. in Bunis 2016, 337; italics and notes from Bunis)

Ultimately, though, it is worth noting that the respective positions of the above three groups are all grounded in a (flawed) classical ontological framework apropos languages, according to which Ladino and each of the linguistic varieties with which it has come into contact since its inception (Spanish, Hebrew, French, Turkish, Greek, etc.) would constitute lexically or structurally based categories. Only from this perspective is it reasonable to pose the ontological question of which words belong (legitimately) to Ladino and from which language(s), even if it is only to answer that all of them can or should belong in Ladino.

By contrast, from the perspective of critical sociolinguistics, these questions cannot be asked (let alone answered) meaningfully. A question formulated about

Ladino *qua* "named language," i.e., as a "cultural object defined by place, memory, identity, history and of course, a socially given (though sometimes contested) name" (Otheguy et al. 2015, 291), cannot be answered in reference to each Ladino speaker's respective idiolect. This is because these idiolects (i.e., the unique linguistic characteristics, including vocabulary, grammar, pronunciation, and usage, of individual speakers) exist prior to the ontological introduction of distinctions and discussions pertaining to the legitimate influence (or lack thereof) between Ladino and other languages understood as self-contained, autonomous, discrete entities that "forcefully shoehorn speaker's linguistically unique idiolects into cultural overdetermined language categories" (Otheguy et al. 2015, 291). As concluded by Ricardo Otheguy et al.:

> Languages (…) are groupings of idiolects of people with shared social, political or ethnic identities that, once so grouped, are described using linguistic terms that tend to give the mistaken impression that the grouping was based on linguistic grounds in the first place.
>
> (2015, 291)

Consequently, while there are undoubtedly large areas of overlap among the idiolects of people who communicate with each other on *LK* in so-called *ladino*, from this we should not surmise that *qua* named language Ladino constitutes a lexically or structurally based category. The reason is that such overlap is not coterminous with the boundaries that the sociocultural category *ladino* supposedly serves to demarcate, particularly in the Internet era, which allows for an unprecedented degree of heteroglossia and, conversely, an unusually restricted overlapping among the participant's respective idiolects. The overlap in question is a necessary condition (but not a sufficient one) for the establishment of externally named boundaries, which ultimately are also predicated on the right social and historical conditions (Otheguy et al. 2015, 290–1). Because of this, all in all, one could argue that in the Internet era, Ladino becomes a real imaginary space premised on nostalgia as much as on imagination (Yebra López 2023b, 87, 95).

Consequently, while seemingly effective for revitalisation purposes, the systematic and uncompromising enforcement of an artificial standardised version of Ladino à la *LK* runs contrary to the spontaneous[18] and empowering use of each Ladino speaker's linguistic repertoire.

Orthography

LK's cyber-standardisation is also largely premised on enforcing a specific Ladino orthography. As seen above, the second of the group rules (as per both *LK*'s website and the group's periodical email reminder of its rules), only after that of writing in Judeo-Spanish/Ladino, is to abide by the orthographic rules stipulated by the Israeli Ladino magazine *Aki Yerushalayim*: "to spread the use of a standardized method for spelling Ladino with Roman characters, according to the rules established by the journal *Aki Yerushalayim*."

Within the recurring email in question, and right before a table of equivalences (featuring the *Aki Yerushalayim* letters, their International Phonetic Alphabet [IPA] correlate, word examples, and explanatory notes concerning their pronunciation), the following instructions and observations are offered apropos the stipulated Ladino orthography:

> **With regards to orthography** (It is EASIER and more phonetic than Castilian Spanish!)
>
> - The vowels are the same as in Castilian Spanish.
> - ***K*** is used for everything that has this sound **(We do NOT use *q, c*)**
> - *S* is used for everything that has this sound **(We do NOT use *c*,** or **use it ONLY in the form of *ch*** for the *ch* sound in "milk" [*leche*] for instance)
> - *y* only for its sound, in grass [*yerva*], or ring [*aniyo*], or very [*muy*]
> - i is used for the conjuction "and" in English.
> - ***J*** has the same sound as the French jour.
> - We use ***dj*** for the *j* sound in English (as in jump): together [*endjuntos*], Jew [***djudio***], to play [***djugar***], etc.
> - ***B, V, S, Z*** have the same sounds as in English.
> - ***X*** can be only used for the sound "***gz***" as in "exam" [*examen*], "to exist" [*existir*], but when it features the *ks* sound, it is written with *ks* (tax [*taksa*], expulsion [*ekspulsion*], Mexico [*Meksiko*], etc.). On LK we also accept the digraph "gz" when the word features this sound.
> - **DIPHTHONGS**: On LK we accept both ways of writing diphthongs *i* or *y*: good–good [*bien-byen*], preparation–preparation [*preparasion-preparasyon*], ate–ate [*komio-komyo*], etc.
>
> As you can see, our rules are VERY logical! (my translation and italics; bold in the original).[19]

In the above section, our discussion apropos prescriptivism related to the language's designation made apparent the clear preference of participants for *ladino* over *djudeo-espanyol* and *djudezmo*, as well as for *djudeo-espanyol* over *djudezmo*, respectively. In turn, this inclination seemed to suggest the privileging of Romanisation (and, to a lesser extent, Spanishness) over Jewishness. After all, it seems reasonable to assume that if *LK* messages had been standardised around Hebrew scripts such as Meruba (block Hebrew letters used in modern Hebrew) or Rashi, *LK* members would have been more inclined to privilege glottonyms such as *djudezmo* and *djudeo-espanyol* over *ladino* and *espanyol*.

In alignment with the current hegemony of Romanisation understood as the widespread use of the Latin script, nowadays and with notable exceptions,[20] Ladino is no longer primarily taught in its traditional Hebrew scripts (Meruba, Rashi, and Solitreo), let alone in any other alphabet historically used to write in Judeo-Spanish, such as Cyrillic.

Consequently, nowadays the main orthographical disputes concerning Ladino do not revolve around the question of in which script to write it. Rather, they focus on two opposite positions on how to romanise Ladino: French-Ottoman Romanisation vs. Castilian Romanisation (see below for an explanation of these labels). This situation raises a two-fold question: (i) how did the Latin script come to prevail over Hebrew scripts when it comes to writing in Ladino? and (ii) why are there two (vehemently opposed)[21] Romanisation systems, and what are the ideological reasons behind this divergence?

Before modernity, it was customary for Sephardic Jewish writers of the Ottoman Empire to think of the most important difference between their everyday language (Ladino) and that spoken by Christians from Spain (Ibero-Romance, mostly Castilian) as scriptural: Jews used the Hebrew script whereas Christians used the Latin script. This sentiment persisted (and grew even stronger *qua* reaction) as Romanisation became progressively hegemonic towards the beginning of the 20th century. Until approximately 1925, Ladino was predominantly printed in Rashi (a semi-cursive Hebrew alphabet) and written in Solitreo (a cursive Hebrew alphabet) (Varol 2008, 22). Indeed, even as late as the middle 20th century, in some communities the use of Hebrew scripts in general and the Rashi script in particular, were still considered integral to Ladino (Bunis 2021, 22), and necessary for its survival in the future. As opined in 1904 by a journalist in Salonika by the name of Samuel Saadi Levy, "the day where a single Judeo-Spanish word is printed in a script other than Rashi, or so-called square Hebrew, that day our language will be dead and buried" (my translation from the Ladino original, published in 1902).[22]

However, towards the end of the 18th century and under the rule of Selim III (1761–1808), who was very much open to foreign dialogue and advocated several reforms, mostly under the influence of French diplomat Horace François Bastien Sébastiani de La Porta, the Westernisation of the Ottoman Empire (and with it, that of Sephardic Jews) began (Bunis 2019, 22).

The increased contact from Jews of the Ottoman Empire with Western European communities and languages, and particularly the re-encounter between Sephardim from the Ottoman Empire and the language of Peninsular Spain (which dates back to the 1859–60 Hispano-Moroccan war), paved the way for the romanisation of Ladino. This process was particularly intense among the most progressive Jewish families, which had already begun to send their children to local modern European schools (see, e.g., Benchetrit 2017, 48).

Already in 1866, one can find in the Ladino journal *El Nasional de Viena* [The National of Vienna] by Yosef Kalvo, an editorial letter suggesting that Hebrew letters be abandoned in favour of Romanisation (cit. in Bunis 2021, 23). In 1875, we witnessed in Balat (Istanbul) the foundation of the first school of the *Alliance Israélite Universelle* in the Ottoman Empire, with students being taught in Judezmo, French, and Turkish. In an announcement on the pages of the Sephardic journal *El Tiempo* apropos the opening of this school, we can already find a bi-scriptural system in place which, in the Latin alphabet, follows the same French-Ottoman Romanisation system advocated by *LK* after *Aki Yerushalayim* (cit. in Bunis 2019, 11).

On the one hand, this system was originally created to suit the needs of those who knew how to write Turkish, and it features letters that are commonly used in the Balkans (notably the 'k'), but not in Castilian Spanish (conversely, it does not contain letters commonly used in the latter, such as 'c' for the phoneme /k/, as well as '*ñ*' and 'll'). On the other hand, the most influential language in the adoption of this transcription system was French (as opposed to Spanish). In addition to being the only vehicular language of the school which was written in the Latin script (for the most part, Ladino was still written in Hebrew scripts, whereas Turkish was still written in the Arabic script), it was the *Alliance's* official language of instruction. Perhaps more decisively, it was the most powerful European language, the most prestigious one for business and politics carried out within the empire, and the language of choice for the most celebrated and renowned authors in France. On these bases, I refer to this Romanisation system as 'French-Ottoman Romanisation,' by opposition to the one that relies on Castilian Spanish at the expense of orthographic aspects from the Balkans, which I am calling 'Castilian Romanisation.'

As clearly shown in the group rules, *LK* moderators strongly privilege French-Ottoman Romanisation over its Castilian counterpart, normalising the stipulation of the former as easier/more convenient and phonetically more accurate than modern Spanish: "It is EASIER and more phonetic than Castilian Spanish!" (caps in the original; see above). Widely praised in scholarly and grassroots circles alike, this form of Romanisation has been adopted by the vast majority of Ladino writers. On the one hand, I agree with Bunis that "the orthography promoted in Ladinokomunita (…) is phonemically almost completely transparent (…) by linguistic criteria, it is an excellent solution for writing Judezmo in romanization" (2016, 333). On the other hand, *LK*'s French-Ottoman Romanisation has not gone unchallenged in either scholarly or grassroots environments. This demonstrates that the choice to adopt French-Ottoman Romanisation is far from self-evident, while also speaking to the importance of examining alternative (extra)linguistic paradigms and considering their motivations.

In particular, the French-Ottoman Romanisation system has been labelled by opponents as a *cacografía* [from the Greek *kakos*, i.e., 'bad' and *graphos*, i.e., 'writing', hence bad, defective, faulty writing] (Shmuel Refael 2018; see also Bunis 2016, 332), in contradistinction with the Castilian Romanisation system developed by Jacob Hassán (1968, 1978) and his disciples (e.g., Elena Romero).

Thus, as early as 1978 (hence prior to Shaul and Bortnick's proposed system), Hassán remarked that neither phonematic nor phonemic forms of transcription satisfy the legibility expectations and requirements of a Hispanophone audience:

> *Ni la transcripción fonemática ni menos aún la fonética, sea o no estricta, satisfacen los deseables requisitos de legibilidad (...) tal transliteración viene a reflejar los desajustes de la imperfecta adaptación de un sistema ortográfico 'ajeno' a una lengua romance.*
>
> (1978, 148)[23]

Needless to say, this attitude raises the question of why Spanish speakers should get special treatment when it comes to accommodating written Ladino.

At a more fundamental level, a paradox obtains from the above discussion: depending on who you ask, French-Ottoman Romanisation is easier, more accurate, more legible, and more phonetic than Castilian Romanisation, and vice versa. This contradiction seems to suggest the existence of extralinguistic factors (e.g., nationalistic motivations) behind the choice between these two Romanisation systems, whose adoption is nonetheless (or precisely because of it) often couched by their supporters in strictly linguistic terms, thus entailing ideological erasure (Gal and Irvine 1995, 974; see above).

Famously, this hitherto largely latent connection between linguistic and extralinguistic factors apropos how to best romanise Ladino surfaced in 2018. It was during the Fourth Tribune of Hispanism organised by the Cervantes Institute, devoted to Ladino and the creation of the National Academy of Judeo-Spanish [*Akademia Nasionala del Ladino*] in Tel Aviv, eventually formed on October 3, 2019. Shmuel Refael, a prominent member of this institution, described the *Aki Yerushalayim* transcription system as a *cacografía*, urging Ladino speakers to reconnect with the culture and tradition of the Spanish language:

> The danger of Judeo-Spanish is that Ladino speakers … are no longer connected with Spanish … it is not a spelling, but rather a cacography. When one does not know the roots of Spanish and does not know the Spanish alphabet, how is it that one can save a culture a great deal of which is based on the Spanish culture and tradition? … and because of this, we are very grateful for the initiatives of the director of the Royal Academy.
>
> (my translation)[24]

The above statement thus made apparent that there is a substantial link between the adoption of Castilian Romanisation for the purpose of writing Ladino, on the one hand, and the unabashed assimilation of Ladino into Spanish as the prestiged (rather than prestigious) linguistic variety within a supposed context of common Hispanophonia, on the other hand. In turn, Hispanophonia is predicated on the seemingly innocuous but deeply ideological claim that Spanish and Ladino (typically referred to as 'Judeo-Spanish' to make it seem derivative) are two varieties of the same language (see Del Valle 2007, 2009, 2011; Calderwood 2019). However, the idea that Ladino needs (and/or would benefit from) re-Hispanicisation is (at least partially) predicated on the modern colonial conceptualisation of the former, as a corrupt, deviant, or otherwise defective variety of 'proper Spanish.' This view is parallel with the longstanding perspective among Ashkenazi Jews that Yiddish is a corrupt variety of German, at least since the late 18th century (though Germanification attempts are limited to the 19th century). Ultimately, both positions incur the postcolonial reproduction of Standard Language Ideology (Lippi-Green 1994, 166; Walsh 2021; see above), from which the pejoration of these minoritised linguistic varieties first emerged (Stroud 2018).

Conversely, and as remarked in 2010 by Moris Shaul in a message to *LK*, the connection between the linguistic and extralinguistic factors behind the French-Ottoman Romanisation of Ladino lies in the belief the dignity of Ladino (and by extension, that of its community of speakers) is found in its distinctiveness from Spanish.

As it happens, the vast majority of members of the global Sephardic community vehemently opposed Refael's proposed language policy in the editorial of

El Amaneser, the only newspaper in the world entirely written in Ladino, in the September issue of that year (Yebra López 2022b, 80). Papo was not wanting in eloquence when he warned readers that "without those who use the cacography proudly, the Academy could turn out to be a "Cacademy" [wordplay between *caca* – feces, spelled à la Castilian Romanisation – and 'Academy']" (2018, 4; my translation).[25] He then drew attention to the assimilationism that animates Castilian Romanisation as advocated by Hassán and Romero, which in Papo's opinion, threatens Ladino's "Jewish autonomy":

> And what do people want? For us to adopt a Jakography [in reference to Jacob Hassán's suggested orthography]-, or an Elenography [in reference to Elena Romeros'] (…) the Elenists (…) want to assimilate and force the others to assimilate, abandoning the Jewish autonomy (in this case, orthography).
>
> (*idem 2018, 4*; my translation)[26]

The *El Amaneser* issue in question further included official statements issued by the ANL (Israel) and the Ottoman-Turkish Sephardic Culture Research Center (Turkey). Shaul himself concluded that these reactions bear witness to a strong and hopeful intellectual defence of Ladino's autonomy against the assimilationist attempt to "Castilianise" Ladino's orthography (see Yebra López 2022b, 80–1).

This retort is also consistent with a 2004 statement where Bortnick framed current Spanish as an ongoing intruder at the levels of orthography, and to a lesser extent, also vocabulary and syntax: "the most persistent problems come from the *intrusion* of modern Castilian, mostly in orthography, but also in vocabulary and syntax" (cit. in Pons 2018, 264; my italics; see the above section for a critical discussion of "foreign" elements in Ladino). *LK* moderator Aldo Sevi has echoed this sentiment on Facebook, stating that Castilian Spanish is the main "enemy" of Ladino (see Chapter 3 for a discussion on how this perspective colours his management on his Facebook group *Los Ladinadores*).

Overall, the above reactions would seem to suggest that even though from a historical perspective, standardisation constitutes a manifestation of the same colonisation and modernity that led to the subordination of linguistic varieties such as Ladino (and their speakers, the Sephardim) (Stroud 2018), this fact only becomes problematic when said standardisation revolves around Castilian Romanisation, rather than French-Ottoman Romanisation. Neda Pons has offered a lucid explanation to this paradox: to the extent to which French-Ottoman Romanisation as purported by *LK* moderators seeks to differentiate Ladino from contemporary Peninsular Spanish, the standardisation of Ladino around this transcription system can be understood as a symptom of a positive valuation of ethnocultural diversity in an increasingly globalised world (2018, 253).

At any rate, it is important to remember that ultimately the rationale behind any prescriptive policy concerning orthography is not just linguistic but also cultural and political. As remarked by Rohen, its implementation can only take place at the expense of impoverishing the speakers' respective unique linguistic repertoires, which is equivalent to not accepting the global community of Ladino speakers for what it is:

> (…) The correct way of writing and speaking Judeo-Spanish does not exist, and no language authority can establish it without throwing into the garbage all the other forms, which would be an impoverishment. I don't throw anything away, I accept everything, with those who accept me, such as I am.
>
> (Ladinokomunita 2011; cit. in Bunis 2016, 345)

Thus, to the extent to which linguistic elements such as orthography, are always-already connected in dialogical fashion to extralinguistic factors, one can (and perhaps should, as I do), prefer French-Ottoman Romanisation on linguistic grounds (or the Castilian one, for that matter), while still scrutinising that option through the lenses of a pertinent and necessary ideological critique. In this sense, as much as French-Ottoman Romanisation and Castilian Romanisation look diametrically opposed (as shown *inter alia*, in the aggressiveness with which their defenders argue in their respective favour), both positions converge in the adoption of the Latin script. Its robust presence in today's world (currently the most widely adopted writing system in the world, used by approximately 70% of the population) might mislead us into forgetting that, as I have explained in this section, this phenomenon is actually a late global trend, particularly among Ladino writers.

Pedagogy

Notwithstanding the above discussion, *LK*'s group rules insist in the moderators' (supposed) authority to enforce what is (putatively) the best way of writing Ladino by couching this effort in pedagogical terms. In other words, the idea is that it is precisely because there are moderators following a strict set of orthographic rules (as opposed to despite it) that members can (and should) follow *LK* rules worry-free, plus they get to (rather than have to) learn from their "mistakes," lest those be incurred again:

> Because of this, don't be afraid to write to us, even with mistakes [*yerros*]. You will see that the message is corrected when it's published, and if you compare what you wrote with what was published, you won't make the same mistake again.
>
> (my translation; bold in the original)[27]

This standardised version of Ladino is also hegemonic in the rest of major Ladino-speaking platforms online, including *Ladino 21* (see Chapter 2), *Los Ladinadores* (see Chapter 3), and *Enkontros de Alhad* (see Chapter 4), as well as for instructional purposes. Thus, in pedagogical initiatives across continental Europe and some parts of the United States, the prevailing geolect is that of Istanbul, almost always presented exclusively in French-Ottoman Romanisation and in a register that is very close to the contemporary spoken language. In this sense, the most widely adopted pedagogical volume is the 2008 English translation of Marie-Christine Varol's *Manuel de judéo-espagnol: langue et culture* (Paris 1998), which employs the *Aki Yerushalayim* writing system, albeit with accent marks (typically absent in that system) (Varol 2008, 22).

Conversely, the predominant standardised variety utilised for educational goals in Israel and certain regions of the United States does not prioritise the contemporary vernacular of a specific city or nation within the Sephardic diaspora (such as Istanbul). Instead, it is predominantly presented in the Rashi script (with occasional employment of Latin, Cyrillic, and Solitreo scripts), drawing from a range of literary genres traditionally cultivated in major Sephardic hubs worldwide, including Jerusalem, Istanbul, Izmir, Salonika, Constantinople, Sarajevo, Belgrade, Sofia, and New York. A prominent example of this instructional methodology is David Bunis' *Judezmo: An Introduction to the Language of the* Ottoman Sephardim (1999), an extensive introductory course at the university level written in Hebrew and utilising the traditional Rashi alphabet (Yebra López 2023b, 104).

As argued above, the enthronisation of any specific way of writing Ladino as the ideal or the best (including *LK*'s) is contingent upon a sociopolitical act of selective legitimation (rather than being an objective process). Consequently, while the ability of *LK* members to perform as fluent writers of this restricted variety of Ladino is a valuable skill, a worthwhile educational goal, and a legitimate aspect for which to test (see Otheguy et al. 2015, 301), reducing *LK*'s pedagogical mission to the implementation and reproduction of this standardised version effectively leaves out several features conventionally associated with Ladino. In the words of Otheguy et al., "it makes room only for those (…) idiolectal features found in the speech of those who share a superior class membership, political power, and, in many cases, an ethnic identity" (2015, 301) (see also Yebra López 2023b, 103–5).

As observed above, while minoritised idiolects and practices (such as those related to Ladino) need protection to grow, from a perspective attentive to diversity, when teaching them educational platforms (from email lists to universities) should not segregate minoritised speakers from their full idiolects and translanguaging practices.

Translanguaging is understood as "the deployment of a speaker's full linguistic repertoire without regard for watchful adherence to the socially and politically defined boundaries of named (and usually national and state) languages" (Otheguy et al. 2015, 281). Initially introduced by Cen Williams during the 1980s within the framework of Welsh education (Lewis et al. 2012), the concept of 'translanguaging' underwent subsequent development to encompass not only discursive techniques but also the educational methodologies derived from them and their role in empowering speakers from minoritised backgrounds (García 2009).

In recent scholarship, researchers including Ofelia García have directed their attention towards the implications of this paradigm shift, critically examining the inaccuracies, essentialism, and inequities inherent in the classical ontological framework concerning 'languages' (García 2013; García and Wei 2014; Otheguy et al. 2015). Specifically, these scholars have highlighted the conceptualisation of 'languages' (such as Ladino in this context) as 'named languages,' underscoring their status as socio-culturally constructed entities, rather than pre-existing phenomena. They argue that named languages represent amalgamations of partially overlapping idiolects (those idiolects being characterised by a unified lexico-structural repertoire) shared among individuals who identify with a common cultural or ethnic heritage (in our case, a Sephardic identity stemming from the expulsion of Jews from Spain in 1492) and who achieve effective communication (Otheguy et al. 2015; Yebra López 2023b, 90).[28]

Through the imposition of sociopolitical restrictions on the idiolects of minoritised speakers, which may involve the suppression of certain linguistic elements, traditional language instruction dissuades learners from integrating new linguistic features and conventions into their linguistic repertoire (Otheguy et al. 2015, 302). Consequently, the incorporation of novel features (in this case, those associated with *LK*'s standardised Ladino) seldom prompts learners to restructure their mental grammar based on these interactions, modify their speech in distinctive ways, or enrich their linguistic repertoire. This, in turn, arguably hinders the ability of many multilingual *LK* members to fully engage as successful, innovative, and critical communicators (Yebra López 2023b, 90). This issue is particularly relevant in the context of Ladino, given its diasporic nature and current status as "severely endangered" (UNESCO 2003; see also Introduction). Indeed, the vast majority of Ladino speakers are multilingual, with most employing other languages more frequently than Ladino in their daily interactions (Harris 1994, 255), thus engaging in consistent translanguaging practices (Yebra López 2023b, 105).

In this context, and in contrast with prevailing misconceptions and the initial prescriptive principle of *LK* (i.e., the requirement to write in Ladino; see above), teaching the target named language (Ladino) does not need to take place exclusively *in* that language, nor is such an approach inherently preferable (see Chapter 4). This assertion is supported by international research conducted over the past two decades, which illustrates that emerging language practices are intricately linked to established ones (García 2013, 3; Yebra López 2023b, 106).

Therefore, and as discussed above, only educational initiatives that enable students to utilise their complete linguistic repertoire (and not just part of it to exclusively develop proficiency in a restricted number of language practices that conform to *LK*'s standardised variety) can lead Ladino learners to effectively incorporate aspects of this named language into the mental grammar of their distinct linguistic repertoire (Yebra López 2023b, 106). As we shall see in the section below, this is the approach embraced by alternative Ladino email lists, where members can publish messages in any 'language,' and they overwhelmingly choose to do so in major named languages relevant to the Sephardic diaspora, such as Spanish, French, Hebrew, or English.

Furthermore, and as regards *LK* moderators' prescriptive-cum-pedagogical labour, monitoring the members' ability to recognise and adhere to *LK*'s standardised version of Ladino is different from assessing the richness and complexity of each member's unique idiolect. While the latter pertains to a genuine evaluation of linguistic competence, the former is (at least partially) about policing cultural and political proficiency. Conversely, when these two elements are combined such that the participant/student is assessed for both, the outcomes will be shaped by and mirror their cultural identity as significantly as their linguistic and communicative skills (Otheguy et al. 2015, 299; Yebra López 2023b, 106–7).

Lastly, prescribing that some learners attempt to restrict their repertoire to the limits of *LK*'s standardised version of Ladino entails requiring individuals to attempt to present themselves as having a cultural and personal identity and background different from their own, including social, geographical, and gender identities (Yebra López 2023b, 107). To the suppressed geolects, sociolects, and even genderlects mentioned above, one needs to add the (attempted) suppression of new realities of the 21st century, such as inclusive language. This process is well illustrated by an anecdote whose relevance will soon become apparent.

For the first time on *LK*, in March 2020, instead of using *karos todos* ['dear all,' in the masculine/neutral form according to the traditional Ladino grammar], or *karas todas* ['dear all,' only when addressing an all-female group], as an *LK* member, I decided to submit an email for publication with the salutation *kar@s tod@s*. To my bafflement, the email was published … but the salutation had been changed to *karos todos* without reporting any errors in the original email, even though it is customary to indicate those in caps in the final message after the moderators have amended any "mistakes" present in the original. In other words, my authorial choice had been suppressed without my consent or right to be informed about it. Upon realising what had just happened, I submitted a further email to the platform, denouncing the facts and explaining my lexical choice in the following terms:

> (…) I believe this is an important subject, and we may or may not agree on what to do about it, and whether it should be written as *'karos todos i todas,' 'kar@s tod@s,' 'karas todas' or 'karos todos'*. But neglecting it doesn't seem like the solution to me. Perhaps in Ladino there is also room to use @ in order not to discriminate. Why not? In any case, I believe it's better to let the speakers decide what they prefer.
>
> (my translation)[29]

Shortly thereafter I received a response from Bortnick, who explained to me that it was the right of the moderators to carry out edits as they saw fit (a point which I had not denied), that mine was one of those "changes that professors want to impose on us" [*"trokamientos ke mos keren impozar los profesores"*] (which I never did), and that they had never come across the use of '@' other than in emails (an informal fallacy known as "appeal to tradition"). Additionally, Bortnick asked me two questions:

> 1. How is this sign pronounced? (how to pronounce it, and how to use it in speech?) 2. Do you believe that 'linguistics professors' have the authority to

> compel native speakers, of any language, to make the changes in their languages that THEY, the professors, order them to make?[30]
>
> (my translation; caps in the original)

Concerning the former, when examining the usage of '@' as an inclusive and non-binary marker, its observed pronunciations in speech indicate that speakers articulate it in manners consistent with the phonological rules of Ladino. In this case, the '@' can be pronounced as the vowel /e/, i.e., as if the salutation read *kares todes*. As for the latter, in addition to being a rhetorical question (to the extent that it presupposes a specific answer – no – to the question being posed), it is one loaded with pernicious assumptions: first, that it was my intention as a linguistics professor to obligate others to adopt my proposed terminology (which was not the case); second, that L1 speakers ("native speakers") are necessarily more competent in (and thus should have more authority, and the last saying in matters pertaining to) that language, which as I have explained above, constitutes a fallacious instance of nativespeakerism.

Further emails were published on the topic soon afterwards which, for the most part, supported censoring the use of inclusive language on grounds that it was "destroying the language" and supposedly revealing of being reckless and insecure.[31] Concerning the former, Rafael Marcelo Díaz wrote as follows on *LK*:

> If everyone writes as they wish, we will destroy the language and also the beauty that Ladino has. Usage changes a language over time, over the years, over the centuries; grammar is never changed by the imposition of a group. I don't like inclusive language and I don't like using '@' to include women and men. I don't believe this language is the correct way to defend women's rights.
>
> (2020; my translation)[32]

"Since you got your degree and you know every fucking thing"

While Bortnick was right to point out that *qua* regulators, *LK* moderators have the right to modify messages as they see fit, by the same token, it was also my right to stop writing on *LK*. In the end, after a brief period of absence on *LK* and notwithstanding the fact that further members sided against the use of inclusive language (see above), I (and the rest of those who wanted to use inclusive language) were allowed to use this salutation and other forms of inclusive language predicated on the @ uneditedly, which we have been doing ever since.

Nowadays there is also a *Ladino 21* video on this issue (Dembowski 2022), and even an edition on the *Pronouns.page* website which allows users to create a personal, multilingual card (including in Ladino) with their names, pronouns, identity words, pride flags, etc., which one can then link in their bio or email footer (*Kooperativa "Konsilyo de Lingua Neutrala"* 2023). Moreover, in March 2024 I published an entire article in the *Aki Yerushalayim* magazine, featuring the first LGBTQIA+ terminology in Ladino (Yebra López 2024a), which will also be published in English as part of a forthcoming edited volume (Kahn and Valijärvi forthcoming).

Revitalisation

Just like the telling fact that the founding of *LK* was suggested within the context of a conference apropos the orthography of Ladino, the statement on the Yahoo! version of *LK*'s website that *LK*'s goals are the "maintenance, revitalization and standardization of Ladino" (cit. in Brink-Danan 2011, 108) would seem to imply an alleged interdependence between revitalisation, on the one hand, and maintenance and standardisation, on the other. While there is nothing wrong with the revitalisation of Ladino understood, as per Zuckermann's definition, as "the revival of a severely endangered language with minimal intergenerational transmission" (2020, 199 – see Introduction), the idea that revitalisation goes/ought to go hand in hand with maintenance and standardisation (let alone that revitalisation might *require* maintenance and standardisation) merits closer inspection.

One could argue that Zuckermann's and my own ontological deflation of languages from well-defined, self-contained entities to mere col-lect-ions, i.e., abstract ensembles of lects (sociolects, idiolects) represents an obstacle to the protection and preservation of these linguistic entities (Ladino, in our case). After all, how can we work towards the preservation of something about which we do not have a clear and distinct understanding? How can we succeed if we do not even know what we are trying to protect?

To this one can simply answer that on the contrary, a revivalist perspective allows us to move away from the otherwise conservative and purist goal of 'language maintenance/preservation,' which often sterilises minoritised named languages, turning them into museum pieces (including 'Ladino'). Conversely, it implies the adoption of sustainable practices by multilingual speakers that thrive on activating (something close to) their full linguistic repertoire without watchful adherence to the socio-politically defined boundaries of a named language (in our case, 'Ladino'). In doing so, Revivalistics facilitates (rather than impeding) the goal of protecting minoritised communities and their idiolects. In sum, revitalisation efforts should be directed towards the affirmation and preservation of Ladino understood as a cultural-linguistic ensemble of idiolects and translanguaging practices deemed valuable by the members of the global Sephardic community, rather than as an essentialised, prescriptivised artefact.

Thus, from the perspective of Revivalistics, when it comes to revitalising Ladino, the goal is to become less puristic and more realistic. This implies encouraging *LK* members to reject the sort of language myths related to Ladino that we have exposed in the above section, instead accepting, embracing, and celebrating inevitable hybridisation: "Revivalistics discards any imprisoning purism prism and makes the community members realize that shift happens. And there is nothing wrong with shift happening. Hybridization results in new diversity, which is beautiful" (2020, 209).

Let us recall that it is precisely this crucial insight that lies at the heart of the "impassioned plea" (Bunis 2016, 337) made by Rohen to raise awareness that, were it not for the fact that Ladino has evolved, it would be already dead (cit. in Bunis 2016, 337) (see above).

In this sense, *LK*'s vigorous advocacy for (non)nativespeakerism and the cyber-standardisation of Ladino can be understood as a symptom of (rather than a solution to) anxiety triggered by the emergence of a new, geographically de-localised, digitally-native sociolinguistic phase in the evolution of Ladino within the Sephardic diaspora (Sepharad 4; see Introduction).

At the same time, a note of caution is in order at this point, namely: while emphasising diversity over standardisation is commendably inclusive, it might not always be the most effective solution for revitalisation purposes, even after we have reconceptualised what that revitalisation looks like (see Chapter 3). In this sense, the relatively low popularity enjoyed by alternative email lists discussing Ladino that do not prescribe its (explicitly standardised) use (see below), would seem to suggest there might be a telling, positive correlation between prescribing and/or monitoring the vehicular use of Ladino, on the one hand, and the popularity of that email list, on the other.

By virtue of what I hope will be insightful juxtapositions, the below sections on further Ladino and Yiddish email lists, respectively, will allow us to further problematise two key assumptions, namely: *LK*'s axiom that revitalisation goes/ought to go hand in hand with maintenance and standardisation and conversely, Revivalistics' presupposition that diversity should always trump standardisation, and that this is not to the detriment of revitalising the endangered language in question (Ladino) but actually conducive to it.

The Ladino Culture Forum (2002–12) and *SefaradiMuestro* (2008 to the present)

While there have been other Web 1.0 Sephardic virtual communities under the form of correspondence circles explicitly seeking to revitalise Ladino (Held 2010; Romero 2017; Yebra López 2021c), none of them have reached the popularity and revitalisation success of *LK*. The most notable examples of alternative Ladino-speaking correspondence circles are the forum Ladino Culture Forum/*Forum Tarbut ha-Ladino* (2002–12), hosted by the Israeli website *Tapuz*, and the email list *SefaradiMuestro* (2008 to present), hosted by Google groups.

Concerning Ladino Culture Forum (LCF, henceforth), just like in the case of *LK*, the ethnic origin of participants with significant control was also partly Sephardic, and the online interaction paradigm followed a many-to-many model, plus discussion on both platforms revolved around similar topics. However, LCF only featured members from Israel (around 350 in total, compared to *LK*'s 1,500+[33]), and relied exclusively on the orthographic system of Ladino in the Hebrew script (initially unregulated, then standardised) (Held 2010, 85–6; Yebra López 2021c, 112). Furthermore, over the years LCF evolved from the use of Ladino as a cyber-vernacular (i.e., as a vehicle of everyday content, and thus akin to *LK*), to a cyber-postvernacular (i.e. symbolic; see Introduction, Chapters 3 and 4). Eventually, members stopped using Ladino, and the last messages were almost invariably in Hebrew (Romero 2017, 280).

Regarding *SefaradiMuestro*, whereas just like on *LK* and LCF, the ethnic origin of participants with significant control is also partly Sephardic and the online interaction paradigm follows a many-to-many model, Ladino is the main language, but not the only one. Spanish, French, and, to a lesser extent, others, are also used. Moreover, *SefaradiMuestro* was founded by Sephardic author Sharope Blanco, who continues to administer it, following a split from *LK* motivated by a number of disagreements with the latter's policies and practices. In a note published by *eSefarad* (see Chapter 4), eight months after the creation of *SefaradiMuestro*, Blanco delineated the defining attributes of her email list. The first two points are diametrically opposed (in fact, they are a direct response) to *LK* in matters of content moderation (where authenticity is equated with the absence of standardisation) and the regulation and discussion of lexical choices:

1 We do not moderate the writings we receive because I think that the messages must remain authentic, to the extent to which they are absolutely intelligible.
2 We are not interested in whether the word is correct, or how this and that should be said, from what etymology is the word, the grammar and the vocabulary, etc.

(cit. in *eSefarad* 2009; my translation)[34]

The longevity of an email list such as *SefaradiMuestro*, centred around the lack of standardisation and dismissing lexical choices as a predominant discussion topic, offers concrete evidence that there is an actual demand for those policies among a decent number of Sephardim. Nevertheless, its relative moderate success when compared to *LK* raises a fundamental question: what factors have contributed to the success of *LK* vis-à-vis alternative correspondence circles seeking to revitalise Ladino? In particular, what importance can be attributed to *LK*'s standardisation around French-Ottoman Romanisation as a distinctive aspect? Is there, as we have hypothesised in the previous section, a correlation between prescribing and/or monitoring the vehicular use of Ladino (conceptualised à la Standard Language Ideology), on the one hand, and the popularity and/or revitalisation success of that email list, on the other hand? A comparative analysis apropos Yiddish correspondence circles might serve to shed further light on this critical issue.

Yiddish Correspondence Circles

The most celebrated Yiddish correspondence circle is the email list *Mendele* (1991 to the present), whose list owners are Victor Bers (Yale University) and Josh Price (Columbia University). It currently features 2,000+ members. Just like on *LK*, the language in question (and in this case, its literature) is itself the most discussed topic. However, standardisation is low (only minor revisions are carried out, and messages can be published in Yiddish with Hebrew letters, Romanised Yiddish, and English), and the language is mostly used in cyber-postvernacular fashion.

Similarly to what happened apropos *LK* (whose cyber-vernacular use led to cyber-postvernacular splits), but in the opposite direction, *Mendele*'s use of Yiddish mostly as a cyber-postvernacular resulted in *Tate-mames* and *Yiddishland qua* cyber-vernacular responses. Nonetheless, just like LCF and *SefardiMuestro* fell short of *LK*'s popularity, these alternative email lists also failed to reach a comparable degree of notoriety.

The Yiddish email list examples, together with the *SefaradiMuestro* case study, would seem to suggest that neither high standardisation nor the exclusive use of the target language in vernacular fashion are necessary conditions for the longevity and/or revitalisation/reinvigoration success of the correspondence circle in question.

Still, one could object that a successful correspondence circle in terms of participation, popularity, and longevity need not imply success at revitalising/reinvigorating the target language. It follows from this that *Mendele*'s prominence as a correspondence circle despite the lack of high standardisation and the extensive and habitual use of the target languages as a cyber-vernacular, does not disprove *per se* the idea that these characteristics might be necessary conditions for the successful revitalisation/reinvigoration of an endangered language.

Nevertheless, Brink-Danan has remarked that scholars of Yiddish have found trends towards purification to be either counterproductive or irrelevant to the "efforts to promote the language" (2011, 116).[35] Instead, the most active users of the language (i.e., the Hasidim), who practice a form of linguistic syncretism that unlike *LK*'s, does not discriminate against "illegitimate" borrowings, do not concern themselves with standardisation, purification, or structural/grammatical forms (2011, 116–7) (see also Chapters 3, 4, and 5).

On the other hand, it has been recently argued that Hasidic online orthography is undergoing a process of standardisation, though not through prescriptivist measures or top-down policies, but rather as an organic process (Benedict 2021), i.e., a form of what I have called 'implicit prescriptivism' (see above). While as observed above, the leaders of this religiously conservative community do not support efforts to standardise the language, a study found that this lack of explicit standardisation coexisted with a form of "rapid implicit standardisation": users that had participated the longest on the platform displayed a tendency to limited innovation, instead adopting the conservative variety (Bleaman 2020).

Research on the popular discussion forum *Kave Shtiebel* ['Coffee Room'] (2012 to present), which features over 400,000 posts by more than 2,000 users, and where Hasidic Jews communicate in Hasidic Yiddish, would seem to support this hypothesis. Here the maintenance of the endangered language in question (Yiddish) is predicated on its use as a cyber-vernacular, reflecting a broader ideology that seeks to fight acculturation into non-Jewish norms (Isaacs 1999).

These experiences would seem to lend further credence to what I have observed about *LK*, i.e., that whether standardisation is explicitly endorsed or rejected, over a sufficient period it seems to be always accompanied by some form of implicit standardisation.

Lastly, as observed by Brink-Danan apropos Simon Bronner's discussion of his mother's culture clubs in Yiddish (*vinklen*), members of the *vinklen* were often suspicious about the attendance of novices. The latter's presence was perceived as a threat to the "total experience they had imagined" (2001, 45; cit. in Brink-Danan 2011, 113). Thus, a look into Yiddish reinvigoration also allows us to better understand the functionality of (non)nativespeakerism in *LK* to reinforce the artificial performance of Ladino as an imagined space premised on nostalgia as much as on imagination, as in the idealisation of a supposed Golden Age where the language was "authentically" and exclusively spoken by "native speakers."

Conclusion

In this initial chapter, I have discussed the first generation of mostly written, mostly read Ladino-speaking online communities, i.e., correspondence circles (including popular email lists and forums). In particular, I have focused on the most celebrated exponent of this digital affordance, namely the email list *Ladinokomunita* (Bortnick 1999), which was the first instance of the successful creation and maintenance of an online community devoted to the revitalisation of Ladino in the 21st century, i.e., a Sephardic Digital Home-Land (Yebra López 2021c), and continues to play a major role in the dissemination of Ladino as a standardised cyber-vernacular.

On the one hand, I have praised *LK* as a remarkable and inspirational case of how to use the global reach of the Internet to bring together thousands of members scattered in diaspora, empowering Sephardim to control the fate of Ladino, getting members to actively participate in the preservation of the unique ethnolinguistic identity of their speakers via functional differentiation (Ferguson 1959; Fishman 1967), promoting intergenerational transmission, expanding its domains of use (Brink-Danan 2011; Pons 2018), and adapting this endangered linguistic variety to the realities of the 21st century (Eisenlohr 2004; Yebra López 2021c).

Additionally, I have stressed that *LK*'s journey demonstrates that the Internet is more than a repository of information, instead actively influencing the fate of languages like Ladino and shaping many of its aspects. Paramount instances include facilitating communication and the incorporation of loanwords across noncontiguous territories, as well as the dissemination of an unprecedented degree of heteroglossia. Ultimately, these elements contribute to the cyber-koinesation of Ladino (i.e., the creation of a new koiné on the Internet – see Introduction) and its eventual cyber-standardisation (explicit around its French-Ottoman Romanisation, implicit in its geolectal, sociolectal, genderlectal aspects, as well as in its vernacularity and adoption by heritage speakers and new learners). It is the ensemble of these features as pioneeringly embodied by *LK* that allows us to speak of the emergence of Sepharad 4 as a disruptive innovation in the history of the Sephardic diaspora in general and the sociolinguistic development of Ladino in particular.

On the other hand, my critique of *LK*'s standardisation from the perspectives of critical sociolinguistics and Revivalistics has highlighted the problematic aspects of the platform's journey from cyber-koinesation to cyber-standardisation. I have nominally divided my examination into four aspects that effectively operate within a continuum: prescriptivism, orthography, pedagogy, and revitalisation.

First, and unlike the previous literature, I have made a distinction between explicit and implicit prescriptivism. The former includes the stipulation of what I have called 'French-Ottoman Romanisation,' which dates back to the late 19th century, and has been widely adopted as the preferred form of writing Ladino. The latter comprises a geolectal bias towards Istanbul and a socio-/genderlectal preference for the popular register (as opposed to rabbinical literature), which is closer to the vernacular used at home and passed intergenerationally, mostly by women. Additionally, I have examined how this strong prescriptivism translates into the overrepresentation of metalinguistic elements as part of *LK*'s discussion topics, particularly concerning glottonyms, speech community (including nativespeakerism), and lexicon (featuring three stands of purism: Spanish and English foreignness, Turkish foreignness, and syncretism). I have read all three less as solutions to the question of what counts as *the* most legitimate/authentic language designation, community member, and Ladino word than as symptoms of the persisting influence of Eurocentric post-18th-century Standard Language Ideology online. I have argued that within this context, Ladino's authenticity (and ultimately, that of its global speech community itself) cannot so much be *described* in accurate terms as *performed* in idealised fashion. This performance relies on ethnic and linguistic stereotypes conducive to the suppression of an otherwise unprecedentedly heteroglossic languaging, which in turn generates the anxiety underlying several censorial and gatekeeping practices and ideologies. In this sense, *LK*'s cyber-standardisation catalyses the portrayal of Ladino as a real imaginary space premised on nostalgia as much as on imagination.

Second, I have observed that this critical analysis carries over into matters of orthography, where I have traced a genealogy leading to the gradual replacement of the Hebrew script by the Latin one, as well as the polemic clash within the latter between proponents of French-Ottoman Romanisation (adopted by the vast majority of speakers, with *LK* serving as a major flag bearer) and Castilian Romanisation (of neocolonial overtones). Ultimately, both positions incur the postcolonial reproduction of Standard Language Ideology, which underlies both the pejoration of Ladino as "broken Spanish" (i.e., a defective attempt at speaking/writing a "modern" language such as Spanish) and its supposed need to assimilate into the Latin alphabet and European languages through Romanisation (particularly of the Castilian sort) (Lippi-Green 1994, 166; Stroud 2018; Walsh 2021).

Third, I have demonstrated that my examination has critical implications for the field of pedagogy. I have contended that *LK*'s prescriptivism translates into a well-intended pedagogical effort whereby the moderators claim that it is precisely because they are enforcing a strict set of orthographic rules (as opposed to despite it) that members can (and should) follow *LK* rules worry-free. While the ability for *LK* members to perform on the platform as fluent writers of a restricted variety of Ladino is a valuable skill (e.g., it is the hegemonic one for instructional purposes in Europe and some parts of the United States), reducing *LK*'s pedagogical mission to this aspect is highly problematic. It erases several features conventionally associated with Ladino, segregates speakers from their full idiolects and translanguaging practices, and discourages learners from incorporating new linguistic features and practices into their own repertoire (Otheguy et al. 2015, 302). Ultimately, it amounts to insisting that speakers try to pass for people with a different cultural and personal identity and background (e.g., socially, geographically, in terms of gender), which is a form of exclusion.

Fourth, I have argued that a Revivalistics perspective allows us to move away from the otherwise conservative and purist goal of 'language maintenance/preservation' and towards a more realistic and hybrid understanding that focuses on the affirmation and preservation of Ladino understood as a cultural-linguistic ensemble of idiolects and translanguaging practices deemed valuable by the members of the global Sephardic community.

Additionally, a look at further Ladino-speaking correspondence circles has allowed us to further relativise the importance of "authenticity" and "legitimacy," as well as of metalinguistic discussions, with some authors even equating the genuineness of Ladino with its very de-regulation.

Furthermore, a comparative analysis of Yiddish reinvigoration through email lists and online forums has granted us the opportunity to better understand that the revitalisation/reinvigoration of endangered languages can take place in absence of explicit standardisation (but hardly in absence of implicit, organic one, which is inevitable). Additionally, it has shed further light on the functionality of (non) nativespeakerism on *LK* to reinforce the artificial performance of Ladino as a real imaginary space premised on nostalgia as much as on imagination.

Last but not least, my analysis in this chapter has yielded not only answers, but also questions, paramount among which are the following: is there a positive correlation between the use of Ladino as a cyber-standardised cyber-vernacular, on the one hand, and the popularity and/or revitalisation success of the email list in question? If, as the *Ladinokomunita* case study suggests, that is indeed the case, it should lead us to problematise a key tenet of Revivalistics, i.e., the idea that linguistic diversity and hybridity are necessarily preferable over standardisation, at least when it comes to utilitarian reasons (in the case at hand, effective online revitalisation of Ladino). On the other hand, we ought to bear in mind that *LK* and Revivalistics hold different (potentially incommensurable) understandings of revitalisation, so that unlike the former, the latter is uninterested in preserving a standardised form of the language, focusing instead on sustaining Ladino as an heteroglossic col-lect-tion. What type of language policies could lead to that?

Furthermore, to what extent does this seemingly positive correlation between the standardised vernacular use of Ladino and a given online platform's success at revitalising the language (conceptualised in close association with Standard Language Ideology) carry over into further endangered Jewish languages and Web 2.0 platforms? Our comparative analysis of Yiddish email lists and online forums, particularly the popularity of *Mendele*, would seem to suggest that neither strict standardisation nor the exclusive or vernacular use of the language in question are necessary conditions for the popularity and/or revitalisation success of that email list/online forums. At the same time, it also seems to beg the question of whether we should disentangle the popularity of the platform, on the one hand, from its revitalisation effectiveness, on the other. This issue will also be at stake in my inquiry in subsequent chapters of this volume, on whether the positive correlation between the standardised vernacular use of Ladino and a given online platform's success at revitalising the language as a self-contained entity (or otherwise) carries over into Web 2.0 platforms.

Indeed, a diachronic analysis of the number of messages posted on *LK* since its foundation in 1999 seems to show a participation decline in the last couple of years, coinciding with the rise and consolidation of *Los Ladinadores* as the flagship Sephardic Digital Home-Land of the Web 2.0, thus indicating a critical mass adoption of and transition into Web 2.0 platforms among Ladino speakers. I shall now turn to the discussion of these.

Notes

1 Standard Language Ideology is the conventional ontological framework employed for the conceptualisation of languages, which became particularly prominent within the context of post-18th-century European nation-states. It refers to the belief system or set of ideas that elevate one particular variety of language as the standard (in our case, traditionally 'modern' Spanish, and now standardised Ladino) against which all other forms of language are judged. This ideology often promotes the idea that there is one "correct" or "proper" way to speak or write a language, typically based on the speech patterns of the dominant or prestigious social group within a society. Varieties of language that deviate from this standard are often stigmatised or seen as inferior (Lippi-Green 1994, 166; Walsh 2021).

2 "*Despues ke votimos kon grande majorita ke keremos adoptar la ortografia ke aviya establesido la revista de Aki Yerushalayim (...) Moshe Shaul (...) mos disho ke siendo ke akseptimos ke este [sic] sera (...) la mijor manera de eskrivir el djudeo-espanyol kon letras latinas, podemos, agora ke tenemos un internet, i munchos de mozotros tenemos kompiuters en kaza (el miyo era muevo, fue mi primer kompiuter), podemos azer un sirkolo de korrespondensia para praktikar i promover esta eskrituria. Me paresio a mi muy buena idea, komo dishe teniya un kompiuter muevo. Vine a kaza, demandi a una persona 'komo se aze un grupo de korrespondensia? ambezame' i me disho ke aviya una ... era antes de Yahoo Groups, aviya otro sitio ... va ayi i dize 'start a group' i lo ... lo avri ... ma antes de esto demandi a unas kuantas amigas i amigos mios, dishi 'mira, me ambezi a avrir ... ansina, un grupo ... ma devesh de suskrivrivos vozotros. Si estash d'akordo, lo vo avrir. Si no, no lo vo avrir.' Me disheron 'si si, buena idea, buena idea.' Empesimos kon kuatro o sinko personas i en supito komo se ekspandio ... esto fue un miraklo, porke no izimos ... ni ... ni eskrivimos artikolos, ni izimos dinguna reklama ... de boka en boka ...*" (my transcription).

3 See below for concrete examples of discussions and messages, intended to offer readers a clearer sense of how *LK* functions and what its content is like.

4 *(...) kuando mos demandan tales preguntas devemos responder de manera optimista, porke ay munchos ke dizen 'si, la lengua esta agonizando, ya no ay mas ken la avla, ya dospues de una djenerasion o dos ya va despareser...' Yo digo, 'esas son profesias ke se realizan si las dizes muncho tyempo. Si tu krees ke la lengua no sera avlada, despues de sinko anyos ya no la van avlar. Si yo digo 'no, la lengua va a bivir (...) es una lengua ke puede kontinuar a bivir komo lengua de kultura'* (my transcription).

5 *El internet es muy, muy emportante. La prova es Ladinokomunita. Kon grande plazer me enkanti de ver ke se engrandesio tan presto (...) i sin dinguna publisidad, solo de la djente bushkando en internet kozas de ladino, de djudeo-espanyol, o de sefardi (...) i de diya en diya ay mas kozas (...) el internet es la manera de ekspandirlo oy en diya, porke mozotros, los ke savemos la lingua de ... de nasimiento ya mos estamos muriendo, no*

vamos a estar aki i grasias al internet (...) mos estan sintiendo a mozotros i esperamos ke muncha djente en los anyos venideros mos van a kontinuar a sentir i tener un poko de ... de kerensia en esta lingua, i el internet es la manera de azerlo (my transcription).

6 *Es kon grande pena ke mos ambezimos la piedrita de Selim Amado, el ermano kerido de Rachel, una persona de muy grande valor por muestra komunidad i kultura/ Ke su alma repoze en Ganeden./ Guler de Estanbol.*

7 *Kon Grande Pena me ambezi la pedrita de Selim Amado/Una persona muy mahpul ke tenia el onor konoserlo/ Una persona de muy grande valor para el mundo de Ladino/ Una persona ke mos va amankar [sic] muncho/ A su famiya kero dizir "Mas por dingunos no/ El Dio bendicho ke vos mande Pasensia"/ Ke tu alma repose en Gan Eden kerido Amigo Selim./ "Menuchatcha Eden"/Moshico Cohen – israel.*

8 *Kerido Carlos, /Pedrites tu kamisa o ganates bastante en las mesas de jugos (21/Blackjack, craps, roulette, poker, ets.) o en las makinas de 'slots' (ke toman o trayen paras) en kryptomoneda para inchir tu armaryo kon vestimientos muevos?!/Jake/Rachel: Carlos estuvo en Las Vegas.*

9 At the same time, it is important to observe that this binary is not necessarily self-evident (see below and Introduction).

10 *Vos rogamos a todos, por favor, de sigyir estas reglas:*
- Eskrivir en djudeoespanyol/ladino.
- Eskrivir segun las reglas de ortografia de Aki Yerushalayim.

11 "Languaging" encompasses any linguistic activity, which is always understood in dialogical relationship with the world and ourselves. As argued by Ofelia García and Li Wei (2014), this conceptualisation offers a more accurate and emancipatory perspective than that of languages as reified entities: "Language is not a simple system of structures that is independent of human actions with others, of our being with others. The term languaging is needed to refer to the simultaneous process of continuous becoming of ourselves and of our language practices, as we interact and make meaning in the world" (8) (see also Introduction).

12 *Ay ke entender ke al alevantarse, un ombre (…) pasava su dia en el charshi kon otros machos; i la mujer, en la kaza i en el kortijo kon otras mujeres. I por esto uvo estratas de lengua totalmente de varones (...) todo lo ke tyene ke ver kon las finansias (...) la politika (...) el govierno (...) los ombres avlavan un djudeo-espanyol muy turkizado (...) i de otro lado, en el momento kuando los machos empesan a avlar sovre las kozas de ley, pasan al ebreo* (my transcription).

13 See Schwarzwald (2019) for a full list of Ladino monikers.

14 *Yo kreygo firmamente ke saver avlar una lingua ke no es tuya, no kere dezir ke perteneses a la nasyón de akeya lingua. Por enshemplo, unos anyos atrás, yo savía avlar el espanyol kon el aksento de la isla de Porto Riko en el Karibe, i lo savía azer tan bueno ke munchos portorikenyos me yamavan Boricua, ke kere dezir portorikenyo. Agora, saver avlar la lingua komo eyos, me izo portorikenyo? Siguro ke no! Yo só sefaradi, de alma i de korasón! A mí me agrada muncho la kultura i la forma de ser de los katalanes de Espanya, i por más admirasyón i karinyo ke tengo por eyos, i mizmo si reusho a ambezarme el katalán, nunka podré ser uno de eyos porke no só katalán. Para mí, los sefaradis son los desendyentes de los djudyós ekspulsados de la península ibérika en 1492.*

15 The notion that an individual's first language aligns with their "mother tongue" has been challenged through various criticisms, with significant concerns including the following: the extent of the mother's influence in the child's upbringing, if any; situations where couples do not share the same primary language; instances where the language spoken in the surrounding environment differs from the predominant language spoken at home; and the effects of migration on these dynamics (Yildiz 2012; Yebra López 2021f) (see also Chapters 3 and 4).

16 My translation from Pons' citation of it in the Serbian original.

17 Drawing upon an anti-essentialist understanding of languages as col-lect-ions, i.e., abstract ensembles of lects (sociolects, idiolects), in his volume *Revivalistics* (2020) Zuckermann encourages linguists to reject myths and accept, embrace, and celebrate

inevitable hybridisation: "Revivalistics discards any imprisoning purism prism and makes the community members realize that shift happens. And there is nothing wrong with shift happening. Hybridisation results in new diversity, which is beautiful" (2020, 209) (see Introduction).

18 Contrary to a common objection, here 'spontaneous' does not necessarily mean 'anarchic' (see Auer 2022; cf. my discussion of Duolingo's Yiddish Course in Chapter 3; see also Conclusion).

19 "***Por la ortografia** (Es MAS FASIL i mas fonetika del espanyol kastilyano!)*

- *Las vokales son las mizmas del espanyol kastilyano*
- ***K** se uza por todo lo ke tiene este sonido **(NO uzamos q, c)***
- *S se uza por todo lo ke tiene este sonido **(NO uzamos c, o la uzamos SOLO en forma de ch** para el sonido de la ch en "le**ch**e" por egzemplo)*
- ***y** se uza solo por su sonido en* y*erva o ani*y*o o muy.*
  i se uza por la konuksion "and" en inglez.
- ***J** tiene el sonido komo en fransez jour.*
- *Uzamos **dj** para el sonido del j en inglez (komo en jump): en**dj**untos, **dj**udio, **dj**ugar, ets.*
- ***B, V, S, Z** tienen sus sonidos komo en inglez.*
- ***X** se puede uzar solo por el sonido "**gz**" komo en "examen", "existir", ma kuando tiene el sonido de ks, ke se eskrive kon **ks** (taksa, ekspulsion, Meksiko, etc.). En LK akseptamos tambien la digrafa "gz" kuando el biervo tiene este sonido.*
- ***DIFTONGOS:** En LK akseptamos las dos maneras de eskrivir los diftongos kon i o y: bien-byen, preparasion-preparasyon, komio-komyo, ets.*
  Komo vesh, muestras reglas son MUY lojikas!"

20 Judeo-Spanish courses at the University of Bar-Ilan, Oxford University (see Chapter 4), and *Ladino 21*.

21 While there are further Romanisation styles (e.g., those adopted by the Paris-based association *Vidas Largas* and the Turkish newspaper *Şalom*, respectively–Varol 2008, 22), the French-Ottoman and Castilian styles are by far the two most popular ones.

22 For the original comment, see Bunis (2021, 24) and accompanying footnote.

23 "Neither the phonematic transcription nor even less the phonetic one, be it strict or not, satisfy the desirable legibility requirements (…) such transliteration comes to reflect the mismatch between the imperfect adaptation of an orthographic system that is 'alien' to a Romance language" (my translation).

24 *El peligro del judeoespañol es que los ladinohablantes ... ya no están conectados con el español ... no es una grafía, sino una cacografía. Cuando uno no conoce los [sic] raíces del español y no sabe el alfabeto del español, ¿cómo es que puede salvar una cultura que mucho de ella está basada en la cultura y la tradición del español? ... y por esto estamos muy agradecidos a las iniciativas del director de la Real Academia* (my transliteration; Refael 2018, cit. in Yebra López 2022b).

25 *Sin la djente ke uzan orguyozamente la Kakografia, la Akademia komo Cacademia salir podria.*

26 *I ke se kere? Ke pasemos a jakografia, o a elenografia? (...) los elenistas (...) keren asimilarse i enforsar a los de mas ke se asimilen, abandonando a la otonomia (en este kavzo grafia) djudia.*

27 ***Por esto, no tengash miedo de eskrivirmos mezmo kon errores (yerros)**. Verash ke el mesaj esta korijado kuando se publika, i* **si komparash lo ke eskrivitesh kon lo ke se publiko no vash azer el mezmo yerro otra vez**.

28 In this volume I understand Ladino as a named language, so that when I refer to it as a "language," it is only metaphorically, rather than as a validation of the traditional ontological framework (see Introduction).

29 *(...) Kreygo ke este es un sujeto emportante, i ke podemos o no estar d'akordo sovre kualo kale azer, i si se deve eskrivir 'karos todos i todas,' 'kar@s tod@s,' 'karas todas' o 'karos todos'. Ama neglijarlo no me sembra la solusyon. Ya puede ser ke en el ladino*

ay tambyen espasio para kulanear @ kon el buto de no diskriminar. De ke no? En kualseker kavzo, kreygo ke es mijor deshar a los avlantes desidir kualo preferen.

30 *1. Komo se pronunsa este sinyo? (komo meldarlo, i komo uzarlo en avlando?) 2. Kreyes ke los 'profesores de linguistika' tienen la otorita de ovligar a los nativo avlantes, de kualkera lengua, a azer los trokamientos en sus linguas ke EYOS, los profesores, les ordenan?*

31 From a historically situated perspective, these reactions were highly predictable, as the global Ladino-speaking community has been traditionally characterised by markedly conservative (language) ideologies, a phenomenon that translates into strong prescriptivism and scarce innovation. Consequently, prior to the advent of the Internet, the only written references to terms we can associate with what we now know as the 'LGBTQIA+ community' were derogatory, including '*karucha*' [homosexual], '*blando/blandiko*'/ '*dulse*' [an effeminate man], '*kulampara*' [A Turkish borrowing from Persian to refer to someone who likes boys; in gay relationships, 'top' or a man who prefers the insertive role], '*kulo alegre*' [gay], '*es o bichim*' [Turkish expression used in Ladino to mean that a gay person 'is that way,' and there is nothing that can be done about it] and *ijoghlan* ['tomboy' for a lesbian. This word is a combination of '*ija*' – Spanish for 'daughter' and *oğlan*-Turkish for 'boy'] (Altaras 2022a; I would also like to thank Prof. Zeljko Jovanovic for related insights as part of our private correspondence). Conversely, Ladino terms concerning the LGBTQIA+ community have entered the everyday lexicon of countries with major Sephardic population, as attested by the incorporation of '*vieja*' into the lexicon of Israeli homosexuals to denote an effeminate and old homosexual male.

32 *Si kada uno eskrive komo kere vamos a destruir la lingua i tambien la ermozura ke tiene el djudeo-espanyol. El uzo troka una lingua en el tiempo, en los anyos, en los sieklos, nunka se troka una gramatika por la imposizion de un grupo. No me gusta el lenguaje inklusivo i no me gusta la @ para inkluir mujeres i ombres. No kreygo ke este lenguaje seya la forma korrekta de defender los derechos de las mujeres.*

33 See Held (2010, 85) and Romero (2017, 280).

34 *1. No moderamos los eskritos ke arresivimos porke kreyo ke los mesajes deven kedar otentikos en la mezura ke se entyenden por seguro.*
2. No mos interesa si el biervo es justo o komo se dize esto i akeyo, de ke etimolojiya es el biervo, la gramatika i el vokabularyo ets.

35 Notwithstanding Brink-Danan's claim, it should be noted that there is still a very strong purist/prescriptivist streak among many Yiddishists, especially among the elderly.

Part 2

Web 2.0

The Participative, Multisemiotic, Multimodal Social Stage (2000s-)

2 Digital Archives on YouTube (2011-)

Autoridad Nasionala del Ladino i su Kultura, eSefarad CCSefarad, Wikitongues, *Ladino 21,* and VLACH

Introduction: Revivalistics and the Ethnography of YouTube Digital Archives

Community-based archives, i.e., those collected, organised, and maintained by members of a particular community or group, have experienced considerable growth over the past 50 years.[1] This has also been the case in Ladino studies, particularly since the beginning of the 21st century. In its first two decades, we have witnessed a proliferation of digital archives devoted to the grassroots documentation and preservation of the Sephardic language and culture on YouTube. This trend includes the digital archives of the *Autoridad Nasionala del Ladino i su Kultura* הרשות הלאומית לתרבות הלאדינו, alternatively referred to as *Autoridad,* henceforth (2011–16), *eSefarad CCSefarad* (2013 to the present), a few Ladino videos (2016–21) from the 'Jewish Languages' playlist of Wikitongues (2011 to the present), *Ladino 21* (2017 to the present), the 'Judeo-Spanish Collection' (2019–20) of Vanishing Languages and Cultural Heritage (VLACH, 2016 to the present), and the 'Ladino (Judeo-Spanish)' playlist (2020) of the Endangered Language Alliance (ELA, 2012 to the present).

These community-based archives have played and continue to play a pivotal role in the revitalisation of Ladino in Sepharad 4 (see Introduction). Indeed, as noted by Ghil'ad Zuckermann in *Revivalistics* (2020), the first stage of any language revival must feature a protracted period of observation and careful listening, which is itself the province of language documentation: "The bread and butter of linguistics are language documentation and analysis. These tasks are front and centre, especially before any language reclamation effort and before and during any revitalisation or reinvigoration effort" (214).

On the other hand, and notwithstanding its occasional (non)nativespeakerism (see Introduction, as well as Chapters 1 and 3; see also the below quote), Revivalistics can and does address many of the ontological blind spots of traditional documentary linguistics. In the absence of this critique, the 'preservation' of minoritised 'languages' becomes hollow, i.e., "a sterile academic or technocratic exercise that cannot really be characterised as genuine language revival" (211–2). Crucially, and much in the vein of my critique of *LK*'s prescriptivism in the previous chapter, when it comes to digital archives, Revivalistics also helps us shift our attention from 'language' *qua* autonomous, discrete, self-contained system to the *speakers*.

DOI: 10.4324/9781003473664-5

This shift transforms the linguist into a community field activist, rather than an armchair intellectual:

> Revivalistics includes Revival Linguistics (…), which is very different from the already-established branch of linguistics called Documentary Linguistics (…). How different is revival linguistics from documentary linguistics? An insensitive linguist can still be a documentary linguist or a typologist but can hardly be a revivalist. Revivalists ought to work with the community. Their work is much more than a laboratory endeavour that analyses a morpheme or a phoneme (…) A revivalist cannot be an armchair linguist, who sits at home and analyses language. A revivalist cannot be a veranda linguist, who observes the natives without engaging them. A revivalist cannot be a caravan linguist, who interrogates a native speaker in a caravan until the native speaker faints out of exhaustion and then the linguist brings the next native speaker in the line. A revivalist must be a community field linguist.
>
> (207, 208)

Thus, community-based archives should focus on the speakers, with the caveat that, as observed by Colett Grinevald and Michel Bert, the isolation of some speakers (particularly in the case of Ladino) and further aspects makes them difficult to identify: "the total number of individual speakers does not comprise a linguistic community in the traditional sense of the term" (Austin and Sallabank 2011, 46). Notwithstanding this difficulty, community-based archives should also seek to revitalise 'languages' (in the case at hand, Ladino), not so much as supposedly autonomous, self-contained entities, in close association with Standard Language Ideology (Lippi-Green 1994, 166; Walsh 2021; see Introduction and Chapter 1), but rather as cultural-linguistic complexes.[2]

In this sense, and just like I remarked apropos *LK* (see Chapter 1), while minoritised idiolects and practices require protection to grow (i.e., functional differentiation – Ferguson 1959; Fishman 1967), such growth should not occur at the expense of isolating them from the interactions of speakers whose idiolectal repertoires are much richer than what the archives are willing to license (Otheguy et al. 2015, 302). Participants must be allowed to speak freely, even when that defeats and challenges monolingual expectations anchored in the classical ontological framework about named languages (in our case, 'Ladino') (Otheguy et al. 2015, 302; see also Chapter 1). This effort entails a move away from conservative and purist idealisations about 'Ladino' as a self-contained language, instead embracing hybridisation as an unavoidable outcome of fieldwork linguistics. Thus, while the name of certain Ladino digital archives may respond to the perceived strategic advantage of labelling the archive through a recognisable language name (e.g., *Ladino 21*), their aim should not (and may not) be to document Ladino as a supposedly self-contained language. Instead, their goal should be to revitalise it as a cultural-linguistic matrix of multiple idiolects with different attrition degrees and translanguaging practices that the community of Sephardic speakers (whether culturally or ethnically so) finds valuable (see Chapter 1) (Yebra López 2023b).

However, while both Zuckermann's position on language revitalisation and the overall impetus behind the above-mentioned Ladino digital archives are primarily descriptive, i.e. to show how Ladino is *de facto* spoken (rather than to prescribe how it should be spoken), ultimately any descriptivist task necessarily leads to and is mediated by various forms of (implicit) prescriptivism (see Chapter 1). As a result of this tension between descriptivist principles and *de facto*, implicit prescriptivism, the community-based YouTube archiving of Ladino for revitalisation purposes in the 21st century operates somewhere on a continuum between two ends: standardised 'Ladino' and the full idiolects and translanguaging practices that already exist in the community and feature plenty of sociolinguistic variation across region, gender, and learnedness (see below).

On the one hand, self-reflexivity apropos such idealism is not missing in Zuckermann's work, which offers specific case studies showing the intricate relationship between linguistic and extralinguistic factors. In particular, Zuckermann acknowledges that the new revivalistic technologies pose "a direct challenge to existing authority structures relating to the everyday management of knowledge, collaboration, and participation" (2020, 233), predicting that how communities of minoritised speakers negotiate these issues will have important repercussions in the results of their related revivalistic efforts. On the other hand, *Revivalistics* offers no systematic treatment of how these extralinguistic dynamics influence the revivalistic process and outcome in the case of YouTube (digital) archives. Such an endeavour, though, can be greatly facilitated by a critical and ethnographical conceptualisation of the archive.

Apropos ethnography, Clifford Geertz (1973) famously noted that rather than being a specific set of methods or techniques, this branch of anthropology relies on the utilisation of "thick description." Deploying "thick description" involves not just the description of video scenes, but also interpreting their meaning within the context of the culture and/or community in which they take place (in our case, the global Ladino-speaking community) (6). Additionally, in *Along the Archival Grain: Epistemic Anxieties and Colonial Common Sense* (2008), Ann Laura Stoler puts forward her own ethnographic approach to archives, placing the accent on the power dynamics that structure them: "ethnography (…) in archives attends to processes of production, relations of power in which archives are created, sequestered, and rearranged" (32). Thus, conceiving of the archive as an ethnographable space entails an understanding of it as an alive and dynamic structure, i.e., a space "that transcends officially designated archival collections" (14).

In the case at hand, the above insights translate into the realisation that any descriptive effort needs to take into account that, in practice, YouTube digital archives in Ladino are embedded in and co-produced with several entities. These include the State of Israel (*Autoridad*), non-profit organisations like *eSefarad*, VLACH, Wikitongues, *Ladino 21* Community Interest Company and the ELA, and last, but certainly not least, YouTube itself (and hence Google – which owns YouTube – and by extension, the big five technology corporations responsible for centralising the Web 2.0, namely: Google, Amazon, Meta, Apple, and Microsoft – GAMAM; see Chapter 6). This last one also encompasses YouTube users posting in the comments section, which is a key aspect of the kind of participative affordances of the Web 2.0., already heralded by the many-to-many interaction model adopted by *LK* in the early 2000s (i.e., every member can interact with any other member).[3]

In sum, just like languaging as an activity offers a more accurate and emancipatory perspective than that of languages as reified entities, rather than conceptualising archives as objects or things, we ought to understand them as part of an "archiving-as-process" (Stoler 2008, 20). Archives are not neutral repositories reflecting the participants' memories and languaging. Rather, they also shape the present and the future of that languaging (1–2). The multiple ways in which audiovisual materials in Ladino are organised, catalogued and classified depends on both YouTube's own structure and functioning, and a constant negotiation with the ways in which academia, the State of Israel (and for that matter, the United States, France, Turkey, and further enclaves with sizeable Ladino-speaking populations), and the wider community of Ladino enthusiasts continue to observe, identify, and discuss Ladino as an "endangered language" in need of (online) "revitalisation." This makes of archives performative spaces where the range, depth, geographical, temporal, and ideological valence of Ladino in the 21st century is navigated and negotiated on an ongoing basis.

For instance, drawing upon the case study of Hebrew reclamation in Israel (1880s–1930s), Zuckermann has observed that such process was accompanied by parallel acts of (conscious) transvaluation, particularly axiological reversal implying extreme amelioration (i.e., a shift from negative to positive consideration) (2020, 127–43). As remarked by Patrick Eisenlohr, this tendency is particularly salient in the contemporary electronic use of languages that had been traditionally deemed "archaic" or unfit for the 21st century (2004, 24), including Irish, Quechua, and Gaelic (29) (see also Chapter 1).

The case study of the digital revitalisation of Ladino in general and on YouTube in particular would seem to lend further credence to the above-discussed dynamic, as the active presence and dissemination of Ladino on YouTube disproves the negative preconception that *qua* minoritised, endangered, and ancient language, Ladino is archaic or unfit for purpose in the 21st century. Regardless of the actual content of these videos, the medium (Ladino + YouTube) is already the message: Ladino is compatible with modernity (a similar procedure is at play in the collocation 'Ladino 21' – see below).

This (*prima facie*) unlikely combination between Ladino, on the one hand, and digitally mediated modernity as articulated through YouTube content, on the other, is further enabled and catalysed by the multimodal affordances (i.e., the written, the visual, the aural, the gestural, and the spatial) and postvernacular semiotic modes (i.e., the symbolic use of Ladino, rather than its referential one – Shandler 2004, 2005) that are facilitated and disseminated by the digital platform in question (more on this below; cf. Chapter 1).

Together, these phenomena further attest to my contention in the previous chapter that the Internet platforms that shape and are shaped by Sepharad 4 as a disruptive innovation in the history of the Sephardic diaspora in general and the sociolinguistic development of Ladino in particular (an email list in the previous chapter, a YouTube archive in the present one), are far from mere passive repositories of information. Instead, they testify to the fascinating fact that the Internet is actively shaping the fate of Ladino, and ultimately contributing to its cyber-koinesation (i.e., the creation of a new koine on the Internet) and its eventual cyber-standardisation (through both explicit and implicit prescriptivism) as a post-geographical variety, both in its vernacular and postvernacular semiotic modes (see below; see also Chapters 1 and 3). Within this process and for the above reasons, Web 2.0 platforms like YouTube constitute a qualitative leap vis-à-vis Web 1.0 ones.

Lastly, the multimodal and multisemiotic affordances of the Web 2.0 vis-à-vis the Web 1.0 would seem to point to the analytical need to distinguish between different qualitative stages within the 'Talknological Revolution' as understood by Zuckermann, i.e., as the fourth linguistic revolution in History, after the emergence of speaking, typing, and typewriting, respectively (xxii, xxiv) (see Introduction).

With this theoretical framework in mind, I shall now turn to the analysis of my case studies.

Ladino Digital Archives on YouTube (2011 to the present)

Since 2011, the field of Ladino Studies has witnessed a proliferation of digital archives devoted to the grassroots documentation and preservation of this named language. These include the YouTube digital archives of the *Autoridad Nasionala del Ladino i su Kultura* *הרשות הלאומית לתרבות הלאדינו* (2011–16), *eSefarad CCSefarad* (2013 to the present), a few Ladino videos (2016–21) from the 'Jewish Languages' playlist of Wikitongues (2011 to the present), *Ladino 21* (2017 to the present), the 'Judeo-Spanish Collection' (2019–20) of VLACH (2016 to the present), and the 'Ladino (Judeo-Spanish)' playlist (2020) of the ELA (2012 to the present).

First, there is the *Autoridad*, with strong ties to the State of Israel. It was created in 1997 thanks to a law passed by the Knesset on March 3, 1996, its declared goal is to preserve and promote Ladino, and it publishes the Ladino-only magazine *Aki Yerushalayim* (1979–2016, 2019 to the present). The first chairman of the board was Yitzhak Navon, who was also the first Sephardic president of Israel (1978–83). Created by Matan Stein in 2011, the YouTube-hosted digital archive of the *Autoridad Nasionala del Ladino i su Kultura* *הרשות הלאומית לתרבות הלאדינו* (2011–16) was the first of its kind. It features 6.26k subscribers and contains 133 videos (in Hebrew and/or in Ladino, almost exclusively set in Israel). These clips are divided into 11 playlists featuring activities by the *Autoridad,* autobiographies in Ladino, *konsejas* [folklore stories] in Ladino, sketches, mixed genres, songs from the *Folklor de Kol Israel* project, two individual collections (Hayim Nahmias and Susana Weich-Shahak), Ladino dialects, and Haketia.

Second, *eSefarad* (2008 to the present) is a non-profit project created by Liliana and Marcelo Benveniste, from Buenos Aires, Argentina, to serve as an information hub apropos Judeo-Spanish culture. Highly successful at fundraising,[4] it comprises the *Raíces de Sefarad* conference cycle, the Ladino/Judeo-Spanish seminar *Savor de Ladino*, the eSefarad.com portal, the free subscription *eSefarad* weekly bulletin (which is sent by email), the weekly radio station *Magacin Sefaradí* on Radio Sefarad (online) from Spain and Radio Jai from Argentina, an online TV channel called *eSefaradTV*, and the weekly Ladino-only Zoom meetings cycle *Enkontros de Alhad*.

The YouTube channel *eSefarad CCSefarad* (2013 to the present) has been active for over a decade, boasts 5.61k subscribers and features 757 videos about Sephardic culture (mostly in Ladino and/or Spanish). This material is divided into 20 playlists, encompassing the network of Spanish Jewish Quarters of Spain *Caminos de Sefarad* [Paths of Sefarad], the 2024 summer edition of the conference cycle *Raíces de Sefarad* [Roots of Sefarad], 2024 events, the compilation of Jewish liturgical poems or hymns *Piyutim para Fiestas y Alegrías* [Piyutim for Festivals and Joy], the cycle of read theatre and songs *Pujados i no Menguados* [Improved and not Impoverished], 2023 events, the Spanish podcast *Perlas Sefaradíes* [Sephardic Pearls] (by Maria Esther Silberman de Cwyner), the Haketia podcast *La Vida en Haketia* [Life in Haketia] (by Solly Levy), *2022 events*, *2021 events*, *2020 events*, a selection of "special videos," a tribute to singer Dina Rot, a selection of "outstanding" videos, the weekly Ladino-only meeting *Enkontros de Alhad* (see Chapter 5), the online world concert *Unidos por el Ladino* (see below, as well as Chapter 5), the *Raíces de Sefarad* conference cycle, the Sephardic music trio Barjan, the first *Shadarim*[5] meeting (2018), and a *soirée* at the CIDiCSef[6] (2013) featuring Liliana Benveniste. The digital archive's unparalleled amount of shorts (short-form sections, featuring videos at a maximum length of 60 seconds) and lives, reveals a very high degree of consistent activity and content output.

Third, Wikitongues is a US non-profit organisation founded by Frederico Andrade, Daniel Bögre Udell, and Lindie Botes in 2014, and aims to sustain and promote all languages. Its 'Jewish Languages' playlist features three videos entirely in Ladino, published between 2016 and 2021. Two of them were recorded on Zoom by the participants themselves through coordination by Noah Usman, while a third one was recorded in person. They all have an autobiographical focus, and none of them include subtitles. The participants are Isaac Azouz (Istanbul, Turkey), Jacky Benmayor (Thessaloniki, Greece), and Sara Yonatan Musnik (Paris, France).

Fourth, *Ladino 21* Community Interest Company (2020 to present) is a London-based non-profit which was founded by myself and Alejandro Acero Ayuda to offer Ladino classes, courses, apps, a digital archive, consultations, talks, transcriptions, and translations. This initiative dates back to 2017, when Alejandro and myself, in conjunction with Sephardic author Benni Aguado (see Chapter 3), created the YouTube-hosted digital archive *Ladino 21*. This archive enables Ladino-speaking members of the global Sephardic diaspora to document the history of their own commonality across several genres, such as semi-structured interviews, autobiographical accounts, stories (inclusive of folk tales), jokes, readings, academic talks, songs, theatre plays, and Ladino apps. It features more than 3,000 subscribers and over 350 videos recorded in more than 20 countries with over 100 Sephardic participants. Not all of these videos are high resolution (particularly the earlier ones) and none of them feature subtitles.

Fifth, VLACH was created in 2016 at the Austrian Academy of Sciences (*ÖAW*). VLACH's declared mission is not just to document vanishing languages for long-term archiving, but also to "aim for more academic engagement with language, an open access policy of user-friendly collections which can better serve both scientific research and the communities whose aim is to preserve their oral heritage" (VLACH 2016). Its *Judeo-Spanish Collection* (2019–20) contains 51 videos (only 50 are in Ladino, i.e., 13.3% of the digital archive), all of which are individual interviews recorded entirely in Ladino, with high resolution, an autobiographical focus, and subtitles in English and Ladino (the latter self-made in the Latin script, albeit not following the *Aki Yerushalayim* orthography – see Chapter 1). The videos were recorded in Istanbul (Turkey) with the local participants.

Sixth, the ELA is a New York City-based non-profit organisation founded in 2010 by linguist Daniel Kaufman and artist and poet Ross Perlin. It emphasises community collaboration, ethics guidelines, and the use of specialised linguistics hardware and software, such as Fieldworks Explorer (FLEx) and ELAN to share its findings with communities and the broader public (ELA 2023). As part of a directly related project, entitled *Software for Enriching Endangered Language-annotated Databases with Crowd-sourced Linguistic and Cultural Input: Travel Supplement,* in 2015 Co-Principal Investigator Daniel Kaufman was awarded over $300,000 by the U.S. National Science Foundation (NSF 2015). The ELA YouTube channel was created in 2012. The 'Ladino (Judeo-Spanish)' playlist of this digital archive appears as a subsection of the playlist 'Europe' (thus implicitly classifying Ladino as a European language) and contains 12 videos. These are part of a high-resolution New York series produced by Roberto Drilea and Colleen Cassingham, mostly in Ladino, but also with a significant portion in English, plus Ladino YouTube subtitles. The videos in question were recorded with local participants. Furthermore, this digital archive features seven videos containing Ladino songs performed live by Sephardic singer Sarah Aroeste.

In addition to the above-discussed initiatives, there are a few other YouTube channels involving songs exclusively in Ladino, though their in-depth analysis falls beyond the scope of this chapter.

Overall, and much in the spirit of Revivalistics, the above Ladino digital archives on YouTube stem largely from non-profit organisations, feature an open-access policy, focus on community engagement and ethical guidelines,[7] and adopt user-friendly interfaces.

In what follows, I will discuss how these YouTube archives contribute to the digital revitalisation of Ladino by analysing them from the perspective of Revivalistics as supplemented by an ethnographic perspective on YouTube (see above). In particular, I will be focusing on four major themes: (i) revitalisation, (ii) the tension between descriptivism and prescriptivism, (iii) multimodality, postvernacularity, and transvaluation, and (iv) pedagogics.

Revitalisation

Like traditional documentary linguistics, Revivalistics posits the idea that any documentation process needs to be preceded by a long period of attentive listening and observation. Unlike documentary linguistics, though, Revivalistics contends that the researcher(s) in question ought to be community field linguists, rather than armchair linguists (see above). To what extent do (Ladino) linguists and archivers partaking in the above YouTube digital archives abide by those two tenets?

"A Protracted Period of Observation and Careful Listening"

Revivalistics agrees with traditional documentary linguistics in the premise that any documentation process ought to be prefaced by a period of careful (and ideally empathetic) observation and listening.

We can safely surmise that Ladino digital archives on YouTube such as the *Autoridad Nasionala del Ladino i su Kultura הרשות הלאומית לתרבות הלאדינו*, the *Judeo-Spanish Collection* of VLACH, and the *Endangered Language Alliance*, all feature a similar preliminary period of careful and empathetic observation and listening. Furthermore, based on my first-hand experience, the initial development phases of *Ladino 21* as a YouTube digital archive also attest to this protracted process. As it happens, the concept of establishing a digital archive for Ladino named *Ladino 21* only emerged through discussions with Acero Ayuda after my recounting of a personal encounter with Ladino L1 speaker Aguado in New York City. During this encounter, I carefully listened to Aguado's narrative and agreed with him that both the story and the language employed were indispensable components of a form of cultural heritage necessitating documentation.

"A Revivalist Must Be a Community Field Linguist"

A crucial aspect underlined by Zuckermann is that practitioners of Revivalistics cannot be armchair intellectuals, or else linguists conducting fieldwork from the comfort of their own caravan. Rather, they need to engage their participants by meeting the latter in their own terms, which often entails working around their preferred time and place. Lest linguists lose touch with the very people that make their efforts worthwhile and relevant. Especially within the context of an online endeavour such as digital archives, conducting interviews in person helps support community engagement: archivers/interviewers collect first-hand knowledge of the current state of the Sephardic diaspora, capturing the local area and experience, and sharing it with viewers. As explained by Paul Axtell,

> in-person meetings provide a sense of intimacy, connection and empathy that is difficult to replicate via video (…) It's much easier to ask for attentive listening and presence, which creates the psychological safety that people need to sense in order to engage and participate fully.
>
> (cit. in Charatan 2020)

Consequently, in what follows I will be assessing the extent to which Ladino digital archives hosted on YouTube fit the bill of community field linguistics à la Revivalistics based on two main criteria: the geographical reach of their fieldwork (given the fact that Ladino is a global diasporic language), and ratio between online and in-person fieldwork (with the caveat that in-person efforts were negatively impacted or altogether discontinued for the better part of the 2020–22 period due to the COVID-19 pandemic).

First, the YouTube digital archive of the *Autoridad Nasionala del Ladino i su Kultura* *הרשות הלאומית לתרבות הלאדינו* (2011–16) was created and managed by Matan Stein, who has taught Ladino at the Hebrew University of Jerusalem (plus Yiddish and Hebrew outside of it). Because this digital archive started and ended its activity before the pandemic, it was unaffected by it. While the overwhelming majority of its interviews (as well as further genres, such as songs), were recorded in person, its geographical location is restricted to the State of Israel.

Second, the founders of *eSefarad CCSefarad* are predominantly Sephardic, and their content features a strong community engagement worldwide: from the *Enkontros de Alhad* (co-organised with 10+ Ladino-related institutions and featuring Ladino speakers from across the globe – see Chapter 5) to the comedy sketches *Pujados i no Menguados* (led by community members Esther Cohen and Rubén Tevah), passing through the podcasts *Perlas Sefaradíes* (conducted by community member María Esther Silberman de Cywiner) and *La Vida en Haketía* (performed by Western Judeo-Spanish speaker Solly Levy). On the other hand, and in terms of fieldwork, interviews are all remote (though there are in-person cultural activities in Argentina and Israel).

For its part, the three Ladino interviews (2016–21) featured on the Wikitongues digital archive hosted on YouTube were facilitated by Noah Usman and John Kazaklis. Usman is a trained linguist with experience in the documentation of Jewish languages. He helped Azouz and Yonatan Musnik record their own videos in Ladino, though he did not interview them *in situ*. John Kazaklis comes from a Mediterranean background and conducted an in-person interview with participant Jacky Benmayor in the latter's hometown of Salonika. Kazaklis, who has recorded further languages from Wikitongues, including Greko, Pontic Greek, five dialects of Circassian in Jordan, Turkmen, and Turkish (Wikitongues 2020), interviewed Benmayor at the Jewish museum of Salonika. In a subsequent interview, Kazaklis reflects back on his recording, emphasising the fact that Benmayor is a community member, and further explaining how he came into contact with him:

> So Jack is a part of that community. His parents were survivors. And um, there's probably about 1,000 members of the Jewish community left in Thessaloniki (…) I connected to, I was connecting with the Jewish Museum of Thessaloniki, Erica, and she was like hey, I have a person for you, the perfect person to come and share, and has a history with the community. And so, she scheduled a meeting and we met at the museum, and we did a recording, in 2016.
>
> (Wikitongues 2020)

Concerning *Ladino 21*, we have stressed community engagement since the beginning, both in terms of geographical reach and in-person interviews. *Ladino 21*'s geographic span is larger than any other YouTube channel (with perhaps the exception of *eSefarad CCSefarad*'s 'Enkontros de Alhad' collection – see Chapter 5), including material from over 20 countries: Argentina, Brazil, Bulgaria, Canada, Chile, England, France, Greece, Israel, Mexico, Morocco, the Netherlands, Poland, Portugal, Serbia, South Africa, Spain, Sweden, Turkey, the United Kingdom, and the United States. Furthermore, from its inception to the outbreak of the COVID-19 global pandemic (early 2020), *Ladino 21* carried out the vast majority of its recordings in person, subsequently adopting a hybrid approach (combining in-person and remote interviews) post-pandemic (since mid-2022, approximately) (see Chapter 5). Our pre-pandemic activity included in-person recordings in the United States, France, England, Spain, Argentina, and Brazil. Post-pandemic, we have recorded interviews in the United States, Spain, England, Morocco, and France.

The shared use of Ladino between interviewer and interviewee has brought us closer to our archive participants, allowing us to build trust with community members, as well as making for a more intimate interaction. In words that have traditionally (yet erroneously) been attributed to Nelson Mandela, "if you talk to a man [sic] in a language he understands, that goes to his [sic] head. If you talk to him [sic] in his [sic] language, that goes to his [sic] heart" (cit. in Mission Forward 2023). Additionally, *Ladino 21* has always had as part of its team both Sephardic advisors (co-founder Benni Aguado, 2017–20, Eliezer Papo, 2020–22, and Aldo Sevi, 2022 to the present) and a Sephardic honorary president (Yuri Sasson, since 2019).

For its part, VLACH's interviews (2019–20) were filmed in person in Istanbul (Turkey) with local residents, which means that the linguists in question had to travel there and meet participants in the latter's place of residence, but also that the digital archive's geographical reach is limited to one city (VLACH's website does feature an additional collection in Bosnia, but its photo and video sections are empty) (2023). The website specifies that the Istanbul interviews were part of a broader PhD project undertaken by Iona Aminian Jazi (also featured as Nechiti) at the University of Vienna, which also includes fieldwork in Ceuta and Tetouan concerning Haketia. Aminian Jazi's fieldwork endeavours concerning minoritised languages also include further named languages such as Zargar Roman, Western Mongolian, and Rumanian varieties. By her own admission, community engagement is at the heart of her work, with an emphasis on reciprocity and catering to the needs of the community: "the main driving force (…) is (…) to cultivate a continuous dialogue with the communities we are investigating, to create an environment for reciprocal exchange where each active member can shape responsible documentation strategies according to their community means" (Aminian Jazi 2019). Additionally, in the VLACH section apropos Judeo-Spanish, Aminian Jazi specifies that interviews were rendered possible by the assistance of a local community member in Istanbul: "This documentation project would have never been possible without the help of the community member, Deyvi Papo, who has given us the confidence of his multilingual insight (L1 Turkish) where our language knowledge reached its limits (…)" (Aminian Jazi 2019).

Lastly, in the case of the ELA, all of its interviews (2020) were in person, and as discussed above, its Ladino archive is reduced to a New York City series produced by Roberto Drilea and Colleen Cassingham, who interviewed 12 participants based in the city. Drilea (a Romanian-American filmmaker) and Casssingham (a Brooklyn-based documentary filmmaker) are both interested in the intersection between storytelling and the human experience. While Drilea has previously worked on endangered languages (Dead Tongues – IMDb 2016), Cassingham has been primarily interested in *engagé* films, or, in her own words, "politically committed artful nonfiction that pushes formal boundaries" (The Video Consortium). Both Drilea and Cassingham's broader intellectual interests, as well as further projects developed by ELA apropos indigenous languages, would seem to testify to the pivotal centrality of community engagement to ELA's *modus operandi* in general and their Ladino series in particular, which is also consistent with its proclaimed ethos on the website: "ELA research, as much as possible, is community-driven, participatory, and grows from the ground up – research *for* and *with* communities" (emphasis in the original).

Overall, Ladino archivers/linguists on YouTube are closer to the ideal of a community field linguist à la Revivalistics than to the figure of the armchair intellectual. They often engage their participants by meeting them in person in their local city and asking them to speak in Ladino (*Autoridad*, *Ladino 21*, VLACH, ELA). On the other hand, the geographical reach of Ladino digital archives on YouTube is typically local or semi-local (*Autoridad*, VLACH, ELA), and otherwise their global reach means the interviews were conducted remotely (Wikitongues, *eSefarad CCSefarad*), so that rarely does global reach imply in-person interviews. *Ladino 21* would be the closest to an exception to this rule, featuring in-person interviews in three continents (for a total of seven countries), though these locations are still a minority within the total amount of countries featured in the archive (21). In this sense, when it comes to the ratio between in-person interviews and remote ones, Ladino digital archives hosted on YouTube can be placed on a continuum ranging from exclusively in-person content (VLACH, ELA), to mostly remote (*eSefarad CCSefarad*, Wikitongues), passing through mostly in person (*Autoridad Nasionala del Ladino i su Kultura הרשות הלאומית לתרבות הלאדינו*, pre-pandemic *Ladino 21*) and hybrid (post-pandemic *Ladino 21*). Additional factors of interest which are nonetheless excluded from Zuckermann's binary between armchair and community field linguists, are Sephardic ethnic ascription and expertise in the target language (Ladino). Unsurprisingly, both components tend to be stronger in digital archives exclusively devoted to Ladino.

The Tension between Descriptivism and Prescriptivism

Both Zuckermann's take on language revitalisation and the overall ethos motivating Ladino digital archives hosted on YouTube are primarily descriptive, i.e., to show how Ladino is *de facto* spoken (rather than to prescribe how it *should* be spoken). At the same time and as we learned in Chapter 1, in the end any descriptivist task leads to and is mediated by several forms of (implicit, unintended) prescriptivism, which ultimately shows the supposed binary between descriptivism on the one hand, and prescriptivism, on the other, to be oversimplistic.

While this self-reflexivity is missing in *Revivalistics*, it becomes easily discernible from a critical and ethnographical conceptualisation of the archive as discussed in the first section of this chapter. In particular, managing an archive requires a number of decisions on the account of the archivers/curators, which can be understood as forms of implicit prescriptivism, because it is unplanned and contrary to the original (descriptivist) intention. This implicit prescriptivism encompasses decisions such as choosing whom (not) to interview, the modality (e.g., *is this interview worth spending a significant part of our budget on an in-person trip?*), what parts to edit out (sometimes at the request of speakers), what thumbnail to use, when to release the videos and in what order, how many videos per interview to publish and of how much length, and how to organise the archive into collections/playlists.

Thus, with the exception of Wikitongues (whose sample, consisting of just three videos, is hardly representative), the working and/or permanent address of the managers of the Ladino digital archives hosted on YouTube has decisively contributed to answering the question of who, where, and how to interview participants. This circumstance has invariably resulted in the overrepresentation of local (or else near) participants, and conversely, the underrepresentation of participants from more remote locations, particularly for the purpose of in-person interviews.

The above pattern helps explain the fact that the YouTube digital archive of the *Autoridad Nasionala del Ladino i su Kultura הרשות הלאומית לתרבות הלאדינו* features only content recorded in Israel, that a significant percentage of the in-person recordings of *eSefarad CCSefarad*'s archive are set in Argentina/Latin America, that the clips from VLACH are set in Turkey (which is close to their Austria headquarters), *Ladino 21*'s overrepresentation of the United States, the United Kingdom, and Spain (Acero Ayuda and myself have had working addresses in the United States and the United Kingdom, plus permanent addresses in Spain), and why the ELA videos were recorded in New York City.

Conversely, these decisions imply a significant opportunity cost, i.e., to date there are no YouTube digital archives featuring in-person interviews in places like South Africa or Canada, which while not being Ladino-speaking hubs, feature significant speech communities.

On the other hand, and perhaps partially due to the above geographical constraints, decisions pertaining to whom (not) to interview and when to release the videos in question and in what order do not seem to have been particularly self-conscious. Instead, digital archive managers and linguists seem to have reached out to Ladino speakers organically, scheduling interviews mostly depending on their willingness and/or availability (or lack thereof), and generally releasing videos in the same order in which they were recorded.

Similarly, Ladino videos on YouTube are not heavily edited, in alignment with the Revivalistics tenet of letting participants express themselves by using their full linguistic repertoire, and then not altering that material in the (perceived) need to live up to the monolingual expectations of the average viewer. In the case of *Ladino 21*, our overall tendency has been to edit out markers of disfluency. In doing so, our goal has been not so much to project an artificial image of fluency (which would underrepresent actual Ladino attrition, contrary to our intention to offer a descriptivist, realistic portrayal of Ladino in the 21st century), but to retain the viewer's attention, which is increasingly important and difficult within the Web 2.0. environment (Wu 2017).

Similarly, the thumbnails of the *Autoridad* and *eSefarad CCSefarad* seem to feature little to no editing, instead corresponding to random frames from the clip in question.

By contrast, VLACH, Wikitongues, and ELA opt for high-resolution thumbnails where most participants are featured either smiling or showing excitement, and/or surprise. This approach is more self-conscious and user-oriented, as it seems to be designed to incentivise clicking on the video. This *modus operandi* is therefore more prescriptive, as it seeks to portray how Ladino (speakers) should be (positive, exciting) as opposed to how Ladino (speakers) is/they are. *Ladino 21* has taken this approach to the next level, often designing ad hoc thumbnails based on the video (as opposed to thumbnails that duplicate its content), superposing eye-catching texts and related images.[8]

Regardless of the thumbnail strategy (or lack thereof), decisions pertaining to thumbnail design reveal a further layer of unintended constraints, i.e., the specific scheme of incentives and disincentives offered by YouTube as a platform. In other words, the ways in which YouTube encourages or discourages certain behaviours among its creators and users, which affects aspects such as posting frequency, genre selection, and many other variables.

To understand these topics, we need to adopt a broader, ethnographic approach. From a critical perspective attentive to the power dynamics that mediate and condition the nature and functioning of digital archives, their (potential) use for organisational, commercial, academic, pedagogical, and/or community purposes implies further restrictions to the overall descriptivist impetus that animates Ladino digital archives hosted on YouTube. Nevertheless, given their extralinguistic nature, the in-depth analysis of most of these aspects falls beyond the scope of the present chapter, with the exception of the community goals and pedagogical objectives (see below).

Regarding community purposes, the dialectal preferences of some voices within the online Ladino-speaking community (particularly, those that enjoy a certain ascendancy, including the interviewees themselves) and beyond (e.g., donors, investors), may incentivise Ladino archivers to adopt a prescriptive curation of the recorded material revolving around the artificial projection of a self-contained national language, in close association with Standard Language Ideology ('Ladino'). Based on my experience as part of *Ladino* 21, there are certainly pressures, particularly from well-established and senior members of the global community of Ladino speakers, to record interviews and other genres with mostly or only the most prestiged (as opposed to inherently prestigious) L1 Ladino speakers. For instance, following the publication of a *Ladino 21* video where I interviewed L1 Ladino speaker Michael Halphie, Rachel Bortnick (*LK*'s founder – see Chapter 1) expressed her appreciation, since Michael speaks Ladino *comme il faut* [*komo se deve*] and shares a similar family background:

> I was really enjoying listening to Michael, because he speaks exactly *comme il faut*, and has the same story as many of us, whose parents did not leave Turkey (in my case, Izmir) since the day they arrived from Spain or Portugal, and who were raised in an entirely [Judeo]Spanish-speaking Jewish environment (…) I am really enjoying these interviews with people that speak good Ladino, and that are, like me, passionate about the language.
>
> (2020; my translation)[9]

At the same time, the type of expectations exemplified in the above passage also represent an opportunity for archivers to challenge the unexamined linguistic assumptions of these petitioners, rather than to cater to them. At any rate and as discussed in Chapter 1, this situation raises a number of critical questions: to what extent do the different Ladino platforms (in this case YouTube digital archives) reflect (pre-Internet) linguistic differences across geolects, sociolects, and genderlects? To what extent do they perform them? Moreover, how do both compare to our discussion apropos *LK* (see Chapter 1) as the flag bearer of Ladino in the Web 1.0?

In terms of overall languaging in the offline world, Ladino is currently experiencing a relatively rapid transition into postvernacularity (Shandler 2004, 2005). In other words, most Ladino speakers nowadays have a limited knowledge of Ladino, using the occasional word or expression for symbolic purposes, rather than being conversational (let alone fluent) speakers of it (see Chapter 3, where, accordingly, Sevi calls them 'semi-speakers'). As we saw in Chapter 1, by its very activity, *LK* reduced the complexity of Ladino languaging to its vernacular aspect, further setting in motion a cyber-vernacular. By contrast to both the offline world and *LK*, YouTube digital archives combine (cyber)vernacularity and (cyber)postvernacularity (see below).

Concerning the geolects of the Ladino-speaking community, nowadays there are two main ones in the offline world: the Istanbuli (which currently features a much larger community of Ladino speakers than other traditionally major speech centres in the Balkans, such as Salonika or Sarajevo), and the Israeli (which draws partially on the Turkish one, as many Ladino speakers of Israel made *Aliyah*[10] from Turkey in the 1950s). While one could argue that there is a third distinct geolect in the United States, this one is mostly predicated on a combination of the Turkey and Israel geolects. Indeed, most (as opposed to many) Ladino speakers in the United States are the descendants of immigrants who arrived there in the 20th century from a plethora of national and ethnic backgrounds, but mostly from Turkey and Israel.

Whereas in the previous chapter we established that *LK*'s privileged geolect is that of Istanbul, when it comes to Ladino-speaking digital archives hosted on YouTube, this preference is only reflected in *VLACH*'s 'Judeo-Spanish Collection,' which as discussed above, is exclusively set in Istanbul. By contrast, the digital archive of the *Autoridad* privileges the Israeli geolect, *eSefarad CCSefarad* combines a very ample diversity of geolects in *Enkontros de Alhad* (overrepresenting the Argentinian/Latin American geolect[s] elsewhere), *Ladino 21* showcases a very wide diversity (while emphasising US geolects), and ELA overrepresents the NYC-based US geolect. While both *Ladino 21* and ELA overrepresent the US geolects, one should bear in mind that already within the United States, there is a very significant geolectal diversity in Ladino, not least because as underscored above, it is spoken by the descendants of immigrants who arrived there in the 20th century from a plethora of nation-state backgrounds.

Lastly, as pertains to the sociolectal and genderlectal diversity of Ladino speakers, the predominant variety of Ladino in the offline world, which relies heavily on Spanish (Castilian) vocabulary at the expense of less Turkish and Hebrew words, is closer to the contemporary vernacular (rather than the more formal rabbinical register). It also aligns with the female genderlect transmitted intergenerationally at home by Sephardic women as part of their children's educational upbringing. It is overrepresented on both *LK* (see Chapter 1) and YouTube digital archives, where L1 speakers typically learned Ladino at home, from their mothers, and in a predominantly secular context.

All in all, Ladino's variety across YouTube-hosted digital archives (as well as in contrast to *LK* and the offline world) is very ample when it comes to overall languaging and geolects, but rather limited in terms of sociolects and genderlects. This sample validates the contention that for the most part and congruent with the Revivalistics perspective, Ladino in the 21st century is best understood as a collection of *lects* (geolects, sociolects, genderlects, and ultimately, idiolects). Or if you will, as the only ever partial, translingual overlap of idiolects shared by people of Sephardic culture, rather than as a supposedly autonomous, self-contained, homogenous, and ethnically overlapping entity, in close association with Standard Language Ideology. Additionally, while the broader organisational, commercial, academic, pedagogical, and/or community context surrounding Ladino digital archives on YouTube has had a rather limited effect on their initial descriptive ambition, these constraints have certainly nuanced it, allowing us to unearth several forms of implicit prescriptivism.

This tension leads us to realise that the content of Ladino digital archives on YouTube mostly shows the diverse idiolects and translanguaging practices that already exist in the global Ladino-speaking community (thus featuring plenty of sociolinguistic variation across region and learnedness). At the same time, though, these audiovisual materials must be inevitably placed within a continuum between that heteroglossia, on the one hand, and various forms of standardised Ladino, on the other.

From my discussion of the tension between descriptivism and prescriptivism on YouTube-hosted digital archives, I would like to derive two preliminary conclusions. First, that as a transdisciplinary field of enquiry, the staunch descriptivism of Revivalistics would benefit from the adoption of a more ethnographic approach apropos the conceptualisation of endangered language archives, *enroute* to the development of heightened self-reflexivity. Second, that an even more heteroglossic portrayal of Ladino on YouTube digital archives would include more rabbinical and male genderlect voices, as well as non-binary and LGBTQIA+ voices and narratives (see below for a discussion on the presence of the latter apropos the Yiddish Book Center's YouTube channel).

Multimodality, Postvernacularity, and Transvaluation

As I discussed in Chapter 1, notwithstanding the current possibility to supplement emails with attachments and hyperlinks, *qua* the foremost exponent of the Web 1.0, *Ladinokomunita* continues to rely heavily and almost exclusively on the written word (see also Chapter 3 on the difficulties experienced by some *LK* users to access the attachments). In contrast, the multimodal nature of the Web 2.0 facilitates the construction and dissemination of a more comprehensive cultural and linguistic representation for Ladino learners. Since the early 2010s, Ladino digital archives have played a pivotal role in the momentous transition from the purely linguistic mode of the Web 1.0 to the more inclusive multimodal communication space that characterises the Web 2.0 (Arola et al. 2014).[11]

Like *LK*, Ladino digital archives on YouTube feature the linguistic mode of communication (though they privilege the spoken word, whereas *LK* focuses on the written one). Unlike *LK*, though, they resort habitually to the visual (images and characters), aural (silence, music, sound effects, ambient, noises, sound volume, tone of voice in spoken language, emphasis, and accent), gestural (body language and interaction), and spatial (the arrangement of elements in space) modes of communication. In turn, this multiplicity results in several different multimodal communication arrangements (Kress 2003).

Furthermore, such a multimodal mode of communication has important repercussions in the digital articulation of the identity, affect, and ideology of the global diasporic community of Ladino speakers. Elsewhere, I hope to have conveyed this phenomenological experience rather vividly when I stated the following:

> the spoon that goes around a cup of coffee in a café in Plovdiv, a sailor's impatient stamping at Thessaloniki's dock, the exchanging of coins in Izmir's market, a grandmother smudging henna in the palm of a Moroccan bride, the leafing-through-the-pages of the Talmud in an Athens's synagogue, and the scratching of the needle of a kippah's clip on the hair-record of a Brazilian Rabbi's headspace, all echo in a game-of-mirrors-like fashion the experiential hermeneutics of the Sephardi home, a circum-Atlantic national event (…).
>
> (Yebra López 2021c, 104)

Ideally, all of these can be conveyed (and stored) worldwide through open-access digital archives such as the YouTube-hosted ones. This much was proven in the early stages of the COVID-19 pandemic (April 2020), when the managers of *eSefarad CCSefarad*, Marcelo and Liliana Benveniste, launched a series of four video concerts entitled 'United by Ladino' ['*Unidos por el Ladino*'], whose first edition assembled the older generation of well-known Sephardic musicians from across the globe to sing together *The Mountain Ahead Burns* ['*Esta Muntanya d'Enfrente*']. The devastating consequences of the pandemic were powerfully conveyed by a multimodal combination of the strictly linguistic (i.e., the lyrics, which talk about lost loves and grief), its aurality, and the on-screen inclusion of the name and country location of each singer (see also Salmon 2021).

At the conclusion of the song, all vocalists were featured singing in unison on the same screen. This served to heighten the performance's emotional resonance and showcase a resilient expression of Ladino-speaking diasporic nationalism (eSefarad 2020; see also Chapter 5 on the Ladino Zoom Boom).

Overall, the multimodal affordances of the online audiovisual format leave room for the digital rearticulation of the Sephardic identity and language through performance. This includes a number of cyber-postvernacular appearances in the form of YouTube videos where the focus is not so much on the content of what is said in Ladino (i.e., its referential meaning, which is characteristic of vernacularity), but on the fact that what is said is *in* Ladino (symbolic meaning, irrespective of the content, which is defining of postvernacularity).

Indeed, the idea of a gradual transition into postvernacularity in the 21st century apropos minoritised Jewish languages was first introduced by Jeffrey Shandler apropos Yiddish in his 2004 article and his 2005 book (see Introduction, Chapters 1, 3, 4 and 5). As part of the latter, he observed the following:

> In semiotic terms, the language's primary level of signification – that is, its instrumental value as a vehicle for communicating information, opinions, feelings, ideas – is narrowing in scope. At the same time its secondary, or metalevel of signification – the symbolic value invested in the language apart from the semantic value of any given utterance in it – is expanding. This privileging of the secondary level of signification of Yiddish over its primary level constitutes a distinctive mode of engagement with the language that I term *postvernacular* Yiddish.
>
> (4)

Moreover, just like we have observed in the present chapter apropos Ladino, Shandler concluded his 2004 article by pointing out that "postvernacular Yiddish performance entails not merely speaking or hearing Yiddish, but 'experiencing' Yiddish as a delimited, totalizing, intensive, multisensory event that entails affective as well as (and sometimes instead of) intellectual or ideological engagement" (33).

While the most representative YouTube-hosted Yiddish digital archives, namely Yiddish Book Center's and *Forverts*', present Yiddish as a (cyber)vernacular, YouTube features additional channels and videos where Yiddish is used postvernacularly. In this sense, in her presentation *Jewbellish and YidLife Crisis: Contemporary Engagement with Yiddish* (UCL 2023), Sarah Benor highlighted the inventiveness of Yiddish comedy in the 21st century, focusing on the YouTube material of JEWBELLish, a comedy brand that embellishes Jewish production. Examples included comedy sketches and the Yiddish reappropriation of pop culture songs such as Jason Derulo's *Talk Dirty to Me* into *Talk Yiddish to Me* (Pellin et al. 2014). In the case of the latter, the highest rated comment, written by @1WoahBubbles, provides evidence of a demand to create similar content in further Jewish languages, including Ladino:

> This is the best thing I've seen! very funny I wish more Jewish channels would do funny and cool things like this, its [sic] been awhile since you guys posted looking forward to your next video! May G-D bless you! <33.

All in all, YouTube Yiddish channels and videos demonstrate the popularising potential of postvernacular use cases for cultural preservation and/or disruptive purposes.

Notwithstanding the innovative multimodality of (cyber)postvernacular uses of Yiddish/Ladino on YouTube, though, (cyber)vernacular ones are still the norm in both languages, in contrast with the offline world (particularly in the case of Ladino).

According to the About section of the Yiddish Book Center's digital archive (5.1k videos, 25.6k subscribers, and over 10 million views), many of its audiovisual materials "are excerpts from in-depth video interviews with native Yiddish speakers [sic],[12] world-renowned klezmer musicians, grandmothers, descendants of Yiddish writers, students, and more from the Center's Wexler Oral History Project." Moreover, the most comprehensive playlists of *Forverts*' (part of the broader homonymous US news media organisation founded in 1897, characterised by a politically progressive focus and primarily targeting a Jewish American audience; 14.3k subscribers and 736 videos) also consist of interviews of various sorts, and thus mostly display Yiddish as a vernacular (with the exception of a few dozens of videos in English).

Similarly, in the case of Ladino, the digital archives of the *Autoridad Nasionala del Ladino i su Kultura הרשות הלאומית לתרבות הלאדינו* and *Ladino 21* rely heavily on the vernacular mode, while those of VLACH, Wikitongues and ELA (plus the *Enkontros de Alhad* playlist of *eSefarad CCSefarad*) do so exclusively.

Nevertheless, the above does not imply that the vernaculars deployed by YouTube digital archives in Ladino and Yiddish, respectively, be interchangeable.

While the topics and genres found in Yiddish digital archives on YouTube greatly overlap with those found in Ladino digital archives (e.g., survivor stories, religious festivities), Yiddish digital archives place more emphasis on (vernacular) written literature. This *décalage* is mostly due to Yiddish featuring a larger population, stronger cultural institutions and literary movements (such as the Haskalah or Jewish Enlightenment, which fostered a rich literary tradition in Yiddish), extensive migration to the Americas, and greater educational support. Consequently, in Yiddish Book Center's there is a playlist devoted to Yiddish writers, and another one to Yiddish poets, while *Forverts*' includes a series of writer monologues (see Chapter 3 for a similar contrast between Yiddish and Ladino platforms apropos Facebook groups and pages).

Additionally, they also underscore Gender Studies. There is a playlist in the Yiddish Book Center's called 'Women in Translation,' plus another one entitled 'LGBTQ+ Pride Month Stories.' This asymmetry is due to a combination of a broader cultural acceptance and visibility of LGBTQIA+ individuals, more progressive and socially engaged artistic movements, and a heightened global influence, particularly in Europe and North America.

Shandler has also drawn attention to the (offline) vernacular revivalistic impulse offered by the organisation *Yugntruf* [Yiddish for 'Call to Youth'],[13] which seeks to encourage people (particularly children) to speak "a good Yiddish" (cit. in Shandler 2004, 32) by producing content about Yiddish *in* Yiddish. Furthermore, and as per its constitution, *Yugntruf* does not seek to just preserve Yiddish, but to raise it "to new heights" (cit. in Shandler 2004, 33) by calling upon young Yiddishists to "contribute new energy" (idem).

A further example worth mentioning is the NYC-based *Yidish Lige* [League for Yiddish] (see also Chapter 3), which was founded in 1979 by Dr. Mordkhe Schaechter with the goal of furthering Yiddish's standardisation and modernisation, and now features Eli Benedict as their online events manager. Its Web 2.0 materials include Zoom conversations, and an online searchable dictionary (*Yidish Lige*/League for Yiddish 2024).

Lastly, there is also *Der Arbeter Ring* [Worker Circle], a Jewish fraternal organisation founded in 1900 in New York City whose aims are to promote social justice, Jewish culture, and community support. It offers Yiddish language classes, cultural events, and publications, thereby fostering a resurgence of interest and fluency in Yiddish (Workers Circle 2024).

On the one hand, and similarly to *Yugntruf*, since its inception *Ladino 21* has aspired to revitalise Ladino by producing the vast majority of its content *in* Ladino (rather than just *about* it, the latter being a habitual practice among many other Ladino online communities). On the other hand, and despite *Ladino 21*'s forward-looking perspective and positive valuation of Ladino as a named language that belongs in the 21st century (see Introduction), it is hard to deny that though increasingly common online (see Chapters 3–6), intergenerational transmission in Ladino is much lower than in Yiddish. The comparatively meagre number of young speakers of Ladino severely restricts the range and depth of its creativity and renewal as facilitated by the affordances of the 21st century in general and the Web 2.0/YouTube in particular.

Concerning postvernacular uses of Yiddish and Ladino on YouTube, there are also significant differences in the way postvernacularity is addressed. First, (cyber)postvernacular Ladino is present on a global scale in the most representative Ladino digital archives, such as *eSefarad CCSefarad* and *Ladino 21*. Thus, to the above example of *Unidos por el Ladino* (*eSefarad CCSefarad*), one has to add several minority genres included in *Ladino 21*, such as Ladino songs, festivals, literary translations into Ladino, and Ladino app demos. First and just like in the case of *eSefarad CCSefarad*, Ladino songs are performed by a combination of speakers and non-speakers of Ladino, in alignment with decreased fluency in this language in the 21st century and conversely, its increasingly symbolic (i.e., postvernacular) value. Given this decrease in fluency, performers cannot assume that their audience's delight at this symbolic (secondary) level of the spectacle (i.e., Ladino "as a signifier of affect or as an aesthetic experience of sound play" – Shandler 2004, 28) is matched by their mastery of its vernacular (primary) dimension. Consequently, in these venues, the programme handouts feature explanatory notes in the local, majoritised language (e.g., English, in the case of *Kantigas Muestras*' performances in Los Angeles), as well as bilingual lyrics (in this case, in both Ladino and English). In the words of Shandler, "the act of translation has thus become intrinsic to postvernacular (…) performance" (idem). Additionally, decreased fluency in Ladino has led to the professionalisation of using Ladino postvernacularly at official events, with a number of pedagogical materials and programmes drawing generously on entertainment activities, including festivals and literary translations (see below).

On a more radical level and not entirely unrelated to the JEWBELLish clip (see above), the performative dimension, with its characteristic use of the cyber-post vernacular, includes a language-dependent performance of the Sephardic self. In an early (2017) and highly acclaimed *Ladino 21* video entitled *Djohá i la supa kayente – Nu York, EE.UU* ['Djoha and the Hot Soup – New York, USA']. Benni Aguado recites a Djoha story[14] by heart.

In the video in question, Aguado chooses to don Sephardic Ottoman clothing, anachronistically echoing sartorial choices and mandates whose development dates back to the nineteenth- and early 20th-century Ottoman Empire. Aguado's attire is fully *a la turka*, i.e., Turkish style (as opposed to *a la franka* – literally 'French style' – but also used to denote Western European style by extension). It includes the *fez* (regulated in 1829), the *entari* (the traditional Ottoman robe) (see Mezistrano 2022), and the *trespil* (string of beads). Queering the modern Sephardic time and space, his vestige persona greets the audience in postvernacular Turkish, whereupon he proceeds to recite the Djoha story by heart.

Aguado's hyperreal portrait of himself further problematises (linguistic) ideologies of authenticity as discussed in Chapter 1 as well as in the present one. If processes of authentication on *LK* were predicated on written competence/proficiency, (non)nativespeakerism, ability and/or willingness to standardise, and alignment with the moderator's view on Ladino maintenance as based on its constant use as a Romanised vernacular, the multimodal characteristics of the digital archive downplay the importance of some of the above elements while bringing new ones into the picture. In particular, written competence (however one chooses to measure it) and standardisation lose relevance in the face of the growing importance of the audiovisual component. In alignment with the (non)nativespeakerism that pervades the global Ladino-speaking community, Ladino digital archives on YouTube combine the uncritical use of the label 'native speaker' as a perceived marker of authenticity (as in ELA's attachment of this label right after Stella Levi, Benni Aguado, and Daisy Bravermann's name in the description box below their respective videos) with new audiovisual modes of performing Ladino-speaking authenticity. This time around these modes are predicated on "sounding" (aural mode of communication) and "looking like" (visual mode) a "native," which in turn opens the door to further forms of discrimination, including image/fashion shaming and accentism.

In the case at hand, Aguado's Sephardic Ottoman cosplay would seem to speak to his awareness of the importance of the visual mode of communication and his desire to project an image of authenticity in this department. While the video received thousands of views (which would seem to be consistent with the postmodern craving for authenticity in an increasingly globalised world – see Chapter 1), ironically, in a *LK* email published shortly after the release of this audiovisual material, a participant criticised Aguado's performance as inauthentic. To that end, his detractor pointed out Aguado's US accent, as well as the fact that Aguado's way of telling the story was somehow unlike that of his (the detractor's) Ladino-speaking grandmother. Aguado's detailed answer is worth quoting at length here:

> Today, I received criticism from a *LK* member. I am not going to mention the name of this embittered person, but I am going to say why he felt the need to write about me. He wrote it in modern Spanish because he comes from a country in Latin America from a Sephardic family from Turkey. I will write it in Ladino. He said that I do not have the accent of those who came from Spain and settled in Turkey, and that I am an American who learned Ladino from his mother, and that I do not tell the stories the way his grandmothers did. To this person, I want to say that it is true that I do not have the accent of those Sephardim who came from Turkey and told these stories with a grace that I lack, as you say, but I do not believe that my accent in Ladino is bad, and I know it is much better than most of the Sephardim who are born and raised in the United States like me and my mother. It is true that I am, as you say, an American who learned Ladino from his mother. Yes, I am one of the very few who know how to speak it and write it correctly in Latin letters, as well as in Solitreo and Rashi. Tell me, can you do that? (…).
>
> Very sincerely,
>
> Benni Aguado, the graceless American (my translation).[15]

The situation was certainly paradoxical: Aguado, who had often criticised Ladino-speaking members' accents and writing as "inauthentic" (that is, vis-à-vis his own), now found himself on the receiving end of this criticism, whereupon he partially admitted to it. Similarly to Aldo Sevi's admission that it took him a couple of years until he was convinced that his Ladino was good enough to create his own content in this language (see Chapter 3), this anecdote further supports my assertion in Chapter 1 that "authenticity" does not have a pre-existing or fixed meaning. Instead, it is the evolving result of an ongoing authentication process that features slightly different parameters in Web 2.0 platforms, particularly because of their multimodality (as opposed to Web 1.0/1.5 ones such as *LK*). Additionally, it lends credence to the increasing prevalence of Ladino postvernacularity, and by opposition to it, the increasing authenticity and prestige associated with being able to express oneself vernacularly in this language: "He wrote it in modern Spanish because he came from a country in Latin America from a Sephardic family from Turkey. I will write it in Ladino," stated Aguado (see above), thus implying that his writing in Ladino proved his Sephardic lineage and authenticity (in contrast with his critic). Lastly, this exchange between Benni and his detractor serves as a powerful reminder of the futility of attempting to hold on to the purist myth of a supposed Golden Age (in this case, 19th-century Ottoman Empire) by opposition to which Ladino would supposedly be nowadays in a state of deterioration (see Chapter 1).

In this sense, Ladino digital archives on YouTube offer more forward-looking possibilities than that of aping Ladino as it was spoken in long-gone periods and remote locations. These include various *Enkontros de Alhad* meetings discussing topics such as Ladino on Netflix and the challenges of teaching this named language on the Internet, respectively (*eSefarad CCSefarad*; see Chapters 4 and 5), as well as the use of Ladino apps, and a drone-recorded aerial 360-degree panorama of the city where the video in question is set (*Ladino 21*).

The second difference between Yiddish and Ladino postvernacularity on YouTube digital archives is that as hinted above, cosplay, drones, and the Internet notwithstanding, in the case of Ladino, its postvernacular presence is seldom as disruptive or innovative as the JEWBELLish example. That clip is part of what Shandler has dubbed "anthologizing" (2004, 30–1), which includes placing side-by-side "Hasidic songs of mystical devotion and anarchist anthems of agitprop" (30). By contrast, Ladino's (cyber)postvernacularity lacks both an Orthodox community of the size and relevance of the Hasidic one vis-à-vis Yiddish, and working-class traditions of the kind that have led to a significant amount of protest songs. The closest instance to it would be a video featuring a hip-hop cover of *La Vida do por el Raki* ['I'd give my Life for Raki'] (2015). In this clip, the music group *Los Serenos Sefarad* (consisting of Rabbi Simon Benzaquen and Alex Hernandez) adapted a classic song from the Ladino repertoire (as opposed to reappropriating a mainstream one from pop culture) to hip-hop culture (though only Hernandez raps) while including a single element from a traditionally religious context (a *kippah*). The impact of this postvernacular innovation (15k views in a channel featuring only 185 subscribers) pales in comparison with its Yiddish counterpart (almost 1M views in a channel followed by over 15k subscribers).

In sum, unlike (cyber)postvernacular uses of Yiddish on YouTube, those concerning Ladino can rarely be understood as "innovative cultural negotiations, responsive to the profound ruptures in Jewish life wrought by the Holocaust and other 20th century upheavals that have left Jewish mimesis in a state of crisis" (Shandler 2004, 24). Instead, at least in their current state, they are more accurately understood as more or less extreme examples of a broad cyber-postvernacular continuum that goes from the most backward-looking efforts of cultural preservation (as unintendedly caricaturised by Aguado's contrived performance) to the most forward-looking attempts to negotiate cultural innovation in Ladino (drones, apps).

Last but not least, while instances of (cyber)postvernacular Ladino on YouTube might not be (yet) as disruptive as their Yiddish counterparts, it is important to remember that it is precisely this juxtaposition between the traditional and the mainstream/futuristic that makes Ladino the ever-evolving linguistic variety that it is still today in the 21st century. While it might be tempting to underanalyse said contrast as an otherwise odd or unlike lumping together of the "old" (Sephardic) with the "new" (technological world, state-or-the-art buildings), as I have argued elsewhere (2021), it is critical to conceptualise these innovations as a disruptive form of ideology critique. Indeed, they effectively serve to challenge many an atavistic prejudice of the kind that are holding back Ladino's revitalisation prospects in the 21st century, paramount among which are misconceptions about Ladino being an "archaic" language, a "dialect of Spanish" or "Castilian frozen in diaspora" (for proof of the persistence of these stereotypes, see below my discussion of user comments in Ladino digital archives on YouTube).

Ultimately and in conjunction with several simultaneous developments in the same direction (e.g., the 2019 foundation of the *Akademia Nasionala del Ladino* in Tel Aviv, Israel – see Chapter 1), this process has transformed the ideological valuation of Ladino in our society: it has made skyscrapers, drones, and the latest language documentation and education technology an integral part of Ladino, and vice versa. This finding is consistent with the emphasis placed by Zuckermann on acts of (conscious) transvaluation from the lens of Revivalistics (though his analysis is confined to "the transition of semantic value" –2020, xxvii – in specific terms as part of Hebrew reclamation in Israel –2020, 127–43–), particularly processes of axiological reversal implying extreme amelioration (i.e., a shift from negative to positive consideration). As remarked by Patrick Eisenlohr, this tendency becomes particularly acute in the electronic use of languages that have been traditionally deemed "archaic" or unfit for the 21st century:

> A central concern of the use of lesser-used languages in electronic mediation is not only encouraging language maintenance and revitalisation by providing speakers with opportunities to hear and maintain skills in the language, but also is achieving a transformation of ideological valuations of the language so that the lesser-used language is viewed as part of the contemporary world and as relevant for the future of a particular group.
>
> (2004, 24; cit. in Yebra López 2021c, 106)

Pedagogical Implications and Awareness-Raising Opportunities

Ladino digital archives on YouTube lend themselves to pedagogical adaptations and purposes. Their Web 2.0 affordances can enrich the students' systematic acquisition of the language (particularly as related to listening/oral practice). In a broader sense, they can also raise awareness of Ladino and positive associations with it as a (post)vernacular linguistic variety among users (particularly through interaction in the comments section).

First, and in a strictly pedagogical sense, the potential use of the audiovisual materials within the context of a class and/or institution that relies on the traditional conceptualisation of languages as standardised entities, can lead archivers to discourage or eliminate their participants' spontaneous translingual practices, to manufacture instead an impression of lexical and grammatical coherence, thus living up to the monolingual expectations of institutional actors (including the students themselves). Thus, addressing the question of whether revitalisation is even possible through education, Nancy Hornberger and Haley De Korne have drawn attention to the fact that the origins and functioning of formal schooling are closely tied to structural monolingualism, which devalues heritage and endangered languages,

> the model of education that emerged in nation-states around the time of the industrial revolution, where children are grouped with a teacher in (largely) government-controlled schools (…) has become a globally dominant form of education (…). This model of schooling has disadvantaged culturally and linguistically diverse groups by promoting one homogenized culture and language as an ideal for all students to attain, and either intentionally or inadvertently stigmatizing and devaluing other cultures and languages (…) The drive to succeed in monolingual schools, to be considered educated within the dominant society, and to be socioeconomically mobile has influenced many students to turn away from their heritage language.
>
> (Hinton et al. 2018, 94–5)

Nevertheless, Hornberger and De Korne also acknowledge that notwithstanding this legacy of monolingualism and exclusion, due to their high prestige as social institutions, schools can also be the place to fight against these injustices, designing new ways to learn endangered languages: “schools (…) can also be sites of struggle to change these norms (…). The challenges of achieving this should not be underestimated, but neither should the possibilities be ignored” (Hinton et al. 2018, 95).

Indeed, it is possible to use online tools such as digital archives in the service of a different kind of pedagogical approach, namely: one that stresses the validity of different accents, speaker backgrounds, and language practices while also managing students’ expectations about the standardisation of endangered languages, particularly by analogy to “modern” languages such as English or Spanish. In the case of Ladino, it is precisely because this named language has been a diasporic, minoritised language, that it has *not* undergone a degree of normativisation comparable to ‘Spanish’ or ‘English.’ As a result, on average students can expect to find audiovisual materials featuring a more heteroglossic and heteronormative reality than they are used to in either their first language or most of the languages they have learned so far.

Additional educational opportunities are presented to YouTube digital archivers through engagement with user comments. With the exception of *eSefarad CCSefarad*, comments are a common feature in most of the videos of the remaining Ladino digital archives on YouTube. Six main themes stand out: (i) who speaks Ladino and their perceived level of proficiency, (ii) praise related to the revitalisation effort, (iii) similarities and differences between Ladino and Spanish, (iv) the desire to learn Ladino, (v) lived experiences related to Ladino, and (vi) engagement from content creators. With the exception of (iv), which is strictly related to the acquisition of Ladino, the above comments provide a number of awareness-raising opportunities. These range from the dismantling of negative language ideologies[16] to the potential implementation of new ideas to further the revitalisation of Ladino on YouTube and the Internet at large.

First, a major theme is judgement of the participant's (perceived) level of proficiency in Ladino. While criticism of (perceived) poor performance in the language is rare, it is arguably discernible as implicit in the praise directed to those whose performance in Ladino is deemed to be of superior quality. For instance, in response to a recent *Ladino 21* interview with L1 Ladino speaker Jacky Benmayor (2022), Ladino student Juan Sanchez Guerra noted the following: "It is necessary to include more recordings of native speakers who speak Ladino well like Jack" (2023; my translation).[17] By the same token, one could surmise, the user in question would seem to be suggesting that he does not enjoy (and therefore would like to see less, or even zero) recordings featuring non-L1 speakers.

Second, comments praising the digital archiver's/interviewer's revitalisation work are common currency, and they often feature further language ideologies that are introduced surreptitiously while presented as objective (rather than as the subjective statements they are). For example, in reaction to the *Autoridad Nasionala del Ladino i su Kultura's הרשות הלאומית לתרבות הלאדינו* video entitled '*Ladino* – Moshe Shaul – לאדינו' (2012) in one of the most upvoted comments, user @mlc08773 stated the following in Spanish: "Sephardim are our forgotten Spanish brothers, today more than ever we love them as part of our culture and their legacy from which we grew together as culture and blood" (2021; my translation).[18] Similarly, in the *Ladino 21* video 'Drita Tutunović and Ivana Vučina Simović: Who will keep the language alive in your family? // Belgrade, Serbia' [*Drita Tutunović i Ivana Vučina Simović: Ken guadrara la lingua en tu famiya? // Belogrado, Serbia*] (2022) user @holofernes1972 congratulates us translingually, adding that Spain is both "their" and "our" home: "How beautiful it is what you do to preserve Judezmo. Congratulations from Spain, our and your home. Shalom" (2022; my translation).[19] Of course, while a significant number of Sephardim conceived of Spaniards as their "brothers" and/or Spain as their "home," not all do.

Generous revitalisation praise is also the norm in Yiddish YouTube archives, as it becomes apparent in the comment section of many *Forverts* videos.

In particular, originality attracts a lot of praise, as in the Yiddish reappropriation of Jason Derulo's *Talk Dirty to Me* into *Talk Yiddish to Me*, where the highest rated comment provides evidence of a demand to create similar content in further Jewish languages, including Ladino (see above).

Third, user feedback abounds apropos the (perceived) similarities and differences between Ladino and Spanish, with an overwhelming majority of comments stating that the user in question understood (almost) everything based on Ladino's (perceived) similarity to Spanish, and/or reproducing the Spanish nationalist myth that Ladino is Castilian/Spanish frozen in diaspora. For instance, in response to VLACH's video 'Which one is our language? – Judeo-Spanish Collection' (Eskenazi 2019), user @Thefermar337 states the following:

> Its [sic] amazing how these people that were expelled from Spain still maintain [sic] the language from the country that expelled them. I am Spanish

> and hearing this language is like hearing a language fossil, this is how don quixote [sic] talked, its [sic] really amazing.
>
> (2023)

Upvoted by 103 people, the comment in question was also the recipient of significant backlash, with users pointing out the obvious, i.e., that all languages evolve and change, including Ladino.

Additionally, reacting to the Wikitongues video 'The Ladino language, casually spoken | Sara speaking Ladino | Wikitongues' (2021) user @enchyxxx claims the following: "Oh wow, I speak Spanish and I can understand almost everything she's saying, it's pretty much the same language but just with some regionalisms or slightly different pronunciations" (2021). Occasionally, some users frame Ladino as a Jewish dialect of modern Spanish, like Connor Murphy in his reaction to ELA's video 'Jake Kohanek [sic] – Ladino' (2020): "Oh wow this is almost exactly like spanish [sic]. It's more of a Jewish dialect than a language" (2020).

Fourth, as stated above, decreased fluency in Ladino has led to the professionalisation of postvernacular Ladino, with several pedagogical materials and programmes drawing generously on entertainment activities, including festivals and literary translations. A case in point can be found in the 2018 *Ladino 21* video 'Sarah Aroeste and Carlos Yebra speak [in Ladino] at the Greek Jewish Festival – New York, USA' [*Sarah Aroeste i Carlos Yebra echan lashon en el Greek Jewish Festival – Nu York, EE.UU*]. In an implicit admission of the prevalence of the postvernacular dimension, the focus of the title is on the fact that Ladino is spoken, what is actually discussed being relegated to a secondary level. In this video, Aroeste (see above) introduces her pedagogical materials, which are bilingual in both Ladino and English, thus seemingly assuming that her audience is not necessarily fluent in the former.

Moreover, 21st-century literary translation is also featured on *Ladino 21*. In total, this type of translation encompasses over 15 works belonging to the genres of Shoah literature, children's fiction for grown-ups (*The Little Prince*, *Alice in Wonderland*), and epic novels (*The Odyssey*, *The Illiad*, *Martin Fierro*, chapters of *Don Quixote*), translated by 8 authors: Avner Perez, Moshe Ha-Elion, Shmuel Refael, Gladys Pimienta, Arnau Pons, Zelda Ovadia, Carlos Levy, and Alicia Sisso. As discussed by Agnieszka August-Zarębska and Natalia Paprocka (2021), the postvernacular dimension of these translations shapes both the form and the functioning of the works, which are published in several scripts and feature the coexistence of Ladino with further languages in which generous paratexts are written and whose role is that of explaining the translations. These characteristics mean that the translations in question assume an incomplete knowledge of Ladino on the part of their audience, the latter being primarily concerned with the acquisition of texts linked to the Ladino-speaking culture (postvernacular level), rather than the detailed understanding of the referential content of these works (vernacular level) (23–4). In particular, *Ladino 21* features Alicia Sisso Raz's reading of her own translation of *Don Quixote* into Haketia (2019), i.e. the Western variety of Ladino spoken by the Jews who settled in Northern Africa, whose postvernacularity is much more advanced than that of Judezmo, effectively being its only dimension left (Bürki 2016; Yebra López 2023b; see also Introduction).

Fifth, occasionally videos in Ladino inspire some users to want to learn this language. For instance, commenting on the *Ladino 21* video 'Nesi Altaras: How Many Speakers of Ladino Remain in Turkey? // Montreal/Istanbul, Canada/Turkey,' [*Nesi Altaras: Kuantos Avlantes de Ladino Kedan en La Turkiya? // Montreal/Estambol, Kanada/Turkiya*] (2022b), user @dzxn3728 expressed her desire to learn Ladino from (and in) Spanish: "I want to know Ladino from Spanish. I was a cryptologist. It is important to save this Romance-Hebrew language. And also to know the Solitreo letter [sic]…" (2022; my translation).[20]

Sixth, numerous users leverage these audiovisual resources to articulate commentary regarding their personal connection with Ladino or its speakers, frequently invoking familial ties and ancestral lineage. For instance, reacting to a VLACH video entitled 'It was wartime and there was nothing – Judeo-Spanish Collection' (2020), where Lüsi Yafet narrates various autobiographical episodes, user @taldrorrouache4021 wrote "How can I contact with the Lady in the video? My grandmother was also there" (2023). Similarly, in response to the *Ladino 21* video 'Marcelo C. Ventura: The Izmirli Dialect and Sephardic Philosophy// Buenos Aires, Argentina' [*Marcelo C. Ventura: El Dialekto Izmirli i la Filosofia Sefaradi// Buenos Aires, Ardjentina*] (2023), user @martaventura noted that everything Marcelo said was also said in her own family, and that they might even be relatives.

> Dear Marcelo, all the things you said … we said them in my house with my grandparents and my parents and the whole family but later with my husband and my mother-in-law!!! ALL FROM IZMIR.!!!!!!! They always asked me if I had anything to do with the Venturas from Tucuman, (I'm from Buenos Aires) and you always said no … but maybe yes … My son is Marcelo too. I don't know much, because I didn't have anybody with whom to learn but now there is more Ladino than back in the day, and it makes me happy (…).
> (2023; my translation)[21]

Last but not least, concerning the archivers' engagement with the comments as content creators, reactions are essentially of two kinds: thanking the many users posting positive feedback and taking advantage of the comment in question to either promote related material or clarify an idea. For example, in response to a praising comment to their video 'The Ladino language, casually spoken | Sara speaking Ladino | Wikitongues,' Wikitongues replied

> *Mersi muncho!* [Ladino for 'Thanks a lot!'] If you're curious about learning more, Wikitongues is part of a network of organisations working to safeguard endangered Jewish languages. We have a page on our website that we'll expand more as the project grows: wikitongues.org/jewish-languages.

Additionally, in response to the above-mentioned comment by Juan concerning the supposed need to feature more Ladino "native speakers," I replied on behalf of

Ladino 21. While doing so, I emphasised the descriptive goal that informs this digital archive, and what that entails for the diversity of Ladino as a named language, and invited him to critically examine his nativespeakerist assumptions.

> Dear Juan, the goal of this channel is not prescriptive, but descriptive. We show how Ladino is spoken in the 21st century, in all its diversity. Aside from this, there is already a lot of critical research on what falls under the category of 'native speaker': https://www.youtube.com/watch?v=aGJkmlCo_t02" (my translation).[22]

An additional example can be found below the *Autoridad Nasionala del Ladino i su Kultura's הרשות הלאומית לתרבות הלאדינו* video *Ladino – Dulse de Bimbrio – לאדינו'* [*'Ladino* – Quince Jam – Ladino] (2013), where Bortnick commented "How beautiful! Is it possible to take the text of Ms. Warshavsky?/Rachel" (2013; my translation).[23] The *Autoridad*'s archiver, Matan Stein, replied with a signed message, providing useful information: "Hello Rachel!/I am going to include this text in my magazine Orizontes, which, with God's help, will publish its first issue soon (Matan Stein)" (2013; my translation).[24]

Conclusion

In this chapter, I have engaged in a critical discussion of YouTube-hosted Ladino digital archives conducive to the revitalisation of Ladino as a cyber-(post)vernacular of the 21st century, including those by *Autoridad Nasionala del Ladino i su* Kultura *הרשות הלאומית לתרבות הלאדינו*, *eSefarad CCSefarad*, Wikitongues, *Ladino 21*, VLACH, and ELA. I have examined these from the lenses of Zuckermann's *Revivalistics* as supplemented by a critical and ethnographic conceptualisation of archives attentive to the power dynamics that structure these spaces as alive, dynamic, and ongoing processes of performative effects co-produced by the state, academia, non-profit organisations, and user comments. As a result of the above, I have observed that the range, depth, geographical, temporal, and ideological valence of Ladino in the 21st century is being constantly negotiated, ultimately shaping the fate of this linguistic variety in Sepharad 4.

Overall, Ladino digital archives on YouTube instantiate many of the conceptual tenets contained in Revivalistics as a transdisciplinary field of inquiry. These include a descriptivist impetus, community field activism, the portrayal of languages as cultural-linguistic complexes, and the development of user-friendly, open-access materials as partially assisted by 'talknology,' and educational opportunities. These pedagogical chances range from enriching the students' systematic acquisition of the language (particularly as related to listening/oral practice) to fostering awareness of Ladino and positive associations with it as a (post)vernacular linguistic variety (particularly among users through interaction in the comments section).

Together, the above-discussed YouTube channels and collections in Ladino provide a valuable blueprint for the Ladino digital archives to come. These encompass the need to upload content consistently, adopting a global reach (*Ladino 21*), paying attention to fundraising (ELA) and output frequency, including shorts and lives (*eSefarad CCSefarad*), utilising specialised linguistics hardware and software (ELA), providing enhanced video and audio quality (ELA, VLACH), and implementing a Ladino–English bilingual subtitling policy, whether using YouTube subtitles (ELA) or self-made ones (VLACH).[25]

On the other hand, my critical discussion of these case studies as supplemented from an ethnographic perspective, has revealed several blindspots in Zuckermann's optimism vis-à-vis the possibility of carrying out a descriptivist task, while also pointing out to the need to adopt a more fine-grained approach to the concept of 'talknology.'

First, as Zuckermann himself shows in *Revivalistics*, including specific case studies such as the reclamation of Barngarla, descriptivist efforts do not take place in a vacuum. Rather, they are mediated by several (prescriptivist) choices, which results in various exercises of implicit prescriptivism that ultimately problematise the alleged binary between descriptivism and prescriptivism. As a result of this tension between descriptivist principles and *de facto* (implicit) prescriptivism, in practice the archiving of Ladino for revitalisation purposes in the 21st century operates somewhere on a continuum between standardised 'Ladino' and the full idiolects and translanguaging practices that already exist in the community (highly diverse in terms of overall languaging and geolects, but rather limited concerning sociolects and genderlects). Consequently, it has been my contention in this chapter that, first, Revivalistics' idealistic descriptivism should be supplemented by a more ethnographic approach apropos the conceptualisation of endangered language (digital) archives (on YouTube), enroute to the development of a heightened self-reflexivity apropos this specific type of platform; second, a more diverse and heteroglossic portrayal of Ladino on YouTube digital archives of the sort advocated by Revivalistics necessitates from the incorporation of more rabbinical and male genderlect voices, as well as non-binary and LGBTQIA+ voices and narratives.

Additionally, the multimodal (combining the written with the visual, aural, gestural, and spatial modes of communication) and multisemiotic (vernacular/postvernacular) and new participative possibilities (user interaction) afforded by YouTube digital archives raise the need to distinguish between qualitatively different stages within the 'Talknological Revolution,' as envisaged by Zuckermann, namely: Web 1.0, Web 2.0, and Web 3.0, each of these stages featuring vastly different affordances.

Lastly, my comparative analysis with YouTube-hosted Yiddish digital archives has yielded a number of lessons, paramount among which are the following: narrowing the gap concerning the hitherto superior longevity and depth of Yiddish channels, being more attentive to and approving of gender and sexual inclusivity, placing more emphasis on the importance of (vernacular) written literature, and exploiting the popularising potential of postvernacular use cases for cultural preservation and/or disruptive purposes.

Notes

1 For an overview of the community-based language archive model, particularly as applied to Native American languages, see Linn (2014). On the technical details of digital archiving, see Austin and Sallabank (2011, 255–74).

2 In this sense, Friedrike Lüpke favours supporting "vital repertoires" over revitalising standard languages (Hinton et al. 2018, 475–84). For an additional critique of Standard Language Ideology, see Olko and Sallabank (2021, 105–6).
3 For a discussion about the role of organisations in language revitalisation, see Hinton et al. (2018, 51–60).
4 On identifying funding sources to revitalise languages, see Olko and Sallabank (2021, 72–82).
5 International group of emissaries of the National Authority for Ladino and its Culture, created in 2016.
6 Spanish acronym of the Argentina-based Centre for Research and Dissemination of Sephardic Culture.
7 For a detailed analysis of ethical guidelines apropos language revitalisation, see Hinton et al. (2018, 216–26), as well as Olko and Sallabank (2021, 49–61), the latter particularly in connection to cultural sensitivity.
8 This task is invariably performed by Acero Ayuda, who has created and edited all the thumbnails, as well as postedited a fraction of them based on my feedback.
9 *Estava tomando grande plazer de sintirlo a Michael, porke avla egzaktamente i tiene la mizma estorya de munchos de mozotros, ke muestros padres no salieron de la Turkia (en mi kavzo, de Izmir) del dia ke yegaron de Espanya o Portugal, i ke mos engrandesimos en un entorno djudio enteramente de avla espanyola (...) me estan plaziendo muncho estas entrevistas kon personas ke avlan bueno el ladino i ke son, koma mi, enamorados de la lengua.*
10 *Aliyah* is a Hebrew term that means "ascent" or "going up." In Jewish tradition, it specifically refers to the immigration of Jews to the Land of Israel (*Eretz Yisrael*). This can be for religious, ideological, or practical reasons. Making *Aliyah* is considered a significant and often deeply meaningful decision for many Jews, as it represents a return to their ancestral homeland and a connection to their religious and cultural heritage.
11 In this sense, David Nathan explains that what makes digital archiving necessary (as opposed to convenient) in our time is the long-term preservation of audio and video (cit. in Austin and Sallabank 2011, 258).
12 See below for my discussion of (non)nativespeakerism and authenticity as language ideologies apropos YouTube Ladino.
13 Its small YouTube channel (17 videos) was only active for a few months between 2021 and 2022, attracting little attention (64 subscribers).
14 'Djoha' is the Ladino name of Nasreddin Hodja, a folklore character of the Muslim world whose short stories and satirical anecdotes were adopted by Sephardim of the Ottoman Empire, such as Aguado's ancestors.
15 *Oy resivi una kritika de un myembro de L/K [sic]. No vo mensyonar el nombre de esta persona amargada ma vos vo dezir lo ke sintió el menester de eskrivir de mí. Lo eskrivyó en el espanyol moderno porke vyene de un país en latino-Amérika de famiya sefaradi de Turkia. Yo lo vo eskrivir en ladino. Disho ke yo no tengo el aksento de akeyos ke vinyeron de Espanya i se aresentaron en Turkia, i ke só un amerikano ke se ambezó el ladino de su madre, i ke yo no konto los kuentos komo los kontavan sus nonas. A esta persona, yo kero dezir ke ya es verdad ke no tengo el aksento de akeyos sefaradis ke vinyeron de Turkia i kontavan estos kuentos kon una grasya ke a mí me manka, komo dizes tú, ma no kreygo ke mi aksento en ladino es malo, i sé ke es muncho mijor ke la mayoría de los sefaradis ke son nasidos i engrandesidos en Los Estados Unidos komo yo i mi senyora madre. Es verdad ke só, komo tú dizes, un Amerikano ke se ambezó el ladino de su madre. Sí, só uno de los muy pokos ke lo saven avlar i eskrivir korrektamente en letras latinas ansi ke en solitreo i rashi. Dime, puedes azerlo tú? (...)*
Muy sinseramente,
Benni Aguado el Amerikano sin grasya.

16 Here I understand 'language ideologies' as the "sets of beliefs about language articulated by users [in our case, those posting the comments] as a rationalisation or justification of perceived language structure and use" (Silverstein 1979, 193; see also Introduction).

17 *Kale meter mas enrejystrasiones [sic] de favlantes nativos ke favlan el Ladino byen komo Jack.*

18 *Los sefarditas son nuestros hermanos españoles olvidados, hoy más que nunca les amamos como parte de nuestra cultura y su legado de los cuales crecimos juntos como cultura y sangre.*

19 *Qué bonito lo que hacéis por conservar el djudezmo. Mis felicitaciones desde España, nuestra y vuestra casa. Shalom.*

20 *Quiero saber ladino desde castellano. Fui criptóloga. Es importante salvar esta lengua romancebreo [sic]. Y tambien saber la letra solitreo.*

21 *Estimado Marcelo todas las cosas ke dishitesh ... las diziamos en mi kasa kon mis nonos i mis padres i toda la familia ma luego con mi esposo i eshuegra!!!! TODOS IZMIRLIES.!!!!!!!*
Sempre me demandaron si tenía ke ver con los Ventura de Tucuman, (soi de Buenos Aires) y siempre diste ke no ... ma tal vez vez si ... Mi isho es Marcelo también. Muncho no se, porke no abia kon ken ambezarme ma ahora [sic] ay más ladino que antier i me pone kontente (...).

22 *Karo Juan, el buto de este kanal no es preskriptivo, ma deskriptivo. Amostramos komo se avla el ladino en el siekolo 21, en toda su diversita. Ahuera de esto, ya ay muncha investigasion kritika en lo ke toka a la kategoria de 'nativoavlante': https://www.youtube.com/watch?v=aGJkmlCo_t0.*

23 *Ke ermozura! Es posivle tomar el teksto de la sinyora Warshavsky?/Rachel.*

24 *Shalom Rachel!/Este texto lo v'a meter en mi revista Orizontes, ke en serka, beezrat a-shem, se publikara su primer numero.(Matan Stein).*

25 Since June 10, 2021, YouTube includes Ladino in its language list. Consequently, when content creators wish to upload a video on YouTube and add subtitles, they can now choose 'Ladino' as the language. On the other hand, automatic subtitling in this language is not an option (yet).

3 Social Media and Language Learning Apps (2017-)

Facebook, X, WhatsApp, TikTok, Duolingo, and uTalk

Introduction

As discussed in Chapter 1, *Ladinokomunita* already heralded many of the participative affordances of Web 2.0 platforms, including user-generated content and the ability of participants to create, share, and interact with content. Additionally, in Chapter 2, we observed that YouTube digital archives offer multimedia content, public visibility, engagement features, algorithmic influence, and follower dynamic, on top of the above affordances. Wherein then, does the innovation offered by the Web 2.0 platforms discussed in the present chapter reside? The answer is real-time interaction (via social network groups and accounts) and gamification (via language learning apps), both of which are complementary concerning their respective targeted skills (reading and writing, in the case of social networks; speaking and listening, on language learning apps) as well as conducive to strengthening intergenerational transmission. In turn, these aspects provide arguments to upgrade UNESCO's current classification of Ladino as a "severely endangered language" (2003; see also Chapter 4).

I shall now turn to the analysis of each platform type.

Social Networks Offering Real-Time Interaction in Ladino

The main Web 2.0. platforms hosting real-time interactive content in Ladino foster more expedient and communitarian communication with higher user engagement than any previous portal. These are, in chronological order, Facebook (2004), X (formerly known as Twitter; 2006), WhatsApp (2009), Instagram (2010), and TikTok (2017). What follows is a breakdown of the idiosyncrasies of each platform, whereupon I will delve into the most popular accounts *in* Ladino (rather than *about* it).

Facebook (2004). The most used social media platform worldwide, with over 3 billion users, Facebook is by far also the preferred social network among Ladino speakers. It enables users to create profiles, share posts, photos, and videos, connect with friends and family, join groups, and create pages based on shared interests, as well as to interact with content through likes, comments, and shares. The most popular standalone groups and pages in Ladino are *Los Ladinadores* and *Ladino*

DOI: 10.4324/9781003473664-6

Forever, with *Ladino 21* (see Chapter 2) and *Ladinokomunita* (see Chapter 1) having the largest followings among non-standalone groups and pages. While concerns have been raised about Facebook's potential decline, despite fluctuations in its popularity and usage trends (as the platform is less favoured among younger age groups, particularly Generation Z), as of 2024 Facebook remains a dominant presence online. In the next subsection, I shall elaborate on Facebook groups and pages in Ladino, adopting *Los Ladinadores* as my case study.

X (former Twitter; 2006). A microblogging platform managed by Elon Musk, X enables users to share short, concise messages (tweets) in real-time. Users can follow each others, engage with tweets through likes, retweets, and replies, and participate in public conversations on a wide range of topics. While there are no salient X standalone accounts in Ladino, the most popular one is *Ladino 21*'s (@LadinoXXI, 2,237 followers). Its activity is supplemented by a number of organisations and Ladino activists that post partly and/or occasionally in Ladino, and boast a significant following, including *eSefarad* (@eSefarad, 7,202 followers), Sephardic Jewish Brotherhood of America (@SephardicBrothe, 3,461 followers), Sarah Aroeste (@SarahAroeste, 2,096 followers), and Bryan Kirschen (@LadinoLinguist, 1,703 followers).

WhatsApp (2009). Created by former Yahoo! employees Jan Koum and Brian Acton, on this messaging platform users can send text messages, voice messages, photos, videos, and documents, create group chats, and share multimedia content with their contacts. In 2014, Facebook Inc. acquired WhatsApp, the latter remaining a separate entity under the former's ownership. The most popular WhatsApp groups in Ladino are *Estamoz whatsapeando* (2018) and *Echar Lashon* (2022).

Administered by Albert Israel, *Estamoz whatsapeando* shares daily pictures, audio clips, and transcriptions in the Latin and Hebrew scripts concerning relevant aspects of the Ladino language and culture. Unfortunately, the interaction in this group is univocal, since participants are not allowed to reply or interact with the content shared by the administrator. As I have argued elsewhere (Yebra López 2021c, 111), this aspect (one-to-many interaction, as opposed to many-to-many) prevents the group from qualifying as a Digital Home-Land, as opposed to a mere online community (see Introduction). Further proof *of it* can be found in the fact that the number of participants in this group has remained constant over the last few years, hovering around 200–50.

For its part, *Echar Lashon* was created by Gabor Szabo as a means to generate new opportunities to speak in Ladino. The main purpose of the group is to coordinate two weekly Zoom meetings (Mondays and Wednesdays at 7 pm Israel time), open to everybody, free of charge, and conducted exclusively in Ladino (without a predetermined topic). These discussions are typically moderated *pro bono* by a senior figure within the global community of Ladino speakers (e.g., Sephardic activist Benni Aguado).

Instagram (2010). Created by Kevin Systrom and Mike Krieger, it is a photo-centred social network where users can share photos and videos, apply filters and editing tools, follow other users, engage with content through likes and comments, and use hashtags to discover and participate in conversations. Popular features include the self-portrait or "selfie," which became viral in 2013, and Instagram Stories (introduced in 2016), which allow users to share photos and videos that disappear after 24 hours. Instagram is not particularly popular among Ladino speakers, partly due to the platforms' overreliance on image over text, as well as on the younger demographic as its main user base. Notable exceptions include the Instagram account of Sephardic Ladino speaker Alexandra Fellus (@ladino.with.lex, 1,078 followers), which focuses specifically on the teaching and dissemination of Ladino in Ladino, as well as accounts with occasional content in Ladino, such as that of the Sephardic artist and Ladino speaker Bella Rios (@bellariosofficial, 17k followers), which revolves around Sephardic music, and that of the Sephardic Jewish Brotherhood of America (@sephardicbrotherhood, 3,886 followers) (see Chapter 4).

During an interview on *Enkontros de Alhad* (see Chapter 4), Fellus admitted that her main motivation to create an Instagram account was to give herself the chance to practise Ladino (which is reminiscent of Szabo's rationale to create the WhatsApp group *Echar Lashon* – see above). Eventually, though, the group gathered over a thousand followers. "At the beginning, this motivation for me was a bit selfish (…) to practise the language (…) I received many messages from people all over the world" (2023). Her ideas draw inspiration from conversations in Ladino with her grandparents, as well as the books she is reading as part of the Sephardic Jewish Brotherhood's book club on Zoom (see Chapter 4). Fellus' primary linguistic reference work is a Ladino-Hebrew dictionary she bought in Israel.

In 2019 Facebook announced plans to integrate WhatsApp, Instagram, and Messenger more closely, with the end goal of allowing users to communicate across these platforms, unifying its messaging services under the umbrella of Meta Platforms Inc. The rebranding took place on October 28, 2021, to "reflect its focus on building the metaverse" (Heath 2021) (see Chapter 6).

TikTok (2017). Created by the Chinese company ByteDance, this platform allows users to make and share short videos set to music, explore trending challenges and hashtags, engage with content through likes, comments, and shares, and interact with other users through duets and video responses. Similarly to Instagram, the format (video, in this case) and demographic target characterising this platform (Generation Z), do not make it particularly palatable to the global Ladino-speaking community, though content in Ladino can be occasionally found on accounts with large followings, such as @litelinguistics (278k followers), @bellariosofficial (9,854 followers), and @jewishlanguageproject (5,427 followers). Similarly to Fellus' narrative apropos the sudden growth of her Instagram account, in an interview with *Ladino 21* (see Chapter 2), Bella Ríos expressed her surprise at discovering that her TikTok video on Ladino had rapidly gone viral:

> I was very lucky to go viral on TikTok with Judeo-Spanish. I made a TikTok asking people if anyone wanted to learn to speak the language, and I really didn't expect people to respond, and then it went viral very quickly.
>
> (2022)[1]

Facebook Groups and Pages: Los Ladinadores (2021)

Founded in 2004 by then Harvard undergraduate Mark Zuckerberg, Facebook emerged just a year before YouTube (2005; see Chapter 2) and swiftly became the new hub of online social interaction, i.e., the new "place to be" (Wu 2017, 295).

Facebook is the only Web 2.0 platform whose name has a Ladino equivalent: *ChehreChitab* [from Ottoman Turkish *chehre* – Face – and *chitab* – book], testifying to its status as the preferred 2.0 social media platform among Ladino speakers. This predilection is perhaps unsurprising. After all, Facebook is the oldest major Web 2.0 platform, and hence that which is most likely to resonate with the elderly, which is precisely the main demographic of (L1) Ladino speakers. Additionally, Facebook also features a very significant number of younger users, thus making it ideal for ameliorating the intergenerational transmission of Ladino. Conversely, not being on Facebook makes it harder for Ladino enthusiasts to communicate in this language in real time with people from a wide variety of backgrounds and age ranges. As Zuckerberg stated in 2009, "think about what people are doing on Facebook today. They're keeping up with their friends and family (…). They're connecting with the audience that they want to connect to. It's almost a disadvantage if you're not on it now" (The Wired 2009).

Moreover, while just like X, WhatsApp, and Instagram, Facebook is also a platform for sharing personal updates and photos, it tends to be more multifaceted than any of the above. It encompasses features like groups, events, and pages that facilitate various forms of interaction, including community engagement and collective action, both of which are key for the purpose of building an online community conducive to an eventual Digital Home-Land (see Introduction). Thus, whereas groups foster community engagement and discussion, pages serve as platforms for entities to establish an online presence and engage with their audience. Additionally, Facebook is more written literature-centred than Instagram and TikTok (which are focused on image and videos), it allows for longer messages than X and WhatsApp, and makes it easier to write longer texts compared to WhatsApp (both because it is desktop native, meaning larger screens and keyboards, and because it provides more space for composing and editing text).

There are several Facebook groups and pages dedicated to Ladino *in* Ladino which capitalise on the innovative integration of visual, auditory, gestural, and spatial communication modes, along with the community-building features of the platform. While many of these groups and pages serve as additional social media platforms for sharing content primarily hosted outside of Facebook, a few Sephardic Digital Home-Lands have exclusively adopted Facebook as their main or sole platform. The most popular ones are as follows:

1 *Los Ladinadores* [Ladino for 'The Ladino People'][2] (standalone, public group exclusively in Ladino; 6.8k members). Created by *Aki Yerushalayim* on November 16, 2020, through its editor-in-chief and *LK* moderator Aldo Sevi, who is also the group's manager, it revolves around the Ladino language and culture and has a strong pedagogical approach. Members discuss various topics related to Ladino heritage, language learning, and cultural preservation.

2 *Ladino 21* (additional platform page exclusively in Ladino; 4k likes and 4.5k followers). Created by myself and Alejandro Acero Ayuda on October 14, 2017, it features content dedicated to the Ladino language(s) (including Haketia)[3] and culture, mostly pertaining to the 21st century.
3 *Ladino Forever* (additional platform page exclusively in Ladino; 4k likes and 4.5k followers). Created by Sephardic performer Michael Halphie on July 5, 2017, it posts traditional Sephardic proverbs[4] on colourful backgrounds.
4 *Ladinokomunita* (additional platform group mostly in Ladino; 1.8k members). Created and managed by *Ladinokomunita* (February 9, 2022; see Chapter 1), *eSefarad* (May 19, 2023; see Chapters 2 and 4), and Marcelo Benveniste (August 15, 2010), it is dedicated to the Ladino language and culture. It serves as a community hub for discussions, sharing resources, and connecting with others interested in Ladino.

Additionally, there are several groups and pages *about* Ladino (albeit with only half or a minority of their content *in* Ladino) which boast much larger followings, suggesting the existence of a trade-off between popularity, on the one hand, and the use of Ladino as a vehicular language, on the other (see below for a similar pattern apropos Yiddish Facebook groups). First, there is the private group Ladino Language of Sephardic Jews – The Basics (4.1k members), created on January 20, 2016, by Keith A. Chavez. Second, there is *שוחרי לאדינו* ['Ladino Lovers,' in Hebrew] (standalone, group mostly in Hebrew; 29.8k members), founded by Eyal Peretz on March 14, 2011, and managed by himself alongside Shmuel Lustman, Sarah Shalom[5] and David Franko. For the most part, it discusses the Ladino language and culture (including plenty of pedagogical materials), but seldom in Ladino or in the Latin script, preferring instead the use of the Hebrew language, and occasionally, Yiddish and Spanish.

It is precisely in response to the absence of Ladino in the Latin script as a vehicular language of *שוחרי לאדינו* that as a former participant, Aldo Sevi decided to create his own Facebook group in 2020, namely: *Los Ladinadores*, arguably the most impactful Digital Home-Land developed in written Ladino on the Internet since *Ladinokomunita*.

According to its About section, the main goal of *Los Ladinadores* is to share vernacular (as opposed to postvernacular)[6] content publicly and exclusively in Ladino (thus rejecting content which is private or in any other language):

> This group is for sharing content in Judeo-Spanish. We do not accept publications in other languages. We do not accept publications that contain hate speech or electoral propaganda. We want substantive content. We do not accept publications of general greetings such as 'Good day,' 'Shabbat shalom,' etc. We are a public group; therefore, we do not accept non-public content.[7]

There are several mentioned and unmentioned functional and ideological elements in the above quote which deserve further scrutiny, and which I had the chance to discuss with Sevi within the context of a private interview on Zoom (March 1, 2024).

1 *Los Ladinadores* operates under the assumption that the online revitalisation of Ladino, along with the community-building endeavours associated with it, are contingent upon the functional differentiation of the language (Ferguson 1959; Fishman 1967) and its cyber-vernacular use (see also the *Ladinokomunita* case study in Chapter 1 and the *Enkontros de Alhad* one in Chapter 4).

Just like in the case of Ladino, on Yiddish Facebook groups and pages such combination of functional differentiation in the target language and a explicitly prescriptivist policy is also rare. The most popular one is the private group *לערן זיך יידיש* [Learning Yiddish] (4.8k members)[8] the public group *ייִדישע שרײַבער גרופּע* [The Yiddish Writer's Group] (1.7k members), created by *מקום-מקלט הײַנטצײַטיקע ייִדישע ליטעראטור: דיגיטאלער* [Contemporary Yiddish Literature: Digital Sanctuary],[9] which focuses on creative writing in Yiddish,[10] followed by the private group *אַ ייִדיש וואָרט און אַ ייִדיש ליד* [A Word and a Song in Yiddish] (1.2k members),[11] *ייִדיש אויף ייִדיש* [Yiddish in Yiddish] (439 members),[12] and *יידיש מיט אלי שרפשטיין* [Yiddish with Eli Sharfstein] (132 members).

Additionally, the page *ייִדיש-ליגע* [League for Yiddish] (3.3k followers), which focuses on pedagogical posts that refer to the League for Yiddish website, is mostly in Yiddish, with English used as an auxiliary language.[13] Moreover, there are a number of bilingual pages whose posts are both in the target language (top), followed by an English translation (bottom), including YiddishPOP (2.6k followers; see below), *Yugntruf* – Youth for Yiddish (1.7k followers), and Yiddish House London – *ייִדישע שטוב לאָנדאָן* (1.2k followers). This bilingual format, which is absent in Ladino Facebook groups, might be reflective of the stronger presence of Yiddish in the English-speaking world and of its enhanced vitality and means compared to Ladino.

Lastly (and perhaps somewhat ironically but also in alignment with my previous observation apropos Facebook groups and pages in Ladino), those Facebook groups whose name suggests a stronger focus on the target language (Yiddish in this case), are conducted mostly in a different language (English, in the case at hand), including *Learn Yiddish* (18.1k members), and *The Yiddish Group* (4.5k members). This paradox would seem to lend further credence to the notion that at least as far as Facebook is concerned, there appears to exist a discernible trade-off between popularity, on the one hand, and the vehicular use of the target language, on the other hand.

2 *Los Ladinadores* abides by the orthographic rules stipulated by the Israeli Ladino magazine *Aki Yerushalayim* (see Chapter 1 apropos *Ladinokomunita*). While *Ladinokomunita* justifies this decision in post-ideological terms, i.e., as easier/more convenient, *Los Ladinadores* only does so apropos the need to write Ladino in Latin characters. When it comes to justifying its use of French-Ottoman Romanisation, Sevi alluded instead to the geographic location of the vast majority of Ladino-speaking participants.

> I don't think it's possible to have this group based on writing in non-Latin letters (…) The group members, just over 20%, are from Israel, and those

> who are from outside of Israel, almost 80%, don't know Hebrew letters (…). Apart from this, the Israelis who know the Hebrew letters, if they try to write Ladino with Hebrew letters, they make a transcription into modern Hebrew and are not familiar with and do not use all the Ladino writing rules in Hebrew letters. This happens a lot on שוחרי לאדינו. They themselves cannot read what they wrote. Half of the discussions there are 'why didn't you write in Latin letters; we cannot read.'[14]

Originally, Sevi envisaged writing in Ladino exclusively in the Latin script, following the *Aki Yerushalayim* orthography as a subsection of *שוחרי לאדינו*. After marinating the idea for two years (i.e., since 2018),[15] especially due to uncertainty regarding his own ability to generate original content in Ladino (rather than sharing preexisting material), he resolved to embark on the endeavour:

> When I entered the Ladino-speaking group … the first intention I had was not to … be an activist for Ladino or Judeo-Spanish, and when I started there, I also began to write mostly in Hebrew, and gradually the decision came to do everything in Judeo-Spanish… It took me two years to be more confident that I could do it in Judeo-Spanish, in Ladino. At first, most of what I wrote in Judeo-Spanish were not my own things, they were songs in Judeo-Spanish, proverbs in Judeo-Spanish, things I found here and there … my own things I wrote [them] more in Hebrew, explaining things about history, culture … things related to my family … when I entered the *שוחרי לאדינו*, I didn't have this concept yet of a group that I wanted to create. (…) At first, I thought I could do it within the framework of *שוחרי לאדינו* but … no … I had hesitations.[16]

By contrast, Yiddish-only and Yiddish-mostly Facebook groups and pages all write the target language in the Hebrew script. This is hardly surprising, given that overall, Ladino Romanisation is much more widespread than that of Yiddish (see Chapter 4).

Moreover, *Los Ladinadores* features a managerial position "correcting mistakes" (though this task is exclusively performed by Sevi, as opposed to a group of moderators, like in *Ladinokomunita* – see Chapter 1). Once again, this circumstance implies the supposed presence of mistakes as per the *Aki Yerushalayim* rules (prescriptivism) and the putative ability and willingness of the administrators to rectify them (self-ascription of authority, which he had previously questioned – see above). However, unlike on *LK*, *Los Ladinadores*' prescriptivism along the lines of the *Aki Yerushalayim* spelling is not explicitly stated as part of the rules of the platform.

By contrast, this prescriptivist aspect is absent in Yiddish groups and pages, suggesting that (YIVO)[17] standardisation is assumed, rather than enforced (see also below concerning Duolingo's Yiddish course). This contrast is partly due to the significant schism between Haredi and non-Haredi Yiddish-speaking cohorts, both in virtual and physical domains, which means scant deliberation has occurred concerning orthographic preferences for specific platforms, groups, and pages. Typically, the orthographic choice aligns with the ideological orientation of the platform, group, or page, either adhering to YIVO standards for Yiddishist sites or following Haredi conventions for those associated with Haredi communities. Although recently there has been a nascent trend of increased interaction between these divergent spheres, partially catalysed by a growing cohort of ex-Haredi Yiddish speakers, this phenomenon remains in its early stages of development (cf. below apropos Duolingo's Yiddish course).

3 Sevi is right to note that there is a stark difference between the respective digital affordances of *Ladinokomunita* (Web 1.0), on the one hand, and *Los Ladinadores* (Web 2.0), on the other, the latter facilitating access to audiovisual content:

> I think that Facebook and email lists are very different things, and on *Ladinokomunita*, I couldn't do what I do on the Ladino group; it's much more … it's different … you can send … photos and attachments, but as a moderator, I know that most people on *Ladinokomunita* can't open attachments, and we have many cases where they don't see the photos and … if I put it in *Los Ladinadores*, it's much more likely that they will see it. Facebook is not more complete, it's different, it's another type of thing.
>
> (my translation)[18]

This aspect also holds true in the case of Yiddish groups and pages, some of which are exclusively devoted to sharing audiovisual content in Yiddish, with no other textual element in the target language, such as the public groups *Yiddish Music* (24k members), *The Forward's Yiddish Word of the Day* (11.6k members), *Yiddish Music & Klezmer* (10k members), and *Events IN* [sic] *Yiddish* (1.6k members).

Additionally, Sevi denies the possibility of having implemented or implementing in the future *Los Ladinadores* on further Web 2.0 platforms, such as X, WhatsApp, Instagram, and TikTok, alluding to his limited acquaintance with them, his demanding schedule, and the incidental nature of his own inclusion on Facebook:

> I'm not someone who uses Instagram and Twitter … the reason for being on Facebook was a coincidence. I don't want to open more accounts in more places, as my time is already full and by chance, I entered Facebook and I use what Facebook can give me.[19]

In this sense, Sevi has made an extensive and commendable use of the pedagogical opportunities afforded by Facebook through active participation in and moderation of the discussion board (see above). Moreover, he has created and shared over 30 guides, which together constitute a "mini library of Judeo-Spanish learning and reading materials."[20] Lastly, his Facebook group boasts a media section featuring photos, videos, and albums, as well as a file rubric containing dictionaries, grammars, advanced courses of Ladino, and further books and manuscripts. This aspect is virtually absent in the case of Yiddish Facebook public groups, with the exception of the *Yiddish Writers Group* (see above), which includes plenty of media and files (mostly focused on written literature in Yiddish), though no pedagogical guides.

4 Concerning the cyber-vernacular use of Ladino on *Los Ladinadores*, during our interview Sevi distinguished between three different generational lects (also known as 'agelects'), i.e., the linguistic differences in speech or language use that occur between three different generations within the demographic of *Los Ladinadores*. His discussion reveals a (non)nativespeakerist approach while also attesting to the ability of Facebook to strengthen the intergenerational transmission of Ladino:

> I think there are three main styles … three main language modes [agelects], and I'm not talking about dialects … there's the generation of my relatives, some of whom participate … in the group. People who … are now over eighty years old. They are native speakers of Judeo-Spanish who in the early years of their lives spoke only Judeo-Spanish. They only learned the second language in school. These people do not have an education in Judeo-Spanish. They were born in the national republics but for much of their lives, the main language of communication with their spouses … and with their friends, was Judeo-Spanish… The other type of Judeo-Spanish was the Judeo-Spanish of their children … people like me, who grew up with Judeo-Spanish, but Judeo-Spanish was never a primary language of communication. It was a language of communication with grandparents, with parents at times, but among themselves, among members of this generation, they did not speak [it] among themselves … Judeo-Spanish was always in second place, third place, but it was never the main language, and then in their lives a part of them learned a bit [of it] … learned Judeo-Spanish, improved their Judeo-Spanish, many of them [taught it] to themselves, by reading things like *Aki Yerushalayim,* by writing. This is one type of lect, and I think their Judeo-Spanish … is … somewhat influenced by foreign languages like French, Turkish, Hebrew, and by written Judeo-Spanish, which is not the same as spoken Judeo-Spanish. And another type of Judeo-Spanish that exists in the group is the Judeo-Spanish of the newcomers, many of whom may have never heard Judeo-Spanish spoken in their families. And this is a different Judeo-Spanish, a Judeo-Spanish that is a mixture of dialects … if they come from the Spanish-speaking world, or South American, it is much more influenced by Castilian or Portuguese.
>
> (my translation)[21]

Additionally, in a post in *Los Ladinadores* (2023), Sevi expressed his disliking for the youngest of the three generational lects used on the platform (which also happens to be the only one that is digitally native):

> I don't like that people who are learning the language nowadays mix in the same sentence the Istanbulite with the Izmirite with the Thessalonian and also add any adjective from Haketia and a bunch of Castilian words that I've never heard in my life from a Ladino speaker. And I'm not exaggerating.[22]

In other words, Sevi acknowledges that there is a strong cyber-koinesation (i.e., the creation of a new koine on the Internet – see Introduction and Chapter 1) characterised by the convergence (rather than divergence) of Ladino dialects. Additionally, he frames this sociolinguistic evolution as a problem, and posits as a solution cyber-standardisation through explicit prescriptivism and around a return to geographically based, standardised varieties, particularly in the vernacular semiotic modes in which he articulates his post (French-Ottoman Romanisation following the specifications of the *Aki Yerushalayim* orthography).

Reading this message against the grain from the perspectives of Revivalistics and critical sociolinguistics, Sevi's prescriptivist impetus and bias becomes readily apparent. It is fundamentally underpinned by a lack of justification for both his negative and positive judgements on what otherwise constitute value-free sociolinguistic evolutions.

First, there is an unwarranted pejoration of the perceived "mixing" of Ladino dialects, as well as of those dialects with Haketia (which is grammatically selective, per the exclusive reference to adjectives, yet it is also said to be uneducatedly arbitrary, per the qualifying of those adjectives as *kualseker- any*). This negative judgement presupposes the previous existence of the dialects in question as separate codes properly mastered and used sometime in the past, thus reproducing the mythology of an ancient Golden Age, which would have gradually declined into modern decadence and corruption (see Chapter 1). By contrast, from the standpoint of (trans)languaging, Sevi is shaming the (unselective) activation of the non-L1 speaker's repertoires around Ladino understood as the partial overlap of idiolects shared by people of Sephardic culture (Yebra López 2023b; see also Chapter 1).

Additionally, we can discern a symptomatic instance of implicit (non)native-speakerism (thus reinforcing the explicit one conveyed during our interview – see above) in the dualistic reference to *djente ke se estan ambezando la lingua en muestros dias*, on the one hand [meaning people who are learning the language from scratch nowadays, in a context devoid of newly born L1 speakers], and *ladino-avlantes*, on the other hand [meaning people whose first language is Ladino]. The conflation between people whose first language is Ladino and speakers of Ladino writ large (which is what *ladino-avlantes* literally means) seeks to legitimise L1 speakers, among which the author counts himself (thus incurring gatekeeping), as much as it serves to delegitimise non-L1 speakers as supposedly deficient speakers (since they are not considered "Ladino speakers," even though they actually speak the language). Such discrimination against new learners of the language also ignores the fact that a significant portion of L1 Ladino speakers feature an advanced degree of language attrition (i.e., gradual loss of proficiency or decline in the use of Ladino). Indeed, some of them have not used the language on a daily basis for decades, so that nowadays they can hardly be said to be more proficient in Ladino than non-L1 speakers (see below, where Sevi acknowledges this through the notion of 'semi-speakers').

In our interview, Sevi admitted his prescriptivism, noting that it does not come from his linguistics education, but rather from his interaction with the first generation of the speakers (as per the above classification). Additionally, when asked whether prescriptivism on *Los Ladinadores* can stifle heteroglossia among the current Ladino-speaking global community (see Introduction and Chapter 1), he argued that its prescriptivism was not entirely so.[23] Even then, he added, prescriptivism can aid in standardising Ladino by establishing clear rules and guidelines, preserving the "character" (i.e., 'authenticity') of Ladino, and serving as a valuable resource within a context where L1 speakers (deemed "natives" in yet another instance of non-nativespeakerism) are scarce.

> My linguistic education is very anti-prescriptivist, and I think that in revitalising a language (…) we have ideologies, and sometimes ideologies conflict with each other. The situation of Judeo-Spanish is special, as we don't have many native speakers, and the native speakers we do have, many of them are now semi-speakers, they're not fluent speakers, but semi-fluent, and I think if we don't want the language to completely lose its character, we need to practice a measure of this prescriptivism. And this is not 100% prescriptivism … it's a form of descriptivism, but descriptivism of what people remember of the language of their relatives. I never learned Judeo-Spanish in a school or in a systematic way, and everything was based on what I heard from my relatives and my family, but a part of the things I heard was, 'this is not said like this, it's said like this,' or 'this can be said among friends, but not…,' and there was a measure of this that I internalised, do you understand?[24]

While there is certainly validity to Sevi's point that a degree of prescriptivism might be necessary (see Chapter 1, as well as my below discussion of Duolingo Yiddish), as I have argued elsewhere (Yebra López 2023b; Chapter 1), the strong emphasis on being a "native" speaker of Ladino or having Sephardic ethnicity as supposed evidence of authenticity, legitimacy, and/or proficiency, is contradicted by two key factors. Firstly, the understanding that authenticity, whether linked to nativeness, heritage, ethnicity, and/or the use of ethereal and esoteric notions like the "character" of Ladino (often referred to as its "flavour" – *savor* – among L1 Ladino speakers), is not inherently meaningful. Instead, it is the result of a socially negotiated and defined process of authentication (Creese et al. 2014, 939).

Incidentally, such nativespeakerism is largely absent from Facebook groups in Yiddish, which nonetheless occasionally incur mothertonguism.[25] For instance, *אַ ייִדיש וואָרט און אַ ייִדיש ליד* [A Word and a Song in Yiddish] states in its About section that "the goal of the group is to hear Yiddish, which is our mother tongue" (my translation). Likewise, *ייִדיש מיט אלי שרפשטיין*[26] [Yiddish with Eli Sharfstein] features the following claim in its About section: "we write, read and speak Yiddish. This is how we preserve our mother tongue" (my translation). Presumably, this means that Yiddish is the heritage language of the participants, as it is common to refer to Yiddish as *mameloshn* [mother tongue], even if it is not actually the first language of the person using the term.

Moreover, even if we were to accept nativeness, ethnicity, or heritage as indicators of representativity, the statistical data tells a different story. To the statistics brought by Brink-Danan (2011, 113 – see Chapter 1) where only 11% of *Ladinokomunita*'s participants answered that Ladino was their "mother tongue," one has to add now Sevi's above point that "we don't have many native speakers, and the native speakers we do have, many of them are now semi-speakers, they're not fluent speakers, but semi-fluent." This suggests that Ladino's authenticity, and by extension, that of the speech community itself, cannot be accurately described but is rather idealised through ethnic and linguistic stereotypes that obscure its diverse reality. By extension, Ladino cannot be defined strictly within the confines of a flawed classical ontological framework in close association with Standard Language Ideology (Lippi-Green 1994, 166; Walsh 2021; see also Introduction and Chapter 1), becoming instead a real imaginary space rooted in nostalgia and imagination (see below for related attempts concerning language learning courses).

As I have argued in previous chapters, this critical perspective is entirely consistent with a similar anti-essentialist understanding of languages as col-lect-ions, i.e. abstract ensembles of lects (sociolects, idiolects, including agelects in the case at hand) in Ghil'ad Zuckermann's *Revivalistics* (2020). This work encourages revitalisation efforts to become less puristic, rejecting myths, instead accepting, embracing, and celebrating inevitable hybridisation: "Revivalistics discards any imprisoning purism prism and makes the community members realize that shift happens. And there is nothing wrong with shift happening. Hybridization results in new diversity, which is beautiful" (209). And yet, as Sevi cautions us, and as we shall see below apropos, e.g., Duolingo's Yiddish course, such hybridity is not necessarily unproblematic, which challenges a major pillar of Revivalistics.

Additionally, Sevi's anxiety towards cyber-koinesation in the above-discussed post is compounded by the realisation that the global diaspora of Ladino speakers meets first and foremost on the Internet. In this context, it becomes imperative to no longer regard the Ladino-speaking Internet, following Held's conceptualisation (2010; Yebra López 2021c), as a mere substitute for offline reality, but rather as *the* central locus of Ladino-speaking activities and innovation, with its influence on the offline world being contingent, if existing at all (see Introduction).

Overall, the contemporary adoption of the Internet as the default platform through which to articulate the enhanced interconnectedness of the global Ladino-speaking diaspora in Ladino seems to be steering this language towards an increasingly well-known, positively transvalued, more accessible, and multimodal cyber-(post)vernacular (including the first generation of a digitally native and geographically decentralised lect). As a result, in Sepharad 4, Ladino is experiencing an increased reach and a spike in publications, as well as more diversified demographics, and a significantly ameliorated digital gap. On the other hand, the permanent and accelerated digitalisation of Ladino has also generated an equal and opposite reaction, this language being now policed into an increasingly standardised and centralised version strongly influenced by Western alphabets and languages (modern Spanish, and to a lesser extent, English and French, all written in the Latin alphabet), at the expense of the vehicular use of Hebrew and Cyrillic scripts, as well as Hebrew and Aramaic lexico-structural elements (see Introduction, as well as Chapters 1 and 4).

5 Much in the vein of the interactive dynamic driving *Ladinokomunita* (Chapter 1) and YouTube channels (Chapter 2), Sevi acknowledged the fact that the Facebook group in question survives off the contributions of the members, and he encourages them to participate as much as possible: "I think we have a core group of people who write a lot and things that others enjoy." [*Penso ke tenemos un nukleo de djente ke eskriven muncho i kozas ke a otros le plazen*] (my translation) This *modus operandi* echoes Bortnick's message on *LK* as part of the group guidelines that "it is YOU who keep the platform alive (and by extension, Ladino itself) ["es VOZOTROS ke lo mantenesh"].

However, just like in the case of *LK*, the above does not imply a for-profit motivation. In fact, the opposite is true apropos both platforms. To begin with, the data on *Los Ladinadores* (and *LK*, for that matter) is not sold to third parties. Moreover, no product is sold by the managers on either platform: "I don't have anything to sell, and I don't sell anything." ["*Yo no tengo nada ke vender i no vendo nada*"], claimed Sevi during our interview. Additionally, the overall ethos is not to allow the promotion of products or services, though exceptions are made in *Los Ladinadores* (less so on *LK*) for sale pitches *in* Ladino:

> I don't care if other people sell things, if it is in Judeo-Spanish. The only thing [is] everything in Judeo-Spanish can enter the group [be published]. The problem is that many who want to sell their songs in Judeo-Spanish, their performances in Judeo-Spanish, don't know Judeo-Spanish, and publish in English and other languages, but in *Los Ladinadores* if it's not in Judeo-Spanish, it doesn't stay [posted] on the group.[27]

Lastly, the manager's content contribution on *Los Ladinadores* is very significant indeed (as it is on *LK*), including open access to a carefully curated "mini library of Judeo-Spanish learning and reading materials," a media section, and dictionaries, grammars, and advanced courses of Ladino (see above).

Consequently, *pace* Sevi's humble response when asked about the reasons behind the platform's success, the audience's contribution cannot be said to be all the platforms survives off. Rather, it would be more accurate to state that while qualitatively different, on both *LK* and *Los Ladinadores* the contribution of the administrator (and moderator/s) is just as important as that of the rest of the participants, both having increased both the activity and popularity of the email list/group in question' after.

Language Learning Apps and Gamification in Ladino

The proliferation of language learning applications as Web 2.0 platforms focused on developing speaking and listening skills through either self-teaching or one-on-one language exchanges with "native speakers" in ten major languages (usually English, Chinese, Spanish, French, Portuguese, German, Japanese, Korean, Arabic, and Russian) on a freemium model[28] has reached mass adoption since the late 2000s and early 2010s. It has also transformed the traditional methods of acquiring new languages, de-emphasising grammar and focusing on vocabulary and audiovisual content, as well as offering convenient and accessible platforms for learners worldwide, while also disseminating pernicious ideologies. These tenets include Standard Language Ideology,[29] (non)nativespeakerism, language ownership (i.e., the idea that a given language is the exclusive prerogative of a specific subset of people), and flaggism,[30] all of which undermine the putatively inclusive ethos of these language learning apps.

Of particular importance for the purpose of our analysis is the fact that these apps rely heavily on gamification, i.e., the implementation of game-design elements and principles in non-game contexts (in this case, language education). The gamified nature of language learning apps plays a crucial role in language revitalisation and community-building by making language learning engaging, interactive, and inclusive. Through leveraging game-design elements, language learning platforms often create immersive and effective learning experiences that not only help learners acquire language skills but also foster a sense of belonging to a vibrant language learning community, one where the intergenerational and digital gaps have been significantly reduced.

Indeed, gamification tends to attract the younger generation, potentially incorporating it into language learning apps featuring endangered languages whose communities suffer from a significant intergenerational gap (e.g., the global community of Ladino speakers). Conversely, because of their user-friendliness, gamified language learning apps are particularly easy to use among the elderly (Reinhardt and Thorneteve 2020). As a result, the digital gap is ameliorated, which proves especially useful in the case of speech communities such as that of Ladino speakers, where the elderly are still vastly overrepresented.

Unfortunately, in the vast majority of language learning applications, including Babbel (2007), Busuu (2008), Rosetta Stone (2009), Memrise (2010), Pimsleur (2010), Duolingo (2011), FluentU (2011), HelloTalk (2013), Tandem (2015), Drops (2015), and uTalk (2016), coverage of endangered languages and especially, rare Jewish languages, remains scarce. For the most part, it can be accurately described as tokenistic, consisting of blog posts and ad-hoc partnerships, rather than courses to learn those languages.

Notable exceptions include Duolingo, HelloTalk (both of which support Yiddish, also offered in apps such as Mango Languages–2007), Memrise and particularly uTalk (more on this below). In the case of Yiddish (but not Ladino), there are even standalone apps aiming to teach users Yiddish, such as Learn Yiddish for Beginners (Sultana 2022), which features ads but no paid content (YiddishPOP is a website alternative, but it does not offer any app – see above for its Facebook group).

The fact that the overall representation of endangered languages in general and rare Jewish languages in particular, remains fairly modest across the top ten apps would seem to testify to the prioritisation of profit over concerns related to linguistics and/or social justice, thus indicating a potential area for improvement in promoting linguistic diversity. As noted by Zuckermann, further collaboration between language experts, app developers, and community stakeholders could enhance the representation of endangered languages in language learning apps, promoting linguistic diversity and cultural heritage conservation (2020, 251).

In this sense, uTalk provides a relevant template. As of early 2024, uTalk's catalogue encompasses more than 150 languages, with a focus on endangered and lesser-known ones like Kinyarwanda, Chibemba, Greenlandic, Oromo, and Cockney, to name but a few. Ladino and Hasidic Yiddish are also among them. Coupled with the fact that any language in the app can be learned from any other one, these characteristics place uTalk as arguably the world's best option to learn, reclaim, reinvigorate, and revitalise endangered languages (including Jewish ones) through language learning apps. As pointed out by uTalk's languages manager Leah Mundy apropos the Hasidic Yiddish course during an email interview in early 2024,

> The fact that users can learn Yiddish from 147 different source languages using the uTalk app is significant. In some cases, our app will be the only option for learning Yiddish from these languages. This widens the availability of Yiddish learning to a huge global audience.

uTalk's Unique Approach to Endangered Languages

Established in 1991 by Richard Howeson and Andrew Ashe, as 'EuroTalk', initially this company focused on interactive language learning software for European languages, employing computer games. Rebranded as 'uTalk' in 2016, the company introduced a new multi-platform app. Since then, uTalk has embraced new technologies and trends in language learning, incorporating features like speech recognition for pronunciation practice, augmented reality for immersive learning experiences, and adaptive learning algorithms for personalised learning paths.

uTalk's main emphasis is on vocabulary acquisition, offering a wide range of words and phrases relevant to everyday conversation and practical situations (2,500 items). The platform provides vocabulary lists organised by 64 topics or themes, allowing users to learn words and phrases related to specific contexts, such as travel, business, or hobbies. To reinforce vocabulary learning and engage users, uTalk offers interactive exercises and games combining visual and verbal memory.

Since its focus is on the oral modality, audio content is pivotal to the functioning of uTalk. This material includes recordings of words and phrases by L1 speakers (which the platform dubs "native speakers" – see below), allowing users to listen to audio recordings and repeat after the speaker to practice speaking while also Improving their listening skills.

Additionally, some versions of the app include video topics, i.e., short clips of L1 speakers ("native speakers") pronouncing relevant phrases and dialogues, meant to enhance the user's understanding of the rhythm and inflection of the spoken language, followed by a number of games designed to help users recall and remember the words and phrases in question.

During our private interview on Zoom (March 11, 2024), Howeson noted that the very fact that the app does not teach grammar explicitly makes producing new courses less time-consuming. In turn, this means a vast number of languages can be incorporated, including endangered ones such as Ladino and Yiddish:

> (…) the way we've designed (…) the product, we don't spend as much making it as they [the competition] do, because they would spend months and months doing the grammar and if we tried to do grammar, with all the languages we've done (…) we would be adding 1,000 (…) years, probably.

As explained in the first paragraph of uTalk's Guidance Notes and notwithstanding the explicit (non)nativespeakerism and treatment of languages as properties,

> the beauty of the EuroTalk system is that for each new language we cover (now yours), the app that you prepare for us will be instantly available to learners all over the world, no matter what their own native language is. The people who will use this app to learn your language could be speakers of Arabic, Turkish, Hindi, Mandarin, Swahili, French, German, Russian, Greek (…), whatever…

This aspect makes uTalk's courses ideal for the community of speakers of any diasporic language (in our case, Ladino, and by the same token, also Hasidic Yiddish), dispensing with the need to know a word of English. As admitted by Bortnick, uTalk learners who are passionate about Ladino can commence their study from any other language, facilitating acquisition regardless of linguistic background. This includes the most common languages of the Sephardic diaspora, such as Turkish, Greek, Portuguese, Hebrew, and French (see below).

Bortnick's intuition was confirmed by Howeson during our interview, where he added that the inclusion of endangered languages in this type of platform is, to some extent, a function of prioritising passion over profit:

> Although we obviously want to be profitable and make money, we also love what we do. We believe in what we do, we believe in what we can do for

> languages, and we see ourselves in a unique position in the world because of the approach we take.

This perspective also allows uTalk to create the very first dictionaries in a vast amount of language pairs, in alignment with Zuckermann's injunction to produce new, user-friendly dictionaries in the revitalised language in question (2020, 210). As admitted by Howeson,

> we can do something that no one else in the world has done before… A lot of the languages we do, there is no dictionary between the two languages, so (…) a Zulu-Icelandic dictionary would not exist. We've got 22,000 combinations. In terms of language-dictionary combinations, it is in the low thousands.

Critically for the purpose of our analysis, for each language there is a distinct and exclusive section of entries tailored specifically to the cultural context of the speech community in question. For instance, in the French learning app, these entries encompass landmarks like the Eiffel Tower, Paris, as well as cultural staples such as baguettes and croissants. This category is managed separately from the standard translation system. In this sense, uTalk Guidance Notes (for corpus translators) emphasise the importance of sociocultural appropriateness as judged by L1 speakers ("native speakers"):

> Very occasionally in the corpus, you may come across an entry that you may judge not to be socially and/or culturally appropriate for many native speakers of your language (…) You may need to use euphemisms for some of your entries, when the English equivalents would be too direct. This can be especially the case in languages with elaborate systems of politeness (like Japanese), or cultures that would take different moral stances on some issues.

All of the above makes the platform ideal for advancing oral vernacularity in Ladino, adapting its vocabulary to the second and third decades of the 21st century. This task entails including content that resonates with the experiences and interests of both younger and older Ladino-speaking adults, thus ameliorating an already-narrowing digital generation gap (Yebra López 2021c).

In what follows, I shall be discussing uTalk's Ladino course (2019) and its upcoming Yiddish course (est. late 2024), comparing and contrasting them with Duolingo's Yiddish course for English speakers.

uTalk's Endangered Jewish Language Courses: Ladino vs. Hasidic Yiddish

Howeson admitted in our interview that as part of the 160 languages initially planned for the uTalk app, "Yiddish was always on the cards," let alone Hebrew ("Hebrew was very high up on the list, for obvious reasons. It was in the top 20"), and before they were even aware of Ladino: "The reason we did Ladino? You."[31]

While language learning app developers and creators tend to advertise their product as descriptive (i.e., showcasing how a given language variety is *de facto* spoken and written), the linguistic corpus that informs these applications, including uTalk's, entails several in-built assumptions about how to speak and write in the target language. Neither the course creation nor the corpus curation can be alien to these constraints, thus revealing a significant degree of implicit prescriptivism (see Chapter 1 on *LK*, and Chapter 2 for a similar discussion apropos the managerial choices shaping *Ladino 21*). As translators of uTalk's main corpus into Ladino, my colleague Alejandro Acero Ayuda and I were faced with a series of linguistic choices we could not avoid (uTalk 2019a; 2019b).

First, in the case of uTalk, the 2,500-item master corpus contains only those words and phrases that are deemed by uTalk to be most relevant for everyday life. Surely enough, this aspect changes across languages, for as Wittgenstein remarked, "speaking a language is to participate in a way of life" (1953, §19), so that each speech community features a unique way of life which in turn corresponds to a different subset of words and phrases. In the case of Ladino, domains such as winter or golf are hardly relevant for the Sephardic way of life, so a number of neologisms were coined to account for them. Additionally, this problem was partially mitigated by the inclusion of the above-mentioned 100-item, culture-specific section. However, this solution generated a further instance of implicit prescriptivism, namely: as content curators, we had to decide the exact words and phrases that would be featured in this section. In the end, we decided to include the main organisations (*Autoridad Nasionala del Ladino i su Kultura*, Be Sepharad, *Centro Sefarad Israel*, CIDiCSef, *Ladino 21*, *Ladinokomunita*, *Kaminos de Sefarad*), personalities (Eliezer Papo, Flory Jagoda, Karen Gerson Şarhon, Mor Karbasi, Moshe Shaul, Rachel Amado Bortnick, Sarah Aroeste, Yasmin Levy, Yitzhak Navon), places (*La Espanya*, *Los Estados Unidos*, *Eretz Israel*, *La Turkia*), products (*Aki Yerushalayim*, *El Amaneser*, *El Ultimo Sefardi*) and cultural as well as religious elements (Hanukkah, *Me'am Loez*, *Agada de Pesah*, *Rosh Hashanah*, *estudio talmudiko*, *haham*, *shabat*, *el kal*) and cultural elements (*boreka*, *bulmas de espinaka*, Jak Esim Ensemble, *kasher*, *kuajado de espinaka*, *Los Pasharos Sefaradis*, *mustachudo*, *Ocho Kandelikas*, *ropa vieja*, *solitreo*, *yaprakes*) of the Sephardic world as we understood it at that time.

Second, we had to decide how to name the target language in question: 'Ladino,' 'Judeo-Spanish,' and 'Judezmo' were all viable options.[32]

Third, since uTalk does not use flags to represent languages,[33] but images, we needed to select a picture which could act as a microcosm for the language. Eventually, we chose the clocktower of Izmir, which is Bortnick's birthplace.

Fourth, we had to decide on a script in which to write Ladino, and we chose the Latin script (cf. uTalk's Hasidic Yiddish below), both because it was easier for us to use and for our audience (uTalk users) to understand.

Fifth, we chose to follow the *Aki Yerushalayim* French-Ottoman Romanisation system because notwithstanding my critique in Chapter 1, it was (and continues to be) the most popular one used for transliterating Ladino into the Latin script.

Lastly, and despite their US accents (which are not traditionally associated with Sephardim), we decided to contact Bortnick and Aguado as speakers because of their experience (and age, which is representative of the average Ladino speaker nowadays), passion about the language, and expertise and credibility as L1 Ladino speakers among the Ladino's global speech community. Both Bortnick and Aguado were flown to London to post-edit *Ladino 21*'s corpus translation and record it with their voices for over four days.

To the above instances of implicit prescriptivism, one has to add the explicit reproduction of (non)nativespeakerism, compounded by the treatment of languages as properties. These language ideologies can be revealed via a critical discursive analysis of the L1 speakers' claims apropos the course, as well as uTalk's description of their role and further press coverage. In particular, the treatment of endangered languages like Ladino as properties is predicated on language ethnicisation, i.e., the process by which a language (Ladino) becomes closely associated with a particular ethnic or cultural group (Sephardim), notably involving the use of a language as a marker of identity and belonging within that ethnic or cultural group, with the ultimate goal of "saving"[34] the endangered language in question.

As an initial point of consideration, upon logging into the app and prior to starting any course, the user can see the following message: "Our male and female voices are real native speakers. Many competitors use artificial voices." The phrasing makes it clear that (non)nativespeakerism is being incurred as means of authenticating the voices of L1 speakers. Additionally, as part of uTalk's press release on the Ladino course, entitled *International Effort to Save*[35] *an Endangered Jewish Language*, Howeson discussed the crucial role played by Bortnick and Aguado in the following terms:

> One of the native speakers we recorded, Rachel Bortnick, is in her eighties but still travelled all the way from Texas to our London recording studio. The other, Benni Aguado, 57, dropped everything to fly in from New York at a short notice after a Ladino speaker from Israel had to pull out at the last minute.

During our interview, though, Howeson nuanced this position, acknowledging that authenticity is just as important as proficiency, so that sometimes the latter trumps the previously perceived need to incorporate "native" speakers.

> We want to be authentic (…) One of our Zulu speakers, she's German, she works for SOAS. She speaks Zulu better than the Zulus… And it's happened in English. There have been English authors who are not native English [speakers], so we will go with the best. It is probably better to say we will go with the best speaker, the most authentic speakers (…) Normally it is [a native/L1 speaker], it is almost bound to be, but not always. There are exceptions. We will have the best possible voice.

Such a position reproduces the (non)nativespeakerist belief that there are "native" and "non-native" speakers while at the same time showing commendable critical awareness vis-à-vis the additional (non)nativespeakerist belief that the former are necessarily superior to the latter.

Similarly, the news article published on December 13, 2019, by journalist Simon Yaffe and entitled *New App Launched in Bid to Save Ladino*, places a very strong emphasis on the supposed intractable link between Sephardic Jewishness, on the one hand, and Ladino, on the other: "CARLOS Yebra López is not Jewish, nor does he have any Sephardi heritage – or at least that he knows of. But it has not stopped the Spaniard becoming passionate about Judeo-Spanish, which is also known as Ladino" (5).

The underlying ideological message is clear: while the fact that I do not identify as a Sephardic Jew did not stop me from developing a fervour for Ladino, it could (and perhaps, it should), thus implying that the language is (and/or should) be, the exclusive prerogative of a certain ethnic group (i.e., Sephardim).[36]

To be sure, as noted in Chapter 1, speech communities should be encouraged to take ownership of their heritage languages, lest they end up being the recipients of all-too-familiar forms of benevolent (neo)-colonialism in the name of humanitarian protection (Spivak 1988; Morton 2003). Sephardic ownership is clearly discernible apropos the uTalk Ladino course, since both L1 speakers, Rachel and Benni, postedited the entire corpus, recording it with their own voices. Additionally, presupposing a neat separation between the Spanish and Judeo-Spanish languages and cultures inadvertently reproduces the same Othering of Jewish (and Muslim) cultures which has been traditionally at the heart of National Catholicism (from the very Catholic Kings who decreed the expulsion of Sephardic Jews in 1492 to Francoist dictatorship). But even if we were to grant that separation for the sake of the argument, the fact remains that vulnerable communities, such as the global Ladino-speaking one, can and do benefit from allyship, the latter facilitating linguistic preservation efforts and promoting cultural awareness globally. Through collaboration and solidarity of the sort exemplified by the creation of this course, allies amplify the voices of language activists from the community and contribute to the sustainability and revitalisation of their endangered linguistic heritage (see Introduction).

Likewise, the article also reproduces (non)nativespeakerism: "two native speakers, Benny [sic], and Turkish-born Rachel Amado Bortnick, recorded words and sentences in Ladino." The closing quote, featuring Howeson's sentiment about the course, serves to drive the point home:

> When we add languages, we work very closely with the community that speaks the language. We do a lot of research. Ladino is special in its own right, especially its history. It is more than spoken words – it is a feeling and a heritage. You can see how important it is to Ladino speakers' identity.
>
> (Yaffe 2019, 5)

Eventually, the course was launched and demoed (by Howeson and Emily Martyn – then uTalk's languages manager) at the academic event *Saved by the Digital: Ladino communities of the 21st Century* (Language Acts and Worldmaking

2019).[37] This gathering was widely covered in the local and international press and events, including reports in *The Jewish Telegraph* (UK), the *Journal of Romance Studies* (UK), *Radio Sefarad* (Spain), *El Amaneser* (Turkey), the conference *Ladino: From the Printing Press to the Smartphone* (University of Washington at Seattle, United States), and *Ladino 21* (online).

Following a demonstration on how to use the app,[38] the event's keynote speaker, Eliezer Papo, admitted that the Ladino course had exceeded any expectations held by the *Autoridad Nasionala del Ladino i su Kultura* [National Authority for Ladino and its Culture] (Israel 1997) regarding the creation of a similar product for Hebrew-speaking children. In particular, Papo stressed the course's relevance to ameliorate intergenerational transmission in Ladino:

> What impressed me the most was the app … for years, the National Authority for Ladino and its Culture has been trying to develop a similar application to help Hebrew-speaking kids in Israel learn the language in exactly this way, through pictures, concepts, quizzes, and this type of things.
>
> (2020a; my translation)[39]

Similarly, in *El Amaneser*, Bortnick remarked that

> (…) it is not necessary to know English to use uTalk apps. They have more than 140 languages, and you can learn one of them based on any other language. This means that you can learn Ladino if you speak French, or English, or Spanish, Portuguese, or Chinese, or whatever.
>
> (2020, 19; my translation)[40]

Since 2024, the roster of languages includes Hasidic Yiddish, which leads us to a fruitful comparison.

As I shall show below, together with the Zoom Boom (see Chapter 4), the language learning app sector is arguably the only sector of the Internet where Ladino has fared better than Yiddish. A significant reason is to be found in the diverging strategies employed in the process of standardisation, partly motivated by the fact that even though the respective standardised versions of Yiddish (YIVO) and Ladino (*Aki Yerushalayim*) have become the norm in their present-day instruction as non-L1 languages, whereas standardised Yiddish is used only by a minority of L1 Yiddish speakers (see below), standardised Ladino is used by most Ladino speakers, including those whose first language is Ladino. In turn, this *décalage* shall help us problematise a key aspect of Revivalistics, namely: the beauty of linguistic hybridity/diversity (Zuckermann 2020, 209), or lack thereof.

According to the Joint UCL Hebrew & Jewish Studies-Linguistics AHRC research project *Contemporary Hasidic Yiddish* (2023–6), approximately 700,000 Hasidic Jews worldwide still use Yiddish as their primary language, mainly in key hubs like New York, London, Antwerp, Jerusalem, and Bnei Brak. However, modern-day Hasidic Yiddish shows notable linguistic differences compared to the pre-war Eastern European dialects and the standardised version primarily influenced by the Lithuanian dialect (Belk et al. 2020) and enforced by YIVO, which is nonetheless used by only a minority of L1 speakers (Birnbaum 1979; Wex 2005).

For instance, a pilot study on the grammar of Stamford Hill Hasidic Yiddish revealed that in traditional and contemporary standardised Yiddish, nouns are assigned gender, dictating the form of the definite article 'the.' For masculine entities like 'father' or 'man,' *der* is used, while feminine nouns like 'mother' or 'woman' take *di* and neuter nouns like 'child' use *dos*. Adjectives must match the gender of the noun they describe. Moreover, the definite article changes depending on the noun's role in the sentence or its association with a preposition, resembling grammatical cases. However, in Stamford Hill Hasidic Yiddish gender and case distinctions are no longer observed, with the definite article uniformly pronounced as *de*, akin to the English 'the.' This shift mirrors historical changes in English and alters the language's linguistic dynamics, impacting aspects like word order rules (Belk et al. 2020). There have also been changes in other aspects of grammar, such as the pronominal system, in which the historically accusative forms of the first person plural and second person plural pronouns are now also used in nominal contexts (Belk et al. 2022).

Additionally, there are also differences concerning vocabulary, spelling, and pronunciation. With regards to vocabulary, Haredi Yiddish displays a greater openness to adopting lexical borrowings from the dominant co-territorial language compared to non-Haredi Yiddish, which typically adheres to prescriptive language norms, and promotes the creation of Yiddish neologisms. Regarding spelling, orthographic distinctions exist between Standard and Hasidic Yiddish, as noted by Benedict (2021) and Yampolskaya et al. (forthcoming). Lastly, regarding pronunciation, there are vowel differences, due to the fact that Hasidic Yiddish is largely based on Polish/Hungarian Yiddish, whereas Standard Yiddish is based on Lithuanian and Ukrainian varieties.

Consequently, language learning apps wanting to incorporate a course in Yiddish are faced with a dilemma. On the one hand, they can create an all-encompassing variety representative of Yiddish diversity across the world (but not spoken or written by any actual Yiddish speaker). On the other hand, they can choose one form of Yiddish between pre-war Eastern European dialects, standardised Yiddish, and Hasidic Yiddish, and stick to its unique conventions in grammar, vocabulary, spelling, and pronunciation (thus admittedly sacrificing Yiddish's global complexity). Whereas uTalk has created a course on Hasidic Yiddish (thus following the latter), Duolingo opted for the former for their Yiddish course for English speakers, with mixed results.

Writing for the Yiddish Studies journal *In geveb*, Sarah Biskowitz has noted that the course in question has generated an unprecedented number of reactions within the Yiddish-speaking realm: "It seems that no Yiddish phenomenon in recent memory has attracted more praise, more criticism, or more excitement than Yiddish Duolingo" (2022).

On its website, Duolingo claims that its Yiddish course, released in April 2021, is "the world's best way to learn Yiddish" (2024). The basic premise behind this course was to gamify an unheard-of combination of standardised Yiddish spelling, on the one hand, and Hasidic pronunciation, on the other hand:

> **The Duolingo team came to an ingenious compromise (…)** they wanted the course to potentially serve as a bridge between secular Yiddishists, who may be learning out of nostalgia or to read Sholem Aleykhem in the original, and Hasidim and other non-secular communities where Yiddish is the lived language of everyday life. If you learn YIVO, you can't speak to native speakers. If you learn Hasidishe Yiddish, you won't grok the grammar in an Isaac Balshevis Singer novel. So what did they do? They chose to ***teach the spelling and grammar of YIVO standard Yiddish with the pronunciation of contemporary Hasidic Yiddish***. This means if you want to speak with people, you'll learn the vocabulary and pronunciation to be able to, and the grammatical changes you'd have to make are to have to do *less* conjugating and declining. If you want to read old books, or take a college class, you will know the academic grammar, and can figure out pronunciation from the standardized spelling. It's literally a win-win. So *of course* everyone is mad about it.
>
> (Jones 2021; bold and italics in the original).

Duolingo courses are developed by volunteers. Involved in the project of creating a Yiddish course were former Hasidic Jews from the United States, as well as L1 Yiddish speakers from Australia and New Jersey who were brought up in Yiddish-speaking households. Although the volunteers for this course unanimously decided to adhere to the spelling and grammar norms of standardised Yiddish (once again proving that in Yiddish standardised spelling is often assumed – see above), they could not determine on their own which dialect to adopt for pronunciation (cf. the above quote):

> Some felt that it was best to use a Hungarian Yiddish pronunciation since that is the predominant dialect among American Hasidim. Others supported the standard Yiddish pronunciation typically used in academic courses, arguing that it is easiest to teach, as its phonology is the closest to how Yiddish is written. Still others proposed a compromise: teaching the Ukrainian Yiddish pronunciation that was historically used in Yiddish theater.
>
> (Kutzik 2019)

Consequently, their volunteers' dialect choice in this regard was prefaced by a survey where Duolingo asked respondents the following overarching question: "The Yiddish for English speakers course on Duolingo is currently being developed. For the audio and pronunciation portions only, what dialect should we use?" (Duolingo 2019) The options were YIVO (with Duolingo noting that it is a "standard literary dialect with many other resources, but not spoken natively as widely"), Hasidic ("spoken most widely among Yiddish speakers, but less phonetically consistent and with fewer external language learning resources"), and Southeastern ("it can be understood by both dialects, and could be a compromise solution"). Participants were then requested to choose one out of the above three options, or else specify an alternative (Duolingo 2019).

Jordan Kutzik, deputy director of Yiddish Forward, has stressed the importance of the dialect question as a symptom of a broader identity struggle: "While the question may seem restricted to the realm of linguistics and language pedagogy, the surprisingly heated [dialectic] debate is also at the heart of larger questions of identity among Yiddish speakers." Ultimately, Kutzik adds, the question is

> to whom does Yiddish belong today? Should it be considered only the language of those who speak it on a daily basis (primarily Hasidim) or is it also a language of students and professors, translators and artists who write, research, and create in Yiddish but don't necessarily use it as their daily vernacular language.
>
> (2019)

From a Revivalistics standpoint, Zuckermann has argued that the legitimate language owners of a language that is being revitalised (reinvigorated, in the case of Yiddish – see Introduction) are "the (native) speakers who are ancestrally tied to the language or those who will carry it into the future" (2020, 211). From a critical linguistics perspective, though, we need to problematise two assumptions, both of which are intractably linked: (non)nativespeakerism (see above) and language ownership. The latter task implies making extensive Zuckermann's claims about lack of ownership (which he applies to, e.g., Israeli Hebrew, but not to Australian aboriginal languages) to all linguistic varieties: nobody needs permission from anybody else to speak any linguistic variety, less we discriminate against a subset of people. Indeed, as explained by David Huddart,

> When language is associated with a very definite community, then obviously there are people excluded from that community in various ways. From this perspective, languages are conceived as belonging to a people (…) even if you speak a given language with great fluency, if it is not your 'proper' language, not the language you 'own,' then you are excluded from the collective understanding that is shared by the community. From this point of view, 'non-native' speakers of English might be unable to share in the supposed common understanding shared by British, Americans, Australians, etc. Further, it might be argued that non-native speakers should not even *want* to share in that common understanding. They have their own languages, their own communities with their own shared understandings, and should use English at most as a mere 'communicative' tool.
>
> (2014, 6–7)

The irony is of course that the romantic assumption of language ownership as the century-long prerogative of a specific subset of speakers is *de facto* challenged by these endangered languages (Ladino, Yiddish) being learned by users coming from a vast diversity of backgrounds on language learning platforms such as Duolingo and uTalk.

Over a year after the release of Duolingo Yiddish, a survey was conducted among 304 Yiddish learners, and posted on the online Yiddish journal *In geveb*. Concerning the most appealing aspects of the course, respondents ranked, in this very order, its free cost (which excludes the use of personal data for commercial purposes, as well as the users' exposure to security breaches compromising their privacy and confidentiality), accessibility regardless of geographical location, and gamification (Biskowitz 2022).

With regards to their experience with the Duolingo Yiddish dialect choices, just over half of the total users (53.5%) defined it as "neutral," with 30.4% framing it as "positive," and 16.2% as "negative."

From a Revivalistics standpoint, I was reminded by Zuckermann in a private interview held on Facebook (March 8, 2024) that something similar occurs with Israeli Hebrew (Yiddish phonetics, Semitic script), and with many Maori tribes in New Zealand, which are reclaiming their own variety, as opposed to its standardised version: "It is either simplification or diversity. I'm ok with diversity (…) It tells the language is more alive," he concluded. After all, and as surmised by Kutzik, every "standard" is the result of a standardisation process (hence why it is more accurate to speak of "standardised" languages, rather than "standard" ones), so that the standardised form of any linguistic variety is predicated on (the reduction of) diversity, including YIVO's: "Standard Yiddish is itself a mixture of elements taken from different dialects (a mostly Lithuanian-Yiddish pronunciation mixed with the grammar of the southern dialects)" (2019).

Duolingo Yiddish volunteer Meena Viswanath has expressed a similar opinion, noting that a Yiddish course with YIVO spelling and Hasidic pronunciation serves the twofold goal of showcasing the diversity of the language while tending bridges between its often-siloed speech communities. In this sense, the course strives "'to make the language taught in the course feel familiar to as many modern Yiddish speakers as possible,' and to foster greater understanding between non-Chasidic Jews and Chasidim, whom she says are often stereotyped and misunderstood'" (cit. in Finlay 2021).

On the other hand, Susannah Finlay has pointed out that the type of hybridity displayed by the Duolingo Yiddish course can often come across as surreal, even downright absurd:

> much of the course has ended up looking like a surrealist game of word association. To help learners get to grips with a different alphabet, they must first wade through a series of absurd sentences featuring zebras, pyramids and avocados – words that are phonetically similar to their English counterparts in Yiddish. Predictably, there is overrepresentation of culinary staples. Students learn to ask crucial questions such as "Where is my babka?," alongside a Curb Your Enthusiasm-inflected "What are you, my mother?"

In the same vein, X user Jewfjan Stevens described it as "Animal Crossing for Ashkenazim" (cit. in Burack 2021).

Similarly, Duolingo Yiddish user Louis Blaine has claimed that trying to please too many speech communities often ends up backfiring: "The main issue with learning Yiddish is that it is a language with multiple dialects. You either chose one, and sound regional, or try to blend them, and make no one happy" (2023). UCL Yiddish university professors Lily Kahn and Sima Beeri have also stressed this point in private correspondence, further observing that to the extent to which beginners might trust Duolingo to offer an accurate representation of how Yiddish is *de facto* spoken nowadays, the course/experiment in question is misleading for new learners. Additionally, it is of very limited pedagogical use, given that nobody outside the Duolingo course speaks this hybrid, intercommunal auxiliary variety of Yiddish.

The above polemic apropos Duolingo Yiddish raises a crucial dilemma concerning the balance between linguistic diversity/hybridity and standardisation. On the one hand, one could argue that hybridity is inherently unproblematic and even beautiful, as it reflects the dynamic and evolving nature of languages (Zuckermann), including their increasing cyber-koinesation in the 21st century. On the other hand, there might be situations where some level of standardisation becomes preferable (Bortnick, Sevi, Kahn, Beeri), even necessary for the purpose of revitalisation, and/or reinvigoration (YIVO) as a means to facilitate communication and comprehension, particularly in formal or professional contexts where clarity and consistency are valued, while also helping maintain linguistic integrity and coherence within a community or across different communities.

The preference for hybridity over standardisation or vice versa would seem to be context-dependent, as ultimately, the (perceived) beauty of linguistic hybridity lies in its ability to reflect the complexity and richness of human communication, while the (perceived) need for standardisation seemingly arises from practical considerations and communicative goals. In the end, languages are meant to be both reflective of the social reality and performative of it (i.e., able to shape it). Consequently, we hit a snag when the performative aspect takes over, leading to a language variety which is not reflective of any pre-existing speech community of an otherwise extant language (e.g., Duolingo Yiddish, but not constructed languages like Esperanto).

Conclusion

In this chapter, I have discussed the online revitalisation of Ladino via groups and accounts on social networks featuring real-time interaction, as well as via language learning platforms operating through gamification.

Apropos social networks featuring real-time interaction, I have noted that Facebook is by far the most popular platform among Ladino speakers to communicate in Ladino, due to its format (focusing on written communication), demographic (inclusive of the elderly), and community engagement affordances. Additionally, I have observed that over the years engagement on Facebook in Ladino has led not only to the consolidation of this endangered language as a cyber-vernacular, but also to the emergence of a new digitally native, geographically delocalised, cyber-koined Ladino *lect*. Drawing upon an original interview with Aldo Sevi, my critique of the case study of the most popular Facebook platform exclusively in Ladino, i.e., *Los Ladinadores* (2021), which I have praised as the most impactful Digital Home-Land developed in written Ladino on the Internet since *Ladinokomunita*, has shed light on a number of critical issues. These include the perceived importance of adopting functional differentiation and standardising Ladino as a cyber-vernacular (in the Latin script, following the *Aki Yerushalayim* orthography) monitored by L1 speakers, plus capitalising on the pedagogical affordances provided by Facebook and disengaging from the platform's increasing commercialisation to optimise the revitalisation of Ladino.

Additionally, I have noted that both Sevi's unwarranted criticism of the new digitally native, geographically delocalised, cyber-koined Ladino *lect* on his Facebook group, on the one hand, and his staunch defence of (non)nativespeakerism and Ladino cyber-standardisation, on the other, are two sides of the same coin. In other words, they are viable solutions (cyber-standardisation) just as much as symptoms of the anxiety provoked by the irruption of a new sociolinguistic stage in the development of Ladino within the Sephardic diaspora (i.e., in Sepharad 4), compounded by the realisation that Facebook is proving pivotal to it, increasingly diversifying Ladino.

My comparison of Ladino Facebook groups and pages with their Yiddish counterparts has further allowed me to conclude first, that there seems to be a trade-off (at least on Facebook; see Chapter 1 for a similar discussion apropos correspondence circles) between the use of endangered languages as vehicular, on the one hand, and the popularity of that group/page, on the other hand. The existence of this offset would help explain the scarcity of platforms devoted to preserving the target language in question *in* that language. Second, I have surmised that there are unexploited opportunities for the creation of Facebook groups devoted to creative writing in Ladino, as well as bilingual Facebook pages in, e.g., Spanish, Hebrew, and/or English, plus Ladino.

Concerning language learning platforms operating through gamification, I have observed that because most of these apps are profit-driven, they tend to focus on ten major languages. In this context, the presence of endangered languages (Ladino, Yiddish) is typically reduced to tokenistic expressions of sympathy under the form of blog posts and/or ad hoc partnerships but rarely resulting in the creation of courses.

Drawing upon my original interview with Richard Howeson, my critique of uTalk's (2016) Ladino course (2019, which I have praised as innovative, revolutionary, and unique in its ability to allow users to learn Ladino from 150+ languages), and its juxtaposition with uTalk's Hasidic Yiddish course and Duolingo's Yiddish course for English speakers, I have derived a number of conclusions.

First, the absence of explicit prescriptivism (cf. *Los Ladinadores*) does not amount to removing (implicit) prescriptivism in issues such as the glottonym, the coinage of neologisms, specific cultural items, the image chosen to represent the course, the script, the spelling, and the actors in charge of recording the corpus.

Second, while flaggism and Standard Language Ideology are not as pervasive in Ladino and Yiddish courses, (non)nativespeakerism and the use of a language as a marker of identity and belonging within an ethnic or cultural group (Sephardim/Ashkenazim) as means to the ends of authentication, establishing language ownership, and/or "saving" endangered languages, plus standardisation, are just as widespread (or even more so). This predicament reveals an underlying anxiety apropos the respective status of Ladino and Yiddish as "contested languages," i.e., those that stand out linguistically from the official languages of the state(s) from whose territories the speech communities of those linguistic varieties were expelled (e.g. Spain/Portugal and Germany, respectively), but are frequently overlooked because of their genealogical similarity to the official languages of the state (Spanish, German). Third, emphasising diversity over (implicit) standardisation might not always offer the best results (particularly when the performative aspect of language overshadows its reflective element), as exemplified by the criticism received by Duolingo's Yiddish course for English speakers.

Overall, my discussion in the present chapter has allowed me to reach a number of overarching conclusions. First, the revitalisation of Ladino by digital means benefits the most from combining the free/cost-effective use of social networking groups and accounts in Ladino through real-time interactions (focused on reading and writing skills, particularly *Los Ladinadores*) with language learning platforms operating through gamification and self-teaching or one-on-one language exchange (focusing on speaking and listening, particularly *uTalk*'s Ladino course). Second, the (combined) impact of these Web 2.0 platforms constitutes a milestone within Zuckermann's 'Talknological Revolution,' particularly when it comes to strengthening the intergenerational transmission of the language, developing digitally native lects, and fostering worldwide community-building. Third, the current presence of Ladino in these platforms problematises the beauty of linguistic diversity/hybridity (or lack thereof), as their success would seem to be partly premised on a cyber-standardisation process that entails setting boundaries to the romanticisation of diversity/hybridity in Revivalistics. In most cases, a balance between standardisation and hybridity is being sought to preserve the linguistic diversity of Ladino/Yiddish while also ensuring effective communication and language vitality.

In light of the above, the best policy would seem to be diversity when possible, standardisation when necessary, yet that would beg further questions: who gets to decide what is possible and what is necessary: L1 speakers, platform creators, users? One whose behalf? At whose expense? On the basis of which (contextual) criteria?

From the perspective of Revivalistics, the speech community should take priority over academic specialists in the language in question. From the perspective of its global community of speakers, unlike Yiddish, Ladino does not present a strong dialectal, pronunciation, vocabulary, or orthographical disagreement, the vast majority of speakers using the geolect of Istanbul written in the *Aki Yerushalayim* spelling and incorporating a rather moderate number of loanwords from Turkish, Hebrew, and Aramaic. Like Yiddish, the question of which script to use is also settled, albeit with opposite results (Hebrew scripts in the case of Yiddish, Latin script in the case of Ladino – except for academic purposes).

Consequently, it would seem both linguistically representative of the *de facto* use of Ladino in the 21st century among the global community of speakers and pedagogically useful to revitalise the language in the Latin script written with the *Aki Yerushalayim* spelling, which is not to say that the latter is unproblematic (see Chapter 1). Notwithstanding the above, and as I will argue in the next chapter, given the historical importance of Rashi and Solitreo, for academic purposes Ladino should continue to be taught also in its Hebrew, and even Cyrillic scripts. Overall, though, it is important to observe that not everyone who wants to learn Ladino conceptualises the language as primarily Jewish (rather than Ottoman and/or Spanish), nor do they all might wish to learn Rashi and/or Solitreo, and as a matter of fact, a significant portion does not.

Notes

1 *Tuve un gran mazal de azerme viral en TikTok kon el djudeo-espanyol. Yo ize un TikTok demandando a la djente si aviya alguno ke keria ambezar a avlar la lingua, i la verdad ke no me esperava ke la djente me ivan a kontestar, i despues dentro de muy poko tyempo se izo viral* (my transcription).

2 Not to be mistaken for *Los Ladineros* [also ‘The Ladino People’], a community of Ladino speakers in Seattle.

3 See Introduction.

4 Most of them are taken from a proverb collection in two volumes, entitled *Trezoro Sefaradi* (comprising both *Folklor de la Famiya Djudiya* and *De Punta Pie a Kavesa*), edited by Beki Bardavid with the assistance of Fani Alyon Ender, a second cousin of Michael Halphie, and thanks to whom Halphie found out about the volume in question (Halphie 2020).

5 Although Shalom is mentioned in the About section as one of the admins, she does not feature as such in the group.

6 See Introduction and Chapter 1.

7 *Este grupo es para partajar kontenidos en djudeo-espanyol. No akseptamos publikasiones en otras linguas. No akseptamos publikasiones ke kontienen diskurso de aboresión o propaganda elektoral. Keremos kontenidos sostansiozos. No akseptamos publikasiones de saludos jenerales komo ‘Buen día,’ ‘Shabat shalom’ ets. Semos un grupo públiko, dunke no akseptamos kontenidos non públikos*.

8 The last line of the About section reads “everything [must be] written in the Yiddish language” (my translation).

9 To the extent to which a sanctuary is typically a place of refuge or safety, often associated with protection or preservation, the “digital sanctuary” metaphor reveals an implicit understanding of the perceived importance of functional differentiation as a means to revitalise Yiddish online.

10 “All correspondence, materials and information exchange will be conducted in Yiddish in this group” (my translation).

11 Writing in Yiddish is mentioned as the first rule of the group.

12 The About section reads as follows: “The rules of the group: the first rule: write in Yiddish. And this is also the last [rule] of the group” (my translation).

13 “The goals of the League for Yiddish are:
to encourage people to speak Yiddish in their everyday life.
to enhance the prestige of Yiddish as a living language, both within and outside the Yiddish-speaking community; to promote the modernisation of Yiddish” (my translation).

14 *No kreo ke es posivle de tener este grupo bazado en eskrivyendo en letras ke no son letras latinas (...) Los miembros del grupo ... poko mas del 20% son de Israel, i los ke son de afuera de Israel, kaji el 80% no konosen las letras ebreas. Aparte de esto los israelianos ke konosen las letras ebreas, si aprovan a eskrivir ladino kon letras ebreas azen una transkripsion al ebreo moderno i no konosen i utilisan del todo las reglas de eskrivir ladino en letras ebreas. Esto afita muncho en Shoharé Ladino [Amatores del Ladino]. Eyos mizmos no pueden meldar lo ke eskrivieron. La meata de las diskusiones aya son 'de ke no eskrivites en letras latinas; no podemos meldar'* (my transcription).

15 Incidentally, this means that COVID-19 (see Chapter 4) was not the main reason why the group was created, notwithstanding the fact that it might have accelerated either its creation or its popularity among users.

16 *Kuando yo entri al grupo de Shoharé Ladino ... la primera entision ke teniya no era de ... ser un aktivista del ladino o del djudeo-espanyol, i yo tambyen kuando empesi aya empesi a eskrivir lo mas en ebreo i a poko a poko vino la dechizion de azerlo todo en djudeo espanyol... Me tomo dos anyos para ser mas siguro ke lo puedo azer en djudeo-espanyol, en ladino. En primero lo mas ke eskrivia en djudeo-espanyol no era kozas mias, era kantikas en djudeo-espanyol, proverbos en djudeo espanyol kozas ke topava aki i aya ... las kozas mias eskrivi mas en el hebreo, eksplikando kozas de la istoria, de la kultura ... koza ke afito a mi famiya ... kuando entre a Shoharé Ladino no tenia dainda este konsepto de grupo ke kero azer. En primero pensi ke puedo azerlo en el kuadro de Shoharé Ladino, ma ... no ... tenia esitaziones* (my transcription).

17 YIVO, or the Yiddish Scientific Institute, is an academic and cultural institution dedicated to the study and preservation of Yiddish language, literature, and culture. It was founded in 1925 in Vilnius, Lithuania, and later moved its headquarters to New York City. YIVO conducts research, hosts educational programs, and maintains archives and libraries related to Yiddish studies. It has played a significant role in the documentation and revitalisation of Yiddish language and culture worldwide (Kuznitz 2014).

18 *Penso ke Facebook i email lists son kozas muy diferentes i en Ladinokomunita no pudia azer lo ke ago en Los Ladinadores. Es muncho mas ... es diferente ... puedes mandar ... fotos i attachments, ma komo moderador se ke lo mas de la djente en Ladinokomunita no pueden avrir los attachments i tenemos munchas keshas i no ven las fotos i ... si lo meto en Los Ladinadores es mucho mas siguro ke lo van a ver. Facebook no es mas kompleto, es otro, es otro tipo de koza* (my transcription).

19 *No so uno ke izo Instagram i Twitter ... la razon ke esto en Facebook fue una koza por azar. No kero avrir mas kuentos en mas lugares, ke mi tiempo ya esta yeno i por azar entri en Facebook i utilizo lo ke el Facebook me puede dar* (my transcription).

20 These guides are, for the most part, modelled after the ones Sevi had created on שוחרי לאדינו, and encompass the following: illustrated vocabularies, verb conjugations, expanding our vocabulary, short articles on different aspects of language/culture, usage issues, spelling issues, pronunciation issues, notes for Spanish speakers, that's how it's said in Judeo-Spanish! for Spanish speakers, literary prose, memoirs and life stories, advice and tips, jokes and humorous advice, Articles, from the press of old times, translations into Ladino of canonical texts, holidays, songs with their words, proverbs and sayings, blessings, curses and jokes, phrases, situations and advice, romances, poetry, for children, cartoons and ideas, concepts, thoughts in visual media, videos, gastronomy, complete numbers from *Aki Yerushalayim*, Books for learning the language (advanced course) [*vokabularios ilustrados, konjugasiones de verbos, engrandeseremos muestro vokabulario, artikolos kurtos sovre aspektos diferentes de la lingua/kultura, kestiones de uzo, kestiones de ortografia, kestiones de pronunsiasion, notas para kastilyano-avlantes, ansina se dize en djudeo-espanyol! para avlantes del kastilyano, proza literaria, rekodros i kuentos de vida, konsejas i konsejikas, shakás i konsejikas umoristikas, artíkolos, de la prensa de altiempo, traduksiones al ladino de tekstos kanónikos, moadim, kantikas kon sus palavras, refranes i dichas,*

augurios, maldisiones i keshas, lokusiones, sitasiones i konsejos, romansas, poezía, para kreaturas, karikaturas i ideas, konseptos, pensamientos en medio vizual, videos, gastronomía, numersós -sic- kompletos de Aki Yerushalayim, livros para ambezarse la lingua (kurso para adelantados)].

21 *Penso ke ay tres stilos prinsipales ... tres modos de lingua prinsipales, i no avlo de dialektos ... ay la djenerasion de mis parientes, ke algunos de eyos partisipan ... en el grupo. Djente ke ... tyenen agora mas de ochenta anyos. Eyos son avlantes nativos de djudeo espanyol ke en los primeros anyos de sus vida avlaron solo en djudeo-espanyol. La segunda lingua se [la] ambezaron solo en la eskola. Esta djente no tyene edukasion en djudeo-espanyol. Nasieron en las republikas nasionalas ma muncho muncho de sus vidas, la lingua prinsipal de komunikasion kon sus espozos ... i kon sus amigos era el djudeo-espanyol... El otro modo de djudeo-espanyol era el djudeo-espanyol de sus kriaturas ... djente komo mi, ke engrandesieron kon el djudeo-espanyol ma el djudeo-espanyol nunka no fue una lingua de komunikasion prinsipal, fue una lingua de komunikasion kon los granparientes, kon los parientes en vezes, ma entre eyos, entre miembros de esta djenerasion no avlaron [en djudeo-espanyol] entre eyos ... El djudeo-espanyol syempre era en segundo lugar, tresero lugar, ma nunka era la lingua prinsipal i despues en sus vidas una parte de eyos ambezaron un poko ... se ambezaron el djujdeo-espanyol, mijoraron su djudeoespanyol, munchos de eyos de si para si, en meldando kozas komo Aki Yerushalayim, en eskrivyendo. Esto es un modo de la lingua, i penso ke su djudeo-espanyol ... es ... un poko enfluensyado por linguas ajenas komo fransez, turko, ebreo i por el djudeo-espanyol eskrito, ke no es lo mizmo komo el djudeo-espanyol avlado. I otro modo de djudeo-espanyol ke ay en el grupo es el djudeo-espanyol de los mansevos, ke munchos de eyos afilu nunka oyeron el djudeo-espanyol avlado en sus famiya. I esto es un djudeo-espanyol diferente, un djudeo espanyol ke es una meskla de dialektos ... si vyenen del mundo ... espanyol, o sudamerikano es muncho mas enfluensyado por el kastelyano o el portugez* (my transcription).

22 *No me plaze ke djente ke se estan ambezando la lingua en muestros dias mesklan en la mizma fraza el estamboli kon el izmirli kon el selanikli kon el sarayli i ademas adjustan kualker adjektivo de la haketia i un alay de palavras kastilyanas ke nunka en mi vida tengo sintido de un ladino-avlante. I no esto exajerando.*

23 For a similar disavowal, see my interview with Liliana Benveniste apropos *Enkontros de Alhad* in Chapter 4.

24 *Mi edukasion linguistika es muy anti-preskriptivista i penso ke en aprovando a revitalizar una lingua (...) tenemos ideolojias i en vezes las ideolojias konfliktan uno kon el otro. La situasion del djudeo-espanyol es espesiala, ke no tenemos munchos avlantes nativos i los avlantes nativos ke tenemos munchos de eyos agora son medioavlantes, no son avlantes halis, son medioavlantes i penso ke si no keremos ke la lingua totalmente pedra su karakter, kale praktikar una mizura de este preskriptivizmo. I esto no es 100% preskriptivizmo ... es un modo de deskriptivizmo, ma deskriptivizmo de lo ke la djente akodra de la lingua de sus parientes. Yo nunka ambezi el djudeoespanyol en una eskola o en una manera sistematika, i todo era de lo ke senti de mis parientes i mi famiya ma una parte de las kozas ke senti era 'esto no se dize ansina, se dize ansina,' o 'esto se puede dizir entre amigos, ma no...' i aviya una mizura de esto ke internalisi, entiendes?*

25 For a critical perspective on the idea that an individual's first language aligns with their "mother tongue," see Chapter 1, endnote 13.

26 Sic, with no *alef* after the *shin*.

27 *No me emporta si otra djente meten kozas para vender si es en djudeo-espanyol. La sola koza ... todo en djudeo-espanyol puede entrar en el grupo. El problema es ke munchos ke keren vender sus kantikas en djudeo-espanyol, sus performansas en djudeo-espanyol, no saven el djudeo-espanyol i puvlikan en inglez i en otras linguas, ma en Los Ladinadores si no es en djudeo-espanyol, no keda en el grupo.*

28 While the app itself is free to download and use, certain premium features and content may require a subscription or in-app purchases.

29 Indeed, as discussed in further chapters in this volume (see Chapters 1 and 5) the idea that meaning-making is structured through distinct "languages" (Gramling 2016) is not universal, but a concept influenced by monolingual ideologies originating in 18th-century European nation-states. These ideologies reinforced the notion of languages as independent entities, distinct from national borders, and were intensified during the 19th century in European nations through colonialism and nation-building efforts, as well as globally through colonialism and education (Makoni and Pennycook 2007, 2012; Yebra López 2022a).

30 Flags typically symbolise countries, regions, institutions, and political causes, but their association with languages is problematic. Many entities represented by flags lack an official language or have multiple languages. Conversely, certain linguistic varieties may lack flags altogether. Additionally, flags often carry controversial political implications (Yebra López 2021a). Thus, using flags in language-related activities is inaccurate and potentially harmful, exemplifying "banal nationalism" as described by Michael Billig, i.e., the normalisation of a shared national identity through everyday representations in the public domain (1995, 39–51), thereby reinforcing the ideological connection between a nation, its state, and its language (Blackledge 2000; Kohn 2019).

31 I entered into contact Howeson in early 2019, proposing the Ladino course for uTalk.

32 See Yebra López (2023b, 83, 92), as well as my discussion of Ladino glottonyms in Chapter 1.

33 See above on flaggism.

34 The perception of "saving" endangered languages can carry connotations of condescension, particularly when it implies a saviour complex on the part of activists, often associated with a "white saviour" narrative. This line of thought suggests that individuals or groups from privileged backgrounds, often culturally dominant or colonising populations, position themselves as the rescuers or guardians of marginalised or endangered cultures, languages, or communities. The concept of "saving" languages can be problematic because it tends to overlook the agency and autonomy of the speakers of these languages. It frames them as passive recipients of aid, rather than active participants in the preservation and revitalisation of their own linguistic heritage. This approach can reinforce power imbalances and perpetuate colonial attitudes that undermine the dignity and self-determination of minoritised speech communities. Moreover, the idea of "saving" languages often implies prioritising certain linguistic varieties over others based on arbitrary criteria, such as perceived linguistic value or cultural prestige. This can lead to the marginalisation or neglect of languages and dialects that do not fit within dominant cultural frameworks or standards (i.e., Ladino, in the case at hand). Instead of adopting a paternalistic approach focused solely on "saving" endangered languages, in line with Revivalistics, efforts should prioritise collaborative, community-led initiatives that respect the rights and agency of minoritised speech communities. This involves empowering communities to take ownership of their linguistic heritage, supporting grassroots language revitalisation efforts, and advocating for policies that promote linguistic diversity and equality. Ultimately, the goal should be to foster a more inclusive and equitable linguistic landscape where all languages and cultures are valued and respected (Austin and Sallabank 2014; Zuckermann 2020).

35 See above.

36 For the discussion of a similar observation made by Yvette Bürki (2021) apropos *Ladino 21*, see Chapter 2.

37 The full programme can be accessed here: https://languageacts.org/events/saved-by-the-digital-ladino-communities-of-the-21st-century/.

38 A demonstration conducted entirely in Ladino, is also available on *Ladino 21* (Yebra López 2019).

39 *Lo ke mas me impresiono fue la aplikasion. Siendo ke la Autoridad Nasionala del Ladino i su Kultura yeva anyos intentando de fazer ansina una aplikasyon para ke los chikos en Israel, ebreo-parlantes, puedan ambezarse el ladino por medio de una aplikasion djustamente ansina, por medio de estampas, konseptos, kuises, i este modo de kozas* (my transcription).

40 *(...) No es menester saver inglez para uzar los apps de uTalk. Tienen mas de 140 lenguas, i se puede ambezar una de eyas de la baza de kualkera otra lengua. Esto kijo dizir ke uno se puede ambezar ladino si avla fransez, o inglez, o espanyol, portugez, o kinezo, o lo ke sea.*

4 Zoom Boom (2020–2)

The Sephardic Digital Academy, *Enkontros de Alhad*, the Oxford School of Rare Jewish Languages

Introduction: The Zoom Boom in the Global Ladino- and Yiddish-Speaking Diasporas

US entrepreneur Daniel Gross posited that 2020 would be recognised by future historians as the epoch when the Internet age genuinely commenced (cit. in Srinivasan 2022, 171). Ultimately, the accuracy of this statement is necessarily subject to how events will unfold over the coming decades. Nonetheless, within his work *The Network State* (2022, see Chapter 6) Balaji utilises it to assert that the COVID-19 pandemic (2020–23)[1] engendered an enduring progression towards digitisation and precipitated a fundamental shift from a predominantly physical world to one largely characterised by digital primacy. Srinivasan's contention does not imply that the pandemic instigated this state of affairs *ex novo*, but rather that it irrevocably expedited a process already underway, ultimately transmuting a cumulative quantitative evolution (whereby an increasing array of activities were conducted online) into a qualitative leap. This disruption permeates all facets of contemporary human existence, with the world now predominantly functioning in a digital-first paradigm, relegating the physical domain to a secondary level, if present at all:

> During the pandemic, every sector that had previously been socially resistant to the internet (healthcare, education, law, finance, government itself) capitulated. Those aspects of society that had been very gradually changing with technology shifted overnight. With vaccination, many of these things have flipped back, but they won't come back all the way. Digitization was permanently accelerated. It used to be that the physical world was primary, and the internet was the mirror. Now that has flipped. The digital world is primary and the physical world is just the mirror. We're still physical beings, of course. But important events happen on the internet first and then materialize in the physical world later, if ever.
>
> (Srinivasan 2022, 172)

This paradigm shift inaugurates a pivotal stage in the sociolinguistic evolution of Ladino as a (cyber)postvernacular language of the 21st century. In a 2021 article published in the Israeli newspaper *Haaretz*, Ladino activist Kenan Cruz Çilli, in

DOI: 10.4324/9781003473664-7

his mid-20s at the time of writing this chapter, spoke of a Ladino "renaissance" following the pandemic, which has had the unintended effect of tending Ladino bridges across continents and generations. Characterising COVID as an "unlikely lifesaver" for Ladino, Cruz notes that "thanks to lockdowns and online learning, the world of Ladino is now flourishing, leading many to reassess whether they'd been too eager over the years to believe rumors of the language's imminent extinction" (2021).

In this sense, the remarkable proliferation of regular meetings conducted exclusively in Ladino using the videoconferencing platform Zoom, also known as 'Ladino Zoom Boom' (Kushner 2020), has both catalysed the revitalisation of Ladino by digital means in quantitative terms and redefined the very nature of the language and (its speech community) in the process. As expressed by Cruz Çilli, "though it's wise to remain cautious about the trajectory of Ladino in the coming decades, it is clear that the online domain has opened up a space for Ladino to grow, and for previously attenuated connections between Sephardic communities to recover and even create new connections and linguistic and cultural networks" (2021).

In contrast and except for a few (temporary) initiatives concerning online classes (see Jacobs 2021; see also below),[2] a comparable surge in Zoom adoption has not been observed among the Yiddish-speaking diaspora. Yiddish usage in the 21st century remains predominantly confined to Haredi (strictly Orthodox, primarily Hasidic[3]) Jewish circles, where there exists a notable portion of individuals or communities expressing reservations towards Internet usage (Basu 2014; YIVO 2014; Fader 2020).[4] Stringent regulations concerning Internet access have been implemented, driven by apprehensions regarding exposure to secular influences, inappropriate content, and potential distractions from religious pursuits and community cohesion, particularly within more conservative factions of the Haredi community.

Conversely, within secular Yiddish-speaking spheres, where the utilisation of Zoom technology could ostensibly thrive, established online practices and lifestyles already existed prior to the advent of Zoom (e.g., the email lists of *Mendele*, *Tate-mames* and *Yiddishland* – see Chapter 1– and the prominent newspaper in Yiddish *Forverts* – see Chapter 2 for its YouTube-hosted digital archive), resulting in a more subdued impact following its introduction within this subset of the Yiddish-speaking community.

Even in the case of Ladino, it is important to note that far from emerging *ex nihilo*, the 'Ladino Zoom Boom' has merely accelerated what was hitherto a latent trend, i.e., the fact that the Internet has been actively shaping the fate of Ladino since the emergence of *Ladinokomunita* at the dawn of the 21st century, ultimately contributing to its cyber-koinesation and its eventual cyber-standardisation as a post-geographical standardised variety (see Introduction, Chapters 1, 2, and 5).

In particular, I would like to argue that the nature of the qualitative changes affecting Ladino in dialogical fashion with COVID-19 and the Zoom boom is predicated upon three fundamental aspects, each of which depends causally on the previous one: (i) the booming of Ladino as a cyber-(post)vernacular of the 21st century, (ii) the global diaspora of Ladino speakers nowadays meeting first and foremost, on the Internet, and (iii) the Internet becoming the default option for Ladino teaching and learning.

In the next section, I will establish a dialogue between the above theoretical framework and claims, on the one hand, and three prominent initiatives within the Ladino Zoom Boom with whose founders I conducted original interviews in January 2024, on the other: the Sephardic Digital Academy (2020 to present), *Enkontros de Alhad* (2020 to present), and the Oxford School of Rare Jewish Languages (2021 to present).

Dissecting the 'Ladino Zoom Boom': Case Studies

Leading the Way: The Sephardic Digital Academy (2020 to Present)

The Sephardic Digital Academy is an initiative launched by Ethan Marcus, the managing director of The Sephardic Jewish Brotherhood,[5] in March 2020 as part of the organisation's pivot to online education in light of the then-incipient pandemic, particularly upon consideration of the social isolation experienced by senior members of the organisation. As such, the pivotal presence of Ladino in this initiative (through language classes across various levels, as well as a vehicular language in religious and cuisine classes) heralded a turning point in the Zoom boom of Ladino as a cyber-(post)vernacular of the 21st century.

The Sephardic Jewish Brotherhood of America, established in 1916 by immigrants from Ottoman lands, is the largest benevolent organisation of its kind in the United States, with nearly 1,000 families across the country, particularly those tracing their lineage to Ladino-speaking Jewish communities in Greece, Turkey, and further territories of the Balkans. Originally offering burial services and financial support, the Brotherhood has adapted to the changing needs of its community, introducing in recent times innovative programs such as a Sephardic Birthright Israel Trip, the annual Greek Jewish Festival in Lower Manhattan, and the Greek Jewish & Sephardic Young Professionals Network. In 'The New Sephardic Generation,' Paula Jacobs discusses the key role played by the younger generation in the United States when it comes to visibilising the history and the future of Sephardim within a traditionally Ashkenormative context: "Indeed, this new generation of Sephardic Jews is actively working to tell its story and secure its solid place within the American Jewish narrative, using social media as a key tool. Their initiatives—from education to culture—speak to the diversity of the Sephardic experience reflecting family roots in Greece, the Balkans, Turkey, North Africa, and across the Middle East" (Jacobs 2021).

It is against this background that we can best make sense of the pioneering establishment of the Sephardic Digital Academy in early 2020, through a collaborative effort with the aim of linking and instructing Sephardic community organisations, Rabbis, educators, and members in the United States. Initially, the Academy provided five weekly classes instructed by unpaid, willing, available, and experienced faculty through which it hoped to offer the broadest possible choice of Sephardic themes to its audiences. This "revolutionary new approach to Sephardic

Jewish education" (Hwang 2021), which had started timidly, eventually "exploded in producing innovative content and individual engagement" (idem), resulting in more than 350 classes and engaging more than 50,000 people around the world in its first year only, with Zoom videos livestreamed and recordings posted on Facebook and YouTube.

The Academy provides complimentary weekly classes whose participation ranges from 10 (in the case of small seminars) to more than 400 attendees (for some lecture series), covering topics such as Sephardic Torah, Halakha, traditions and customs and Sephardic cooking, and sure enough, Ladino language instruction. Ultimately, the Sephardic Digital Academy, as expressed in its own words, strives to "help you feel a little more connected to our Sephardic Community, identity, history, and heritage" (Sephardic Digital Academy 2020, cit. in Yebra López 2021c).

In a further piece published by *The Jerusalem Post* (Beede/Jewish Telegraphic Agency 2020), Marcus spoke to the ability of the Internet in general and the Sephardic Digital Academy in particular to attain a global reach while retaining a physical location confined to the United States, redefining in the process the very idea of a (Sephardic) national community: "This has been a moonshot in more ways than one, just connecting people really spread out across the world," he remarked. "We have participants in Turkey, in France, in Argentina — we even had a participant in Japan. It's really elevated our profile (…) But more importantly it really made us rethink what it means to be a national community, how do we play a role in people's lives daily today" (cit. in Beede/Jewish Telegraphic Agency 2020). Moreover, attesting to Zoom's ability to spark action in the offline world and as per Marcus' own admission during our private interview, many of the participants in the Sephardic Digital Academy would go on to become members: "[The Sephardic Digital Academy] acted as a huge boom for our membership recruitment (…) we recruited hundreds of new members" (2024). A case in point is Ladino-speaker Lexi Fellus, who became a member after taking Bryan Kirchen's class on Ladino, and then went on to launch a Ladino profile on Instagram, named *Ladino with Lex* (see Chapter 3).

As of early 2024, the overall activity of the Sephardic Digital Academy had decreased, due to a decline in the number of attendants and less energy for sponsorship from the general public (which might lead the Academy to switch to a non-profit focus on community service).[6] At any rate, Marcus notes, the Sephardic Digital Academy plans to offer between 4 and 6 classes a week (with an emphasis on book talks), and remains very popular among senior members. On the other hand, Marcus emphasises, the younger demographic has been consistently interested in Ladino introductory courses, partially attracted by the perceived "coolness" of the language (thus, demonstrating how the inclusion of Ladino into new domains contributes to its positive ideological transvaluation – Eisenlohr 2004; see also Introduction). While such perception may occasionally drift into a romanticisation of this linguistic variety, as concluded by Marcus, "at least we are getting recognition that Ladino is a very important language to the common Jewish community" (2024).

Courses and classes in Ladino taught at the Sephardic Digital Academy include not only beginner-level Ladino (taught by Bryan Kirschen, Rachel Bortnick – see Chapter 1–, Daisy Braverman, and Karen Şarhon), and intermediate level (taught by

Bortnick and Braverman), but also Ladino music classes (featuring Ian Pomerantz and Sarah Aroeste – see Chapter 2), Sephardic liturgy classes (alongside Hebrew and English), and courses on the *Me'am Lo'ez*[7] conducted in Ladino (by Eliezer Papo – see Chapter 1), as well as in that language and English (by Al Maimon).

During our interview, Marcus showed remarkable linguistic self-awareness by acknowledging that the inclusion of Ladino as a pivotal aspect of the Sephardic Digital Academy was not a mere matter of passively incorporating this language from the offline world to the Internet, but actually carried specific metalinguistic implications pertaining to aspects such as script use, language demarcation, standardisation, and glossaries.

First, just like we have already seen apropos *Ladinokomunita* (Chapter 1), *Los Ladinadores*, and uTalk's Ladino course (Chapter 3), and we will see below apropos *Enkontros de Alhad*, the Latin script was adopted as the vehicular one, particularly for introductory courses, with Marcus citing its relative ease of use and learning. On the other hand, and somewhat closer to the spirit of the Oxford School of Rare Jewish Languages (see below), intermediate courses would also highlight Rashi and Solitreo, though not as vehicular scripts. Second, Marcus observed that there has been a deliberate push for the "narrative" that Ladino is its own language (as opposed to being a 'dialect' of Spanish). Third, and following the precedents of *Ladinokomunita* (see Chapter 1), *Los Ladinadores* and uTalk's Ladino course (see Chapter 3), the *Aki Yerushalayim* standardisation had been implemented for transliteration into the Latin script, which in turn has reinforced the above narrative. Fourth, both the Spanish-to-Ladino glossary of *Ladinokomunita* and the Ladino-to-English glossary by Marie-Christine Varol (2008, 299–318) (see Chapter 1) had been disseminated as part of the activities of the Sephardic Digital Academy. Lastly, the use of Ladino as a feature of these initiatives' classes and courses has expanded into other areas of the Sephardic Jewish Brotherhood. These encompass the inclusion of Ladino pieces in its magazine, weekly Ladino Zoom classes for high schoolers (taught by Aaron Shapiro) as part of the *Bivas* [Ladino for 'May you live'] initiative (a Sephardic Teen *Shabbaton* in New York City), and the adoption of translingual practices, such as the so-called 'Ladinglish,' understood as the postvernacular functional inclusion of Ladino terms within an utterance or a conversation conducted in English, and vice versa (e.g., '*Mashallah*, that was great!') (cf. below apropos *Enkontros de Alhad*'s draconian measures concerning translingual practices).

During our interview, Marcus remarked that Ladinglish was used several times during the 2023 Sephardic Gala, which was organised by the Sephardic Jewish Brotherhood. Similarly, in 2024, the Brotherhood launched a National Essay Competition in partnership with the University of Washington, where writers were expected to compose in English, interspersing words and references in Ladino. Lastly, to a lesser extent, further instances of Ladinglish can be found in the use of English words, mostly by senior members, whenever the speaker (often a heritage one) fails to remember the equivalent term in Ladino.

In the next section, I shall discuss the case study of *Enkontros de Alhad*, which distances itself from translingual practices and posits an intractable link between building a community of Ladino speakers online, on the one hand, and doing so *in* Ladino, on the other.

Ladino Speakers Meet Online First: Enkontros de Alhad

Marcelo and Liliana Benveniste (founders of *eSefarad*, 2008 to the present; see Chapter 2) established *Enkontros de Alhad* in late summer 2020, the first program airing on August 9. *Enkontros de Alhad* is an online Ladino show devoted to weekly meetings ['*enkontros*' in Ladino] on Sunday ['*alhad*'], which take place under the form on an interview between a *balabay* ['host'] and a *musafir* ['guest'].

In a private interview (2024), co-founder Liliana Benveniste acknowledged the fact that the pandemic accelerated the online implementation of Ladino. She even admitted that *Enkontros de Alhad* might have never come into existence were it not for (the online activism sparked by) COVID 19: "First, it is important to consider that the pandemic accelerated the process of Ladino's arrival to the online mode. If this global catastrophe had not occurred, even though I had been thinking about this idea, it might be that we would still be thinking about it and not doing it" (my translation).[8]

Enkontros de Alhad has managed to fill a gap that many had identified and communicated prior to the pandemic, i.e., a virtual space (or any space at all, with the exception of Turkey and/or Israel, which still feature pockets of Ladino speakers) allowing speakers and enthusiasts to both listen to content in Ladino and interact in this language: "Before the *Enkontros de Alhad*, the majority of Ladino speakers, excluding Israel and Turkey, lamented the lack of places to express themselves and even speak the language. It is true that Ladino speakers could only engage in conversation with each other in person; in person, there was no other way" (2024).[9]

It is within this context that Benveniste had a prophetic dream of a place where people could only speak Ladino. Upon waking up, the sweet taste this dream had left in her heart prompted Liliana to share it with her husband and collaborator, Marcelo Benveniste, who encouraged her to implement this idea:

> *Enkontros de Alhad* (…) came from a dream of mine. I dreamt that we were all in a place where only Judeo-Spanish could be spoken. And I woke up that morning with this pleasant feeling of having a place where the language was the most important thing, where in order to enter, you only had to know this language. And well, I told Marcelo about it that same morning and he said, 'well, do it' and I said to him, 'what, do you think I should ask somebody if they want to participate? It would please me if this truly became a community of the world.' So, I spoke with some very good and very active friends in the field of Sephardic culture and language in particular, and wonderfully, right after I finished explaining it to everyone, they all said to me, 'yes, count on me' (…) in a very short time this turned out wonderfully, as if it were a sign from God.
> (2021a; my translation)[10]

The above quote reveals a clear ideological gap between the community's vocalised desire, on one hand, and the implemented solution, on the other, namely:

whereas Ladino speakers and enthusiasts longed for a place where they could speak Ladino, Liliana Benveniste's vision and implementation were to create a place where *only* Ladino was spoken. Thus, the community-building aspect was made contingent on the functional differentiation of the language (Ferguson 1959; Fishman 1967). This element is largely absent in both the Sephardic Digital Academy (e.g., through the use of Ladinglish and the coexistence of Ladino with other named languages, particularly in the courses related to religion and cuisine; see above) and the Oxford School of Rare Jewish Languages (whose policy is to use English as a vehicular language in which to teach the rare Jewish language in question; see below).

The *balabays* of these meetings, most of whom were introduced in the first *enkontro*, come from 13 Sephardic institutions worldwide, which are responsible for inviting the *musafires* in question each week. By chronological order of incorporation, these institutions are as follows: *Autoridad Nasionala del Ladino i su Kultura* (Jerusalem, Israel; see Chapter 2), *Sentro Kultural Sefarad* (Buenos Aires, Argentina), *Instituto Salti* (Tel Aviv, Israel), *Ladinokomunita* (Internet, managed from Dallas, United States; see Chapter 1), *Los Shadarim* (Internet, managed from New York, United States; see Chapter 2), *Aki Estamos-Les Amis de la Lettre Sépharade* (Paris, France), *Sentro Sefaradi de Estambol* (Istanbul, Turkey), *Sentro Moshe David Gaon* (Beer Sheva, Israel), The Sephardic Jewish Brotherhood (New York, United States; see above), The Stroum Center for Jewish Studies (University of Washington, Seattle, United States), *Voces de Haketia* (Internet, managed from New York), the *Muzeo del Patrimonio Djudio de las Komunidades de Salonika i Grecha en Memoria de Leon Recanati* (Tel Aviv, Israel; no longer collaborating), *Ladino 21* (Internet, managed from United Kingdom), *Federasion Sefaradi de Palm Beach* (Boynton Beach, Florida, United States), and *Aki Yerushalayim* (Internet, managed from Israel; see Chapter 1).

This format, which was chosen by the founders of the show, makes room for a collaborative space conducive to the eventual crystallisation of a global community of Ladino speakers (i.e., a Digital Home-Land in my re-definition of it – see Held 2010; Yebra López 2021c; see also Introduction). During our interview, Liliana Benveniste delved into this layout, describing it as global in its impetus and democratic in its spirit:

> My thinking was always to create a global community of Ladino speakers, a collaborative, and not a personal activity. For this reason, I thought of giving the responsibility to one person from each institution to organise their meeting, and freely choose the topic and guest. I cannot say that I decided that this is better than anything else, but no one gave me an alternative idea, and everyone accepted to do it this way (in my opinion, quite democratic).
>
> (2024; my translation)[11]

Over time, Benveniste confided, *Enkontros de Alhad* became a virtual community of weekly attendance where people (split between 60/70% of regulars and 30/40% of casuals) come to feel closer to their roots and language (thus echoing the

Sephardic Jewish Brotherhood's mission statement apropos the Sephardic Digital Academy – see above). The *enkontros* allow attendants to find out and hear about Ladino speakers from different geographies and ages that can speak Ladino in virtually all discourse domains, and for all purposes ["*todo modo de sujeto*"],[12] making it possible people to meet for the first time or reunite after decades of not having heard from each other: "*Enkontros* became a community where those who want and can, come every week to be close to their roots, their language, to meet and hear people from different geographies and ages who can speak Ladino, not only apropos stories and proverbs but about all kinds of subjects" (my translation).[13]

Additionally, and as remarked at the beginning of this subsection, Benveniste noted that what was specifically lacking was not only a place where Ladino speakers could meet to communicate, but a space where they could do that *exclusively in Ladino*, as opposed to using other languages to speak *about* Ladino. Her statement belies a monolingual ideology whereby languages (whether it is Ladino, Spanish, Hebrew, or French) are assumed to be discrete, self-contained entities among which there would be a pre-existing separation that ought to be respected:

> For a long time, I was looking through our website [esefarad.com] and noticed that there were many activities for Sephardic culture and language, as well as research, but some were in English, others in Spanish, and others in French … in Israel, the activities (even in the advertisements!) to invite you to participate were in Hebrew … so this aroused in me a feeling of … how are we going to revive the language if we are talking about the language but not speaking *with* [in] the language?
>
> (2021a; my transcription; emphasis in the original)[14]

To the above, she added the following in our recent interview: "*Enkontros* ignited in others the idea that conducting activities online *in* Ladino, and not just in other languages talking *about* Ladino, is possible" (2024; my translation; emphasis in the original).[15]

Benveniste acknowledged the fact that this form of enforced monolingualism in the endangered language implies the exclusion of some people who otherwise would like to participate but cannot do so because they are not fluent in Ladino. Instead of viewing this aspect as problematic, she articulated her perplexity regarding the apparent challenge faced by prospective participants in embracing the policy: "at times we encounter people who want to participate (…) for them, it seems difficult to understand that they cannot participate if they cannot speak fluently" (2021a; my translation).[16]

While undoubtedly well intended, such a position is entirely at odds with a descriptive (rather than prescriptive) and empowering revitalisation process premised on the acknowledgement and reflection of the translingual discursive practices of the speakers (rather than on their repression). As discussed by Ofelia García in 'The Role of Translanguaging in Bilingual Education in the United States' ['*El papel del translengüar en la enseñanza bilingüe de los Estados Unidos*'] (2013), drawing upon Charles Ferguson's notion of "diglossia" (1959), Joshua Fishman hypothesised that only the functional differentiation of two languages in separate domains of different social functions (e.g., Ladino from Spanish/English/Hebrew/Turkey/French for the purpose of the *Enkontros de Alhad*) could result in a stable form of social bilingualism (1967). However, in practice, García argues, the exclusive use of the target language in a given domain or for a given social function (e.g., *LK*, *Los Ladinadores*, and in the case at hand, *Enkontros de Alhad*) maintains that very language (Ladino) in a position of inferiority, excluding discursive practices deemed inappropriate by the powers that be. As pointed out by Makoni and Pennycook (2007), the idea of named national languages (including that of stateless nations, such as the global community of Ladino speakers) is a deliberate social construction that reproduces dynamics of colonial oppression which, in the case of Ladino, lie at the very origin of this language (see also Chapter 3). Consequently, from the perspective of translanguaging, while seemingly conducive to an emancipatory end, the creation of virtual spaces premised on a Ladino-only policy also constitutes an exercise of gatekeeping which reproduces past injustices and power imbalances in the name of their remediation:

> Educational diglossia, as much as social diglossia, maintains in place both the subordinate language and any practices that do not adhere to the linguistic patterns of those who hold power, always reluctant to share their sacrosanct domains (…) diglossia in education only serves to exclude linguistic practices that are not considered appropriate by the nation-state and its agents of power.
>
> (García 2013, 362; my translation)[17]

Additionally, and as noted in previous sections of this volume (see Chapters 1, 2, and 3), this policy of enforced monolingualism in the target language fails to measure up to the complexity of the discursive practices of 21st-century multilingual speakers as facilitated by new technologies (including in our case, the Internet and Zoom):

> The bilingual speaker with true 'agency' utilises their linguistic repertoire, which encompasses practices and features normally associated with one system or another, in a dynamic manner to signify and construct meanings. It is these dynamic discursive practices, which enable the bilingual individual to access all aspects of their social life with dignity and freedom, that I have termed 'translanguaging' (…) and which I refer to here as '*translenguar*.'
>
> (García 2013, 363; my translation)[18]

This circumstance is particularly true of Ladino, whose advanced degree of attrition among its remaining speakers lends itself to the emergence of translingual practices such as the Ladinglish exchanges discussed by Marcus apropos the Sephardic Digital Academy (see above).

Unaware of the above-discussed implications, Benveniste reasoned that some speakers have tried to replicate the success of the *Enkontros,* but fell short precisely because (rather than despite the fact that) they failed to enforce a Ladino-only policy. Nevertheless, she added with a certain patronisation, they seem to be making progress towards it: "Some (…) jealous of the *Enkontros de Alhad,* began to hold meetings solely in the language, but the rules are somewhat loose and some speak in other languages, but they are on their way…" (2021a; my translation).[19] Even when ironic, such a statement implies a journey towards successfully enforced monolingualism in Ladino as the ultimate object of desire and recipe for success, thus validating this ideological assumption.

At any rate, the fact that other platforms face challenges in maintaining a monolingual virtual space for Ladino would seem to suggest the inherent difficulty of such an undertaking (due to its dependence on the host's ability to regulate and discourage translingual practices). However, Benveniste argued that the *Enkontros de Alhad* (whose success is, by her own admission, predicated on her ability to enforce monolingualism in the language) is not prescriptive. Rather it merely describes the current global usage of Ladino:

> (…) the *Enkontros de Alhad* (…) are showing how those who know the language today speak. It directly reflects the use of the language by individuals who are familiar with it from home, as well as those who are learning it in the present times.
>
> (2024; my translation)[20]

At the same time, though, Benveniste admitted to sometimes encouraging guests to write down their piece so they can feel more confident in their speaking ability and "do not make a lot of mistakes" ["*no agan munchos yerros*"] (2024), implicitly acknowledging the prescriptivism of the *Enkontros*.

Additionally, one could speculate that over the years regular online interaction exclusively in Ladino might be leading to some changes in the way the language is used as a vehicle of communication (regardless of whether those are prescribed or arise more or less organically–implicit prescriptivism), as we have seen apropos *Ladinokomunita* (see Chapter 1) and *Los Ladinadores* (see Chapter 3). One could point, for instance, to the increased use of languages such as 'modern' Spanish and English, which have an overwhelming influence on the Internet (thus reproducing a pre-existing offline imbalance)[21] that contrasts with the scarce impact they have historically had on Ladino when its predominant space was the offline realm. After all, Ladino developed in virtual isolation from the Iberian Peninsula for three centuries (16–19th) (Quintana 2010) and then mostly isolated from English up to the present day (with the exception of some communities in the United States).

The increased influence of Spanish (and to a lesser extent, English) on Ladino within the Internet would help explain why participants at the *Enkontros de Alhad* have come to use '*ola*' [from Spanish '*hola*'; i.e, 'hello'] to greet each other, which was once considered a 'mistake,' i.e., the result of 'mixing' Spanish with Ladino. However, Benveniste believes that this phenomenon comes from the fact that participants find themselves in all sorts of different time zones, so that typing *buenos dias*, ['good morning'] *buenas tadres*, ['good afternoon/evening'] and *buenas noches*, ['good evening/night'], respectively, would be less accurate than using a more general form of greeting like *ola*. However, such generic greeting already existed in the form of e.g., *shalom*, so Benveniste's explanation does not suffice to explain the emergence and spreading of *ola* among attendants of the *Enkontros*.

To be sure, it seems to me that the challenge that critical sociolinguists like García and myself are levelling on functional differentiation has less to do with functional differentiation *per se* than with the nature of what is being isolated. On the one hand, Ladino understood as a self-contained linguistic variety, in close association with Standard Language Ideology (Lippi-Green 1994, 166; Walsh 2021; see also Introduction and Chapter 1) and to be used vernacularly only within the domain or for the function for which its exclusive use has been agreed/negotiated (e.g., *LK*, *Los Ladinadores*, and to a lesser extent, *Enkontros de Alhad*,[22] which opens the door to over-prescriptivist standardisations that reify Ladino as a living reality, removing it from further domains and functions). Alternatively, Ladino as a cultural-linguistic matrix of multiple idiolects with different attrition degrees and translanguaging practices that the community of Sephardic speakers (whether culturally or ethnically so) finds valuable (e.g., *Ladino 21* – see Chapter 2; see also Otheguy et al. 2015; Yebra López 2023b).

In this sense, in a concession to descriptivism, Benveniste claimed that Ladino's online resilience as facilitated by the 'Zoom boom' will never amount to Ladino's apogee in the offline world back in the Ottoman Empire. Instead, it will be premised on the speakers' ability to understand that in the words of Zuckermann, "shift happens,"[23] i.e., that whether the global community of Ladino speakers likes it or not, the language will continue to change and evolve, and there is hardly anything wrong with that:

> It's not that I think this [the Zoom boom] will revive and become flourishing again like it was in the communities in the Ottoman Empire, but I think it will evolve towards a different path. If we think that the language is alive and that we want to keep it alive, for sure the language will have to develop in some way (…) we can see a light at the end of the tunnel. It will be a different thing.
>
> (2021b; my translation)[24]

Needless to say, Ladino's ability to admit change would imply that people's interaction in this language in the *Enkontros de Alhad* does not only reflect Ladino but actually *shapes* it, a possibility Benveniste had hitherto denied for the most part (see above). Indeed, as concluded by Julia Sallabank and Jeanette King, "linguists have found that ironically, endangered languages change faster than larger or more vital languages. This is often due to influence from other languages, especially the dominant one(s), which can be difficult for some language supporters to accept, although it is impossible to prevent" (Olko and Sallabank 2021, 40).[25]

Contra Judith Olszowy-Schlanger (see below), Benveniste does not consider the Hebrew elements (be they articulated through the Hebrew language or Hebrew scripts such as Rashi and Solitreo) to be necessary conditions for the preservation of Ladino, labelling advocates of this paradigm "traditionalists." Rather, and not unlike the beginner-level classes in Ladino offered by the Sephardic Digital Academy, Benveniste's vision for the future of Ladino revolves around fluency in a language written in the Latin script, if at all:

> I know that the traditionalists think that the era of the grandparents will not return anymore and all of this, and that it is necessary because initially it was written in Hebrew… It would be very good to know Hebrew because there is a lot of Ladino material in Hebrew, there is also a lot in Solitreo, but you can speak Ladino without knowing any writing.
>
> (2021b; my translation)[26]

Such observation is symptomatic of Benveniste's place of enunciation (i.e., a Spanish-speaking country like Argentina, no advanced knowledge of Hebrew). It is also idiosyncratic of a significant demographic among the Ladino-speaking community (with the notable exception of Israel), where unlike in the Jewish Linguistics approach (including the Yiddishist one), learning the Hebrew scripts is not considered a necessity.[27]

Lastly, when inquired about the future of Ladino on Zoom, particularly as pertains *Enkontros de Alhad*, Benveniste rightly claimed that while many have returned to in-person activities after the pandemic, to the extent to which a great number of people continue to lack a physical place to come into contact with the language, it is important to continue organising the *Enkontros de Alhad*:

> When the pandemic subsided, many abandoned the online activities and returned to doing what they had always yearned for: in-person meetings only. In my opinion, it is important to continue with the *Enkontros* on the Internet because I think there are many people who do not have another way to have contact with the language.
>
> (2024; my translation)[28,29]

While this conclusion might seem to leave the door open for the continuation of the *Enkontros de Alhad* as a virtual space where people can interact in Ladino (but not just in this language, i.e., minus enforced monolingualism), that would contradict her statement from 2021, where she clearly made the continuation of the *Enkontros* (and the preservation of the language on the Internet at large) contingent on perpetuating Ladino-only virtual spaces. As long as these platforms continue to exist, Benveniste resolves, we might not have a physical community, but we will continue to have a virtual one (i.e., a Digital Home-Land, as I have defined it – Held 2010; Yebra López 2021c) in which to develop Ladino for the foreseeable future:

> If we can maintain places like you with *Ladino 21*, like us with *Enkontros de Alhad* (…) I think we won't have a physical community, but we will have a virtual geography where we can develop Ladino in the future.
>
> (2021b; my translation)[30]

That virtual geography, Benveniste concedes, may be articulated on Zoom, or alternatively, in some sort of upgrade to this platform. At any rate, the virtual space choice seems to be of secondary importance to her, as long as people continue to interact (only) in Ladino: "Perhaps a better platform than Zoom may come along, and then we will switch to this other mode, but people will continue to be involved to speak, listen, and participate" (2024; my translation).[31]

In the ensuing section I will examine the community-building endeavours undertaken by an additional Zoom initiative, namely, the Oxford School of Rare Jewish Languages. The distinctiveness of its scholarly methodology and emphasis on Ladino as a Jewish linguistic entity contribute to a paradigm shift in the way Ladino preservation is approached through the medium of Zoom.

Online Ladino Classes Take Over: The Oxford School of Rare Jewish Languages

In addition to the plethora of online educational resources discussed in this volume (including digital archives in Chapter 2, WhatsApp groups, apps, Facebook groups, Instagram, and TikTok accounts in Chapter 3, Netflix in Chapter 5, and the Metaverse in Chapter 6), nowadays there are myriad of options to attend formal Ladino classes online. From Liliana Benveniste's classes via *eSefarad*,[32] to myself and Alejandro Acero Ayuda's courses via *Ladino 21*, passing through the Sephardic Jewish Brotherhood of America's Ladino courses (see above), Bryan Kirschen's 16-session, 20-hour Ladino course through his platform Ladino Linguist, and Karen Şarhon's Judeo-Spanish classes at the Sephardic Center of Istanbul.

To be sure, one could argue that the same holds true for the offline realm, where Ladino classes can be taken, inter alia, at the following institutions: University of Washington (Seattle, United States), the Frankel Center for Judaic Studies (University of Michigan, United States), University of California, Berkeley (United States), Harvard University (United States), Hebrew University of Jerusalem (Israel), Salti Institute (Bar-Ilan University, Israel), Aristotle University of Thessaloniki (Greece), The Moshe David Gaon Center for Ladino Culture (Ben-Gurion University of the Negev, Israel), the University of Salamanca (Spain), the University of Wrocław (Poland), the National Institute of Oriental Languages and Civilizations (INALCO, Paris), and University College London (United Kingdom).

However, what sets online Ladino classes apart from their offline counterparts is the former's unrivalled capacity to maximise enrolment and global reach. The immense importance of both factors for the revitalisation of Ladino in the 21st century can hardly be overstated, as Ladino is currently spoken only by a few tens of thousands scattered across the globe, without any community with control over or majority within a given physical territory (not even as small as a neighbourhood, let alone a city or a country). Consequently, nowadays only the Internet can and does platform a large community of interacting Ladino speakers/learners.

In this sense, it is perhaps unsurprising that as we already began to see apropos the Sephardic Digital Academy (see above), the Internet has become the default option for Ladino teaching and learning on a global scale, and inevitably, it will continue to consolidate itself as such. In what follows, I will be discussing the case study of the foremost exponent of this dynamic, as its enrolment figures and global reach alone comfortably surpass that of all in-person students combined: the Ladino classes (including both Judezmo and Haketia, both taught by myself) of the Oxford School of Rare Jewish Languages (henceforth, OSRJL).

Established in August 2021, it was founded through a collaborative effort between the Oxford Centre for Hebrew and Jewish Studies (created in 1972; henceforth OCHJS) and the *Institut des Langues Rares* (ILARA) at the École Pratique des Hautes Études (EPHE) in Paris and benefits from the financial backing of two philanthropic foundations that have opted to maintain anonymity. The OSRJL offers free, web-based instruction in less common Jewish languages, accompanied by an exploration of their cultural and historical underpinnings.[33]

As acknowledged in a private interview by Olszowy-Schlanger, founder and director of the OSRJL,[34] COVID-19 had a decisive impact on the implementation of this initiative, as only the online pivot that followed the pandemic offered concrete evidence that it was possible to teach and learn several Jewish languages simultaneously on the Internet: "The pandemic gave us experience (…) [the OSRJL] came out clearly as a result of that. We did not know that we could do it. It simply made us realise that it is possible" (2024). Furthermore, this breakthrough, which was described by Olszowy-Schlanger as "really revolutionary" (thus echoing the description utilised by Marcus concerning the irruption of the Sephardic Digital Academy – see above), led to significant innovation in the areas of teaching methodology and community-building: "COVID did help (…) it is a horrible thing that happened but (…) it did change our approach to the transmission of knowledge (…) and forced us to think about new ways (…) of contacting, of interacting" (2024).

While people were not able to meet each other face to face, the pivot to online education allowed instructors and students to make the most of the effective use of visual and audio elements, facilitating the worldwide distribution of pedagogical content:

> It had disadvantages because it is nice to meet (…) and be together, but it does give you other possibilities (…) now everyone is at the same distance to the screen, to the PowerPoint, so you can use visual elements in teaching, more than you did before (…) and also all the audio possibilities that the computer gives you (…) so yes (…) it became possible [thanks to the pandemic].
> (2024)

Unlike the beginner courses of the Sephardic Digital Academy and in stark contrast with the overall policy of *Enkontros de Alhad*, the OSRJL's markedly academic approach to the preservation of (mostly European) rare Jewish languages implies a prominent focus on Hebrew writing (as opposed to oral fluency) as a defining feature of these linguistic varieties. It also entails the creation of a community of scholars around them, as opposed to a community of Ladino speakers from all walks of life (*Enkontros de Alhad*), and a community of Sephardic Ladino speakers (the Sephardic Digital Academy). In turn, this approach means that unlike on

Enkontros de Alhad, (oral) fluency in Ladino is neither a prerequisite for participation nor even a pedagogical goal.

Hebrew Writing and Preserving Rare Jewish Languages Away from Revivalistics

Whereas traditionally Hebrew and Aramaic have held significance as the Jewish languages for prayer, education, and elevated literary forms, other vernaculars have served as communal languages, spoken by mothers to their children and used to express emotions and daily matters. When writing in these languages, Jews typically utilised Hebrew characters, imparting their writings with a distinctive Jewish identity.

Themes conveyed in Judeo languages often revolved around everyday or light-hearted subjects such as wedding songs, lullabies, tales featuring knights, princesses, and dragons, homemade medicinal recipes, and simplified retellings of biblical narratives tailored for women and children. Over time, these languages evolved to encompass discussions on science, philosophy, and medicine. They extended beyond the confines of synagogues and study spaces, aiding Jews in comprehending foundational texts of Judaism and facilitating religious instruction.

As a consequence, the oral and written traditions of Judeo languages flourished as valuable repositories of family and community customs. Regrettably, the tumultuous events in Jewish history, including persecutions and expulsions across the ages, and particularly the devastating occurrences of the 20th century that led to the decimation of entire Jewish language-speaking communities in Eastern Europe and the Balkans, coupled with subsequent displacements and the disappearance of Jewish communities from North Africa, the Near East, Yemen, and Central Asia, posed significant threats to the survival of many of these languages.

Discussing the above-summarised historical and academic rationale behind the emergence of the OSRJL, Olszowy-Schlanger has made the argument that what underpins its creation (but also, I would like to argue, the very existence of –Digital Jewish– Revivalistics and further related initiatives, such as the Jewish Languages Project –Benor 2002–, the Journal of Jewish Languages–Tirosh-Becker and Benor – 2024– and the Routledge book series Studies in Jewish Languages –2024) is the contention that there is a distinct and discrete group of languages that are best characterised as Jewish, thus justifying the label 'Jewish languages' (Weinreich 1937, 1953, 1959; Weinreich 1967; Wexler 1981; Szulmajster-Celnikier and Varol 1994). Despite variations among different communities, the numerous 'Judeo' or 'Jewish' languages' would share common characteristics, notably the use of Hebrew scripts (Bunis 1981) and the incorporation of Hebrew and Aramaic words to convey distinctively Jewish concepts. In this sense, Olszowy-Schlanger notes that the OSRJL is the only institution combining an entirely online format with instruction across several Jewish languages:

> Teaching (…) Jewish languages is clearly something that people want very much (…) our school is (…) as far as the online school and only Jewish languages (…) probably the only in the world now (…) Jewish languages as a

> group are extremely important (…) it is a good idea to have a reference point where people can consult.
>
> (2024)

Moreover, there is also an economic argument to be made: only the online format, she observes, allows the simultaneous teaching of so many Jewish languages at no cost for students and very cheaply for the institution: "what online teaching did is that we can teach 18 languages at the same time very cheaply for the institution. No university in the world could afford to employ 18 teachers full time, bringing them into the university" (2024). In the case of Ladino, initially taught by Ilil Baum and myself (and as of early 2024, just by myself), the OSRJL has allowed not only the immediate implementation of classes that had been planned for but had not previously been financially viable, but also a much vaster reach than if they had been taught offline:

> when I applied to Oxford [in 2018] what I promised was to bring Ladino into Oxford. That is what I wanted. We had Yiddish, I wanted Ladino. But suddenly, this way of teaching (…) as an experience, as well as a small salary (…) even as an economic model, we are getting the best of all worlds.
>
> (2024)

From a pedagogical perspective, while there are no prescriptions to the methods utilised by OSRJL instructors, Olszowy-Schlanger has made the argument that it is reasonable to assume that audio is commonly used by fluent instructors of the target language. This is particularly true if there is not much written evidence in the latter (e.g., Judeo-Moroccan, Haketia). Conversely, transcription is likely to predominate when dealing with languages that are no longer spoken.

> We have tried to strike a balance (…) we let our teachers (…) teach for instance in transcription (…) to teach from audio (…) we have some teachers who are native speakers[35] of the language, and there are languages which have very limited (…) written tradition (…) We all know that when you learn a language, the written form and the spoken should come together. It is much more different for the languages which are no longer spoken.
>
> (2024)

Notwithstanding that equilibrium, Olszowy-Schlanger stressed the writing aspect, insisting that the use of Hebrew scripts is necessary, as according to her, it constitutes a defining feature of Jewish languages (cf. Benveniste above). The centrality of Hebrew scripts also explains why manuscript transcription has been incorporated into OSRJL Tutorials, i.e., the OSRJL's homework platform:

> the Hebrew script (…) is extremely important, because when we talk about the Jewish languages of the past, if these languages are not written in the Hebrew script, it is very difficult to talk about a Jewish language (…) This is why

> on our tutorial platform (…) we have the (…) possibility of transcribing from manuscripts and automatic checking on the transcription from manuscripts.[36]

She further noted that, as discussed above, the introduction of (Hebrew) scripts makes the learning process more academic. In this sense, Olszowy-Schlanger is very aware of the OSRJL's unique positioning vis-à-vis initiatives revolving around (cyber)vernacularity (e.g., *Enkontros de Alhad*) and projects focused on Revivalistics (reclamation, reinvigoration, and revitalisation) (Zuckermann 2020):

> We provide something completely different (…) we try to have an academic perspective with structured grammatical exercises, and all the hard stuff (…) but [this] may not be the easiest way for people to learn how to speak it for a family reunion (…) but I am aware of that and that is the choice of our school (…) yeah, in Oxford we do an academic approach.
>
> (2024)

Thus, the OSRJL's foremost aim is the preservation of rare Jewish languages understood as a repository of cultural heritage that has evolved over centuries (and it certainly seeks to rekindle an interest in these linguistic traditions, spurring intellectual curiosity and fostering a deeper appreciation of their significance). However, in the case of Jewish languages that are no longer spoken, this exercise does not amount to a reclamation à la Hebrew (i.e., the revival of a no longer spoken language – Zuckermann 2020–, such as Haketia, as opposed to Judezmo):

> Our aim is to preserve these languages from oblivion, but not necessarily by making them into (the) modern Hebrew experience, and trying to influence that people speak them. This is not the objective. This is why we teach many different languages: some of them are dead languages,[37] and some of them are still spoken.
>
> (2024)

Moreover, since Ladino is still spoken nowadays (vernacularly as Judezmo, and postvernacularly as Haketia),[38] both the audio and writing approaches discussed above remain equally valid, though Olszowy-Schlanger rightly stressed that Hebrew (scripts) are required for a scholarly understanding of Ladino:

> you can teach Ladino by ear and in transcription. [The former] might be easier for Spanish-speaking people (…) people who do not know Hebrew. If they want really to be scholars in Ladino (…) they would have to pick up Hebrew at some point (…) Looking at the comments of the students, we have decided to include the Hebrew alphabet into the student's booklet (…) telling them 'you learn the alphabet before you come to the class' (…) we are going as well to (…) introduce the printed semi-cursive, which is called 'the Rashi script.'
>
> (2024)

Building a Global Community of Scholars of Rare Jewish Languages

The OSRJL is also driven by a commitment to democratising access to rare Jewish Languages, ensuring that it transcends geographical boundaries and is readily available to individuals from diverse backgrounds. Ultimately, and much like in the case of the Sephardic Digital Academy and *Enkontros de Alhad*, this effort is intended to create a sense of belonging and community. As remarked at the beginning of this subsection, though, the OSRJL's intended community is a markedly academic one. This does not mean, however, that it is not open to incorporating people from outside of academia (it is; see below for a discussion of its enrolment policy and figures). It simply means that its approach is academic, which translates into an increased focus on reading and writing, as well as an active involvement in further scholarly activities.

Consequently, the OSRJL community-building tools encompass not only a comprehensive curriculum, but also the above-mentioned Tutorials website (spearheaded by Michael Allaway),[39] the 'OSRJL Café' (a virtual gathering held once per term, providing a platform for students and instructors from diverse OSRJL language courses to engage in discussions), the publication of teaching manuals on rare Jewish languages in collaboration with UCL Press' Open Access Textbooks of World and Minority Languages series (2020 to the present), edited by Lily Kahn and Riitta-Liisa Valijärvi (including a Ladino edition authored by myself and a volume on Baghdadi Judeo-Arabic by Dr Assaf Bar Moshe), a series of public lectures,[40] an academic blog named 'The Jewish Languages Bookshelf,'[41] a Visiting Fellows program, and specialised classes focused on Jewish music.[42] All of them are accessible without charge to accepted students and the global populace at large.

Furthermore, in yet another proof of the interconnectedness between Zoom and further Web 2.0 platforms contributing to the online revitalisation of Ladino, OSRJL students have proactively created WhatsApp and Facebook groups (see Chapter 2), along with a LinkedIn page, to enhance sustained connections and discourse among themselves, irrespective of geographical constraints. Further evidence of such porousness can be found in the fact that the promotion of course offerings is often conducted through the OCHJS website, social media channels, and email distribution list. To this, one has to add the collaboration with the Oxford Language Centre, dissemination via diverse academic mailing lists across institutions, and inclusion in 'The Jewish Chronicle.' All of the above efforts have collectively contributed to a substantial expansion of the OSRJL's global audience and outreach.

Lastly, as a means to further facilitate (academic) community-building, the OSRJL made the decision not to record classes: "this choice was motivated by the aspiration to cultivate a dynamic and interactive learning environment, one where students could actively engage and participate without the encumbrance of recording devices (…), facilitating their active involvement and practice during sessions" (Trivasse 2023).

At the time of writing this chapter, the OSRJL had released two annual impact reports, corresponding to each of its first two academic years, namely: the 2021–22 and the 2022–23 impact reports (Trivasse 2022, 2023). As per the 2021–22 edition, in the inaugural year there were 649 applications to the OSRJL from prospective students across 47 countries, out of which 338 students were eventually accepted. As per the 2022–23 impact report, the following academic year there were 514 applications from 54 countries,[43] and eventually 349 students were accepted. In other words, the number of applications declined, but their global reach increased *vis-à-vis* the first year, as did the overall number of accepted students. Lastly, for the first term of the 2023–24 academic year alone, the OSRJL received 671 applications, surpassing all previous figures. Out of all the languages taught at the OSRJL,[44] Ladino has consistently received over a hundred annual applications, proving to be the most popular language after Yiddish.

These numbers and figures are in stark contrast with the highly limited enrolment and global reach of Ladino offline classes, where the former is usually restricted to 1–10 students per course (e.g., in my in-person classes at UCL for the 2022–23 academic year, there were five students enrolled), and the latter is of course restricted to one country alone. The kind of increased online reach exemplified by the OSRJL becomes crucial within a context where a growing number of people are interested in Jewish Studies but not involved yet, while at the same time, more and more countries find themselves in the early stages of implementing Jewish Studies as an academic field:

> we reach across the globe (…) to people who are not necessarily involved in Jewish Studies (…) or to the countries where Jewish studies are at their beginnings, for example in Algeria (…) India (…) Turkey (…) suddenly we became a hub which (…) allows people from across the world to learn.
>
> (Olszowy-Schlanger 2024)

The OSRJL's global impetus notwithstanding, such an initiative is explicitly and implicitly Eurocentric. Explicitly, because as acknowledged by its director,

> most importantly is Europe (…) most of these Jewish languages are very much based on European culture and European languages, linguistically but also culturally they have roots in the past, and most of the languages that we teach (…) are European or Mediterranean. And there is an enormous interest in the departments of let's say, French, or Spanish (…) in the Jewish component (…) 65% per cent of our students are from Europe (…) both applicants, and the ones we have chosen (…) Why should we study Jewish languages? (…) As a European scholar I see Jewish studies (…) as a very important part of the contribution to national histories [of Europe] (…) Jewish languages should be important for Europe because they are museums of local languages (…) Jewish texts and Jewish literacy in the past was higher (…) so we have more texts (…) Ladino should be a part of the Spanish course (…) this is a language of contact, resulting from the contact but also contributing to the contact.
>
> (2024)

Additionally, the OSRJL could be considered implicitly European, to the extent to which it operates only during UK working hours, thus favouring students based in Europe, rather than those who live far away, who might (and do) find it hard to attend the class at e.g., 3 am local time for eight consecutive weeks per term.

The selection process for these courses is conducted through a competitive application procedure, with limited enrolment slots (capped at 30 students per section[45]; a waiting list is also in place for each class, with up to ten applicants queued, and placements are extended as they become available). While priority is accorded to existing university students enrolled at institutions worldwide (particularly those coming from Philology and History, as well as those with a very specific need to learn the target language in question), applications from the general public are also actively encouraged and, in numerous instances, result in successful admissions. All individuals accepted into the program are eligible to receive certificates of participation provided they do not miss more than the equivalent of two sessions per term for the classes they are enrolled in. On the other hand, the OSRJL language courses are not formally graded or accredited through the OCHJS, though by deploying their certificates of participation, students can and do arrange to receive official recognition of their OSRJL studies via their local universities. In turn, the fact that these courses do not include rigid assessment structures means that they typically lean towards being more descriptive than prescriptive.

The duration of each course is one hour per week for a cumulative total of eight weeks, thus adhering to the Oxford term structure. For those languages offered over multiple terms, rather than commencing each term anew, they follow a continuous progression, allowing for the organic development and expansion of material from one term to the next. It is worth noting that both sections of Ladino (Judezmo) and all levels and segments of Yiddish are featured as part of the program's three-term offerings (though Haketia – see below – lasts only two), reflecting the OSRJL's commitment to comprehensive and sustained language instruction in these particular linguistic traditions. Moreover, after the inaugural year, an Intermediate Ladino class was implemented as well to complement the existing two sections of Beginners Ladino, and a Haketia class was also implemented during the third year. For their part, after the first year the Yiddish courses were restructured and configured into Beginners, Advanced Beginners, Lower Intermediate, and Yiddish Literature classes.

Concerning the link between Yiddish and Ladino, during our interview Olszowy-Schlanger specified that since its inception, the OCHJS has played a crucial role in reinvigorating Yiddish. It was already a pre-existing field with its own diploma at the OCHJS, and now it retains its a special status at OSRJL (as mentioned above it, is the most popular one among applicants, followed by Ladino), serving as a model for the preservation of lesser-known rare Jewish languages, particularly Ladino:

> This is one of the roles of our School (…) This is Oxford (…) once we start it, new similar projects will be created at different universities, so the contribution to the study of these languages will be enormous (…) Teaching Yiddish

> was not obvious. Teaching Yiddish was summer schools, you know, Medem in Paris, you know, all these old Bund organizations, it was very much culture-oriented and less language-, history-, tradition-oriented. Now we have no problem (…) Yiddish is spoken but Yiddish is also studied, and Yiddish literature since the medieval period is studied in many different universities, but it was not the case 50 years ago, so Oxford was really very important with Yiddish. And I thought (…) that now what happened with Yiddish should be happening with Ladino. With completely different communities, with completely different history, but very, very important history, important literature, important spread of settlements (…).
>
> (2024)

Lastly, and by contrast with a lack of coordinated solicited feedback as part of either the Sephardic Digital Academy or *Enkontros de Alhad*, surveys are systematically deployed by the OSRJL to gather immediate and firsthand feedback from both students and instructors throughout the program's progression and at the conclusion of each academic term. Alongside the structured surveys distributed to all participants, a number of students and instructors willingly provide informal reflections on their experiences with the program, and this feedback is very much taken into account for the purpose of improving the OSRJL teaching and learning experience.

In concluding and concerning the near future, Olszowy-Schlanger points out that the OSRJL would like to be a model for similar projects while also remaining operational. In this journey, the financial aspect is the biggest obstacle, particularly considering that all classes are offered to students for free, and that the OSRJL would like to keep functioning on this model. After all, the OSRJL is a non-profit focused on "the scientific contribution to the study and preservation of these languages (…) we really do not want to transform this school into a language school business. This is one of my worries for the future" (2024).

Future plans include increasing the current offer in terms of languages and levels, continuing to build (a scholarly) community, and stressing the importance of Hebrew writing, as well as the production of written pedagogical materials as a means to ensure the preservation of rare Jewish languages, including Ladino and Haketia.

New languages will include Malayalam, Judeo-Berber, and Ethiopian Jewish languages, plus more levels and courses, particularly advanced-level (oral/written) literature courses/reading groups, with the Yiddish experience continuing to act as the benchmark model:

> For Yiddish (…) we have opened something that I would like to open for most languages. We have a class of Yiddish literature (…) where (…) very advanced students can come and read texts together, literature. And I would like very much to reach this kind of higher level for all languages, for really advanced students, so they can have a platform for exchange.
>
> (2024)

Additionally, the OSRJL would like to further develop a heightened sense of (academic) community:

> having a platform of exchange for different languages (…) coming together, (…) bringing the identity to the School, in a way (…) listening to the students, I have realised that we need (…) another page on our website where we could publish articles which deal with (…) teaching and revival, which could include orality, computer treatment (…), peer-reviewed (…).
>
> (2024)

Lastly, there are plans to rewrite the Student Handbook to include Hebrew scripts (with the demand that students learn them in advance), making the online tutorial platforms more user-friendly, and furthering the publication of textbooks for rare Jewish languages as part of the book series Textbooks of World and Minority Languages.

"It is an adventure that we want to continue" (2024), concludes Olszowy-Schlanger with undisguised excitement.

Conclusion

Drawing upon the notoriously successful initiatives of the Sephardic Digital Academy (2020 to the present), *Enkontros de Alhad* (2020 to the present), and the OSRJL (2021 to the present), in this chapter I have undertaken the examination of the consequences stemming from the Ladino Zoom Boom as a pivotal occurrence catalysed by the impact of COVID-19.

I have demonstrated first, that as acknowledged by the founders of all three initiatives, partially aided by the advanced age and geographical isolation of most Ladino speakers, the COVID-19 pandemic played a key role in the adoption of Zoom-mediated solutions by the global community of Ladino speakers. Additionally, I have observed that the consequences of their implementation, paramount among which are the accelerated digitisation and transformation of the Ladino-speaking world from offline to online–first, seem to be permanent, including educational solutions (in contrast to Yiddish). After all, the three initiatives will continue to exist for the foreseeable future, and while the Sephardic Digital Academy and, to a lesser extent, *Enkontros de Alhad* seem to be following a downward trajectory, the Oxford School of Rare Jewish Languages is peaking as of early 2024, i.e., within a clearly post-pandemic scenario. Such uninterrupted extension in time suggests that a new phase has been inaugurated within Zuckermann's 'Talknological Revolution,' marking the most important milestone in the sociolinguistic development of Ladino within Sepharad 4 since the emergence of *Ladinokomunita* at the dawn of the 21st century. This disruptive development carries momentous consequences for the cyber-koinesation and eventual cyber-standardisation of Ladino as a post-geographical variety, both in its vernacular and postvernacular semiotic modes.

Second, my case studies have revealed idiosyncratic (and oftentimes diverging) approaches to the multimodal (audio, writing), multisemiotic (education, traditions, religion, cuisine), (post)vernacular and communal functioning of Ladino on Zoom. The Sephardic Digital Academy targets the global Sephardic population, combines the vehicular and vernacular use of Ladino in some language and religious courses with its auxiliary and postvernacular one in others, and favours translingual practices. For its part, *Enkontros de Alhad* is in principle open to everybody, but in practice through the strict implementation of a Ladino-only policy (where Ladino is presented and encouraged as a vernacular, writing playing a secondary role and being confined to the Latin script), the show restricts meaningful participation to those who can either understand Ladino and/or express themselves exclusively in this language understood as a self-contained variety, policing and suppressing translingual practices. Lastly, the OSRJL adopts a distinctively academic approach that translates into its desire to preserve (rather than revitalise) Ladino by following a model that has proved successful in the case of Yiddish, namely: fostering a global (but Eurocentric) scholarly community around the language that is able to read it and write it in Hebrew scripts (fluency being relegated to a secondary role), as well as to participate in further scholarly events featuring the target language.

Moreover, to the extent to which the OSRJL experience leaves the door open for the preservation of Ladino away from Zuckermann's Revivalistics paradigm (the latter including the existence of speakers of the language), it tasks us with a critical question lacking a readily discernible solution, namely: which scenario is more likely and/or desirable, preserving Ladino as a language which is no longer spoken, but continues to be read and written in Hebrew scripts, mostly in scholarly circles, or else revitalising Ladino orally as well as in written form, though the latter not necessarily in Hebrew scripts?

Third, I have demonstrated that the above differences notwithstanding, all three case studies seek to preserve Ladino (not necessarily to revitalise it) by engaging the younger generation and operating, for the most part, independently from financial profit. Additionally, their functioning reveals that Ladino's evolution in the early 2020s is largely premised on the ability of this language to serve as a vehicle of communication and/or learning on Zoom, though this does not need to entail a process of functional differentiation premised on isolating Ladino as a self-contained entity to be used only for specific purposes. In turn, this sociolinguistic development is redefining in real time what it means to belong to the Sephardic nation, the contours of the global community of Ladino speakers, and the nature and functioning of Ladino itself.

In particular, I would like to argue that the evolution of Ladino over the last three years in light of the Zoom boom, warrants a renewed critique of pivotal factors contributing to its current status as a "severely endangered" language (see UNESCO 2003, 8),[46] paramount among which are intergenerational transmission and response to new domains and media.

First, concerning intergenerational transmission, UNESCO's framework distinguishes six endangerment levels (5 being the least, and 0 the most), which are as follows:

> *Safe* (5): The language is spoken by *all generations*. There is no sign of linguistic threat from any other language, and its intergenerational transmission seems uninterrupted.

Stable yet threatened (5-): The language is spoken in most contexts by all generations with unbroken intergenerational transmission, yet multilingualism in the native language[47] and one or more dominant language(s) has usurped certain important communication contexts (…)

Unsafe (4): Most but not all children or families of a particular community speak their language as their first language, but it may be restricted to specific social domains (such as at home where children interact with their parents and grandparents).

Definitively endangered (3): The language is no longer being learned as the mother tongue[48] by children in the home. The youngest speakers are thus of the *parental generation*. At this stage, parents may still speak their language to their children, but their children do not typically respond in the language.

Severely endangered (2): The language is *spoken* only by *grandparents and older generations*; while the parent generation may still *understand* the language, they typically do not speak it to their children.

Critically endangered (1): The youngest speakers are in the *great-grandparental generation*, and the language is not used for everyday interactions. These older people often *remember* only part of the language but *do not use* it, since there may not be anyone to speak with.

Extinct[49] (0): There is no one who can speak or remember the language.[50]

(UNESCO 2003, 7–8; emphasis in the original)

By these standards, according to UNESCO, Yiddish is a "definitively endangered language,"[51] (3) whereas Ladino would be a "severely endangered language" (2) (UNESCO 2003, 7–8).

However, in the present chapter I have shown that whether it is through the Sephardic Digital Academy, *Enkontros de Alhad* or the OSRJL, the 'Ladino Zoom Boom' has attracted a significant number of young students from all over the world to this language, thus significantly strengthening its intergenerational transmission. As noted by Jacobs, and notwithstanding the explicit (non)nativespeakerism contained in her statement (see also above), "with the continuing demise of elderly Ladino and Yiddish native speakers, the future of these languages rests on the shoulders of younger generations. Online classes can play a critical role in preserving this linguistic legacy" (2021).

One may object that the type of intergenerational transmission facilitated by the 'Ladino Zoom Boom' is rather unconventional, in that it no longer takes place at home (but online), or necessarily from parents to their children (but rather from older to younger speakers, irrespective of family ties). At the same time, it is hard to dispute that the 'Ladino Zoom Boom' does disprove the idea that "the language [Ladino] is spoken only by grandparents and older generations" (2003, 8), which is mentioned by UNESCO as a defining feature of 'severely endangered languages.' In light of this realisation and for the sake of consistency, within a post-Zoom boom context and for intergenerational transmission purposes, UNESCO should reclassify Ladino as a 'definitively endangered language.'

Finally, and as regards the "response to new domains and media" (comprising among others, "school … new media, including broadcast media and the Internet" – UNESCO 2003,11), UNESCO's framework distinguishes six endangerment levels (5 being the least, and 0 the most), which are as follows:

> *Dynamic* (5): The language is used in all domains.
> *Robust/active* (4): The language is used in most new domains.
> *Receptive* (3): The language is used in many domains.
> *Coping* (2): The language is used in some new domains.
> *Minimal* (1): The language is used only in a few new domains.
> *Inactive* (0): The language is not used in any new domains.
> (UNESCO 2003, 11; emphasis in the original)

UNESCO's perspective here is dated in at least two respects. First, the Internet is not just another media, like the radio or the TV. Rather, the Internet can be considered a media of media, in the sense that it aggregates various types of content from different sources. It is a transformative force that has not only absorbed elements of traditional media but has also given rise to new modes of communication and content creation (see Introduction). Consequently, Ladino's significant presence on the Internet (as demonstrated in this volume), and in particular, on Zoom, makes this language increasingly relevant and destigmatised in ways that do not necessarily fit UNESCO's classification but that definitely make Ladino rank above the equivalent degree of a 'severely endangered language,' i.e., "the language is used in some new domains (2)" (UNESCO 2003, 11). Therefore, the latter claim is somewhat of an understatement.

Second, UNESCO proceeds to discuss the importance of time limitation (e.g., let us suppose that the language in question is broadcasted on the radio, but only 30 minutes per week, resulting in limited exposure) (2003, 11). This yardstick is also dated, as it fails to take into account the subsequent irruption of media content on demand,[52] which nowadays allows consumers to access said content an unlimited amount of times, regardless of live attendance (the exception would be the OSRJL's classes, whose policy is not to record lessons, precisely to incentivise live interaction). Regarding the educational realm, UNESCO observes that two measures need to be considered, namely: up to what level and how broadly is a given language featured across the curriculum. The case studies of the Sephardic Digital Academy and the OSRJL show that Ladino is mostly taught from beginners to intermediate level a few hours per week, and not necessarily used as a vehicular language, all of which would make it rank around degree "*coping* (2)" (UNESCO 2003, 11). However, thanks to content on demand platforms such as YouTube, some of these lessons (i.e., the Sephardic Digital Academy's) can be accessed via different recording repositories.

In sum, a balanced critique of the 'Ladino Zoom Boom' attentive to its ability to engage the younger generation and achieve significant presence on the Internet, notably through platforms like Zoom, demonstrates Ladino's current relevance and impact beyond UNESCO's framework assessment. Consequently, it warrants a more positive revaluation of Ladino's endangerment level as per this organisation's classification in a manner which incidentally and sometimes as a result of explicit language planification and policy (e.g. OSRJL's),[53] brings it slightly closer to the status of Yiddish.

Notes

1 The World Health Organization (WHO), which announced the outbreak of COVID-19 as a global health emergency on January 30, 2020, officially lifted this declaration on May 5, 2023.

2 In contrast to the Ladino-speaking community, the majority of these endeavours reverted to their initial offline structure following the conclusion of the pandemic. This regression manifested in reduced accessibility and geographical outreach, alongside a conspicuous rise in tuition costs.

3 For further details on Hasidic history and culture, see Biale et al. (2018).

4 Cf. my discussion of *Kave Shtiebel* ['Coffee Room'] (2012 to the present; see Chapter 1).

5 This organisation includes further Zoom initiatives such as the Sephardic Young Professionals Network's Zoom book club.

6 During our interview, Marcus pointed out that donations were not a necessary condition for the Sephardic Digital Academy, and that they merely facilitate its work. Regardless of those donations, he noted, maintaining the Sephardic Digital Academy as a public forum was pivotal to the community mission of the Brotherhood.

7 Begun by Rabbi Yaakov Culi in 1730, this volume extensively examines interpretation of the Tanakh and is composed in Judeo-Spanish, written in Rashi characters.

8 "*En primero ay de tener en konta ke la pandemia akselero el prochezo del arrivo del ladino al modo en linea. Si esta katastrofa mundiala no mos uviera akontesido, mizmo ke i yo venia pensando esta idea, puede ser ke todavia estamos pensando i no aziendo esto.*"

9 "*Antes de Enkontros de Alhad la mayorita de los ladinoavlantes, sin kontar Israel i la Turkia, se keshavan ke no tenian ande sintir i mizmo avlar la lingua. Verdad es ke los ladinoavlantes solo podian echar lashon en persona kon otros, non avia otra manera.*"

10 "*Enkontros de Alhad* (…) *salio de un suenyo mio. Me sonyi ke estavamos todos en un lugar ande solamente se podia avlar en djudeo espanyol. I me esperte esa manyana kon este savor agradavle de tener un lugar ande la lingua fuera la mas emportante koza, ke para entrar solamente tenias ke saver esta lingua. I bueno, se lo konte a Marcelo esa mizma manyana i me disho, 'bueno, azelo,' i le digo, 'ke, te parese ke le demande a alguno si kere partisipar? Me plazeria ke esto verdaderamente fuera una komunidad del mundo.' Ansina ke avle kon unos amigos muy buenos i muy* (…) *aktivos en el kampo de la kultura sefaradi i de la lingua en espesial i maraviyozamente al punto ke lo eskapi de eksplikar kada uno me disho 'si, kuenta konmigo'* (…) *al punto esto salio maraviyozamente, komo si fuera un sinyo del Dio*" (my transcription).

11 "*Mi penserio syempre fue de azer una komunita globala de ladinoavlantes, kolavorativa, i no una aktividad personala. Por esto pensi en dar la responsabilidad a una persona de kada institusion para organisar su enkontro i eskojer livremente sujeto i musafir. No puedo dizir ke dechize ke es mijor esto de otruna koza, ma dingunos no me dieron otra idea i akseptaron todos de azer de este modo, a mi pareser abastane* [sic] *demokratiko.*"

12 While universal use is mentioned by UNESCO as the ideal stage of language vitality (2003, 9) and *Enkontros de Alhad* does feature an abundance of topics, most of these continue to be confined to the Sephardic traditions and *modus vivendi*.

13 "*Enkontros se troko en una komunita virtuala ande los ke keren i pueden vienen kada semana a estar serka de sus raises, de sus lingua, konoser i sintir personas de diferentes*

jeografias i edades ke pueden avlar ladino i no solamente para kuentos i reflanes sino para todo modo de sujetos."

14 "*Por muncho tyempo, estava mirando yo atraverso de muestra pajina web [esefarad.com] ke ay munchas aktividades por la kultura sefaradi i por la lingua, i la investigasyon, ama una era en inglez, la otra en kasteyano, la otra era en fransez ... en Israel las aktividades (i mizmo en los reklames!) para invitarte a partisipar eran en ebreo ... entonses esto me esperto a mi un savor ke ... komo vamos a arebivir la lingua, si estamos avlando de la lingua ama no avlamos kon la lingua?*" (my transcription).

15 "*Enkontros asendio en otros la idea de ke azer aktividades online 'en' ladino, i no solo en otras linguas avlando 'del' ladino, es posivle.*"

16 "*a vezes mos enkontramos kon djente ke kere partisipar* (…) *para eyos parese difisil de entender ke no pueden partisipar si no pueden avlar korrido*" (my transcription). In this sense, the fact that *Enkontros de Alhad* permits the vehicular use of Ladino, placing the language at the heart of the interaction, allows Benveniste to trace the show's genealogy back to *Ladinokomunita*'s pioneering efforts in this department (see Chapter 1), thus enhancing the prestige of her own show by association: "In a certain sense, therefore, with different modalities, *LK* and *Enkontros* opened a space where the language is protagonist and fundamental, not an accessory" (2024; my translation) ["*En sierto senso, dunke kon distintas modalitas, LK i Enkontros avrieron un espasio ande la lingua es protagonista i fundamental, no un aksesorio.*"] Such family resemblance across various Ladino-mostly or Ladino-only platforms of Web 1.0 and 2.0 environments would also include *Ladino 21*, as acknowledged by Benveniste in a previous interview for this digital archive: "I think the same happens with *Ladino 21*. You cannot participate in *Enkontros de Alhad* if you do not speak Judeo-Spanish" (2021a; my translation). ["*Penso ke pasa lo mizmo kon Ladino 21. No puedes partisipar en Enkontros de Alhad si no avlas djudeo-espanyol*"] (my transcription), yet the translingual practices of the latter are very much at odds with *Enkontros*' (and *LK*'s) enforced monolingualism, which is closely related to Standard Language Ideology (see above).

17 "*La diglosia educativa, tanto como la social, mantiene en su lugar tanto a la lengua inferior como a todas las prácticas que no se ciñan a los patrones lingüísticos de quienes ostentan el poder, siempre renuentes a compartir sus sacrosantos dominios* (…) *la diglosia en la educación solo sirve para excluir aquellas prácticas lingüísticas que no son consideradas apropiadas por la nación-estado y sus agentes de poder.*"

18 "*el hablante bilingüe con verdadera 'agencia' utiliza su repertorio lingüístico, que abarca prácticas y rasgos normalmente asociados con un sistema u otro, de una manera dinámica, para significar y construir significados. Son estas prácticas discursivas dinámicas, que sirven para que el bilingüe acceda a todos los aspectos de su vida social con dignidad y libertad, lo que he denominado* 'translanguaging' (…) *y al cual me refiero aquí como 'translenguar.*'"

19 "*algunos* (…) *enselados de Enkontros de Alhad empesaron a azer enkontros solamente en la lingua, ama tyenen un poko floshas las reglas i algunos avlan en otras linguas, ama van en kamino…*" (my transcription).

20 "(…) *los Enkontros de Alhad (...) estan amostrando komo avlan los ke konosen la lingua oydiya. Reflekta en modo direkto el uzo de la lingua de personas ke la konosen de kaza ansi komo de personas ke se la ambezan en los dalkavos tiempos.*"

21 For a study on how the Internet reinforces offline biases, see Noble (2018), and Chapter 5.

22 In this sense, *Enkontros de Alhad* encompasses more lects than *LK* and *Los Ladinadores*, particularly through the regular inclusion of cyber-vernacular Haketia, thanks to the contribution of *Voces de Haketia,* as a collaborating organisation.

23 "Revivalistics discards any imprisoning purism prism and makes the community members realize that shift happens. And there is nothing wrong with shift happening. Hybridization results in new diversity, which is beautiful" (2020, 209).

24 "*No es ke penso ke esto* [el *ladino despues del Zoom Boom*] *va a arebivir i va a ser otra vez floresiente komo era en las komunidades en el imperio otomano, ama penso ke va a evolusionar asia un kamino diferente. Si pensamos ke la lengua es biva i ke la keremos mantener biva, por siguro la lingua va a tener ke dezveloparse asi alguna parte (...) podemos ver una luz a la fin del kamino. Va a ser una koza diferente*."

25 Additionally, for an overview of language contact and change in endangered languages, see O'Shannessy (2011, 78–99).

26 "*Yo se ke los tradisionalistas se pensan ke ya no tornara mas la epoka de los abuelos i todo esto, i ke es menester porke al empesiyo se eskrivia en ebreo ... seria muy bueno konoser el ebreo por mor ke ay muncho material del ladino en ebreo, tambyen ay muncho en solitreo, ama puedes avlar el ladino sin konoser la eskritura ninguna*" (my transcription).

27 See below for Judith Schlanger's elaboration on this idea apropos the Oxford School of Rare Jewish Languages.

28 "*Kuando la pandemia eskapo, munchos abandonaron las aktividades en linea i tornaron azer lo ke siempre oraniavan* [sic for '*anioravan*'], *enkontros en presensia solamente. A mi pareser es importante kontunear kon los Enkontros en Internet porke penso ke ay muncha djente ke no tiene otro modo de tener kontakto kon la lingua*."

29 In this sense, some of the participating institutions, alongside others that do not participate, make monthly or yearly donations, which cover the Zoom and email costs. *Enkontros de Alhad* is a non-profit and in the absence of donations (which continued to be notable at the time of our private interview in January 2024), the managers pay for the costs. In other words, just as in the case of the Sephardic Digital Academy, while donations facilitate this initiative, they are not a *conditio sine qua non*. Above all else, Benveniste concludes, those who make a donation show that they find *Enkontros*' activity "interesting, valuable, and important" (2024; my translation) ["*interesante, valutoza i importante*"].

30 "*Si podemos mantener lugares ande komo vozotros kon el Ladino 21, komo mozotros kon Enkontros de Alhad* (…) *me penso ke no tendremos una komunidad fizika ama tendremos una geografia virtuala ande podemos dezvelopar el ladino en el avenir*."

31 "*Puede ser ke venga otra plataforma mijor de Zoom i entonses trokaremos a este otro modo, ma las personas kontunearan a estar adientro para avlar, sintir i demandar*."

32 During our private interview, Benveniste acknowledged that the 'Ladino Zoom Boom' contributed to the increased attendance of her online Ladino students, particularly among the younger generation: "With the pandemic, many online courses were also created on the Internet. People started because it's something exotic that you can do online, they were all confined to their homes, there was a lot of free time… Then some did it out of interest, others who had been wanting to learn the language for a long time but couldn't come to Argentina [did it] to immerse themselves, and well … from one point to another we found many young people interested in learning the language and grateful to know the Jewish customs and traditions as well" (2024; my translation). ["*Kon la pandemia tambyen se kriaron munchos kursos online en la internet. I la djente al empesijo, porke es una koza eksotika ke puedes azer por la internet estavan todos konfiandos a las kazas, aviya muncho tyempo livre ... dospues algunos si, por interes, otros ke ya me aviyan demandado por muncho tyempo de konoser la lingua ama no podian vinir a la Ardjentina a ambezarsen i bueno ... de un punto a otro mos enkontrimos kon munchos djovenos enteresados en ambezar la lingua i agradesidos de konoser las kostumbres i las tradisiones djudias tambyen*."].

33 The OSRJL's advisory committee comprises Sarah Bunin Benor (Hebrew Union College), Yehudit Henshke (University of Haifa), Lily Kahn (University College London), Geoffrey Khan (University of Cambridge), Laurent Mignon (University of Oxford), Ofra Tirosh-Becker (Hebrew University of Jerusalem), and Ronny Vollandt (Ludwig-Maximilians-Universität München).

34 Olszowy-Schlanger's leadership is complemented by Madeleine Trivasse, who manages funding, operations, and development as the OSRJL Coordinator. Celeste Pan

serves as the OSRJL Administrator, handling daily administrative tasks. Priscilla Lange aids the OSRJL by arranging public lectures and Jewish music classes. Kerry Maciak and Jun Tong manage the financial aspects of the program's administration.

35 For a discussion of (non)nativespeakerism as a language ideology apropos Ladino, see Chapters 1, 2, 3, and Yebra López (2023b, 94).

36 The categorisation of Jewish languaging into self-contained entities corresponding to different individual courses partakes from the conceptualisation of writing used in a given Jewish community as a bound system, by contrast to code-mixing, code-switching and/or translingual discursive practises involving Hebrew terms, as Marcus' discussion of *Ladinglish* (see above) and Benor's reference to a Distinctively Jewish Language Repertoire (2009), both of which include the insertion of Jewish words in a 'modern' language other than Hebrew.

37 See below for my critique of terminology pertaining to language 'death' and 'extinction.'

38 See Introduction, Chapters 1 and 2, for a detailed explanation of these juxtapositions.

39 The website serves as a resource for both instructors and students, facilitating the creation and dissemination of a wide array of self-correcting exercises tailored to the diverse spectrum of rare Jewish languages featured in the curriculum. It also accommodates the uploading of supplementary resources, encompassing textual, visual, auditory, and video materials, all of which complement the exercises and contribute to an enriched learning environment. In the case of Ladino, it is worth mentioning that the platform facilitates the use of scripts other than Latin, including Meruba and Rashi, plus the fact that the exercises are automatically graded allows students to learn from their mistakes in real time, while exonerating instructors from additional and uncompensated grading and correction duties.

40 These lectures delve into topics relevant to rare Jewish languages, providing insights into their historical, cultural, literary, and linguistic contexts. Conducted online via Zoom, they have been attracting diverse global audiences, and they are being recorded and made accessible through the OCHJS's Vimeo account, where other OCHJS lectures are also archived.

41 Often shortened to 'The Bookshelf,' this project offers concise and accessible articles that delve into specific facets of material and book culture pertaining to less common Jewish languages.

42 Conducted by Diana Matut (University of Halle-Wittenberg).

43 These were Albania, Algeria, Argentina, Australia, Belarus, Belgium, Bosnia and Herzegovina, Brazil, Brunei, Canada, Chile, Colombia, Croatia, Cyprus, Czechia, Denmark, Egypt, Estonia, Ethiopia, Finland, France, Germany, Greece, Guatemala, Hong Kong, Hungary, India, Indonesia, Iran, Iraq, Israel, Italy, Jamaica, Japan, Latvia, Malaysia, Malta, The Netherlands, New Zealand, Norway, Peru, Poland, Portugal, Romania, Russia, South Africa, South Korea, Spain, Sweden, Switzerland, Turkey, Ukraine, the United Kingdom, and the United States of America (Trivasse 2023).

44 In its inaugural year, the OSRJL offered an array of courses spanning 12 vernacular languages historically spoken and/or written by Jewish communities: Baghdadi Judeo-Arabic, Classical Judeo-Arabic, Judeo-French, Judeo-Greek, Judeo-Italian, Judeo-Neo-Aramaic, Judeo-Persian, Judeo-Tat, Judeo-Turkish, Karaim, Ladino, and Yiddish. The following academic year, the OSRJL augmented its curriculum by incorporating courses on three additional rare Jewish languages (Beginners Judeo-Moroccan, Old Yiddish, and Advanced Beginners Judeo-Provençal). Lastly, in its third year, the OSRJL added three beginners' sections in three additional languages, namely, Haketia, Judeo-Hamadani, and Kivruli/Judeo-Georgian, thereby imparting instruction in a cumulative total of 18 vernacular languages employed by Jewish communities spanning the historical continuum from the Middle Ages to the contemporary era. Furthermore, several languages were presented across multiple classes and proficiency levels, a strategic approach intended to address heightened enrolment demands while concurrently catering to students possessing diverse linguistic backgrounds.

45 While this figure is arguably very high for a language class, since consistent attendance is mandatory and the courses typically last 2 or 3 terms, dropouts are not uncommon, significantly reducing the number of attendants by term 2, and especially term 3: "I actually think that the class should be 15 people and I count on the fact that some people will drop out" (Olszowy-Schlanger 2024).

46 In the 1990s, UNESCO released the *Red Book of Endangered Languages*, a comprehensive compilation of the world's endangered languages. This publication was followed by the *Atlas of the World's Languages in Danger*. In 2002/03, UNESCO enlisted an international team of experts to devise a framework for assessing language vitality. This framework delineates nine major evaluative factors of language vitality: (1) intergenerational language transmission, (2) absolute number of speakers, (3) proportion of speakers within the total population, (4) trends in existing language domains, (5) response to new domains and media, (6) materials for language education and literacy, (7) governmental and institutional language attitudes and policies, including official status and use, (8) community members' attitudes toward their own language, and (9) amount and quality of documentation (see below).

47 See above for a critique of (non)nativespeakerism as a language ideology.

48 The assumption that one's first language corresponds to their 'mother tongue' has been problematised via a number of objections, paramount among which are the following: How much influence does the mother have in raising the child, if any? What if the couple, if there is one, does not speak the same primary language? What if the language spoken in the environment differs from the dominant language spoken at home? What impact does migration have on these dynamics? (Yildiz 2012; Yebra López 2021f).

49 Much like the terminology of 'language death,' (see above for the OSRJL's reference to 'dead languages') speaking of languages in terms of 'extinct' may erroneously convey the impression that the extinction of languages is an inherent and inevitable occurrence, which is why they are often rejected by Indigenous people. Such a representation obscures the historical context of political violence integral to the linguistic metamorphosis, and fosters the normalisation of prevailing and historical linguistic disparities. Substituting the term 'extinct' with alternative conceptual frameworks like 'extinguished' (which already implies the existence of a process), 'glottophagy' (Calvet 1974) and 'linguicide' (Skutnabb-Kangas and Phillipson 1995), according to which languages do not die, but rather, are killed, serves to counteract this inclination, fostering a heightened consciousness of both ongoing and historical linguistic injustices.

50 From the perspective of Revivalistics, though, we ought to bear in mind that as pointed out by Zuckermann, these languages are not necessarily 'extinct' or 'dead' (see the previous footnote), but dormant, and as such, they are subject to future reclamation, even in the absence of L1 speakers (e.g., Hebrew). To express this idea, he coined the term 'sleeping beauties,' justifying it as follows: "I use the term 'sleeping beauty' as a positive, poetic way to champion and celebrate these dormant tongues, and to avoid the negative connotations of alternatives such as 'dead' or 'extinct,' which are often rejected or rebuked by indigenous people" (2020, xxii).

51 Nevertheless, one might argue that UNESCO's classification ignores the Haredi Orthodox communities (see above), where transmission is quite stable, thus placing the language anywhere within the spectrum between '*stable yet threatened* (5-)' and '*unsafe* (4).'

52 See Chapter 2 for Ladino content on YouTube, and Chapter 5 for Ladino content on Netflix.

53 For an overview of LPP (Language Planning and Policy) for endangered languages depending on specific goals (e.g., academic achievement, as in the OSRJL vs. conversational proficiency, as exemplified by *Enkontros de Alhad*), see Coronel-Molina and McCarty (in Austin and Sallabank 2011, 354–70).

5 Video-On-Demand and Streaming Services (2021-)

The Netflix Shows *Kulüp* and *The Beauty Queen of Jerusalem*

Introduction

In the 21st century, the consumption of audiovisual content through video-on-demand (VOD) and streaming services has disrupted the TV industry, significantly altering both *what* we watch and *how* we watch it. In particular, VOD and streaming services have revolutionised the multi-semiotic forms in which to articulate many diasporic and subalternate groups in their own endangered voices (Fernández de Arroyabe Olaortu et al. 2018).[1]

As remarked by Thomas Eriksen (2007), the non-territorial character of the Internet is compatible with the possibility of maintaining a shared sense of national identity, especially in the case of nations with large diasporas overseas, like that of the Sephardim. In particular, the tension between Netflix's transnational reach and its subservience to state-based domestic legislation has further problematised the supposed continuity between the *home* (nation) and the *land* (the state), thus arguably leading to a unique subtype of Digital Home-Land (Held 2010; Yebra López 2021c; see also Introduction).

In a recent article entitled 'Digital Nationalism: Understanding the Role of Digital Media in the rise of 'New' Nationalism' (2020), Sabina Mihelj and César Jiménez-Martínez placed the accent on three qualitative changes brought about by the proliferation of digital platforms: diversification, polarisation, and commodification.

First, the participatory affordances of digital technologies have allowed a wider range of actors to partake in the production and dissemination of public communication, including previously stifled or censored voices (see Netflix's 'Inclusion and Diversity Statement' – Netflix 2023). This change has led to more diverse and unpredictable forms of national imagination and nationalism. For starters, it has weakened state attempts to reproduce the hegemonic version of national identity. Additionally, it has transformed digital media into potential tools of bottom-up discourse, political opposition, and even resistance against authoritarian regimes, including the use of rare languages and alternative conceptualisations. Indeed, as discussed by Sofia Savoldelli and Giselle Spiteri Miggiani (2023), Netflix's policies and dubbing specifications (2022) show a "strong tendency to mark and preserve multilingualism" (2023, 20), including cases of minoritised languages such

DOI: 10.4324/9781003473664-8

as Yiddish (2023, 20; see also below). Nevertheless, this democratisation has not resulted in either the establishment of an even playing field for all parties involved (due to disparities in funding, accessibility, skill, and knowledge related to digital technologies) or the end of top-down common national narratives.

Second, this diversification has given rise to a greater fragmentation and polarisation of national imagination, leading individuals and groups to a disjunction: on the one hand, more inclusive, pro-diversity and pro-immigration forms of national belonging and, on the other hand, more exclusive, ethnonationalist ones. Such polarisation has been fuelled by the more affective and personal engagement with nationalism afforded by the digital environment, which might otherwise have positive psychological effects (Fox and Miller-Idriss 2019).

Third, and as regards commodification, Netflix, which currently features over 270 million subscribers and is available in almost 200 countries, made its debut as a streaming service in 2007. Its innovation lay partially in the adoption of VOD services, thanks to which for a relatively cheap flat monthly fee, consumers could now enjoy any program and any time, uninterrupted by commercials and on a host of devices (from a TV screen to a computer, passing through tablets, phones, and gaming platforms). In 2013, Netflix transitioned from distribution to production, releasing original content of its own. In stark contrast to traditional TV services, Netflix does not develop around or cater to either the state or businesses and advertisers, but it directly sells to audiences, which means that neither government nor businesses have direct control over its content (Khalil and Zayani 2021). The popularity of Netflix as a digital capitalist affordance that seemingly transcends nation-states caught the attention of the latter, particularly where the content of its shows was related to culture and politics. This is precisely the case of the series I shall discuss in this chapter.

Kulüp

Introduction

Directed by Seren Yüce and Zeynep Günay Tan, *Kulüp* [Turkish for 'Club'] premiered in late 2021, and was the first Netflix series to feature Ladino. The plot focuses on a Sephardic family in 1950s Istanbul. A Sephardic mother by the name of Matilda has just been released from prison, where she ended up after killing her Muslim lover (Mümtaz) for betraying her family. When she applies at the local community centre to get the necessary documents to make *Aliyah*,[2] she learns from the local Sephardic gentleman Davit Pinto that her estranged daughter, Raşel, has been jailed for breaking into a nightclub (hence the title of the show) managed by a Turkish gentleman named Çelebi. Additionally, Raşel is torn between marrying Mordo (Mordiko), i.e., a Sephardic young man, or İsmet (a Muslim taxi driver). In other words, between tradition and assimilation.

The action occurs in the aftermath of the infamous wealth tax of the 1940s (known as '*Varlik Vergis*') and the 1955 Istanbul Pogrom, both of which resulted in the impoverishment and persecution of many Turkish Jews (Güven 2011; Ağır and

Artunç 2019). In conjunction with the creation of the State of Israel in 1948, these events led to a massive exodus of up to 50% of the Sephardic Turkish population between 1948 and 1951. While Muslim discrimination again minorities in general and Sephardic Jews in particular is a well-known story among Turkish Jews, it has remained taboo in Turkish public discourse to date.

Summary

The first season of *Kulüp* is divided into two parts. The former features six episodes, with the latter comprising four.

Turkish Jews in general and the Ladino language in particular play a more prominent role in the first part, which revolves around the impact that the *Varlik Vergis* had on the non-Muslim population of Turkey, and particularly, on Sephardic Jews (for a total of 21 scenes featuring Ladino). The second part, where Ladino is much scarcer (just three scenes), focuses on the Istanbul pogroms of 1955, popularly known as "the Turkish Kristallnacht" (Erdemir 2016). During my private interview with İzzet Bana (2022), *Kulüp*'s main adviser on Ladino and a prominent member of the local Sephardic community, he admitted that this imbalance concerning the use of Ladino across both parts of the first season was due to the perceived need on the account of the directors to downplay Judaism and expand the scope to local minorities beyond Sephardim in the second part.

Overall, there is a fair balance between vernacular (conversations) and postvernacular instances (i.e., symbolic ones, as exemplified via songs, isolated words, and expressions) of Ladino. In terms of genre distribution, conversations account for 45.8% of the scenes in Ladino, followed by words/expressions used in postvernacular fashion (33.3%), and songs (20.8%).

Discussion

Community Engagement

Community engagement is critical to any process of language revitalisation by, of, and for the community of speakers of the endangered linguistic variety in question. In the present volume, I have discussed two key tenets of community engagement understood from the perspective of Revivalistics: placing Sephardim at the centre of major decision-making processes affecting Ladino (Chapter 1) and engaging in in-person fieldwork (Chapter 2).

Kulüp excels at both aspects. The TV series deployed two language advisers: Forti Barokas, in the early stages, and then İzzet Bana for the bulk of the season. Both are local L1 Ladino speakers and Sephardim who were born and raised in Istanbul, surrounded by other Ladino-speaking Sephardim. Moreover, as per Bana's insights during our interview, while the initial cast, which was carefully trained by him to speak Ladino from scratch, consisted largely of non-Sephardic Turks speaking Ladino in tokenistic (i.e., mostly postvernacular) fashion, upon his request more instances of vernacularity were included (notably, background dialogues in Ladino), some of the existing Ladino content was post-edited, and he was allowed to recruit 90 members from the local Sephardic community. Barokas and Bana were further consulted on aspects pertaining to the faithful recreation of the broader Sephardic culture, from the decoration of Sephardic houses to the garments worn by Sephardic characters.

(Post)vernacularity

Overall, there is an even balance in the show between vernacular and postvernacular uses of Ladino, which is historically accurate, considering that the series is set in 1950s Istanbul. This semiotic range further allows the audience to familiarise itself with quintessential elements of the Sephardic culture (songs, proverbs, cuisine, endearing terms) while enjoying a glimpse into the use of Ladino as an everyday language at home, which has disappeared in 21st-century Istanbul.

In what follows, I will break down the use of Ladino in *Kulüp* into each of these semiotic modes, and then delve into specific subtypes and themes.

Concerning vernacular instances, there was a time (and a few places) in 20th-century Turkey when Ladino could be heard conversationally in the streets and courtyards, as well as at home (particularly in the kitchen and the dining room, but also in the living room). Some areas in 1950s Istanbul, notably around the neighbourhood of Galata, were a case in point.

The first scene of *Kulüp* shows one such *kartier* [Ladino for 'neighbourhood'] in its now long-gone vernacular splendour. Upon her release from prison, the protagonist, Matilda, is depicted walking the streets of the multicultural and back-then Ladino-speaking neighbourhood of Galata, with its iconic tower in the background. We are barely at the three-minute mark, when a myriad of Ladino voices can already be heard as part of the everyday interaction of a lively Sephardic community. Among the plethora of inaudible voices, some words can be discerned, which are not even subtitled: "Are we invited to eat? Tomorrow? Alright, talk to you later" [*Estamos invitados a komer? Amanyana? Avlamos, ayde*].[3] In the first full Ladino sentence with subtitles, a little girl calls on her friend to go downstairs and play in the street: "Esther, come! Let's play!" [*Esther, Esther. Abasha, abasha!*].

Only two scenes later, the proverbial Sephardic courtyard makes its appearance. A middle-aged woman[4] meets and greets Matilda and Mordiko, showing the former around as she gives instructions to a number of neighbours: "Come on, Davitiko. Hurry up. Go get the goods. Shut the door, Mishon" [*Davitiko, ayde. Va tomar los panes. Aserra la puerta, Mishon*]. Then she explains to Matilda where her room is, when to shut the main door, and her concern about the fact that the pardon thanks to which she was just released from prison, might have let out many dangerous criminals: "There's a vacant room upstairs. The curfew is at sundown. They let all the shady bunch out with the pardon. God help us. Come on" [*Arriva ya ay una kamereta vaziya. La puerta se serra kuando se eskurese. Eh, ya salio el afia. Desharon a todos los perros de ursuses afuera. El Dio ke mos guadre. Ayde ven, ven*].

The *kurtijo* reappears again towards the end of Episode 4. First, when Matilda finds herself there, hearing again the same Ladino song from Episode 1, *Yo era ninya* ['I Was a Girl'] (see below), and using it as an opportunity to explain to

Haci, a fellow immigrant and nightclub employee, that Sephardim are like him, immigrants in Turkey. Second, when she joins there fellow local Sephardic Jew Hayim[5] during a Purim celebration, Ladino is present in this scene in a number of background voices, which is most likely intended to convey a vernacular use. The only sentence that can be discerned is "let's go home" [*mos iremos a kaza*], uttered by a Sephardic woman as celebrations come to an end.

Additionally, the depiction of Ladino as a home language also starts early in the series, and it recurs until the end of the season, with a focus on the dining room and the *mupak* ['kitchen'] as emblematic settings.

Already in the second scene of the first episode, Matilda reaches a house full of Sephardic women around her age whom she knew from before entering prison. The initial scene shows them interacting in the living room in fluent Ladino. One woman asks an older one about the colour of her own dress: "Do you like this colour?" [*Te plaze esta kolor?*] Then she poses a similar question to another woman, this time using a Turkism: "Should I go with this colour?" [*Me yakishea*[6] *esta kolor?*] In the meantime, they are also waiting on a seamstress, so when the latter arrives, the girl who opens the door mistakes Matilda for said sewer and introduces her as such: "Mom, the seamstress is here" [*Mama, la kuzendera ya vino*]. When her mother sees Matilda, she pauses for a second until eventually she recognises her: "Matilda?" Although sceptical, she invites her to sit down and after exchanging a couple of sentences in Turkish, both women activate their Ladino. As expected, Turkisms abound:

> –Were you pardoned too?
> –Yes. Is Monsieur Davit…?
> –(interrupting Matilda) Monsieur Davit's on the phone. It's a very important call. It'll take a while (pauses). Why are you here? Can I help you?
> –I'll come back later.[7]

Then in Episode 5, Raşel has decided to marry Mordiko, and the concomitant Jewish celebrations have just begun around the dining table of a restaurant. A Sephardic woman uses Ladino to congratulate Matilda on Raşel's engagement to Mordiko while also expressing relief at the fact that she finally got out of prison: "Mordo is a great boy. Your daughter is very lucky" ["*Mordo es pasha*[8] *por ijo. Tu ija es muy mazaloza*"]. "Merci" [*Mersi*], responds Matilda. "I'm happy you got out [that is, of prison] too" [*I a ti, pasado ke sea*], adds her interlocutor.

And yet a later scene set in the dining room shows Raşel mortified at the prospect of following in the footsteps of her female relatives by becoming a stay-at-home mother. At times, the conversation takes place in Ladino:

Sephardic woman 1:	Everything is ready.
Sephardic woman 2:	Give him a son and he'll worship you.
Raşel:	I'll help in the kitchen.
Sephardic woman 3:	What are you doing? Stop embarrassing the girl.
Sephardic woman 2:	What did I even say?
Sephardic woman 4:	She's right. You talk too much.[9]

The season ends too with a beautiful scene around the table as a place where family and friends can come together to forge the strongest bonds in the face of adversity and *ressentiment* (here embodied by the 1955 Istanbul pogrom, against whose background this sequence is taking place). Undoubtedly, the sequence also alludes to the further symbolism in Judaism of the *shulḥan*, i.e., the intricate, golden table that was in the *kodesh* ['holiness'], that is, the Holy Temple's outer chamber.[10] Eventually Matilda recognises her family among the people at that table, thus solving her personal-cum-political riddle of family, ethnic and national belongingness. It is the same table that also spelt a new fate for Raşel, or in the narrator's own words: "That table was where my mother changed her destiny."

Notwithstanding the above-shown accurate vernacular instances of Ladino, one could object that this linguistic variety (and Turkish, for that matter) is often portrayed as a self-contained, entity, in close association with Standard Language Ideology (Lippi-Green 1994, 166; Walsh 2021; see also Introduction and Chapter 1). Ironically and while seeking to revitalise Ladino, this portrayal would reinforce the very colonial and language-planning policies that contributed to Ladino's current predicament as a severely endangered language (see Stroud 2018; see also Chapter 1).

On the other hand, the representation of Ladino as self-contained in *Kulüp* is nuanced by the presence of several postvernacular instances, which can be classified into six different genres: songs, proverbs, cuisine vocabulary, endearing terms and reassuring words, hate speech, and Ladino as a cryptolect.

Concerning songs, the multimodal affordances that characterise the Web 2.0, which combine the written register of the Web 1.0 with the visual (images and characters), aural (silence, music, sound effects, ambient, noises, sound volume, tone of voice in spoken language, emphasis, and accent), gestural (body language and interaction), and spatial (the arrangement of elements in space), can be (and have been) instrumentalised to articulate an enhanced cultural and linguistic picture conveyed to learners of Ladino (see also Chapter 2 for a discussion of YouTube's multimodality). Such multimodal arrangements have important repercussions in the digital articulation of identity and affects. In this sense, songs in particular often function "as a signifier of affect or as an aesthetic experience of sound play" (Shandler 2004, 28), ultimately crystallising into a form of Ladino-speaking diasporic nationalism.

This phenomenon becomes most apparent in *Kulüp* via the recurring reproduction of the classic Ladino song *Yo era ninya* ['I Was a Girl'], which appears strategically at crucial moments of the plot development, each time seemingly conveying a different layer of meaning. We can first hear it at the end of the first episode, during a flashback to the moment when the protagonist, Matilda, handed her daughter Raşel over to Davit Pinto so that he could place her in an orphanage. The lyrics and melancholic overtones of the background Ladino song eloquently convey how this moment changed Matilda's life forever, from an comfortable childhood to pregnancy as a single mother, condemning her to enduring hardships for the rest of her life: "I was the daughter/of a wealthy family/I never knew what suffering was/But then/I fell for you, you scoundrel/You made me a servant" (x2)

[*Yo era ninya/de kaza alta/No saviya del sufrir/Ma al kayer kon ti, bebe/Me metites a servir*]. The song then reappears towards the middle of the season. Close to the end of Episode 4, Matilda chances upon a Sephardic *kurtijo*, whereupon she hears *Yo era ninya* again.

According to Derrida (1971), iterability (that is, the repetition of a text in a new context) allows texts to function again beyond their context of production and their original destination. Similarly, the reiteration of *Yo era ninya* in this new context makes the song lose its hitherto dramatic overtones to acquire a healing aura that makes Matilda smile with nostalgic reassurance.

Then Haci passes by and casually enquires about the song, to which Matilda replies "It is an old Sephardi song." Realising that he is unfamiliar with the term 'Sephardi,' Matilda proceeds to explain: "The Sephardi [sic] are the Jews who migrated here centuries ago. Like me." His colleague, who is also an immigrant, chimes in: "Like us, you mean." This riposte is of course a powerful pro-diversity statement, whereby further immigrants in Turkey recognise the story of the Sephardim as their own.

Lastly, Episode 10, the last one of the first season, features once again the song in question, whose iteration from Episode 1 helps bring the plot full circle: from Matilda's dependence on Mümtaz and Raşel to Raşel's liberation from İsmet, thus breaking off the cycle of family misery. As the 1955 Istanbul pogroms ravage the city, Raşel, about to give birth, wanders the streets desperate for help. Suddenly, she hears somebody calling her name, and the camera goes slow-motion as *Yo era ninya* plays in the background… It's Matilda. İsmet then arrives at the scene and calls her too. The same song plays again, conveying the message that Raşel is now torn between Matilda (her mother) and İsmet (her Muslim fiancé), both fighting for her just as hard. Raşel chooses Matilda and leaves the scene with her, abandoning İsmet. The last verse is played again, now against the background of İsmet's stunned expression, in poignant antiphrasis: "You made me a servant" [*Me metites a servir*].

Of less significance, yet still highly relevant, is the introduction of two further classic songs in the Ladino repertoire: *Kuando el rey Nimrod* ['When King Nimrod'] and *Adio' kerida* ['Goodbye, Dear Love']. *Kuando el rey Nimrod* is played in Episode 2, when in an effort to make things right with Raşel, Matilda visits her at the synagogue. Against the background of a choir of Jewish girls singing the song in question, Matilda offers her the keys to her home, inviting Raşel to move in with her:

> When King Nimrod went out to the countryside/He was looking at heaven and at the stars/He saw a holy light in the Jewish quarter/[A sign] that Abraham, our father, was about to be born./[Chorus] Abraham our Father, beloved father,/Blessed father, light of Israel.(x2)/Then he told the midwives/That every woman who was still pregnant/If she gave birth to a male child at once he will be killed/because Abraham our father was about to be born. [Chorus] Abraham our Father, beloved father,/Blessed father, light of Israel.(x2)/Terach's wife was pregnant/and each day he would ask her/'Why do you look

> so pale?'/She already knew the blessing that she had./Abraham our Father, beloved father,/Blessed father, light of Israel (x4).[11]

Lastly, *Adio' kerida*, which is inspired by the instrumental of Verdi's *La Traviata* [Italian for 'The Fallen Woman'] (1853), and whose lyrics tell the story of a bitter farewell to a beloved person, is introduced at the end of Episode 3 to make the scene in question more poignant and memorable. As Raşel and İsmet are conversing in the latter's taxi, it starts pouring down. Raşel goes outside and starts dancing under the rain. She leaves the taxi against the background of prominent Ladino singer Yasmin Levi's rendition of the staple Sephardic song in question. The juxtaposition serves to emphasise the lyricism concomitant to Raşel's will to emancipate herself from Matilda's shadow, breaking away from traditional and family values, and into everything else life has to offer (excitement and adventure as embodied by İsmet). But İsmet does not have time for games: he leaves Raşel stranded under the pouring rain and goes on a date with another girl (Pazike). Raşel finds out minutes later, as still soaked under the pouring rain, she catches İsmet red-handed, which compounds her perceived isolation:

> [Chorus] Goodbye, goodbye beloved,/I don't want to live/You made my life miserable (x2)/When your mother delivered you/and brought you to the world/she did not give you a heart/to love with (x2)/[Chorus] Goodbye, goodbye beloved,/I don't want to live/You made my life miserable (x2)/I'll go look for another love,/knock on other ports/in hope there is a true hope,/because for me you are dead (x2)/[Chorus] Goodbye, goodbye beloved,/I don't want to live/You made my life miserable (x2).[12]

Second, proverbs and idioms are of pivotal importance to every culture, as they serve to offer advice, guidance, and knowledge, as well as to relieve interpersonal tensions and make arguments. Their symbolic nature is particularly important within a predominantly postvernacular context, such as the one already emerging at the time when the series is set (1950s). In Episode 1, for instance, Davit Pinto draws upon a Sephardic proverb to encourage Matilda to visit her daughter: "there's no better friend to a girl than her mother" [*no ay mijor amiga ke la madre kon la ija*]. In the very next scene, and as we saw above, a middle-aged woman resorts to an idiom of religious overtones to express concern about the fact that the pardon thanks to which Matilda just came out of prison might have let out many dangerous criminals, as well as to ask for God's favourable intervention: "They let all the shady bunch out with the pardon. God help us" [*Desharon a todos los perros de ursuses afuera. El Dio ke mos guadre*]. In Episode 2, worried that she might be pregnant, Matilda resorts to similar idioms to express shock and then ask God for help: "Oh, my God. God, help me" [*Atyo Santo. El Dio ke me ayude*]. Then in Episode 3, Raşel is feeling sorry for herself, and seeks solace in Mordiko. She expresses her deep emotions to him with a classic Sephardic proverb: "I have no wings, but I want to fly" [*Alas no tengo, volar me kero*]. This proverb, which according to Bana, was taken alongside similar ones by Rana Denizer (co-writer of

Kulüp) from a book of Sephardic sayings, is the exception to Raşel's consistent use of Turkish instead of Ladino (in stark contrast to Matilda).

While it could be argued that this intergenerational gap reflects to some extent the realities of the 1950s Jewish community in Istanbul (though for the most part, Ladino was still spoken vernacularly by the younger generation), or perhaps more plausibly, that it bears witness to Raşel's desire for assimilation into the local culture, it is also a practical adaptation for the TV show. As per Bana's own admission, it is hard to script Ladino dialogues, not least because some actors might find it particularly challenging to learn the lines in the target language (see also my discussion of *Unorthodox* below, where the star Shira Haas does not actually speak Yiddish). Subtitling these dialogues is even more arduous (see below). It is also difficult to have language coaches in the studio for extended periods (sometimes over six hours and on a very short notice), particularly under the extenuating circumstances of the COVID-19 pandemic, during which *Kulüp*'s first season was shot (see also Chapter 4).

Finally, in Episode 5, a Sephardic woman uses an idiom to express relief at the fact that Matilda finally got out of prison: "may it be in the past" [*pasado ke sea*] see above.

Third, cuisine is of paramount importance as a form of cultural bond within Sephardic culture, particularly in connection with Ladino understood as a language of the home. The kitchen's centrality to Sephardic culture is most conspicuously conveyed in the habitual characterisation of Ladino as a language of the *mupak*. *Kulüp* offers further proof of its realistic and accurate portrayal of Ladino by both adopting the kitchen (and sitting around the table in general) as the frequent setting for Ladino conversations (see above), as well as peppering the series with cuisine vocabulary, particularly as pertains to classic Sephardic dishes. For instance, at the beginning of Episode 4, Matilda discovers that İsmet slapped Raşel, and confronts her about it: "Is this what love is to him?"[13] Raşel breaks down and starts crying, but is comforted by Matilda, who prepares for Raşel Sephardic baked pastries, known in Ladino as *börekitas*. Similarly, in Episode 9, food (and its mentioning in Ladino) is also used to strengthen family relationships. Matilda treats her brother Ishak to some *lalangas*, a Sephardic-Ottoman deep-fried dessert. "I missed it so much," expresses Ishak. Witnessing his first bite brings tears of joy to Matilda's face.

Fourth, the consistent use of endearing terms and reassuring words further attests to the centrality of home, family, and affection to the Sephardic way of life. By way of illustration, in Episode 1 as Davit Pinto's son enters the room to offer Matilda some coffee, Pinto addresses him with an endearing vocative in Ladino: "*Mordiko*? Come in, *payshiko*.[14]" In the above-quoted very next scene, where a middle-aged woman meets and greets Matilda and Mordiko (see above), she addresses Davit via the endearing *Davitiko*: "Come on, Davitiko. Hurry up. Go get the goods" [*Davitiko, ayde.* (Inaudible) *Va tomar los panes*]. Then in the same episode, when Matilda goes back to the house of the Sephardic women to meet Mr. Davit and claim the travel papers for Israel, one of them lets her know that Mr. Davit is at the police station because of Raşel's altercation with her boss Çelebi, referring to the former as *ijika*: "One of the girls at the orphanage, Raşel, she assaulted a Muslim guy. The manager of Club Istanbul" [*Una ijika del orfelinat, Raşel, yaraleo a un ombre vedre. El mudur, el mudur del Klub de Estambol*]. Similarly, and as quoted above, in Episode 5, a Sephardic woman advises Raşel to give Mordiko an *ijiko*: "Give him a son and he'll worship you" [*Si le pares un ijiko, te va a azer la korona en la kavesa*]. Additionally, a further Sephardic woman in the conversation reprimands the previous one while referring to Rachel herself as an *ijika*: "What are you doing? Stop embarrassing the girl" [*Ke estas aziendo? Le averguensates a la ijika*] see above. Finally, in Episode 7, while at home, Raşel tells Matilda she is not feeling well at all, and her mother resorts to Ladino to make her encouraging words all the more intimate and reassuring: "These days will pass. Don't worry. I'm here" [*Estos dias van a pasar. Yo esto aki. No te merikiyes*].

Fifth, and in contrast with the above usage, Ladino is also deployed in *Kulüp* to express hate, though to a much lesser extent, and not always by Sephardim. Thus, in Episode 2, in an eerie display of discrimination against Sephardim/non-Muslim minorities at the workplace in modern Turkey, Çelebi makes his employees skip Shabbat. First, he pretends to be flexible, offering Matilda to go home before sundown, should she finish her job early. But his ironic use of Hebrew/Ladino at the end of the sentence reveals his true intentions: "Maybe you'll finish before sundown. *Shalom!*" On the other hand, in Episode 4, Mordiko resorts to hate speech in Ladino to label İsmet and his father pejoratively: *vedres* [Ladino for "green people," meaning Muslims, the green colour being characteristic of Islam], he utters with an angry look in his face.

Sixth, Ladino is also used as a cryptolect in both *Kulüp* and offline historical reality, which is symptomatic of the century-long persecution of Sephardim *qua* minority and the concomitant need for their communication to remain private within a (potentially) hostile environment. Thus, in Episode 3 and with Raşel missing, Matilda is at Çelebi's when the phone rings: it is a call for her. She picks up the phone and knowing that Çelebi will not understand anything (in contrast to what would happen if she was to speak in Turkish), she states the following in Ladino: "Raşel hasn't come home. I'm worried sick. Is she there? Merci. If you hear anything…" [*Raşel no vino a kaza. Esto muy enkudiado.*[15] *Eya vino? Mersi.*[16] *Si toma un haber…*] Thus, based on her language choice, the audience can surmise both that Matilda's interlocutor is Davit (or alternatively, Mordiko), and that she does not want Çelebi to know what she is saying.

Dubbing and Subtitling

Notwithstanding its remarkable Ladino language advising and performance in the show, *Kulüp* falls short of taking advantage of the multimodal affordances of VOD streaming services in general and Netflix in particular to further the online revitalisation of Ladino in two key aspects: dubbing and subtitling.

First, Ladino can only be heard as part of the Turkish (original) audio, and it is therefore entirely absent as part of the audio in any other language (e.g., Spanish, English). Moreover, Ladino itself cannot be selected as an audio language. This is contrary to Netflix's 'Dubbing Audio Style Guide' (2022), which notwithstanding the negative framing of minor(itised) language varieties as "foreign," recommends the following for lip-sync dubbing: "Do not dub over foreign dialogue" (cit. in Bangkok Video Productions).

Additionally, the show does not feature any Ladino subtitles (not even as part of the original subtitles, hence why the above transcription of Ladino is mine), regardless of whether the dialogues in Ladino are meant to be understood or not. This too is in stark contrast with Netflix's guidelines:

> Foreign dialogue should be translated in the forced subtitle stream only if it is meant to be understood. If it is unclear whether or not the foreign dialogue is meant to be understood, seek advice from Netflix or the production.
>
> (2022)

Only the Turkish and English closed captioning features the disclaimer "[in Ladino]" before any Ladino audio in the original version, and even then, some instances are wrongly captioned as 'modern' Spanish (or even French – see above).

In a private interview in late 2022, *Kulüp*'s main linguistic adviser, Bana, clarified that he did not partake in the subtitling of the show (possibly because it was done centrally by Netflix and/or freelancers commissioned by Netflix, though this was not elucidated). In principle, the paradoxical coexistence of an otherwise careful and accurate presence of Ladino in the show with its misrecognition and/or absence as part of its dubbing and subtitling could be reconciled in light of Safiya Noble's concept of the 'algorithms of oppression' (2018). According to Noble, algorithmic bias exists because while mathematical formulations might be neutral, ultimately, they are created by people. As humans, we carry all sorts of biases and prejudices that are then written into the algorithms we create. As a result, the algorithms of the Web 2.0 (Google, YouTube, Netflix) reproduce the social inequalities from which they originate.

For the purpose of our analysis, the above would mean that because Ladino is a minoritised language offline, this marginalisation carries over into the digital world, leading to Ladino's erasure (Gal and Irvine 1995, 974; see also Chapter 1) or alternatively, to its misrecognition as 'modern' Spanish and/or further 'modern' languages,[17] very much so against the intentions of *Kulüp*'s producers and language advisers.

However, as Savoldelli and Spiteri Miggiani (2023) have demonstrated apropos multilingual occurrences in Netflix's Italian dub streams, extensive neutralisation of the sort utilised in *Kulüp*, where language variation (in this case in Ladino) is dubbed over/omitted, was not encountered in any linguistic variety, even in the case of a minoritised Jewish language like Yiddish. Instead transfer unchanged combined with subtitles (i.e., maintaining the original voice track for the specific language variation, while adding part subtitles to convey the meaning to the audience) turned out to be the most frequently employed, once again including in the case of Yiddish (27).

On the one hand, it could be argued that Ladino's extensive neutralisation could still be due to the fact that unlike Yiddish, which is currently classified by UNESCO as a "definitively endangered" language (i.e., children no longer learn it at home as their L1),[18] Ladino is a "severely endangered" one (i.e., the language is mostly spoken by the elderly, and while the parent generation might understand it, they do not speak it to children or among themselves) (2003; cf. my critique of this classification in Chapter 3). In other words, it could be due to the fact that Ladino is more endangered than Yiddish and thus more affected by the 'algorithms of oppression' (Noble 2018). On the other hand, Savoldelli and Spiteri Miggiani's study offers conclusive evidence that Netflix can (and does) further the revitalisation of endangered languages in the dubbing and subtitling departments, in addition to encouraging it at a macro level.

Conclusion

Overall, the use of Ladino in *Kulüp* is best understood as part of the show's broader and careful portrayal of Sephardic minorities in 1950s Istanbul. Notwithstanding the difficulties associated with shooting scenes in Ladino (particularly during a global pandemic) and thanks to the generous effort of *Kulüp*'s main language adviser, the series boasts a high level of community engagement, as well as a fair balance between vernacular and postvernacular instances, which are for the most part representative of the Istanbul geolect[19] of the 1950s.

On the other hand, Ladino (and Turkish, for that matter) are often represented as autonomous codes isolated from each other, in close association with Standard Language Ideology (see above), thus arguably reinforcing the very colonial and language-planning policies that contributed to Ladino's current predicament as a gravely endangered language (see Stroud 2018). Additionally, the presence of Ladino is very scarce in the second part of the first season. More importantly, Ladino is extensively neutralised in the dubbing and subtitling, which runs contrary to Netflix's overall policy on multilingualism.

The paradoxical coexistence of an otherwise careful and accurate presence of Ladino in the show with its misrecognition and/or absence as part of its dubbing and subtitling, can only be partially accounted for by the so-called 'algorithms of oppression' (Noble 2018). Their reproduction has taken place despite the best intentions of the show's producer and language advisers, and is also in contrast with Netflix shows featuring further Jewish endangered languages (Yiddish), where transfer unchanged combined with subtitles has been the preferred strategy (Savoldelli and Spiteri Miggiani 2023).

The Beauty Queen of Jerusalem

Introduction

Directed by Oded Davidoff and based on a best-selling novel by Sarit Yishai-Levi (2015), *The Beauty Queen of Jerusalem* aired in early June 2021. This Ottoman-era

Israeli melodrama jumps back and forth through the years of 1917–49 to tell the story of four generations of the Ermozas, a wealthy Sephardic family who owns a delicatessen shop in *Machane Yehuda*, Jerusalem's major market. Not unlike *Kulüp*, the series focuses on family (and by extension, Ladino as a language of home), but also pays attention to the use of Ladino with and in the broader local community of Sephardim. Accordingly, the main characters are Gavriel Ermoza (the son of Mercada[20]), his wife Roza,[21] and their three daughters: Luna (her father's favourite), Rachel, and Becky. Additionally, the show features prominently Luna's relationship with her Sephardic neighbour David, son of Victoria, who has a short affair with Ephraim,[22] Roza's brother and a right-wing revisionist who engages in violent attacks against the British. Lastly, it also displays rather frequently two Sephardic characters from the local community: the fortune-teller Jilda and the amanuensis/lender Avram.

The action is set against the backdrop of the fall of the Ottoman Empire, the British Mandatory Period in Palestine, and Israel's War of Independence. In 1916, Britain and France made a secret agreement (named 'Sykes-Picott' after Britain's Sir Mark Sykes and France's Charles George Picot) to divide the Ottoman Empire among themselves. Although Palestine was supposed to be internationalised, eventually it came under British control. In 1917, the British government issued a statement ('The Balfour Declaration', named after Althur Balfour, the British Foreign Secretary who signed it on Britain's behalf) that recognised the right of the Jewish people to a national home in Palestine. Finally, in the San Remo Conference of 1920, Turkey ceded Palestine to Britain.

As illustrated in *Kulüp*, for Jews in the Balkans, the end of the Ottoman Empire resulted in increased anti-Semitism, poverty, and violence. As their lands were no longer safe, many Sephardim migrated to Palestine, whose modern-day territory was colonised by the British and named 'The British Mandate of Palestine' from 1923 to 1948. Here, though, as shown in *The Beauty Queen of Jerusalem*, they would also experience many challenges, not least because the significant increase in Jewish population led to more religious, national, and ethnic conflicts.

Hence the establishment in the early 1920s of the mainstream and reactive Zionist militia *Haganah* [Hebrew for 'Defense'], to protect the Jews from the violence of the Arabs and the British, subgroups of which would eventually give way to the more proactive Revisionist *Irgun* ['Organisation'], also known as *Etzel* [acronym for *Irgun Tzvai-Leumi*, which translates into 'National Military Organisation'], featuring violence against the Arabs, and *Leḥi* [acronym for *Lohamei Herut Yisrael*, which translates into 'Fighters for the Freedom of Israel'], which contrary to the previous two, focused on fighting the British through intimidation and assassination.

Unrests became particularly conspicuous during the Arab riots of 1920, 1921, and 1929 in Jerusalem, and the 1936–39 Arab Revolt, which saw Palestinians attacking both Jewish and British targets. During the 1930s, each uprising was followed by an investigative commission and a White Paper encouraging cutbacks in Jewish immigration and land acquisition (e.g., The Shaw Commission in 1930, and then The Peel Commission in 1936, which recommended partitioning the country into Arab and Jewish states). Eventually, the situation prompted the British to retreat from the Mandate's promises as approved by the League of Nations in 1922. These included recognition of the historical link between the Jewish people and Palestine, and assistance in rebuilding their homeland in that region. Then in 1939, the British government closed the doors of Palestine to European Jews, effectively condemning them to the death camps. By 1945, all three Zionist militias teamed up to drive the British from Palestine, in a postwar struggle against colonialism that inspired analogous efforts in Africa, India, and the Far East (Oren 2021). The characters of *The Beauty Queen of Jerusalem* both shape and are shaped by this complex matrix of historical circumstances (Karabelnicoff 2022).

While British, Arab, and Ashkenazi discrimination against Sephardic Jews in Israel is a well-known story among local Jews, it remained taboo in Israeli public discourse until the tenure of the first Sephardic prime minister of Israel, Yitzhak Navon, between 1978 and 1983 (Refael 2008). Until the present day, a substantial demographic of the media-consuming public is yet to learn of such horrors. The shows' problematisation of the mainstream national narrative from a Sephardic perspective further translates into its heterogeneous linguistic composition, featuring Hebrew (the main language), English, Ladino, Arabic, and Turkish, not only as seemingly autonomous codes (like *Kulüp* apropos Turkish and Ladino), but also often enough as named languages (Heller and Martin-Jones 2007; Makoni and Pennycook 2007; Jørgensen et al. 2011) cross-pollinating in (limited) forms of translanguaging (Otheguy et al. 2015) (see also Chapter 1).

Summary

The first season of *The Beauty Queen of Jerusalem*, which was filmed in Safed (Israel) during the COVID-19 pandemic, is divided into two parts, each featuring ten episodes.

As remarked above and much in the vein of *Kulüp*, the TV series travels back and forth in time to problematise a neat distinction between past, present, and future when it comes to both individual and national identities. Accordingly, Part One jumps back and forth between the 1917 and 1929 and the 1937 and 1939 periods, whereas Part Two travels between the 1929 and 1938 and the 1939 and 1945 periods, for a total time lapse of 27 years (1917–45).

The use of Ladino is abundant throughout Parts 1 and 2 of Season 1, and quantitatively much higher than in *Kulüp*, for a total of 2,139 Ladino instances (472 different words). Endearing and family terms are the most widely used, including *kerida* ['darling,' 'beloved,' addressed to a female] [110 instances], *ijo* ['son'] [43], *ermana* [42], and *amor* [31], as does profanity, via recurring words like *putana* ['prostitute,' 'b*tch'] [25], *mierda* ['sh*t'] [16], and *tetas* ['tits'] [9].

Discussion

Community Engagement

As intimated by Yishai-Levi (2015), the first draft of the script featured very little Ladino, and even those few words (the work of a local Hebrew-Ladino translator) were of questionable quality. While Yishai-Levi had a basic grasp of the language (that is, of the postvernacular sort), as it was spoken at home by her grandparents, eventually the show decided to hire a local Ladino-speaking Sephardic Jew, namely, Shmuel Refael (Vivante) (see Introduction and Chapters 1 and 2) as a language adviser and coach for the cast.

In a private interview (2022), Refael described the initial bits of Ladino as "not Ladino," but rather a Spanish translation (from Hebrew) via Google Translate. Moreover, the cast had no previous knowledge of Ladino. The closest thing to an exception was perhaps Hila Saada (Roza)'s command of Spanish (not Ladino), after having studied it for three years, which facilitated her Ladino pronunciation in the series. In a Zoom interview with Refael (Saada 2021), Saada admitted this much, praising him for this pedagogical endeavour:

> Shmuel was a wonderful teacher (…) I have been studying Spanish for three years now, so it was like going back to the basics [of Spanish] and the [historical] sources (…) I really fell in love with this language through Shmuel.[23]

While Roza's performance in Ladino is satisfactory, the overall absence of local Sephardim and Ladino speakers results in a significantly lower level of community engagement in *The Beauty Queen of Jerusalem vis-à-vis Kulüp*. In turn, this shortage raises questions about the authenticity and accuracy of the former concerning Ladino-speaking Sephardim based in Jerusalem/Israel, including several instances of lacklustre pronunciation that occasionally make it even difficult to understand what is being said in Ladino.

(Post)vernacularity and Translanguaging

Vernacular uses of Ladino are hardly present in *The Beauty Queen of Jerusalem*. This is perhaps unsurprising, given the absence of local Ladino-speaking Sephardim. It also contrasts with *Kulüp*, where Ladino is much less used, but vernacular and postvernacular instances are evenly distributed, the former group including a number of fluent conversations involving several local community speakers. On the other hand, in *The Beauty Queen of Jerusalem* Ladino bits never go over two consecutive sentences (unless they are one-word long). Consequently, rather than speaking of vernacularity vs. postvernacularly, it might be more accurate to conceptualise the entire presence of Ladino in the show from the perspective of (a limited form of) translanguaging (García 2013; Otheguy et al. 2015; Wei 2018) (see also Introduction and Chapter 1).

By way of illustration, consider the use of Ladino in the following three scenes.

In the first one, as Gavriel is relaxing in the courtyard, smoking a pipe, Mercada arrives. As she sits down, Mercada initiates an exchange with him which Roza joins later on. The conversation takes place in Hebrew and the ensuing transcription draws upon the show's English subtitles with captions, enhanced with my own additions for clarification purposes. Ladino words, the vast majority of which are nouns, are introduced occasionally. While on the surface this is done either in a funnily manner for humoristic effect (Gavriel) or to be more eloquent (Mercada), one could also argue that the presence of Ladino is ultimately tokenistic. Ladino words are italicized below, the footnotes including my own translation[24]:

Mercada [as she sits down]:	Gavriel, I'm talking to you. What's that smell, huh?
Gavriel:	What, *ima*?[25]
Mercada:	The smell from your pipe is like … the smell of the Arabs who smoke at the market.
Gavriel:	This is tobacco I brought from Beirut. They have good tobacco.
Mercada:	I was at the shop earlier. Matzliach said the goods you bought in Beirut, arrived, but there's quite a lot missing.
Gavriel:	It's certainly stuck at the port. Ah, these Lebanese are all *tronchos*,[26] that much I can tell you.
Mercada:	We're almost out of pistachios. We got two tins of Syrian olives instead of ten [grunts]. The French chocolate, the *lokum*…[27] Maybe they stole from you.
[Rosa shows up]	
Gavriel:	I have documents for everything I sent.
Mercada:	What will we do with your documents? If a client comes to buy olives, what should I give him, documents?
Gavriel:	Fine. I'll have to go there and see what happened.
Mercada:	You just got back. That's absurd.
Gavriel:	Do you want to go?
Mercada:	*Por favor, por favor*…[28] A boat ticket, a hotel, you know how much that costs?
Gavriel:	So I'll swim there, *komo pesh en la mar. Komo dolfino*.[29] [puckered squeaking] [laughs]
Mercada:	You are completely *loko, loko*.[30]
Roza:	Are you leaving again for Beirut?
Gavriel:	Do I have a choice?
Roza:	Good night to you [leaves the scene]
Gavriel:	What? Rosa, what? It's really early. Roza! Look at your watch, it's early!

From an external perspective, one could look at the above exchange in terms of the classic language mixing/code-switching approach, assuming that Gavriel and Mercada are "switching" back and forth to a single language default (Hebrew). This approach relies on the assumption that Hebrew and further languages, like Spanish, English, or Ladino are codes that occupy separate spaces with clear boundaries, thus constituting separate nameable languages. However, such perspective is rooted in Western European language ideologies of language boundaries (Blommaert and Verschueren 1992; Gal and Irvine 1995, Irvine and Gal 2000; Irvine 2008; Bonfiglio

2010), intrinsically linked to the 'one nation, one language' ideology (Carlsson 2021), which inevitably led/leads to the downplaying, misrecognition, and/or erasure of other regional and non-official varieties, namely, Ladino, in the case at hand.[31]

However, as the following two scenes show, this would be the wrong assumption to make about the main characters, such as Gavriel, Mercada, Roza, Victoria, or Avram, *qua* community of multilingual speakers in *The Beauty Queen of Jerusalem*. My below transcription of both scenes demonstrates that in contrast to *Kulüp*, in the Ladino speech community presented in the Israeli show, perceived "shifts" between each "code" cannot be viewed as marking boundaries between distinct languages, but as part of a complex continuum.

Consider, for instance, a second scene, where Victoria, who is illiterate, pays a visit to Avram to ask him to write a letter to her son David, who is fighting the Nazis in Greece. Once again and as it typically happens in the show, the bulk of the conversation takes place in Hebrew, with Ladino being introduced via idioms and nouns that help make the speech in question not just more eloquent, playful, or humorous, but above all, more plausible (though, as pointed out above, its presence also comes across as tokenistic). In other words, while it would have been impractical to do most of the show in Ladino (as opposed to Hebrew),[32] its occasional postvernacular inclusion via a limited form of translanguaging kills two birds with one stone: it serves to increase the historical accuracy of the show, authenticating it, while also dispensing the series with the onerous shooting and (post)editing of vernacular Ladino. The series' portrayal of Ladino is thus arguably tokenistic and anachronistic (at the time in which the series is set, during the 1923–48 period, Ladino was spoken much more fluently), instead being close to the current situation of Ladino in Israel. Thus, while historically incongruent, this postvernacular representation turns out to be of great help for the purposes of teaching/learning, and revitalising Ladino in the 21st century (see below). The same transcription conventions apply as in the previous scene:

Avram: [after reading headlines about Jews killed in the war in Greece] *Dios* mio…*[33][sighs]

[Victoria shows up]

Avram: Good morning, Mrs. Franco. What can I do for you?

Victoria: Oh, come on, Avram. Why do I come to you here all the time?

Avram: Another letter to your son? You sent one yesterday.

Victoria: I haven't heard from him in a couple of months.

Avram: Yes, but, you know, it takes time for a letter to arrive on a ship. I should add that, unfortunately, some ships never reach their destination. The Germans, may their name and memory be erased, they crawl around the sea with *submarinos*[34] and throw *torpedos*.[35]

Victoria: *Ke submarinos?*

Avram: *Submarinos* are … You know … They're like boats, or *amama*.[36]

Victoria: Mm-hmm.

Avram: They swim beneath the water, almost *komo pishkados*.[37] And they throw bombs at the ships from underwater.

Victoria: Oh, God help me.

As this scene illustrates, rarely does a whole conversation take place in Hebrew, Ladino, English, Turkish, or Arabic as codes. Instead, there is a "back and forth" between these in an organic, determined, selected, and in-group accepted manner, which results in a language practice that seems to transcend the classical framework of switching between self-contained codes. Rather, conversations featuring Ladino as depicted in the show would constitute another example of "dynamic and creative linguistic practices that involve flexible use of named languages and language varieties" (Wei 2018, 14), which outside of the community are seen as separate nameable languages, but within the community are accepted as one language practice.

From the lenses of this paradigm, the characters in *The Beauty Queen of Jerusalem* (particularly Sephardim, because of their linguistic capaciousness), would be expressing themselves linguistically (i.e., languaging), activating their full linguistic repertoire, without watchful adherence to the socio-politically defined boundaries of any given named language. In this sense, what we call 'Ladino' would be one more fluid set of lexico-grammatical aspects of their diverse linguistic reality as influenced by the sociopolitical context in which the action is set, and these elements would be organically and selectively activated depending on a number of factors, such as the intentions of each character and the (perceived) identity of their interlocutors. In particular, in the show, Sephardim expect other Sephardim to understand Ladino and/or communicate in it, but not Ashkenazim, or non-Jews, except occasionally British officers with a basic grasp of Spanish (see below).

Thus, what is occurring in the use of Ladino in *The Beauty Queen of Jerusalem* is best understood as a limited form of translanguaging (as opposed to an entirely arbitrary one). As such, this subtype is "primarily concerned with everyday language practices of multilingual language users" (Wei 2018, 11), and premised on the Revivalistics-influenced realisation that "shift happens. And there is nothing wrong with shift happening. Hybridisation results in new diversity, which is beautiful" (Zuckermann 2020, 209).

More specifically, this particular form of limited translanguaging, as illustrated in the above scenes (themselves highly representative of many similar exchanges in the show), seems to follow predominantly a grammar/vernacular versus lexicon/postvernacular divide: the lexicon usage is selectively activated within the grammar matrix of Hebrew as the dominant vernacular. While one could argue that in the exchange between Victoria and Avram (as well as the dialogue below), Ladino is used vernacularly (to convey meaning, to explain a concept), in the vast majority of scenes Ladino words are used postvernacularly and in fact, rather tokenistically, within this form of limited translanguaging.

Lastly, and as I have anticipated above, occasionally Ladino-speaking Sephardim in *The Beauty Queen of Jerusalem* resort to Ladino hoping that its (limited) mutual intelligibility with Spanish will allow British officers with a basic background in the latter to understand them. The complexity and richness of these exchanges cannot be explained from the classical perspective of switching between supposedly autonomous codes. Instead, they bear witness to the "flexible ways in which bilinguals actually practice bilingualism" (Martínez, et al. 2015, 27), thus leading us to abandon idealised theories that emphasise language separation. Conversely, this dexterity prompts us to embrace translanguaging as a more refined paradigm that allows us to account for "the complex languaging practices of actual bilinguals [including multilinguals] in communicative settings" (García 2009, 45).

Thus, whilst for explanatory purposes in the transcription of the scenes of *The Beauty Queen of Jerusalem,* I am carrying out an approximate identification of the nameable languages and varieties in use (e.g., my claim above that Ladino words are italicized), ultimately, my contention is that, as concluded by Wei apropos the everyday language practices of ethnic Chinese Singaporeans, "there seems to be little point in asking what languages or varieties they are speaking or counting how many languages are being spoken here" (Wei 2018, 14). Moreover, in some cases, this distinction is simply impossible. For example, if a Hebrew word which is also used in Ladino, like *beraha* (blessing) appears in a dialogue, should it be classified as a Ladino word or a Hebrew one? This question cannot be meaningfully answered. Nevertheless, and as discussed above, the presence of Ladino in the show should not be overstated, since elements of this linguistic variety (as opposed to Hebrew) are certainly much more restricted and tokenistic than bilingualism in the case of Chinese Singaporeans (Wei 2018), Yiddish/English bilingualism in Hasidic speakers as accurately portrayed on Netflix (see below), and even the type of bilingualism that would actually correspond to the time and place where *The Beauty Queen of Jerusalem* is set (1923–48 Palestine) (see above).

In the third scene in question, alarmed after her conversation with Avram in the same episode (scene two), Victoria pays a visit to the police station and enquires about the whereabouts of his son. Later on, Luna, who is dating David, also decides to inquire about him at the police station. As the ladies bump into each other, together with the British officer, all three interlocutors are forced to activate their full linguistic repertoire to get their message across while navigating any difficulties on the fly. The same transcription conventions apply as in the previous scenes, and the conversation is taking place in English, unless otherwise signalled by the Ladino transcription or the captions referring to the use of Hebrew:

Victoria:	Kalamata.
British officer:	Yes, Mrs. Franco, they've already told me.
Victoria:	*Mi ijo,*[38] uh, [in Hebrew] is at war. He's fighting for the British.
British officer [in English]:	I know. The situation in Kalamata is not good. Mrs. Franco.
Victoria:	[in Hebrew] What?
British officer:	In Kalamata… [In Hebrew] not good,
Victoria:	[in English] Y-Yes. I know that.
British officer:	Yes
Victoria:	*Kuatrosientos muertos*![39]

British officer: Yes, yes.
Victoria: [in Hebrew] Do you have names?
British officer: What?
Victoria: [In Hebrew] Names. *Nombres*.[40]
British officer: Ah. Yes, yes, uh … Yeah. Here. These are the names and the numbers of Jews that died in Kalamata.
Victoria: [in English] I uuh … no read.
British officer: I have no other lists.
Victoria: [in English] Read! Read!
[Luna shows up]
British officer: I'll be with you once I attend to this lady.
Luna: [in English] I think we are here for the same thing.
[British officer hands over the list]
Victoria: [in Hebrew] It's a list of those who died.
[hands it to Luna]
[Luna reads it]
Luna: [in Hebrew] David is not here.
[Victoria sobs]
Victoria: [In Hebrew] Praise the Lord! Praise the Lord.
British officer chimes in: The list is not final. There will be more names.
Victoria [asking Luna]: [in Hebrew] More names?
Luna [smiling, holding Victoria's hands]: *Vamos a kaza, Victoria. Vamos*.[41] [in Hebrew] David is not here.

What self-contained language is Victoria using when she asks the British Officer about *nombres*? Spanish or Ladino? And when she tells Luna *Baruch hashem* ['praise the Lord']? Is she using the Hebrew or the Ladino code? While the algorithm-informed subtitles answer the question unambiguously (Ladino in the former case, Hebrew in the latter), this question cannot be answered meaningfully from a perspective indigenous to the conversation at hand. Rather, the exchange defeats both the idea of 'code-switching' and the very concept of 'code' as an autonomous linguistic entity. In doing so, it prompts us to look for more encompassing, nuanced, and complex paradigms from which to make better sense of the dialogue (i.e., translanguaging).

On the other hand, and notwithstanding the fact that in the show, most linguistic exchanges involving Sephardim are best understood from the perspective of the sort of limited translanguaging I have outlined in this subsection, a reduced number of characters do engage in a very limited number of semi-conversational/vernacular exchanges in Ladino. In decreasing order of fluency and accurate pronunciation, these are Jilda, Roza (presumably both because of her centrality to the plot and the actor's background in Spanish), and Gavriel (whose actor was coached in Ladino for the specific purpose of the series). Interestingly, Jilda is a Sephardic fortune-teller and medium, often shown reading coffee grounds to predict the fate of the Ermozas, as a result of which she makes a number of unsettling yet accurate predictions fully and fluently communicated in Ladino to Mercada and Roza.

For instance, in Episode 2, Jilda prophesies that Roza will have a boy who nonetheless will die soon due to an evil eye. Then in Episode 4, Mercada visits Jilda, who tells her that "heaven is very angry, Mercada" ["*los sielos se aravian, Mercada*"], and asks God not to listen to Mercada: "God, forgive me. She's crazy" [*Adyo perdoname. Esta es una loka*]. Jilda then claims that she is seeing "two" [*dos*]. When Mercada asks her two of what, Jilda resorts to Ladino to urge her to be patient "Hold on a minute" [*Aspera un minute**[42]]. "You're seeing two boys?" [*Dos ijos?*], insists Mercada. Jilda begs the hereafter to communicate with her: "Talk to me, I beg you. Talk to me. Please, talk to me" ["*Avlame, por favor. Avlame. Avlame, por favor*"]. Jilda then says she sees a sin. Baffled, Mercada asks her whether she really sees a "sin" [*pekado*], whereupon Jilda adds "And water … Lots of water" [*I agua ... Mucha**[43]*agua*"]. Mercada cannot quite comprehend why: "I … I can't understand" [*No entiendo*]. Jilda repeats the same sentence. She continues in trance: "The ocean, far … Far off [*Mar i eyos ... leshos ... Leshos, mar i eyos*]. Then in Episode 20, Luna visits Jilda and the latter asks the former who she is to her boyfriend David. Luna responds in Ladino: "He's my fiancé" [*Su prometido**[44]]. Jilda repeats after Luna "Your fiancé, huh?" [*Su prometido…*] Jilda tells Luna he is alive, and she asks her why he is not writing to him in that case. Jilda resorts to Ladino to excuse herself: "I don't know" [*No lo se*]. "When will he come back?" Luna inquires further. Jilda issues the same response: "I don't know" [*No lo se*]. "He will though?" she asks. The same response ensues "I don't know" [*No lo se*]. Jilda then tells Luna somebody who already died loves her. Whereupon she tries to serve as a medium, and uses Ladino to conjure up the presence of someone who is dead: "Talk to me, talk to me!" [*Avladme. Avladme!*] Then she reports to Luna as follows: "He loves you. He loves you so much" [*El te ama. Komo te ama!*]. Luna wonders who he is, and Jilda explains that the British hanged him, adding that "He's a hero" [*Es un banagan*]. Eventually, Luna guesses it right: the man who loves him is dead, and he is her ex-boyfriend Itamar.

These and similar scenes seemingly introduce a dose of magical realism into the plot while also reinforcing the Orientalist and exoticising prejudice against Ladino as a language of superstition (rather than science), and by extension, against its community of speakers (traditionally, Sephardim) as backward, and/or stuck in the so-called "Middle Ages."[45] Still, one may object that the introduction of Ladino-mediated superstition in the show is tongue-in-cheek, as humour plays an important role in the TV series (as well as being characteristically Sephardic). The subsequent exoticisation of modern Spain in the late episodes of the first season would seem to lend credence to this observation. Thus, in Episode 18, in what looks like a reverse-diaspora thought experiment (see Chapter 6), Mercada decides to act upon Gavriel's suggestion to leave Israel for "Spain" (x2) [*Espanya*] to live there with her cousin. Although Gavriel is concerned about the situation in *Espanya* (at that time, undergoing the most repressive years of Francoism), Mercada does not mind going there, because as per her own admission, she already feels dead inside. In the following episode, Mercada goes back to Jerusalem after a decade in Spain, where she has bought "castanets" [*castañetas**] from "Spain" [*Espanya*] and "two fans" [*dos abanikas*] from Spain's "flamenco dancers" [*bayladeras de flamenko*].

Lastly, there is an instance where just like we saw apropos the third scene, the (limited, contested) mutual intelligibility between Spanish and Ladino is exploited by James (whose linguistic repertoire includes so-called 'English,' and 'Spanish,' but not 'Hebrew'), and Victoria (whose linguistic repertoire here includes the named languages of Hebrew and Ladino, but not English) to communicate with each other apropos an urgent matter. In Episode 15, Victoria's son, David, gets hurt by accidentally shooting himself. Victoria then grabs the gun, brings it to the police station, and reports the finding to James. In Hebrew, she says she found the gun at her place. James double-checks whether he understood the last bit: "…your house?" Then Victoria answers in Ladino: "Yeah" [*Si*] She wants to say there was much more at her place and keeps speaking in Ladino/Spanish: "Not only this" [*Mucho**[46] *mas*]. James understands the message, and replies in Ladino/Spanish and English: "[More stuff] like this? Weapons?" [*Mucho* mas?*] Victoria replies in Ladino: "Yes … Yes" [*Si … Si*].

All in all, whether essentialising or not in cultural terms, *The Beauty Queen of Jerusalem*'s portrayal of Ladino is certainly more humoristic and playful, but above all, more tokenistic, than in *Kulüp*. In linguistic terms, this contrast translates into a less strict separation between languages as supposedly autonomous, self-contained codes, and conversely, a more fluent, translingual one that while hardly reflective of Ladino's vernacularity at the time and place where the action is set (1923–48 Palestine), accurately portrays the current predicament of Ladino in Israel, with positive repercussions in the fields of pedagogics and revitalisation (see below).

Postvernacular instances of Ladino in *The Beauty Queen of Jerusalem* concern, in decreasing order of frequency, endearing vocatives, family vocabulary, obscene terms/hate speech, idioms, and cuisine terms. This suggests that this linguistic variety is predominantly used at home to express affection, intimacy, and profanity (thus similar to *Kulüp*, minus the obscenity). It is also consistent with the context in which Yishai-Levi acquired her basic grasp of Ladino prior to writing the story, as it was spoken at home by her grandparents (see above). On the other hand, traditional songs and proverbs feature much less prominently than in *Kulüp*, which suggests that notwithstanding copyright issues, the producers of *The Beauty Queen of Jerusalem* did not prioritise offering a representative sample of Ladino in historical terms. Lastly, and just like in *Kulüp*, Ladino is used as a cryptolect, though unlike the Istanbul-based show, *The Beauty Queen of Jerusalem* includes instances where this strategy backfires.

First, the overwhelming use of endearing terms becomes apparent through the high frequency of "dear" [*kerida*, in the standard French-Ottoman Romanisation, but also occasionally presented in Castilian Romanisation[47] – *querida*], which appears 110 times (more than twice as much as the next word) and *amor* ['-my-love'], which comes sixth (31 instances). These are often used in conjunction with and close proximity to family vocabulary, which is also extremely common in the show, as attested by the presence of *ijo* ['son,' including its variations of spelling and ending – namely *hija*, *ijiko*, etc.] and *ermana* ['daughter,' also featuring ample variation across spellings and endings] coming second [43 instances] and third [42], respectively, as part of the most frequently used words.

For instance, in Episode 1, after Roza earns her first salary, she uses it to bring food to her little brother. Whereupon she resorts to an endearing term in Ladino: "Hey, little brother" [*ermaniko*]. "Do you like it, *hermaniko**?"[48]

Then in Episode 14, one of Roza's daughters, Becky, is crying, and the former comforts the latter in Ladino as follows: "My darling. I'm here, I'm here. … What is it, darling? … What's wrong? What's wrong? … My love, what's wrong? What's wrong? What's wrong, my love?"[*Kerida mia, esto aki, esto aki (...) Ke pasa,mi amor? Ke pasa, ke pasa? (...) Mi amor, ke pasa, ke pasa? (...) Ke pasa, mi amor?*] Additionally, in Episode 3 Roza asks Ephraim whether he committed the terrorist attacks, to which he admits implicitly, using a Ladino vocative to elicit his sister's benevolence: "Listen, *ermana* 'sis', if you don't know, you can't tell them." When he adds that he does not have a place to stay, and that he is just roaming around town, Roza resorts to Ladino to convey her unconditional love for him: "Listen to me, sweetie. You and I only have each other. I'm here for you, and you're here for me" [*Mi amor, sienteme. Tu i yo es lo ke kedimos. Yo para ti i tu para mi*]. Ephraim agrees, deploying the endearing vocative once again to show emotional proximity: "You're all that I've got, *ermana* 'my dear'."

Indeed, conflict is very frequent in the show (within the family, across genders, between different political factions, among Ashkenazim and Sephardim, Jews and Arabs, Palestinians, and English soldiers, etc.). As a language of intimacy and affection, Ladino is often resorted to within the family to appease those conflicts. Hence the high frequency of words such as *basta* ['enough,' 'stop it'], the fourth most-used word [38 instances], *durme* ['sleep' – imperative], fifth in the ranking [32], *favor* [overwhelmingly used as part of *por favor* –'please'], eighth [21], and *avlame* ['talk to me,' 'let us communicate'], eleventh [11].

For instance, in Episode 1, Gavriel asks Ephraim if he has a job. Ephraim, who is a right-wing revisionist (see above), explains to him that he does not, because he is not part of the *Histadrut* ['Organisation'/'Federation'], Israel's national trade union. Roza resorts to Ladino to try to calm Gavriel down: "I know, sweetie. Calm down, please, for me" [*Ya esta kerido, por favor, para**[49]*mi*]. Then in Episode 3, Gavriel and Roza manage to diffuse a very tense situation by using Ladino as a language of intimacy and affection. As the British Army surrounds the house, looking for Ephraim, who eventually surrenders after threatening to shoot Gavriel, the latter resorts to Ladino to implore him not to do so: "*Por el amor del Dio* [For the love of God], not in front of my family, Ephraim." Roza mirrors Gavriel's strategy, using Ladino to implore him to put the gun down: "Ephraim, put it down" [*kerido, por favor*]. Gavriel asks Luna if she is okay, to which she answers by using a Ladino vocative: "Yes, *papa* [abba]."

Lastly, the use of affectionate terms in postvernacular fashion transcends the intragroup, family setting. For instance, in the first episode Gavriel has a romantic affair with an Ashkenazi woman, and the latter resorts to Ladino to convey her affection to him, thus making the statement all the more intimate: "I love you, Gavriel" [*Te amo, Gavriel*].

Intimacy and love–hate relationships are also frequently articulated under the form of obscene terms/hate speech, only in limited overlap with *Kulüp*'s use of Ladino to express emotion. Indeed, unlike the Israeli series, the Turkish show did not feature obscene terms in Ladino, and only one instance of hate speech by a Sephardic persons (see above). This contrast seems to be consistent with the markedly higher presence of postvernacular Ladino in *The Beauty Queen of Jerusalem* (similarly, in the case of Yiddish, heritage speakers are often most familiar with curses and insults).[50]

It also reinforces the negative stereotype that Ladino is a marginalised language variety best suited for informal and vulgar purposes, rather than formal or prestigious ones (the latter being featured in *Kulüp*). Thus, 4 out of the 22 most frequently used words are obscene terms: *putana* ['b*tch,' 'prostitute'; including its variation across different endings], which is the seventh most-used word in Ladino in the entire show with 25 appearances, *mierda* ['sh*t'], eleventh in the ranking with 16 cases, *kulo* ['ass'], sixteenth [12], and *tetas* ['tits'], twenty-second [9].

For instance, in Episode 8, as the Ermoza family is sitting at the table, Ephraim tells them that the place where he leaves is now full of Russian-speaking Jews, and then discusses the local Russian girls, resorting to Ladino to express obscenity as she mentions their *tetas* ['boobs'], which according to him, are like those of "whores at the brothel" [*putanas de bordel*; my transcription of the last two words]. When Gavriel tells Ephraim not to be so vulgar, Luna, who is still a child, says *putanas*, giggling, and making Ephraim laugh, to Gavriel's dismay. Then in Episode 7, Gavriel returns home and sugarcoats to his family the story of how he lost his money and belongings in Beirut, omitting his affair with a local prostitute. He resorts to Ladino to be as graphic as possible, claiming that he was left with only his *bragas* ['underpants.'] But his audience is not buying it. Mercada tells him that his was a "half-assed story there, Gavriel" [*estoria del kulo, Gavriel*].

Additionally, in Episode 11, Ephraim begins working at the Ermoza's shop. When he finally shows up, significantly late, his colleague Leito uses a Sephardic expression that translates roughly into "speaking of the devil," but is couched in much more vulgar terms in the Ladino original: "Speaking of *dolor de kulo*, here comes *dolor de kulo*" ["Well, speaking of pain in the butt, here comes the pain in the butt"]. A similar vulgarism is used in Episode 3 to express political defiance by undermining the proverbial British solemnity. James shows up at the Ermozas' and demands that Luna go to the police station to help provide information about a "terrorist" attack. "I work according to the dictates of mandatory law," he adds gravely, only to receive Gavriel's sarcastic rebuttal in Ladino: "Yeah right, the 'mandatory law'" [*del mandado de mi culo*, which literally translates into "the mandatory law of my a**"].

Vulgarisms also abound in reference to further bodily parts and functions. Thus, testicles and penis are often referred to as *guevos* ['balls,' 'eggs'] and *chuchunika* ['penis'], respectively. Poor-tasting drinks are described as *pisha* [piss] (Episode 1) or even *pisha de viuda* ['widow's piss'] (Episode 5), or alternatively as tasting like *el kulo de un maymun* ['a monkey's ass'] (Episode 5). Food deemed unsavoury is often referred to as simply *mierda* ['sh*t.']. Thus, it should come as no surprise that in Episode 12, while Ephraim and Victoria are getting dressed up for their wedding, when Roza takes his hands and calls him in Ladino "my sweet little brother" [*chiko ermaniko*], Ephraim has no problem in answering back bluntly in Ladino: "I gotta chop a log" [*Me muero para kagar*].

Cursing is also extremely common in the show. The insult *troncho* ['jerk,' 'idiot'] (twice in Episode 12, and then in 13, 17, 19, and 20), once compounded as *troncho de Tiberia* ["colossal idiot"] (Episode 12) is very common, and we can also find its synonym *bovo* ['idiot'] (Episode 16). Then in Episode 5, upon hearing the name of Gavriel's mistress, Mercada reacts viscerally: "That b*tch … That b*tch! The wh*re. May God help me!" [*una putana … una putana! Ija de un perro … El Dyo ke te tome!*] Similarly in Episode 13, Victoria sees David talking to Luna in the patio and reprimands him for mingling with the Ermozas, as well as Luna for targeting her son. She then looks at the latter with disgust and utters a curse in Ladino: "May God strike the head off this family" [*Ke el Dyo le kite la kavesa a esta famiya*]. Finally, cursing becomes almost sadistic in Episode 20, when Gavriel finds out that the money Ephraim had given to Roza, which would allow the family to repay its multiple debts and offer Luna a beautiful wedding, was actually stolen from some local workers. Upon his realisation, Gavriel curses Ephraim in Ladino while setting fire to all the money:

> That bastard. I'll kill him. He's a beast in … in the form of a human. I will kill him. Bastard. May the Devil take you. God give you the plagues of Egypt. Son of a mutt. Let the evil haunt you for the rest of your days. May you leave, never to return, you accursed bandit. May you burn yourself, Ephraim Siton. May you burn.
>
> *[Ijo de un [*inaudible*] ke te mate. Beema en forma de benadam. Figura negra. Satan. El diablo que te tome. El Dio ke te de las asmakot de Mizraim… Ijo de un perro. Ijo bueno ke no veygas. Ida sin venida. Kulsus. Ke te kemas**[51], *Ephraim Siton. Ke te kemas**[52]].

Finally, just like *Kulüp*, *The Beauty Queen of Jerusalem* offers a faithful rendition of the centrality of cuisine as a form of bond within Sephardic culture, particularly in connection with Ladino understood as a language of the home. To begin with, and as mentioned above, the family's business is a delicatessen store in *Machane Yehuda* (Jerusalem's major market), which is why unsurprisingly, its Ladino equivalent, '*delicatesa*,*'[53] makes it to the top ten of most frequently used words in Ladino (ninth) [19 instances]. Food mediates a lot of the action in the show. It is used to feed the Ermoza family in times of scarcity, bought by Gavriel to contribute to the Ashkenazi charity where his mistress Rochel works as a cook, and fetishised as an article of luxury (e.g., through the recurring appearance of Martinique chocolate as the ultimate luxury good) in which one indulges (e.g., Ephraim, who steals it from Gavriel's store). It is also depicted as something one can weaponise to put the family out of business (like a character named Mordoch the Kurd does), traded with the English soldiers to pay the bills (an opportunity deftly exploited by Mercada), and of course, shared at the table with one's dearest and nearest, whether it is in everyday life or celebrations (this last use being common currency in both *Kulüp* and *The Beauty Queen of Jerusalem*).

For example, in Episode 2, Roza is cooking. Taken aback by the smell in the kitchen, Mercada asks her rhetorically whether she is cooking "a cat." [*gato*][54] Roza responds that it is just "kidney pie" [*pastelico**].[55] In the next scene, as Mercada advises Roza on how to be prettier for Gavriel, she also warns her that she can still smell on her the "sh*t" [*mierda*] that Roza had cooked the night before. Meanwhile, Gavriel, who is still very much in love with Rochel, buys the finest Lebanese merchandise to send it to her charity. At home, Mercada tells him to donate instead the kind of food they eat regularly at home, such as the "beans and rice" [*abas kon arroz*] that she just cooked for that night. Then in Episode 17, a British soldier enters the delicatessen shop and asks for plenty of kidney pies. Although there are none in stock, Mercada accepts the request, and then asks Roza to do said "pies made of kidneys" [*pasteliko*][56] and black pudding[57] if she wants to be able to afford a doctor for "the little one [Becky]" [*pizgada*, literally 'the heavy/burdensome one']. When Roza asks Mercada whether she can cook them outside, she refuses, expressing her disgust in Ladino: "You want the whole neighbourhood to smell of that *mierda* [sh*t] with the blood?" Back at the delicatessen store, Mercada is very happy with the sale, and she asks Gavriel to let the British soldier know that from now on, they will be selling "kidney pies" [*pastelikos*[58]]. Further Ladino terms related to cuisine pepper the show, including the *pitom* ['tip'] of the *etrog* [yellow citron used by Jews during Sukkot], *kofetika* [pie] (Episode 4), *bizkochos* ['cookies'] (Episode 7), *fritikas* ['meatballs'] (Episode 14), *vaca**[59] [cow] (Episode 17), *fritikas kon arroz* ['meatballs and rice'] (Episode 19), and *kaveiko* ['coffee'] (Episode 19).

When it comes to songs, unlike *Kulüp*, *The Beauty Queen of Jerusalem* does not feature classic songs of the traditional Sephardic repertoire, like *Yo era ninya*, *Kuando el rey Nimrod*, or *Adio' kerida*. Instead, it includes lullabies, a birthday song, and a final song in contemporary Spanish. As observed above, notwithstanding potential copyright issues, this contrast suggests that offering a representative sample of Ladino in historical terms was of lesser importance to the producers of *The Beauty Queen of Jerusalem* than it was to those of *Kulüp*. Instead, the marked presence of lullabies, which appear in episodes 4, 6, 7, 8, 11 (twice) and 18, is consistent with the persistent portrayal of Ladino as a language of the home, as well as the preponderance accorded to family relationships and intimacy. Nevertheless, and as in *Kulüp*, this use is combined with the interaction in Ladino within the broader community (in the case at hand, with characters like Victoria and Avram).

The most frequent lullaby is often cut short. Indeed, it is precisely because its function is postvernacular or symbolic (as opposed to vernacular or referential) that spectators do not need to hear every single word for them to get the overall point: "Sleep, sleep, my little darling/to sleep, dear child/Sleep without fear or pain/Close your beautiful eyes/Sleep, sleep in peace/You will graduate school/And then, my dear daughter/You will have your own children…" [*Durme, durme, kerida ijika/Durme sin ansia i dolor/Serra tus lindos ojikos/Durme durme kon savor/De la kuna saliras/A la eskola tu entraras/I entonses, kerida ijika/Kriaturas tu tendras…*].

This lullaby is sung by Gavriel to put either Luna (episodes 4, 6 and 11) or Becky (Episode 12) to sleep. Alternatively, when Roza puts Rachelika to sleep, she uses slightly different lullabies. Thus, in Episode 7, Roza sings as follows: "Go to sleep, my soul/your father is coming/ with great joy/nanny, nanny..." [*Ay, ay, durmete ya, ay/ke tu padre vyene/kon muncha alegriya/nani, nani...*], before falling asleep herself. Then in Episode 8 she sings "Go to sleep, my little girl/go to sleep, my little girl/Go to sleep, my little girl" [*Ay, durmete mi alma/ ay durmete mi alma/ija mia*]. In Episode 12, as the whole family celebrates Becky's birthday, to encourage Roza, Rachelika, and Luna to lift up Becky, Gavriel addresses them in Ladino: "Come, sweethearts, come!" [*Vamos, mis keridas, vamos!*]. The whole family holds hands and sings in unison in Ladino: "It's her birthday, it's her birthday, lovely Becky. It's her birthday, it's her birthday. It's her birthday, lovely Becky. It's her birthday, it's her birthday. Happy birthday, dear Becky" [*Tyene kumpleanyo, tyene kumpleanyo, kerida Becky, tyene kumpleanyo, tyene kumpleanyo, tyene kumpleanyo, kerida Becky* (inaudible) *Tiene kumpleanyo, kerida Becky*].

Finally, the last scene of the season features David and Luna's Sephardic wedding. As the credits roll down, a Spanish song is played in the background: *'Mi amor'* ['My love'] (2021), sung by Israeli singers Daniel Salomon and Yasmin Levy, who usually sings in Ladino (see Chapter 3). The lyrics speak about love as a language and are entirely in Spanish, the song seemingly implying and/or performing mutual intelligibility between Spanish and Ladino (as seen above apropos the dialogue between James and Victoria). One could even argue that they hint at the supposed convenience of re-Hispanicising the latter to make it survive and thrive in the 21st century (in stark contrast with Yiddish, where there have been no equivalent calls among current Yiddishists to assimilate Yiddish into German).

In a private interview (2022), the show's Ladino adviser (Refael) stated that a different piece had been translated from Hebrew into Ladino as an alternative track, but in the end, the Spanish song was favoured over it, without him having had any influence on this decision.

Similarly to songs, traditional proverbs feature much less prominently in *The Beauty Queen of Jerusalem* than in *Kulüp*, once again implying that offering a historically representative sample of Ladino was of lesser importance to the producers of *The Beauty Queen of Jerusalem* than it was to those of *Kulüp*.

More specifically, there are only two proverbs in Ladino in the entire show, and both are remarkably obscene. In Episode 3, Mercada advises Roza to please Gavriel sexually. To illustrate this, she resorts to a Ladino proverb: "Men have a small organ they care about. Satisfy it, and your man will ask you for more. And if you don't give him more, he'll leave you" [*Un chiko organo tyene el ombre. Si lo artas keda ambriento i si lo deshas ambriento, keda arto*"]. Then in Episode 12, Mercada tries to justify Ephraim's infidelity to Victoria by claiming that it is in his nature as a man to cheat, which Mercada seconds with a lapidary Sephardic proverb: "When the d*ck is erected, the brain goes to the *culo**"[60] [*Kuando la chuchuna se alevanta, la kavesa se abasha al kulo*]. While profanity is not uncharacteristic of Sephardic sayings, it seems caricaturesque to reduce the breadth and depth of wisdom encapsulated in Sephardic proverbs to the above two instances.

As remarked before, this phenomenon is very similar to the postvernacular tendencies seen among the descendants of Yiddish speakers (Epstein 2006; Gusoff 2012).

Additionally, *The Beauty Queen of Jerusalem* features plenty of idioms, which much like in *Kulüp*, are related to the semantic fields of religion and superstition, accurately attesting to the centrality of these domains in the Sephardic *Weltanschauung*. *Adyo/Atyo Santo* ['My God'] is the most frequently used, complemented by *inshallah*, ['God willing'] *kol akavod* ['congratulations'], *el Dio ke mos guadre*, ['may God protect us'], and *pishgado ilim* [no evil eye upon us].

Lastly, and just like in *Kulüp*, Ladino is used as a cryptolect, though unlike the Istanbul-based show, *The Beauty Queen of Jerusalem* includes instances where this strategy backfires. Indeed, the first use of Ladino in the initial episode concerns the deployment of the language as a cryptolect to hide from a political enemy, which we also saw in *Kulüp*. In this case, the time-space coordinates are 1917 Jerusalem, i.e., during the last days of the Ottoman Empire. An Ottoman guard shows up at the front door of the Siton family to inquire about the whereabouts of Rachamim Siton. Upon realising they are coming for her brother, Roza wakes him up in Ladino ["They're looking for you. Go hide. Hurry. Hurry!" (my translation) [*Te estan bushkando. Vete, vete presto. Presto*]. When the Turks finally enter, their first question is telling, as it reinforces what we already saw throughout *Kulüp*, namely: the intractable link in Turkification ideology between speaking Turkish, on the one hand, and being a subject of the Ottoman Empire, on the other: "Do you speak Turkish?" "A little," Roza answers, which leads the Ottoman guards to further inquire: "How did you learn Turkish?" "I picked it up from the streets," she answers.

Then within the same episode we see the use of Ladino as a cryptolect backfire. The action fast-forwards to the 1918–19 period of British occupation. Gavriel is marrying a Sephardic woman named Esterika Malki. However, he is temporarily dazzled at the sight of a young, working-class Ashkenazi woman (Rochel; see above). As he is about to approach her, the illiterate Roza shows up, asking him for a job, to Gavriel's great inconvenience. Mercada is initially reluctant to hire Roza based on her appearance, as she confides to Gavriel in Ladino "look at her. Seriously. She'd scare all of our customers away" [*kon la kara ke tyene, todos los klientes se van afuera*]. Whereupon Mercada changes her mind when looking her in the eyes, as Roza responds in Ladino "but I can help with the cleaning for you" [*para limpiar esto pronta*]. Roza's command of Ladino dismantles Mercada's previous use of it as a cryptolect while also indexing Roza's ethnicity, showing that she belongs. Indeed, Roza's response sparks Mercada's curiosity: "You're good at this?" [*De onde saves?*]. "I do the cleaning for British families. I can speak five languages, including Turkish" [*Yo esto limpiando las kazas de los inglezes. Tambyen avlo inglez i un poko turko*], Roza answers, as she nods confidently. Her response triggers Mercada's in-group loyalty and out-group rejection, as attested by her subsequent remark to Gavriel: "well, at least she's one of us. Our Arab woman does a terrible job."

Finally, in Episode 5, the Ermozas resort to Ladino to keep their conversation private while in a dialogue with the British authorities where anything they say may be used against them (provided, of course, that it be understood). It is 1937, and Ephraim has killed a warden and managed to escape from prison. When the British Army checks the Ermoza's house looking for Ephraim, Rachelika pisses her pants, and Roza uses Ladino as a secret language to calm her down in front of James: *ke paso, kerida*?

In sum, it is fair to conclude that the use of Ladino in *The Beauty Queen of Jerusalem* is more humorous and playful but, above all, more postvernacular, tokenistic and anachronistic (relative to 1923–48 Palestine) than in *Kulüp*, including several instances of non-standardised uses and mispronunciation that occasionally affect intelligibility. On the other hand, I have also argued that it is precisely the fragmentary, mostly postvernacular and often humoristic (including vulgarisms) presence of Ladino as a named language (rather than its traditional presentation as a reified, autonomous code) which, cultural stereotypes notwithstanding (i.e., the implication that Ladino is best suited for informal and vulgar purposes, rather than formal or prestigious ones), prevents the show from essentialising Ladino-speaking Sephardim as the seats of monolingual/bilingual speech communities. Instead, it reflects the predominant use of Ladino in Israel and abroad, ultimately vindicating the Revivalistics principle that "shift happens. And there is nothing wrong with shift happening. Hybridization results in new diversity, which is beautiful" (2020, 209).

In this fashion, *The Beauty Queen of Jerusalem* creates a playful space where (limited) forms of translanguaging can flourish, which in turn can have positive repercussions in the fields of pedagogics and revitalisation (see below). The danger, though, resides in the fact that the postvernacularly inflected presence of Ladino in the show goes oftentimes hand in hand with its re-Hispanicisation, thus seemingly making the revitalisation of Ladino ancillary to its assimilation into and standardisation along the lines of contemporary Spanish (see Yebra López 2022b). This is a position that the show's main linguistic adviser has explicitly endorsed in the past (see Chapter 1), and that as I have notice above finds no parallel among contemporary Yiddishists when it comes to making the reinvigoration of Yiddish contingent upon its assimilation into German.

Dubbing and Subtitling

Just like in *Kulüp*, notwithstanding the remarkable efforts of the show's Ladino adviser, *The Beauty Queen of Jerusalem* also falls short of taking advantage of the multimodal affordances of Netflix to further the digital revitalisation of Ladino in the dubbing and subtitling departments.

Similarly to what happened in *Kulüp* apropos the Turkish original audio, in *The Beauty Queen of Jerusalem,* Ladino can only be heard as part of the original (Hebrew) audio, and it is therefore entirely absent as part of the audio in any other language (e.g., Spanish, English). Nor can Ladino itself be selected as an audio language. Once again, this runs contrary to Netflix's 'Dubbing Audio Style Guide' (2022), which in alignment with an overall impetus to favour multilingualism, states the following: "Do not dub over foreign dialogue" (cit. in Bangkok Video Productions) see above.

On the other hand, and in contrast with *Kulüp*'s subtitles, where Ladino is entirely absent, the English subtitles (with captions) (and only them) include a few Ladino words, though most of them do not. Additionally, and just like in *Kulüp*, only the English closed captioning and that of the original audio (Hebrew) feature "[in Ladino]" before any Ladino audio in the original version. Even then, though, just like in *Kulüp*'s English closed captioning, some instances are wrongly captioned as Spanish. Hence why as part of my discussion, all the above transcriptions were mine, and what followed between brackets were the English subtitles with captions, which do not always accurately convey the original meaning in Ladino. If there was no English translation following the Ladino transcription, it meant it was the show's own, rare Ladino transcription. Just like in the case of *Kulüp*, *The Beauty Queen of Jerusalem*'s linguistic adviser has clarified that he did not partake in the subtitling of the show.

Once again, in principle, the paradoxical coexistence of an otherwise careful and professional presence of Ladino in the show with its misrecognition, and/or absence as part of its audio and subtitles (though in the case of *The Beauty Queen of Jerusalem,* now we have to add an inconsistent and often Hispanicised transcription of the few Ladino words that are subtitled) could be reconciled in light of the so-called 'algorithms of oppression' (Noble 2018). Yet we need to remember that as showed by Savoldelli and Spitteri Miggiani (2023), the extensive neutralisation of the Ladino audio is in stark contrast with the adoption of transfer unchanged (maintaining the original voice track for the specific language variation – Ladino in our case – in audio versions other than the original – Hebrew) for another Jewish endangered language, (Yiddish), in the case of multilingual occurrences in Netflix's Italian dub streams in *Unorthodox* (more on this below). Notwithstanding these circumstances, the subtitling of *The Beauty Queen of Jerusalem* (rarely) featuring part subtitles to convey the meaning of language variation in Ladino to the audience, represents a step forward in the right direction *vis-à-vis* the extensive subtitling neutralisation shown in *Kulüp*. Moreover, this would show that there is nothing intrinsic about "severely endangered" languages like Ladino, as opposed to merely "definitively endangered" ones like Yiddish (UNESCO 2003; cf. Chapters 3 and 4), which unlike the latter, would prevent shows featuring linguistic varieties belonging to the former group from benefiting from more inclusive subtitling policies (and potentially also dubbing ones), in line with both the treatment received by Yiddish and the principles advocated as part of Netflix's 'Dubbing Audio Style Guide' (2022) and 'Inclusion and Diversity Statement' (2023).

Nevertheless, the question remains of whether the otherwise algorithm-induced re-Hispanicisation of Ladino in the subtitles is actually consistent with the intention of the show's language adviser, who did not partake in either the show's dubbing/subtitling or the choosing of the concluding Spanish song over a different piece that had been translated (with his help) from Hebrew into Ladino as an alternative track. While this information would seem to exonerate him from the bulk of the ostensive Hispanicisation of Ladino, such policy is nonetheless consistent with his stated desire during the Fourth Tribune of Hispanism, organised by the Cervantes

Institute in 2018, apropos the recently established Judeo-Spanish (Ladino) Royal Academy of Israel (of which he is a prominent member). There Refael expressed his wish that Sephardim "reconnect" with (Peninsular) Spanish, stressing the need to educate them in the "proper" writing of Ladino, by opposition to the current Ladino orthography (*Aki Yerushalayim*), which he derogatorily labelled "cacography" (2018) (see Chapter 1; Yebra López 2022b). The danger is, of course, that through its acculturation into the prestigious linguistic variety (Spanish, in the case at hand) Ladino might well transition from a fragmentary state to its downright disappearance in the name of its own revitalisation. This is why such forms of unabashed linguistic assimilationism into the colonial language have been dubbed *cannibalisme* ['cannibalism'] by Louis-Jean Calvet (1974) and "ontological predation" by Eduardo Viveiros de Castro (2008), thus stressing the aggressive neocolonial lust behind the policy in question. While it is perfectly possible for Refael to have changed his thinking on this topic since 2018, when asked during our 2022 interview whether that was the case, he did not produce a direct answer.

Last but not least, it is worth noting that if based on what I have argued above, Ladino as depicted in *The Beauty Queen of Jerusalem* is best understood from the perspective of a limited form of translanguaging, Netflix's dubbing and subtitling (most of the latter, in the case of *The Beauty Queen of Jerusalem*; all of it, in the case of *Kulüp*) is problematic not only at the more apparent level of misrecognition and erasure of Ladino *qua* linguistic variety. It is also troublesome at the more fundamental, metalinguistic level of reproducing the conceptualisation of languages in close association with Standard Language Ideology (Lippi-Green 1994, 166; Walsh 2021; see also Introduction and Chapter 1), compartimentalising them into boxes. Even when the Ladino box happens to be empty, it still exhibits the contours of (a standardised) one. By contrast, my approximate identification of the nameable languages and varieties in use (e.g., 'Hebrew,' 'Ladino,' 'English') ought to be understood as strategic for explanatory purposes, rather than congruent or in agreement with Standard Language Ideology (see above).

The Awareness-Raising, Revitalisation, and Pedagogical Implications of Netflix Ladino

Regardless of the commonalities and differences between the nature and use of Ladino in *Kulüp* and *The Beauty Queen of Jerusalem*, respectively, our comparative analysis raises a critical question: what are the repercussions that the presence of Ladino on Netflix as articulated via these two shows is currently having among their audience when it comes to raising awareness about the existence of this linguistic variety (and its concomitant speech community), revitalising, and learning it?

Methods

To elucidate these questions, in late 2022, I inquired about the above aspects as part of my private interviews on Zoom with the language coaches behind

Kulüp (İzzet Bana) and *The Beauty Queen of Jerusalem* (Shmuel Refael), respectively (see above). Then in early 2023, I designed my own original survey about these elements on Google Forms, and disseminated it for a week among people who had watched at least one episode of at least one of these series. The answers were anonymised and no data (e.g., email address, gender, age, etc.) was collected from participants, each of whom were limited to one response from an authenticated, unique Google account. The survey contained four multiple-choice questions:

> (i) Which Netflix TV series have you watched (at least one episode)? (ii) If you watched both, which series' depiction of Ladino had the most positive impact on you? (iii) What impact did Ladino in *Kulüp* have on you? and (iv) What impact did Ladino in *The Beauty Queen of Jerusalem* have on you? (2023a)

Results

Half of the participants had watched both shows (24). Among the other half, spectators of *Kulüp* only (15) outnumbered the audience of *The Beauty Queen of Jerusalem* only (5) by a 3:1 ratio. Lastly, four of the participants declared not having watched either show (consequently, they did not answer any of the ensuing three questions).

Second, among participants who had watched both shows (24), 17 (70.83%) picked *Kulüp* as the series that had the most positive impact on them, while 7 (29.17%) selected *The Beauty Queen of Jerusalem.*

Third, the majority of *Kulüp*'s audience declared that the show did raise their awareness about Ladino and its community of speakers (78.95%), followed by 47.37% of participants who expressed that *Kulüp* had encouraged them to revitalise this linguistic variety, and 23.68% who claimed they had also been inspired to learn Ladino. However, none of the participants declared that the show had encouraged them to just learn Ladino.

Finally, when asked what impact *The Beauty Queen of Jerusalem* had had on them, the majority of the audience declared that the show did raise their awareness about Ladino and its community of speakers (79.31%), followed by 48.28% of participants who expressed that *The Beauty Queen of Jerusalem* had encouraged them to revitalise this linguistic variety, and 34.48% who had been inspired to learn Ladino in addition to the former two impacts. Only 6.90% of the participants declared that the show had encouraged them to just learn Ladino.

Discussion

Notwithstanding the rather reduced sample size, the survey results yield some clear and clarifying conclusions.

First, on a general level, Netflix shows featuring Ladino contributed to raising awareness about this severely endangered language and its community of speakers among the vast majority of the audience (78%–80%), to revitalise it as well among half of it (47%–48%) and lastly, to learn it as well only among a minority (23%–34%). In both cases, the show in question only managed to do all three (raise awareness, encourage to revitalise the language, and encourage to learn it) among a minority of the audience, and almost nobody (0%–7%) whose awareness was not already raised and had also been encouraged to revitalise Ladino, felt motivated to learn it.

These findings are mostly consistent across both series: almost identical concerning the awareness-raising and revitalising impact (around 1% difference), and only slightly different in the pedagogical implications (almost 11% more of participants wanted to learn Ladino after watching *The Beauty of Jerusalem*, compared to *Kulüp*). Lastly and across the board, they are further consistent with the intuitions expressed in private interviews by the main language coaches behind both shows, as well as those disseminated in mainstream media by the shows' respective producers and further members of the audience.

Thus, regarding *Kulüp*, the reaction of prominent members of the Sephardic community would seem to attest to the ability of the show to increase awareness about Ladino and its community of speakers. Ivo Molinas, editor-in-chief of the Turkish Jewish newspaper *Şalom*, celebrated this inclusive aspect apropos *Kulüp* as a pleasant surprise: "I was amazed (…) we never thought that this kind of series, from the perspective of non-Muslims, could be shown in Turkey" (cit. in Pitel 2022). Much in the same vein, in a recent interview for *Al Jazeera*, Nesi Altaras, a Sephardic Jew from Istanbul, stressed the extent to which (the presence of Ladino in) *Kulüp* might facilitate inclusive, pro-diversity, and pro-immigration forms of national belonging (in this case, as applied to Turkey): "Mainstream Turkish society has become a stranger to Jews who live in Turkey, who have lived here for hundreds of years, so I think the show [*Kulüp*] really presents itself as a teachable moment" (Farooq 2021; see also Klein 2021). Additionally, and prior to my survey, Rana Denizer, co-writer of the show (see above), had already expressed hope that the series would be of help to the revitalisation of Ladino, particularly among the new generation: "I wish the young people would get excited now and revive Ladino (…) Hopefully good things have happened" (cit. in Stroum Center for Jewish Studies 2022). Lastly, the limited impact of the series depiction of Ladino when it comes to enticing the audience to learn the language was also anticipated by Bana (*Kulüp*'s main Ladino adviser), as he sided with Netflix in conceptualising the show as an entertainment product first and foremost. In particular, he remarked that while the audience enjoyed watching *Kulüp*, for the most part, they lacked the desire and/or motivation to learn Ladino. Even those who were personally recruited by him and featured in the show as Ladino speakers oftentimes had just a rudimentary knowledge of the language, he claimed, their performance being primarily motivated by the desire to be watched and paid (2022).

Concerning *The Beauty Queen of Jerusalem*, in late 2022 its main language adviser had already expressed his belief that the use of Ladino in the series could well contribute to the dissemination of this linguistic variety in Israeli culture, not only among Ladino speakers and Sephardim at large, but also among the entire populace. As evidence of this dynamic, he cited recent Yiddish theatre plays in Israel where Ladino was featured side by side with the language of the Ashkenazim, such as Shoki Wagner's *It's Never Too Late* (Baub 2022).

Finally, it is worth noting that as per my survey, *Kulüp* had three times more audience than *The Beauty Queen of Jerusalem*, and this translated into the former being perceived as having 2.42 times more positive impact than the latter. In other words, controlling for the audience size, *The Beauty Queen of Jerusalem*'s depiction of Ladino was actually perceived to have a more positive impact than that of *Kulüp*, particularly in the pedagogical department, as per responses to questions (iii) and (iv). While this is consistent with the fact that *The Beauty Queen of Jerusalem*'s language coach and adviser has a strong background in the pedagogics of Ladino, which is lacking in his counterpart from *Kulüp*, it should also prompt us to consider the fact that the very nature of what is being presented to the audience as a potential object of revitalisation (i.e., Ladino) varies significantly across shows, with momentous implications.

In the case of *Kulüp*, what we are being encouraged to appreciate, revitalise, and learn is Ladino understood as a language code that while suffering from severe attrition, still enjoys a certain degree of autonomy (as implied in the presence of several vernacular instances), and is anchored in a prestiged[61] corpus featuring a number of classical/traditional texts (e.g., songs such as *Adio' kerida*, *Kuando el rey Nimrod*, and *Yo era ninya*) that can be universally recognised as quintessentially Sephardic. Thus, Ladino is presented as a decaying, yet fully fledged language whose lexico-structural aspects and corpus would have to be learned from scratch.

By contrast, the Ladino portrayed in *The Beauty Queen of Jerusalem*, though anachronistic for the time and place of the action (1923–48 Palestine) and tokenistic (see above), consists less in a self-contained code anchored in a clearly discernible and traditional corpus, than in a fluid number of lexico-grammatical elements shared by people with a common Sephardic culture that are and/or should be mutually intelligible with Spanish, and can be activated both organically and selectively depending on a number of circumstances, including the desire to index and/or perform a number of realities. In this case, the entity to be revitalised is not a language understood in the traditional sense, but the only ever partially overlapping of idiolects shared by people of Sephardic culture (Yebra López 2023b). As such, learning 'Ladino' should be a less systematic process consisting in the incorporation of a few hundred words and cultural references into one's pre-existing linguistic repertoire, plus it should be fairly useful in giving one partial access to over 500 million Spanish speakers. Overall, this makes for a more attractive pedagogical proposition, and it is perhaps in light of this contrast that we can better account for the fact that the percentage of participants who watched the *Beauty Queen of Jerusalem* and felt compelled to learn Ladino was higher than that of the participants that felt inspired to learn this linguistic variety after having watched *Kulüp*.

Ultimately, though, the above results do not only provide useful answers. They also raise further questions, namely: how many of those who declared that the show inspired them to revitalise Ladino were already speakers of the language? Is this expressed desire to revitalise and/or learn the language a feasible plan, or just a theoretical one? What does "revitalise" mean for them? How consistent is this conceptualisation with the key tenets of Revivalistics? Where do we draw the line when it comes to determining whether we have successfully learned a language like Ladino?[62]

Comparing Ladino and Yiddish on Netflix

Notwithstanding the fact that Ladino shows on Netflix are historical, whereas those featuring Yiddish are set in the present, comparing and contrasting the above discussion with the use of Yiddish in *Shtisel* (2018–21) and *Unorthodox* (2020–22), respectively, can enrich our understanding of the revitalising and empowering potential behind the use of Ladino on Netflix.

Originally released in 2013, *Shtisel* only arrived on Netflix in 2018, spanning three seasons. It tells the story of a fictional Haredi (i.e., ultra-Orthodox Jewish) family living in Geula, Jerusalem (Israel), an Internet-free neighbourhood where the violation of norms often results in chaos within the family.[63] This strictness is nuanced by the presence of several characters ready to embrace a secular lifestyle, in contrast with the more stringent community of adjacent *Mea She'arim*.

Much in the vein of *Kulüp*, *Shtisel* features a limited use of the minoritised language in question (Yiddish, minoritised *vis-à-vis* Hebrew) and to do so, it draws upon the local community, which enhances the authenticity of the series. Additionally, *Shtisel* also combines the vernacular and the postvernacular registers to show the linguistic landscape of the host country (Israel, in the case at hand), thus forcing us to think about the politics of multilingualism in the territory at large, as well as the extent to which a perspective embracing linguistic diversity and translanguaging might contribute to an enhanced understanding of the country's national and popular culture. In particular, and similarly to Rachel's use of Ladino within interactions in Turkish in *Kulüp*, postvernacular instances in *Shtisel* are the prerogative of the younger generation of heritage speakers, which uses the minoritised language (in this case, Yiddish) within conversations in the main one (Hebrew, in the case at hand).

In this sense and much like *The Beauty Queen of Jerusalem*, *Shtisel* also shows that Jewish immigrants in Mandate Palestine were hardly monolingual, often engaging in translingual exchanges. Finally, and similarly to *Kulüp*, during the first season *Shtisel* ended up minimising the use of the endangered language in question, both to avoid alienating potential audiences and because writing and filming scenes in that language proved too burdensome a task for writers and actors alike. And yet, while the second part of the first season of *Kulüp* features much less Ladino than the first one, in *Shtisel* the staff decided to include more Yiddish, in hopes of offering a more accurate reflection of the Haredi life (Weiss 2016).

For its part, *Unorthodox* (Schrader 2020–22) was the first Netflix series predominantly spoken in Yiddish. Inspired by Deborah Feldman's 2012 memoir *Unorthodox: The Scandalous Rejection of My Hasidic Roots*, it tells the story of Esther Shapiro, a 19-year-old Hasidic Jewish woman living in an unhappy marriage in the Satmar[64] sect of the ultra-Orthodox community of Williamsburg, Brooklyn. Esther flees to Berlin, where she attempts to navigate a secular life. Following the order of their rabbi, her husband and his cousin travel to Berlin to try to find her.

Unorthodox's methodological repertoire includes the frequent use of flash forwards and backwards, thus accounting for ethnolinguistic continuity, just like in *Kulüp* and *The Beauty Queen of Jerusalem*. It also features the recruitment of local speakers as actors and/or consultants, just like in *Kulüp* and *Shtisel* and to a minor extent, *The Beauty Queen of Jerusalem* (though the Yiddish-speaking community is admittedly much larger than the Ladino-speaking one, which greatly facilitates this effort). Lastly, it shows the pervasiveness of the Jewish language in question (in a sense, like in *The Beauty Queen of Jerusalem*, though this time used very much as a vernacular, rather than in postvernacular/tokenistic fashion). Crucially, this includes accurate dubbing and subtitling via the use of transfer unchanged combined with subtitles. This practice is consistent with Netflix's overall policy on multilingualism (2022 -cit. in Bangkok Video Productions; 2023) and in stark contrast with both Ladino shows, but particularly *Kulüp*, where the extensive neutralisation of the Ladino audio in the dubbing department was also accompanied by the extensive neutralisation of Ladino in the subtitles (whereas *The Beauty Queen of Jerusalem* featured the odd word subtitled in Ladino). It should be noted, though, that having many more speakers, Yiddish must not have suffered as much as Ladino from the pernicious influence of the 'algorithms of oppression' (Noble 2018). At any rate, in the case of *Unorthodox*, the above approach results in a strong process of language ethnicisation (Linke 2004; Eisenlohr 2006) and reinforces a sense of "diasporic intimacy" (Boym 1998) and citizenship (Weheliye 2005, 145–97) where "the national and the transnational are quasi-dialectical partners in the movement of globalization" (149) (Yebra López 2021c, 111). For all the above reasons, arguably *Unorthodox* functions as a compendium of best practices when it comes to revitalising (Jewish) endangered languages through Netflix.

Conclusion

In this chapter, I have shown that since the mid-2010s, VOD and streaming services (paramount among which is Netflix) have disrupted the TV industry, reshaping both *what* we watch and *how* we watch it, while also problematising the supposed continuity between the *home* (nation) and the *land* (the state), thus arguably leading to a new and unique subtype of Digital Home-Land (Held 2010; Yebra López 2021c).

I have first outlined the main utilities of Netflix, emphasising its ability to visibilise diasporic voices (namely, that of Sephardim) and marginalised languages (i.e., Ladino), further noting that this is in alignment with its pro-multilingual dubbing and subtitling policies (Netflix 2022 - cit. in Bangkok Video Productions-; 2023). On the other hand, I have also cautioned the reader that Netflix is part and parcel of digital capitalism and as such, it reproduces its many blind spots and shortcomings, including the commodification of culture, and the preponderance of entertainment.

Second, concerning how Ladino is used on Netflix, I have concluded that *Kulüp* (2021 to present), which was the first series to feature a significant use of Ladino on the platform, draws upon this language as part of its careful portrayal of Sephardic minorities in 1950s Istanbul. The show is consistent with the main tenets of

Revivalistics, paramount among which are high community engagement (including the notable influence and decision-making power granted to its main language adviser, L1 Sephardic Jew İzzet Bana), and a fair balance between vernacular (conversations) and postvernacular instances (i.e., symbolic ones, as exemplified via songs, isolated words, and expressions), which is representative of the most frequently used idioms, songs, and expressions in Ladino, particularly among users of the Istanbul geolect.[65] On the other hand, the presence of Ladino is very scarce in Raşel's performance and the second part of the first season (due to the plot's own development, but also to the impracticality of shooting extensively in Ladino, particularly with non-fluent speakers), Ladino is mostly portrayed as an autonomous code, in close association with Standard Language Ideology, and more importantly, Ladino is absent as an audio language and as part of any audio language other than the original version (Turkish), plus no Ladino words appear in any subtitles. These dubbing and subtitling practices are in glaring contradiction with Netflix's overall policy (2022, – cit. in Bangkok Video Productions 2023).

In this sense, on the one hand, I have observed that the paradoxical coexistence of an otherwise careful and accurate presence of Ladino in the show with its misrecognition and/or absence as part of its dubbing and subtitles, could be excused in light of the so-called 'algorithms of oppression' (Noble 2018). On the other hand, I have stressed that as Savoldelli and Miggiani (2023) have demonstrated apropos multilingual occurrences in Netflix's Italian dub streams, extensive neutralisation of the sort utilised in *Kulüp*, where language variation (in Ladino) is dubbed over/omitted, was not encountered in those streams, even in the case of a minoritised Jewish language like Yiddish. Instead, transfer unchanged combined with subtitles was the most frequently employed strategy (2023, 27).

Third, as regards *The Beauty Queen of Jerusalem*, I have demonstrated that similarly to *Kulüp*, in this show the work of its language adviser, Shmuel Refael, played a key positive role in the visibilisation of Ladino. On the other hand, the overall absence of local Sephardim and Ladino speakers resulted in significantly lower community engagement than in *Kulüp*. Partly because of this, while in *The Beauty Queen of Jerusalem* the presence of Ladino is very significant across virtually every episode of the season (including more playful, humorous, and eloquent appearances), it is mostly postvernacular and tokenistic (and hence, anachronistic, since at the time in which the series is set, during the 1923–48 period, Ladino was spoken much more fluently), including several non-standardised uses and mispronunciations which occasionally affect intelligibility. Nevertheless, I have also argued that it is precisely the fragmentary, mostly postvernacular presence of Ladino as a named language which, cultural stereotypes notwithstanding (i.e., the implication that Ladino is best suited for informal and vulgar purposes, rather than formal or prestiged ones), prevents the show from essentialising Ladino-speaking Sephardim as monolingual, uniform speech communities, instead reflecting how Ladino is predominantly spoken nowadays in Israel and elsewhere. In turn, this creates a playful space where (limited) forms of translanguaging can flourish, which has positive repercussions in the fields of revitalisation and pedagogics, though it would be exaggerated and inaccurate to put this limited form of translanguaging on equal foot with that of Yiddish/English Hasidic bilinguals as accurately portrayed on Netflix. An additional danger is that the postvernacularly inflected presence of Ladino in the show occasionally comes across as Orientalist and exoticised, plus is oftentimes accompanied by its re-Hispanicisation. This last aspect seemingly makes the revitalisation of Ladino ancillary to its assimilation into and standardisation along the lines of contemporary Spanish, a position that the show's main linguistic adviser has explicitly endorsed in the past (Refael 2018).

Finally, similarly to what happened in *Kulüp*, in *The Beauty Queen of Jerusalem* Ladino can only be heard as part of the original (Hebrew) audio, and it cannot be selected as an audio language. On the other hand, and in contrast with *Kulüp*'s subtitles, the English subtitles (with captions) do include a few Ladino words, though just like in *Kulüp*, only the English closed captioning and that of the original audio (Hebrew) feature "[in Ladino]" before any Ladino audio in the original version, and even then, some instances are wrongly captioned as Spanish, or even French, or Yiddish. In this sense, Netflix's dubbing and subtitling remain problematic in both shows not just at the more obvious level of misrecognition and erasure of Ladino as a language, but also at the more fundamental, metalinguistic level of taking for granted the conceptualisation of languages in close association with Standard Language Ideology, compartimentalising them strictly.

Then with regard to the question of how does/can the use of Ladino contribute to raising awareness about this linguistic variety, revitalising, and/or learning it in the digital era, I have reached a number of conclusions. First, on a general level, Netflix shows featuring Ladino contribute to raising awareness about it and its community of speakers among the vast majority of the audience, to revitalise it among half of it and lastly, to learn it only among a minority. Moreover, since the first season of *Kulüp* enjoyed a considerably larger audience (based on the amount of participants who reported having watched *Kulüp* only versus *The Beauty Queen of Jerusalem* only), its impact on these three categories can be assumed to be similarly stronger in absolute terms. At any rate, in both cases the show in question only managed to do all three (raise awareness, encourage to revitalise the language, and encourage to learn it) within a small portion of the audience, and almost nobody whose awareness was not already raised and had been also encouraged to revitalise it, felt motivated to learn it. These findings are mostly consistent across both series, as well as with the intuitions expressed in private interviews by the main language coaches behind both shows, and those disseminated in mainstream media by the show's producers and further members of the audience.

Ultimately, a significant portion of the issues I have discussed in this chapter boil down to the blessing and the curse of digital capitalism as embodied by Netflix *qua* mainstream VOD platform: while useful for the purpose of raising awareness about minoritised communities and languages, it is mostly conceived as a form of passive entertainment, which as reflected by my interviews and survey, makes it difficult to transition into language activism, particularly in terms of enticing the audience to devote additional effort to learning Ladino. Moreover, this task seems to be particularly challenging when that learning effort is implicitly conceptualised like in *Kulüp*, i.e., as the protracted acquisition of fluency in Ladino understood as an autonomous code anchored in a vast corpus of traditional works. By contrast, presenting Ladino as the only ever partially overlapping of idiolects shared by people of Sephardic culture (Yebra López 2023b) in the manner of *The Beauty Queen of Jerusalem* might make this learning task seem less onerous and more rewarding.

Lastly, and while still subject to some of the most persistent constraints posed by the digital affordances of VOD and streaming services, I have shown that the use of Yiddish in the Netflix show *Unorthodox* can serve as a blueprint for the upcoming creation of Ladino content on Netflix in particular and VOD/streaming services in general, be it for future seasons of the same series or for new series. In particular, I have argued that *Unorthodox* features a superior methodological repertoire based on a combination of the recruitment of local speakers as actors and/or consultants (just like in *Kulüp* and *Shtisel* and to a minor extent, *The Beauty Queen of Jerusalem*), and the pervasiveness of the Jewish language in question (as in *The Beauty Queen of Jerusalem*), including also careful dubbing and subtitling (unlike *Kulüp* and *The Beauty Queen of Jerusalem*, though it is possible that Yiddish, having a larger number of speakers, has not suffered as severely from the effects of the 'algorithms of oppression' – Noble 2018). All the above results in a strong process of language ethnicisation (Linke 2004; Eisenlohr 2006) and reinforces a sense of "diasporic intimacy" (Boym 1998) and citizenship (Weheliye 2005, 145–97) where "the national and the transnational are quasi-dialectical partners in the movement of globalization" (149) (Yebra López 2021c, 111).

All in all, and as shown in further chapters, the revitalisation and pedagogical policies supportive of language sustainability, including the desire to recognise, use, and transmit a language inter-generationally, can be achieved only by endorsing initiatives (in this case, Netflix shows) that are not just tolerant of the full complexity of Ladino languaging, but explicitly aimed at creating spaces where these language practices can flourish. In turn, the ability to reach this goal is largely rooted in two activist premises congruent with *Revivalistics* (Zuckermann 2020) whose combination we can already observe in *Unorthodox*, but not in any Ladino show, namely: high community engagement manifest in the hiring of local L1 speakers, and the careful dubbing and subtitling of the endangered linguistic variety in question as a named language (in alignment with Netflix's policies on multilingualism; see Netflix 2022- cit. in Bangkok Video Productions).

Notes

1 See also Chapters 2 and 4 for further use cases.
2 Emigration by Jews to the land of Israel (see also Chapter 2).
3 Unless otherwise stated, my discussion of *Kulüp* is based on the use of Turkish audio (the only one featuring spoken Ladino) and English subtitles, from which I am quoting in this chapter for the purpose of translating Ladino (but which do not always accurately convey the original meaning). The transcription of the latter is mine (see also below).
4 Played by prominent Ladino speaker Karen Şarhon, editor-in-chief of Istanbul-based *El Amaneser*, the only journal in the world published entirely in Ladino (see also Chapters 3, 4, and 6).
5 Played by İzzet Bana (see above).

6 Verbalisation of the Ladino term '*yakishikli*,' Turkish for 'beautiful, handsome.' Consequently, a more accurate translation would have been "Does this colour look great on me?"
7 *Salites kon el af?*
Si. Musyu Davit esta…?
Musyu Davit esta avlando kon el telefon. Es muy emportante. Se puede alargar. Para kualo vinites. Te puedo ayudar?
Dospues vengo.
8 Originally the title of a Turkish office of high rank, it is frequently used as a term of endearment for boys/men (see below).
9 Sephardic woman 1: *Ya esta todo pronto.*
Sephardic woman 2: *Si le pares un ijiko, te va a azer la korona en la kavesa.*
Raşel: *Yo me ire al mupak.*
Sephardic woman 3: *Ke estas aziendo? Le averguensates a la ijika!*
Sephardic woman 2: *Atyo, ke dishe agora?*
Sephardic woman 4: *Avla poko. Tyene razon.*
10 The table is, of course, the centre of the home and such, symbolic of the centre of Jewish life. For their part, food and drink represent livelihood, and sharing them symbolises love for everybody at the table.
11 *Kuando el rey Nimrod al kampo salia/mirava en el sielo i en la estreyeria/vido una lus santa en la juderia/Ke avia de naser Avraham Avinu/Avraham Avinu, Padre kerido Padre bendicho, lus de Israel(x2) Luego a las komadres enkomendava/Ke toda mujer ke prenyada kedara/si paria un ijo, al punto la matara/Ke avia de naser Avraham Avinu/ Avraham Avinu, Padre kerido/Padre bendicho, lus de Israel(x2) La mujer de Terah kedo prenyada/i de dia en dia el le preguntava (or demandava)/'¿De ke tenesh la kara tan demudada?'/ Eya ya savia el bien ke tenia./Avraham Avinu, Padre kerido/Padre bendicho, lus de Israel* (x4). The song in question is rooted in a *piyyut* (a Jewish lithurgical poem designed to be sung) which was written in the 18th century by anonymous Sephardic authors of the Ottoman Empire and then eventually adapted by an anonymous author from Morocco. The latter shortened the lyrics, of which the quoted version is just the initial part.
12 "[Chorus] *Adio, Adio kerida/No kero la vida/Me l'amargates tu* (x2)/*Tu madre kuando te pario/I te kito al mundo/ Korason eya no te dio/Para amar segundo* (x2) [Chorus] *Adio, Adio kerida/ No kero la vida/ Me l'amargates tu (x2)/ Va bushkate otro amor/Aharva otras puertas/Aspera otro ardor/ Que para mi sos muerta* (x2)[Chorus] *Adio, Adio kerida/No kero la vida/Me l'amargates tu*" (x2). Mistakenly, when the song is played in the Ladino original, the captions read "Spanish music playing."
13 Ironically, later on in the episode İsmet is found confronting his mother on why she stays with his father, even though he beats her up regularly.
14 Diminutive form of '*pasha*' (see above).
15 Surely a mistake, as the subject (Matilda) needs to agree in gender and number with the verb. Since Matilda is a woman, she is '*enkudiada*,' as opposed to '*enkudiadas*,' '*enkudiado*,' or '*enkudiados*.'
16 Mistakenly, in the subtitles it is claimed that this is French (as it is similar to the French '*merci*').
17 For a decolonial deconstruction of the category of 'modern languages,' see Yebra López (2021d).
18 UNESCO's classification notwithstanding, many Hasidic children do still learn Yiddish at home as their first language.
19 More on this in Chapters 1 and 2.
20 In Jewish communities across the world a gravely ill child will sometimes be given an additional name indicating that the child was (ritually) sold or abandoned to fool the forces of illness. Mercada (sold) is a primary example, and her ability to escape from the eye of evil (or lack thereof) is a recurring theme in the series. Additionally, while not wrong *per se*, the transcription of the voiceless velar plosive /k/ as *c* (hence the spelling

of the Sephardic surname 'Merkada' as 'Mercada') runs contrary to the French-Ottoman orthography adopted by *Aki Yerushalayim*, instead following the rules of Castilian Romanisation, thus being a mark of re-Hispanicisation (see Chapter 1). The same applies to subsequent (proper) nouns such as 'Franco' (see below).

21 Although in the original Hebrew subtitles with captions 'Roza' is spelt with a *zayin* (whose equivalent in Latin script is *z*; this is both the *Aki Yerushalayim* spelling in Ladino and reflective of how the characters pronounce it), as it is common in standardised Ladino, in the English subtitles with captions this name is spelled as 'Rosa,' following Castilian Romanisation. In this chapter, I will stick to the original subtitles and spell her name as 'Roza.'

22 Although in the original Hebrew subtitles with captions 'Efraim' is spelt with a *fey* (whose equivalent in the Latin script is *f*; this is also the standardised spelling in Ladino), in the Spanish subtitles with captions this name is spelt as 'Ephraim.' The same goes for 'Rafael,' which is spelt with a *fey* in the original Hebrew subtitles with captions (in line with the standardised spelling in Ladino), but in the Spanish subtitles is spelt as 'Raphael.' In both cases, the standardised Ladino version seems to have been Anglosaxonised. However, since for the purpose of this chapter, I am writing in English and using English subtitles with captions, plus both 'Ephraim' and 'Raphael' are the standardised spelling in English and convey the same sound as the original in Hebrew and Ladino, I will keep the spelling of these names as 'Ephraim' and 'Raphael,' respectively.

23 My translation from the Hebrew original.

24 Unless otherwise stated, my discussion of *The Beauty Queen of Jerusalem* is based on the use of Hebrew audio and English subtitles (with captions), the only ones to include Ladino words, though just a few. Similarly, unless otherwise stated, all transcriptions are mine, and the parts in English are quoted from the English subtitles with captions, which do not always accurately convey the original meaning in Ladino. If there is no English translation following the Ladino transcription, it means it is the show's own Ladino transcription. Non-standardised/Hispanicised uses are marked with an asterisk (*).

25 A Hebrew word meaning "mum," left in the original in the English subtitles.

26 "Stupid."

27 An Ottoman Turkish delight.

28 "Please, come on…"

29 "Like a fish in the sea, like a dolphin."

30 "Crazy, crazy."

31 See below, as well as Chapter 2, for a critical discussion of the pedagogical repercussions of this approach.

32 See above for a similar discussion apropos *Kulüp*.

33 "My Goodness…" In standardised Ladino it would be "*Dio*" as opposed to "*Dios,*" "*Dios mio*" (Spanish) being translated into '*Atyo/Adyo santo.*'

34 "Submarines".

35 "Torpedoes".

36 Arabic-derived Hebrew slang for "something (like that)" preserved in the English subtitles.

37 Like fish.

38 "My son".

39 "400 dead!".

40 "Names".

41 "Let's go home, Victoria. Let's go".

42 My accurate spelling of the original pronunciation, possibly influenced by Italian. In standardised Ladino it is '*minuto.*'

43 Hispanicised pronunciation and spelling. In standardised Ladino it is '*muncha.*'

44 Either a grammar or a pronunciation error. In standardised Ladino it is '*prometida*' (referring to Luna) instead.

45 For a critical analysis of the 'Middle Ages' invention as defined by opposition to 'the myth of Modernity,' see Dussel (1993).

46 Hispanicised pronunciation and spelling of the standardised Ladino '*muncho*.'
47 On Romanisation systems, see Chapter 1.
48 Often in Ladino the use of diminutives is exclusively affectionate and need not refer to the supposed small size or young age of that which is alluded. In this case, the suffix '*-iko*' conveys both the fact that Ephraim is Roza's younger brother and her affection for him. In the scene in question, Roza says '*ermaniko*' (which is the standardised form), but the subtitles show '*hermaniko*' (a mixture of re-Hispanicisation – via the *h*- and French-Ottoman Romanisation – via the *k*-). In contrast to contemporary Spanish, where the *h* is silent, in Ladino it corresponds to the phoneme represented by the Hebrew letter *ḥet*, which sounds similar to the Spanish *j* in '*jamón*.' ['ham']
49 The show's own transcription. It is '*por'* in standardised Ladino.
50 See Epstein (2006); Gusoff (2012).
51 It is '*kemes'* (subjunctive mood) in standardised Ladino, instead of '*kemas'* (indicative mood).
52 It is '*kemes'* (subjunctive mood) in standardised Ladino, instead of '*kemas'* (indicative mood).
53 Castilian Romanisation of the standardised Ladino '*delikatesa*.'
54 Mistakenly, the Hebrew subtitles with captions allude to a further word in this scene being in Ladino: 'cat,' which is actually in Hebrew (in the Hebrew subtitles with captions), in English (in the English subtitles with captions), and in Spanish (in the Spanish subtitles).
55 Hispanicised spelling of the standardised Ladino '*pasteliko*.'
56 Yet the Hebrew subtitles treat it as a Hebrew word with the equivalent spelling in Meruba.
57 Not a Sephardic food, since it has blood in it (which is not *kosher*, i.e., food that adheres to Jewish dietary laws as prescribed in the *Torah*, the central religious text of Judaism), but the Ermozas are ready to cook it for the Brits because they need to repay their debts.
58 Once again, the Hebrew subtitles treat it as a Hebrew word with the equivalent spelling in Meruba.
59 Hispanicised spelling of the standardised Ladino '*vaka*.'
60 Hispanicised spelling of the standardised Ladino '*kulo*.'
61 I.e., deemed prestigious over time, rather than being intrinsically so.
62 For my discussion of the conceptualisation of Ladino as a pedagogical object, see Yebra López (2023b), as well as Chapters 1 and 2 in this volume.
63 For a discussion of Haredi reservations towards Internet usage, see Basu (2014); YIVO (2014); Fader (2020). See also Chapter 4.
64 Yiddish for 'Satu Mare,' in present-day Romania (like most Hasidic sects, it is named after the place where they emerged). This town was a significant centre of Jewish life in pre-World War II Hungary.
65 See Chapters 1 and 2.

Part 3

Web 3.0

The Decentralised, Blockchain- and Token-Based Stage (2010s-)

6 Sepharad 5? (2022-)

The Metaverse and the Network State

Introduction

Since 2020, the digital affordances of Web 3.0, including advancements in artificial intelligence (AI), virtual reality (VR), augmented reality (AR), the Metaverse, Non-Fungible Tokens (NFTs) and cryptocurrencies, have garnered increased attention worldwide. The Arts and Humanities, and more specifically language studies, have not been alien to this trend.

A case in point can be found in recent editions of the MLA (Modern Language Association) Convention, widely considered the main professional association in the United States for scholars of language(s) and literature. Its 2023 edition, for instance, featured sessions such as *Adaptation and the Metaverse* (Leitch et al. 2023), presentations like *The Metaverse Is a Lie: Dreams of Escape in Facebook's Connect 2021 Announcement Video* (Kalinka), and posters such as *Immersive Technologies for Arts and Culture*, where organisers Anne M. Lambright and Stephan Caspar (Carnegie Mellon University) discussed the recent creation of a digital space for modern languages and humanities known as 'The Askwith Kenner Global Languages & Cultures Room.' This project was spearheaded by the need to adapt to remote learning following the global pandemic (see Chapter 4), and now features sessions taught using Oculus VR headsets (see below), as well as VR storytelling carried out by students (Caspar 2020). Additionally, the 2024 edition of the MLA Convention included sessions such as *AI and What It Means to Create: A Cross-Disciplinary Conversation* (Frost et al. 2024) and *Teaching First-Year Writing to the Post-pandemic, AI Generation* (Boyd et al. 2024). plus presentations like *#GrahPoem: Analytical-Creative AI for Minority Languages and Community-Involving Performance* (Tanasescu and Tanasescu), and *How AI Large Language Models like GPT Are Disrupting, Redefining, and Revitalizing the Academy* (Chun).

These and similar events stress the importance of the Web 3.0 in a post-pandemic context, not just as speculative fiction, but also as part and parcel of the present and future of the Internet[1] and by extension, of its intersection with the Arts and Humanities in general and language studies in particular. To the extent to which the present and future of Ladino and its speaking communities is becoming increasingly contingent upon their online fate, comprehending the Web 3.0, with a focus

DOI: 10.4324/9781003473664-10

on its exciting potential for Ladino revitalisation purposes, is critical for a thorough understanding of the prospects of Ladino and its community of speakers (and by extension, that of further diasporic languages, among which rare Jewish languages feature prominently).

Consequently, the above predicament raises a critical question: how can researchers interested in the online revitalisation of languages in general (and that of rare Jewish languages like Ladino in particular) leverage these technological developments to further their humanitarian efforts in the Web 3.0?

What Is the Web 3.0? Decentralisation, Blockchain Technology, and Language Preservation

The history of the evolution of the Internet from the Web 1.0 to the Web 2.0 and beyond offers us some valuable insights. First, as humans we favour digital models that closely resemble the world as we inhabit it: complex, multisemiotic, and with an accompanying sense of aliveness (see Chapters 2, 3, 4, and 5). Second, as our virtual experiences become more realistic, we invest more of our time, money, and further resources in the online world, as well as in mixed-reality environments (online-to-offline and/or vice versa), which in turn acquire an increasing influence in our offline lives (see Chapter 4). Third, the strongest indicator of this transition is the mass adoption of innovative technologies, which have a tendency to be first embraced by younger generations (see Chapters 3 and 4).

In this sense, the Web 3.0 is best understood as a new version of the Internet whose main disruptive characteristics are decentralisation and blockchain technology, both of which are intimately linked to the digitalisation of our world. First, the Web 3.0 is built around a decentralised network of independent developers and users, in contradistinction with the big five centralising technology corporations in charge of the Web 2.0, namely: Google, Amazon, Meta, Apple, and Microsoft (GAMAM) (see Chapter 2). As I have discussed in previous chapters, most current virtual Ladino-speaking communities, including some of the most successful Digital Home-Lands (such as *Ladino 21* [YouTube, owned by Google], *Los Ladinadores* [Facebook, whose parent company is Meta], *Estamoz whatsapeando* [WhatsApp], acquired by what is now Meta], are partially or entirely hosted (and oftentimes owned) by GAMAM.[2]

By contrast and at least in theory, in the Web 3.0's decentralised version of today's Internet, power and value will experience a relevant shift from corporations to developers and end users. This transition is best facilitated by blockchain technology. Blockchains are a type of distributed ledger technology (DLT) consisting in growing lists of publicly available records (called 'blocks') securely linked together via cryptography.[3] They are also programmable payment rails, of which the first mainstream one was Bitcoin, created by Satoshi Nakamoto in 2008 and released in 2009 to serve as a public distributed ledger for its own cryptocurrency: bitcoin.[4]

The self-sustaining nature of blockchain technology, which is premised on the attributes of trustlessness (i.e., there is no need to trust a third party such as a bank, a person, or any intermediary that could operate between cryptocurrency transactions or holdings) and permisionlessness (i.e., no permission is required from any of these agents), allows it to increase capacity, decrease cost, and improve security, while the revenue and profits derived from operating its payment network are set by the market.[5]

The simplest production originating in crypto-based development are NFTs (Non-Fungible Tokens, meaning unique, non-replicable ones), through which developers and individual users can engage in 'minting,' i.e., placing ownership of an item (e.g., an image) onto a blockchain. Whereupon their right to the asset in question is managed just like any other cryptocurrency transaction (Chohan 2024).

Following a very successful 2021, the cryptocurrency market experienced a pronounced dip in 2022, featuring the collapses of LUNA, Terra USD, as well as the centralised cryptocurrency exchanges FTX and Three Arrows, losing billions and dragging many investors down. While these disastrous events triggered renewed scepticism and calls for heightened regulation, FTX (and Three Arrows) were centralised cryptocurrency exchanges, i.e., intermediaries between individual investors and crypto assets. Consequently, their collapse in 2022 was akin to that of major banks (which served as intermediaries between regular people and fiat currency such as USD, EUR, and GBP) in the 2008 financial bubble bust. Just like the demise of major banks did not spell the end of fiat currency, that of centralised cryptocurrency exchanges did not and will not spell the end of crypto, either, as demonstrated by its strong early 2024 recovery (including bitcoin's all-time high). This is particularly true if we take into account that cryptocurrencies emerged in the first place as alternatives to banks *qua* institutions that revolve around centralising currency, which means that centralised cryptocurrency exchanges are fundamentally at odds with the decentralising drive behind crypto assets.

While cryptocurrencies are primarily associated with new monetary systems and financial networks, the public blockchain networks on which they are built can be used for a variety of purposes, including language revitalisation. Entrepreneurs and engineers are quickly creating new products and services that take advantage of these networks, which are constantly being improved by a worldwide community of developers through an open-source software ecosystem (World Economic Forum 2020).

Additionally, just like in the case of previous revolutionary disruptions such as fire, the wheel, the written word, the printed press,[6] electricity and the Internet, making sense of blockchain requires us less to offer an essentialist definition of it than to actually show how it solves certain problems.

For the purpose of this chapter, we will be focusing on specific use cases where blockchain is leading to the preservation of (the) cultural heritage (of Sephardim) through the online revitalisation of a language like Ladino. The question then becomes as follows: how do blockchain in particular and the Web 3.0 in general function in connection with the revitalisation of Ladino in the 21st century?

The Tokenisation of Cultural Heritage and Language Preservation

Can blockchain save endangered languages? Although in the past I have engaged this question at face value (Yebra López and Alejandro 2021), as remarked by

Christina Comben (2020), blockchain cannot really "save" anything (be it a physical object, such as land, or an activity like languaging[7]). However, this technology grants us the chance to preserve (i.e., to record) data in general and languages in particular in a way that is more decentralised, transparent, and permanent than any other solution to date.

The progressive tokenisation of cultural heritage in our time implies precisely this: taking aspects of cultural heritage (e.g., a heritage language like Ladino) that are particularly valuable to us and converting them into digital form, storing them permanently in the blockchain public ledger: "In tokenising culture, your heritage, your traditional values basically you are opening up another economic sector for your community, building it, enriching it and telling your story to the world and giving it back to your own community" (Pentas NFT Market Place 2021).

While blockchain technology is not typically used for language revitalisation, it can be instrumentalised to store and protect language-related information. For example, blockchain can be used to create a decentralised database of language resources, such as dictionaries, grammars, and historical texts, which can be easily accessed and preserved by speakers of endangered languages. Additionally, blockchain-based smart contracts (i.e., agreements stored on a blockchain whose execution is automated, provided that the predetermined conditions are met) can be used to create decentralised platforms for language learning and teaching. Contrary to common misconception, this does not necessarily imply reifying cultures and languages (i.e., sterilisation, reducing them into museum objects that are only preserved on the proviso that they remain fixed), because the blockchain is a constant work-in-progress whose digital record can and does contain dynamic use cases, such as unscripted oral speech within the context of semi-structured interviews (e.g., à la *Ladino 21* – see Chapter 2).

A case in point is Indigen, a company that seeks to preserve the heritage of Indigenous cultures by storing their historical data on the blockchain. As discussed above, *qua* repository, blockchain is superior to any other type of online database in that its content is open-access, transparent, immutable, and virtually impossible to counterfeit, plus its administration is decentralised (no single ownership), trustless (no need to trust third parties, such as intermediaries) and permissionless (no permission required from these agents). Indigen's most ambitious undertaking is the creation of an unabridged Indigenous languages database named the B.U.I.L.D. project (Blockchain Unabridged Indigenous Language Database). Furthermore, as it can be discerned from the words of Larrimar Tia, Lead Developer of Indigen, B.U.I.L.D. offers a glimpse not just into how to use blockchain to preserve languages, but also into how to combine blockchain with further Web 3.0 disruptive technologies such as AI and machine learning to facilitate coexistence by eliminating language barriers:

> We are using distributed ledger technology (DLT) as the repository of data due to the immutable nature of blockchain and the ability to time stamp information and to keep track of historical records (…) Furthermore, once the

> data have been recorded on the blockchain, we will apply Artificial Intelligence (AI) or machine learning technologies to allow real time translations between native languages or tribal dialects. This way, we hope to bridge the gap between various tribes and eliminate the thought of cultural differences and language barriers.
>
> (Comben 2020)

In the case of African languages, OBTranslate is a deep learning company developing online CAT (computer-assisted translation) tools, neural machine translation (NMT), and AI platforms for African languages. The expansion of these Web 3.0 disruptive technologies into Ladino (within which Haketia would already count as an African linguistic variety) would be of tremendous benefit, not least because it would contrast with the current Web 2.0 misrecognition of Ladino as either Spanish or Hebrew, or else its erasure (for a discussion of this issue apropos Ladino on Netflix, see Chapter 5).

A further example is to be found in the Global Heritage Fund, which has adopted blockchain as a promising (if not perfect) technological solution towards the preservation of heritage culture and languages:

> Blockchain may not be a perfect solution for saving endangered cultural heritage, but it can provide assurances about historical data and accuracy by establishing unalterable records (…) In addition, blockchain can also help heritage conservation organizations appeal to new donors through cryptocurrency, which are built on blockchain technology (…) The rhetoric of blockchain "saving" heritage obfuscates the truth – that blockchain is just the latest in a long series of technologies contributing to the documentation, conservation, and restoration of our world's historic places.
>
> (Global Heritage Fund 2018)

Ultimately, the future use of blockchain technology for language preservation would depend on the development of specific solutions or platforms designed for this purpose, and on the extent to which they would be adopted and utilised by the communities they are intended to serve (itself a key tenet of Revivalistics – see Zuckermann 2020). In this sense, the younger generation of speakers of the endangered language in question is poised to play a major role in the intergenerational transmission of these solutions. In the case of Ladino, the educational process will most likely have to take place from a minority of young speakers to a majority of elderly ones.

On the one hand, it might be argued that cryptocurrency does not offer a stable basis for language revitalisation and cultural heritage in general as well as Ladino in particular. On the other hand, the Web 3.0 venture offers the opportunity to use technology-aided language revitalisation to push a discipline of the past (most of Sephardic/Ladino studies focus on pre-21st century – see Introduction) into the future, and to offer massive scale support for its ethnolinguistic cause from a borderless industry that continues to be packed with (volatile) investment.

We can already discern an initial implementation of specific solutions in the recent launching of cryptocurrency as payment rail on *Ladino 21* (where students can pay in bitcoin and Ether, in addition to any traditional fiat currency), as well as in the development and popularisation of machine learning applications of AI on Web 2.0 Ladino-speaking platforms (*Ladinokomunita*, *Los Ladinadores*). The latter includes the Ladino course *Ambezandomos Muestra Lingua* (Yebra López 2018). hosted under the AI-assisted language-learning app *Memrise* (which runs on a space repetition system [SRS] algorithm), and *LadinoType* (Berman 2006, 2022), which was relaunched in 2022 as a smart transliteration engine between the Latin, Rashi, and Solitreo scripts. This updated version of *LadinoType* features live conversion (including approximately 300 algorithms), warnings of potential errors, instant font switching, text utilities and tooltips showing Latin characters, strong privacy controls, a public document directory, and email or live chat for help.

In the next section, I turn my attention to a specific development that has attracted a great deal of investment from some of the biggest technology companies of the Web 2.0, and that could have a revolutionary impact on the survival prospects of Ladino, namely: the Metaverse.

The Metaverse

The Metaverse is increasingly thought of as the next great disruption in computing and networking, which could transform virtually every industry and reshape modern society and politics (Arkontaky et al. 2022; Darby et al. 2022; Evans et al. 2022; Van Rijmenam 2022).

The term 'Metaverse' was coined by Neal Stephenson in his novel *Snow Crash*, published in 1992. There it was first used to refer to an all-encompassing virtual world permeating every aspect of human life, from business to pleasure, passing through self-actualisation and physical exhaustion.

In line with its disruptive potential, the Metaverse features no consensus definition or consistent description, which means that industry leaders often adapt the term to serve their own respective worldviews and/or the expertise of their specific companies. Once more, although a working definition of the Metaverse can be useful, ultimately, rather than asking what it is, we should be primarily concerned with finding out how it functions, and in particular, how it could function in the case of preserving cultural heritage and endangered languages such as Ladino.

As far as I am concerned, the most lucid and comprehensive characterisation of the Metaverse has been offered by Matthew Ball in his 2022 book *The Metaverse: And How It Will Revolutionize Everything* (notice how already in the title, the *what* of the Metaverse is intractably linked to the *how* it will change something else). Ball characterises the Metaverse in these terms:

> a massively scaled and interoperable network of real-time rendered 3D virtual worlds that can be experienced synchronously and persistently by an effectively unlimited number of users with an individual sense of presence,

> and with continuity of data, such as identity, history, entitlements, objects, communications, and payments.
>
> (580)

In Chapter 3, he further unpacks the above definition.

First, the Metaverse is an ensemble of virtual worlds, i.e., a set of environments simulated by a computer. There is a sheer abundance of virtual world models, depending on the following criteria: fidelity to the outer world (a virtual world can be a reproduction of the material world, a fictionalised version of it, and/or a wholesale fictional reality), purpose (game-like – where the main goal is to win, score, or solve – and/or non-game-like – such as educational, commercial, and/or socialising), amount of creators, professionalism (i.e., whether computer-generated simulations are carried out by professionals or amateurs), persistence (i.e., the extent to which what happens inside them is permanent), and governance model (centralised, reliant on self-governance, and/or autonomously operated).

Second, the above-characterised virtual worlds are rendered in 3D, which means that their featured 3D objects and environments are computer-generated. Real-time rendering allows a virtual world to react live to user-generated input, thanks to which the user(s) experience(s) a sense of aliveness. This component is key to eventually generating the feeling of 'home' that underpins Digital Home-Lands (Held 2010; Yebra López 2021c).

Third, the virtual worlds of the Metaverse work within an interoperable network, that is, they are articulated by computer systems or software that are capable of exchanging and making use of information sent from one another. This translates into the user's ability to carry their virtual content across several virtual worlds, exchanging and/or remixing them with further 'assets' (see below).

Fourth, as already implied by its etymology (from the Greek prefix 'meta-,' i.e., 'beyond,' and the stem 'verse,' referring to a universe) the Metaverse is massively scaled, i.e., it features a seemingly infinite number of virtual worlds. In turn, networks of these virtual worlds operating under a single authority and connected by a visual layer would function as 'metagalaxies.' These would be to the Metaverse what the big five technology companies (GAMAM) are to the Internet in the Web 2.0.

That the Metaverse is experienced synchronously and persistently means that all its data is read, written, synchronised and rendered permanently, thus ensuring its continuity as part of an experience of events shared by an effectively unlimited number of users at the same time and place in a way that is nonetheless unique to each of them (e.g., through their own avatars and bodily sensors). This requires every participant to enjoy a high bandwidth (i.e., capable of transmitting large volumes of data), low-latency (fast) and continuous (uninterrupted) connection to and from a server of a virtual world.

Ultimately, as surmised by Ball, "the computational, network and hardware demands of the Metaverse will be unprecedented" (772–3). Moreover, the Metaverse is likely to require novel forms of infrastructure, including overhauls to the Internet Protocol Suite (which facilitated the Web 1.0 and 2.0), and new devices and hardware. Lastly, the Metaverse will likely exacerbate the main issues that are already present online, which will become increasingly critical in the years to come, namely: free speech, data rights, data security, misinformation and radicalisation, platform power and regulation, abuse, and user satisfaction.

What Would Sepharad Look Like within the Metaverse?

Based on the above and taking the metaphorical nature of the Metaverse to its logical conclusion, how should we conceptualise the hypothetical and relatively likely existence of Sepharad within the Metaverse? First, Sepharad would not be *the* Metaverse, understood as "a unifying layer that sits across all individual, computer-generated 'universes' as well as the real world, just as the universe contains, by some estimates, 70 quintillion planets" (Ball 2022, 43). Second, it would not even be a subset of it, which as mentioned above, Ball dubs a "metagalaxy." Rather, Sepharad would be a collection of virtual platforms cutting across GAMAM (e.g., *Los Ladinadores* is hosted on Facebook, which belongs to Meta; *Ladino 21* is hosted on YouTube, which is owned by Google; *Estamoz whatsapeando* is hosted on WhatsApp, which is owned by Meta). Consequently, it would be more accurate to conceptualise the nature of Sepharad within the Metaverse in terms of a meta-intergalactic star (or alternatively, a metaintracluster star or a metarogue star), i.e., a metastar that is not bound to any metagalaxy but cuts across several metagalaxies of the Metaverse, that is, the current and next generation of GAMAM sites.

Furthermore, as a meta-intergalactic star of the Metaverse, Sepharad would not just be a mere collection of present and future virtual platforms, but would also feature emergent properties, i.e., interacting components within a system that do not belong to the individual platforms themselves. As per Ball's definition of the Metaverse, paramount among these attributes would be interoperability (the ability for members of Sepharad to carry their virtual content across several virtual worlds, exchanging and/or remixing them with further assets), real-time rendering (which would allow users to react live to user-generated input, thus providing them with an enhanced sense of aliveness), and an enhanced individual sense of presence (each member would have their bodily sensors and avatars, the latter reflecting and/or performing their Sephardic ethnolinguistic identity – Yebra López 2021c).

Last but not least, the crystallisation of Sepharad as a meta-intergalactic star may or may not result in the adoption of a different governance model that no longer requires centralised control and/or ownership. The opposite is true of the main Ladino-speaking platforms in the Web 2.0: e.g., *Los Ladinadores* is managed by Aldo Sevi; *Ladino 21* is administered by myself and Alejandro Acero Ayuda; *Estamoz whatsapeando* is managed by Albert Israel. As a meta-intergalactic star, Sepharad could rely instead on self-governance and/or be autonomously operated.

Moreover, since in the words of Mark Zuckerberg, "the best way to understand the Metaverse is to experience it yourself" (cit. in Stern 2021), to make things more specific, we should imagine an average Ladino speaker spending 24 hours in the Metaverse.[8] How would that look like?

Let us take the case of the editor of the Ladino-only newspaper *El Amaneser* (see Chapter 1), Karen Sarhon, born in Istanbul on May 25, 1958, in a community of Sephardic Jews. Although Sarhon continues to live in that city, as of 2024 the number of local Ladino speakers with whom she can to interact in person has drastically decreased. In light of this fact and her desire to reconnect with other Ladino-speaking Sephardim, we could imagine her acquiring a Meta Quest 2 Advanced All-In-One VR Headset (256 GB) on Amazon for an approximate bundle price of £430.

Following a gerontechnologically[9]-accommodated briefing by a Meta representative, Sarhon would put her VR headset on and log into the Metaverse in its current work-in-progress state to get together with friends, work, learn, play, and shop. In the meantime, she would still be able to see the offline world around her by tapping on the headset. In the Metaverse, the first step would be to re-create Sarhon as an avatar, which would probably (but not necessarily) look like a realistic-enough, but also highly curated version of her offline self. Given Metaverse's currently suboptimal interoperability, Sarhon would likely have slightly different avatars for each of the metagalaxies she visits.

After customising her avatar, she would log into her first metaverse world. Given that socialising with further Ladino speakers was the rationale behind her visit to the Metaverse, Sarhon could choose an app like *AltSpace VR*, which allows users to hang out with other avatars in virtual venues for mixed-reality events and experiences.[10] There we can imagine her participating in a Ladino-themed event created by other users of Sepharad as a meta-intergalactic star on the occasion of the annual Ladino day (hitherto held in person) to reconnect with Ladino speakers who due to health reasons (e.g., reduced mobility), travel restrictions, economic hardships, and/geographical location did not have the chance to attend in person. For that purpose, she would need to slightly customise her avatar (e.g., in line with a more formal dress code).

Tickets for the event could have been acquired with a cryptocurrency exclusively used within the Sepharad meta-intergalactic star (e.g., *e-groshiko*). Sarhon's share of tokens would likely come as retribution for her main contribution to the Sepharad meta-intergalactic star, i.e., the editing and publishing of *El Amaneser*. Upon entering the event in question, she would start hearing people talk and chat, and would likely recognise a few familiar voices that in turn correspond to avatars that resemble Sarhon's real-life Ladino-speaking friends, who are hundreds of miles away at home, using a similar device to access this metaversal event.

As other users start recognising her, she could be invited to partake in VIP experiences (such as her own private table with other illustrious members of the Sephardic community) by clicking on a portal button superimposed on the event environment. Given how multisemiotic and detailed this experience would be (e.g., courtesy of high-quality, low-latency spatial audio that allows users to hear the people around them based on where they are standing, just like in offline reality), the presence of further Ladino speakers would likely feel real, potentially leading to a flow state where Sarhon would lose track of time in the offline world.

After the event, Sarhon could exit *AltSpace VR* and briefly enter a 3D web browser displayed in a giant curved virtual monitor simultaneously showing windows of her respective activities on *Estamoz whatsapeando* (Meta), *Los Ladinadores* (Meta). and *Ladino 21* (Google).[11]

Then even if other members of the *El Amaneser* editorial board do not have access to the Metaverse, Sarhon would be able to attend a work meeting with them through *Meta Horizon Workrooms*, which are Metaverse meeting rooms where participants can join a meeting as an avatar native to the Metaverse or dial into the virtual room from their computer via video call (i.e., à la Zoom, Teams Skype, and Microsoft Team). This room brings together into one technology functionalities such as a mixed-reality desk and keyboard tracking (whereby Sarhon can bring a physical desk and a compatible tracked keyboard into the virtual room with her, where she can see them sitting on the virtual meeting table in front), spatial audio (as in offline reality), hand tracking, and infinite, exportable whiteboard space. and remote desktop streaming.[12]

To decompress from the stressful meeting, Sarhon could then log into the *Wander* app (Meta), which allows her to join other *turkanos* (Sephardim from Turkey – see Chapter 1) and use the historical jumping feature to reminisce together about the many architectural changes undergone by Istanbul over the last 30 years, or to teleport as a group to Israel (no need to make *Aliyah*![13]), taking advantage of Wikipedia integration for location-based learning in Yad Vashem, The World Holocaust Remembrance Centre, in Jerusalem.

To finish off the day, Sarhon would be able to either watch *Kulüp* (see Chapter 5) alone in stereoscopic view (thanks to Oculus' Netflix app) or perhaps hanging out with other Turkish people while watching a film like *Saved by Language* (which tells the story of Moris Albahari, a Sephardic Jew from Sarajevo – Kirschen and Zaraysky 2015) through the *Social VR* movie theatre Bigscreen by selecting the Balcony environment and the Turkish public room (Bigscreen 2023).

Overall, at its worst, the Metaverse could very well exacerbate many of the modern and/or digital challenges already faced by the online Ladino-speaking community, paramount among which are cultural appropriation, socio-gerontechnological issues (such as the digital gap), virtual isolation (see Chapter 4), and the algorithms of oppression (see Chapter 5). At its best, though, it also offers a generational chance to empower Ladino speakers and their allies *qua* end users and developers, respectively (as opposed to GAMAM), increase national consciousness (via personalised avatars, shared experiences, and an enhanced sense of aliveness), and bring community members closer together (courtesy of the portability of their data and the interoperability across Ladino-speaking platforms). Lastly, some of the perceived disadvantages could turn out to be advantageous, and vice versa. For instance, the Metaverse could amplify the tension between using avatars to reveal a different, and potentially more genuine version of ourselves, on the one hand, and the need to reproduce our identity faithfully, on the other. For instance, would it be acceptable for non-Sephardic Ladino speakers like myself to choose an avatar of a Sephardic individual? (see Introduction).

At any rate, it will mean that more and more of our lives, labour, leisure, time, spending, wealth, happiness and relationships will be digitally native, i.e., they will exist online first and foremost, and only then perhaps offline, rather than being online copies of previously existing offline realities (see also Chapter 4, on how the irruption of Zoom heralded the digital-first world).

The Metaverse is both the present and the future: while most of the technology to power the Metaverse already exists, the Metaverse does not exist yet as a finalised product. This is because its arc is likely to resemble that of most consumer electronics: in the early stages, they serve as a toy for the wealthy (think of Mark Zuckerberg back in 2019, already wearing an 2019 Oculus Quest Immersive All-in-One VR Headset); then early sales enable more investments, which results in cost improvements, which means greater sales, which leads to greater production efficiency, which reduces lower prices, and so on. This is where we are right now, as illustrated by the evolution of VR headset unit sales, which has grown steadily since 2019 (Alsop 2023).

Eventually, provided this trend continues over a long-enough timeframe, mass adoption will be reached, i.e., enough members of a society or community, such as Sephardim, will have adopted this innovation to make its subsequent rate of adoption self-sustaining. This is likely to become the case for the Metaverse. When that happens, it is reasonable to infer that it will significantly and finally transform Ladino as a language that has long resisted disruption and that must evolve in sync with the times, if it is to survive (see Introduction).

Ultimately, though, none of the Metaverse's characteristics and innovations as discussed above (or their sum, for that matter) would justify conceptualising Sepharad in the Metaverse as Sepharad 5, i.e., a qualitatively different new stage in the development of Sepharad in general and Ladino in particular. Rather, the hypothetical and relatively likely existence of Sepharad as a meta-intergalatic star of the Metaverse is to be more accurately understood as a (significantly) new stage of Sepharad 4 (which one could perhaps dub 'Sepharad 4.5'). There, an increasing portion of our lives will be spent in virtual worlds, encompassing various aspects such as work, recreation, time allocation, financial resources, well-being, and social connections, becoming a parallel plane of existence for millions that unites our physical and digital economies while not replacing any of them *ex novo*.

By contrast, and as we will see below, while the (open) metaverse[14] is also featured in *The Network State* (Srinivasan 2022), the idea of a network state is much more ambitious and revolutionary, so that we could be justified in conceptualising the latter as the inaugural platform of Sepharad 5.

The Network State

Some authors have argued that whereas capitalism and techno-feudalism (see above) have a tendency to serve the market and GAMAM, respectively, at the expense of the individuals, blockchain technology allows for self-organising structures that promote growth through cooperation, which in turn empowers individuals and increases social justice (Cuende 2018; Alejandro 2021):

> Capitalism tends to do what's best for the market [and one could add with Varoufakis, techno-feudalism tends to do what's best for the digital platforms

> of GAMAM]. Maybe not what is best for all the individuals who comprise the market and, those platforms like Silicon Valley, they tend to fund projects of companies that are trying to solve very much first-world problems. How do you get your food five minutes quicker? How do you get your Uber 2 minutes faster? Whereas with blockchain technology, we have the ability to fund initiatives that will provide true social good and provide value to the most undervalued parts of humanity.
>
> (Cuende 2018)

In sum, the creation of Web 3.0 communities constitutes a case in point of the potential of blockchain technology to empower individuals and increase social justice. These communities are commonly referred to as 'DAOs,' which stands for 'Decentralised Autonomous Organisations,' i.e., entity structures where governance is decentralised and distributed across token holders who participate in management and decision-making. A particular subset of DAOs lends itself to the preservation of cultural heritage in general and endangered languages in particular: network states.

Network states are Web 3.0 communities that share with DAOs key aspects such as decentralised governance and a bottom-up management approach. Nevertheless, the network state is more helpful than most blockchain-powered DAOs, because it implies implementing blockchain technology to decentralise the functions of the nation-state *enroute* to the accomplishment of a moral imperative related to social justice, namely: economics through cryptocurrencies; law through smart contracts (see above); governance, just like DAOs; and physical territories and immigration through blockchain cities. In the network state model, the crypto economy is a tool for the furthering of a moral principle, rather than the other way around (as in most DAOs), which makes network states particularly amenable to the preservation of cultural heritage, including endangered languages (Alejandro 2021; Jur Team 2022):

> if a tech company is about technological innovation first, and company culture second, a startup society is the reverse. It's about community culture first, and technological innovation second. And while innovating on technology means forecasting the future, innovating on culture means probing the past.
>
> (Srinivasan 2022, 19)

In early 2021, Balaji Srinivasan released his manifesto *How to Start a New Country*, later on expanded into the volume *The Network State: How to Start a New Country* (2022). In his book, Srinivasan characterises the network state as a digital-first, land-last iteration of the post-Westphalian nation-state requiring diplomatic recognition from the latter: "A network state is a highly aligned online community with a capacity for collective action that crowdfunds territory around the world and eventually gains diplomatic recognition from pre-existing states" (9). He then proceeds to offer a much more nuanced definition whose discussion constitutes the bulk of this section, namely:

> a social network with a moral innovation, a sense of national consciousness, a recognized founder, a capacity for collective action, an in-person level of civility, an integrated cryptocurrency, a consensual government limited by a social smart contract, an archipelago of crowdfunded physical territories, a virtual capital, and an on-chain census that proves a large enough population, income, and real estate footprint to attain a measure of diplomatic recognition.
>
> (9)

In its most embryonic form, a network state is just a startup society, or in more simple terms, an online community (albeit different than those that populate the Web 2.0 – see below). When that digital community acquires the capacity for of collective action, it becomes a network union. When that network union manifests that collective action in the material world, it becomes a network archipelago. Eventually, when that network archipelago obtains diplomatic recognition from an existing government, it becomes a network state. In particular, Srinivasan lists and elaborates on 12 necessary and (collectively) sufficient conditions of network states.

In what follows, I will break down the various stages that lead to a network state as the final form of a social network, while unpacking each of the aspects that characterise such state (including the role played by the Metaverse).

Startup Society Stage

A Social Network

The network state is an online-first nation, which implies that the core organising principle is not geographic (as in land-first nation-states) but social. However, this social network is not the traditional one from the Web 2.0 (e.g., Facebook, X), but a 1-network. A 1-network is a social network constructed on the basis of one coherent community, rather than many different ones hosted under the same corporation, such as Meta or X. It is premised upon an opt-in model (that is, every member has applied to join), which is characterised by selective admission and revocable account privileges (in case of undesirable behaviour).

A Moral Innovation

Every member of the social network or startup society gathers around what Srinivasan calls 'One Commandment,' namely, they think a given principle X is good, even though the rest of the world thinks it is bad, or vice versa (social justice) (136–44); hence why the network state is a proposition nation. This proposition infuses the network with a sense of purpose and attracts people from the outside world, even when they do not necessarily agree. Srinivasan argues that the moral innovation plays a key role in a potential network state, not only because in theory and practice "missionary societies perform better than mercenary ones" (101), but also because it is what makes the community ideologically disruptive in an increasingly profit-driven environment:

> Without a genuine moral critique of the establishment, without an ideological root network supported by history, your new society is at best a fancy Starbucks lounge, a gated community that differs only in its amenities, a snack to be eaten by the establishment at its leisure, a soulless nullity with no direction save consumerism.
>
> (28)

A Sense of National Consciousness

A feeling of belongingness permeates the whole community, whereby each of its members feels as if they share the same values and culture. This is stronger than the same of aliveness that permeates the Metaverse experience (see above) and similar to the feeling of 'home' that underpins Digital Home-Lands (Held 2010; Yebra López 2021c).

A Recognised Founder

The network state, particularly in the early stages, requires a leader that those who consent and buy in can listen to and follow while simultaneously being allowed to exit peacefully, including for the purpose of founding and scaling a new (perhaps even competing) startup society into a network state.

A Capacity for Collective Action

This is premised on a combination of collective purpose (which helps unify the nation, thus strengthening its national consciousness) and the ability to act upon it. A digital community capable of collective action towards their purpose (as measured through team dashboards, rather than individual scores for likes and followers on, e.g., X or Facebook) becomes effectively a network union.

Network Union Stage

An In-Person Level of Civility

While high trust comes from alignment with a collective purpose and a strong sense of national consciousness, it also requires in-person levels of civility *vis-à-vis* community fellow members, both online and offline.

An Integrated Cryptocurrency

A native digital currency using encryption algorithms manages every bureaucratic process across the borders of legacy nation-states, including smart contracts, internal digital assets, public national statistics, web 3 citizen logins, property registries, and birth and marriage certificates.

An Archipelago of Crowdfunded Physical Territories

This is the physical materialisation of the network union, which takes place by crowdfunding physical real estate (including office space, homes, shops) scattered across the globe, rather than in contiguous territories. The clustering together of crowdfunded physical territories via the Internet crystallises into a network archipelago.

Network Archipelago Stage

A Consensual Government Limited by a Social Smart Contract

At this stage, the organic people of the network nation set up laws that reflect their moral consensus concerning which aspects are encouraged and discouraged, acceptable and optional, mandatory and forbidden. Regardless of the voting system and election method, what legitimises this government are the consent of the governed, a specific way of measuring such consent (e.g., on-chain evidence of a contract) and the right to leave if that (contractual) agreement is no longer congenial. According to Srinivasan, users can be said to have consented to be governed by a startup society if they have signed a social smart contract that grants a system administrator limited privileges over the digital life of those users in return for admission to the startup society. Thus, the notion of "social smart contract" (which effectively transforms government into digital government) combines Rousseau's 'social contract' with blockchain's 'smart contract' (225). The former is premised upon the axiom that freedom can only be experienced in a civil society ensuring the rights and well-being of its citizens (i.e., through law as contractually encoded), whereas the latter refers to agreements stored on a blockchain whose execution is automated (i.e., certain and instantaneous), provided that the predetermined conditions are met. As an example, Srinivasan offers the use of blockchain credentials, such as the Ethereum Name System (ENS), to log in to both a startup society community within the "open metaverse" (see above), and the offline territory owned by the same startup society. Conversely, he also mentions having our deposits frozen and our ENS locked out of all physical access for a time period as a punishment for our misbehaviour in the digital (and eventually, physical) sphere constituted exclusively by those who have opted in by signing a social smart contract with their ENS names.

A Virtual Capital

Although its members are physically distributed, a network archipelago assembles in one place digitally. This cloud assembly point could initially be a Telegram group, or a Discord channel, but according to Srinivasan, eventually it will evolve into a private network of the open metaverse. This implies a VR-*cum*-AR environment that allows members to see offline reality digitally, as well as to perceive digital reality in the offline world. A Web 3.0 login limited to network members serves as an access gate to the network's virtual capital.

Thus, Srinivasan claims, the (open) metaverse constitutes the last, ineluctable iteration of one of the twelve necessary and collectively sufficient conditions of network states, further affecting additional ones, such as consensual governance as mediated by a social smart contract.[15]

An On-Chain Census Demonstrating a Large Population, Income, and Real Estate Footprint

A distributed census is required which can be conducted in real time. It establishes the network's population, income, and real estate via on-chain data and incorporates that census to an all-encompassing site that allows people to track in real time the number of network members, their on-chain GDP, and how much real estate they own.

Attaining Diplomatic Recognition

The network archipelago can once again resort to on-chain data to generate a publicly verifiable census of population income and real estate to seek diplomatic recognition by a pre-existing government, whereupon the network archipelago becomes a network state.

Network State Stage

As of May 2024, Srinivasan's The Network State Dashboard, which tracks startup societies around the world, features 95 instances, subdivided into the following development stages: not a community (7), pre-launch (11), physical society (23), and digital society (54).

Only a minority are focused on culture, including the pan-African digital nation Afropolitan (which comprises both Africa and the African diaspora), a borderless society for digital nomads known as 'Plumia,' and a global community known as the 'Panarmenian Network State.'

Concerning Afropolitan, the notion of afropolitanism revolves around human mobility to, from, and across Africa,[16] which is a lived experience that lends itself to the accelerated development of creative and critical thinking in local and global settings. In their manifesto, the authors define the Afropolitan Network as a "Curator of Black and African (…) Talent (recruit, partner up), Culture (art, media, fashion), Capital (investment, DAOs), Information (newsletter, blog, Twitter) [and] Experiences (events, curated offerings)," stressing the diasporic component as a cornerstone of the project.

> With the advent of cryptocurrency, the next Facebook will not be a social network with a passive online community but rather a full-blown digital republic coordinated by its native currency and a unifying mission. What, then, could Afropolitan be? If it were a country, the African diaspora would

> be the 10th largest globally (~150 Million). The diaspora is our North Star (Afropolitan).

Similarly, Plumia insists upon a declining trust in institutions and nation-states, the importance of global mobility rights, and the relevance of thinking across local and global lines as rationales behind its creation:

> Plumia is an umbrella project for SafetyWing's[17] efforts to increase the global mobility rights of people everywhere (…) It's also the name of the internet country we're building through our work (…) We believe that connecting local communities with global solutions is the best way to establish foundational infrastructures for modern life.
>
> (Plumia)

Unlike The Afropolitan Network, though, Plumia memberships do not (yet) imply citizenship (featuring next-generation passports).

Lastly, the Panarmenian Network State focuses on uniting its members globally so as to revitalise the Armenian civilisation, ultimately facilitating a transition towards a harmonious world by uniting similar civilisations, cultures, and peoples worldwide (in the case at hand, Sephardim), leveraging spiritual, intellectual, and material resources (in our case, the Ladino language).

In sum, notwithstanding the embryonic development of the above projects, they offer concrete proof that there are already instances of network states à la Srinivasan, a minority of which revolve around cultural heritage preservation, including diasporic communities.

What Would a Sephardic Network State (SNS) Look Like?

In light of the above-discussed conceptualisation of the network state by Srinivasan, we could speculate about the forthcoming existence of a SNS, understood as an all-encompassing network state where the (open) metaverse would be a necessary condition, but not a sufficient one.

Not unlike the example of Afropolitan, the creation of a SNS would be prompted by the realisation that "the nation-state experiment has failed for Black [Sephardi, in our case] people worldwide." Overall, we could distinguish between five stages of the nation-state, with Sephardim in general and Ladino in particular, having been invariably at the receiving end of discrimination.

From the Creation of the Shtetl to the Dynastic Union of Spain as a Proto-Nation-State (13th–15th Centuries)

Shtetlekh [singular '*shtetl*'] were small Jewish towns or villages in Eastern Europe whose origin dates back to the 13th century. As the Yiddish term suggests, the population of these islands within the surrounding non-Jewish populace was predominantly Ashkenazi.[18] No equivalent exists in the case of Sephardim, which means that Ladino speakers never had a territory or group of territories for themselves, jumping instead from one non-Ladino-speaking land to another. The first variations of Ladino began with the interaction of Jews with the local population of Hispania. Their expulsion from the Iberian Peninsula in the late 15th century, which would give way to the gradual crystallisation of Ladino as a Mediterranean *lingua franca* among Sephardim, is a direct result of the dynastic unification of Spain by the Catholic Kings in 1492 (Bunis 2018).

The Peace of Westphalia (1648)

With the end of the Thirty Years War in 1648, courtesy of the Peace of Westphalia, a new model of international legal order and governance came into play which would have profound sociolinguistic effects. According to that model, which posits a tripartite correspondence between nation, state, and language, citizens of a given sovereign nation-state are monolingual, and any other linguistic variations pose a threat to its social cohesion (Gobbo 2017; Carlsson 2021). This ideological model implies either the erasure of Ladino as a national language (since it is not the official language of any state) or its reduction to a sub-state, minoritised language/dialect.

The Congress of Vienna (1814–15)

This assembly reorganised Europe after the Napoleonic Wars, focusing on the balance of power to prevent further conflict. This process emphasised states at the expense of nations, largely ignoring the idea of nationality (i.e., the wish of inhabitants to come together as a community), and thus had a negative impact on the (potential) recognition of Ladino speakers as a legitimate nation with a language.

The Franco-Prussian War (1870)

This conflict hastened nation-state building in Europe and beyond, leading to the creation of the German empire and deeper involvement in state-wide education, with France implementing a free, mandatory, and secular one for children. Consequently, this process strengthened the equivalence between nation, state, and language while assimilating minoritised communities into major European languages. In 1860 when the troops of Leopoldo O'Donnell entered Tetouan (Morocco), they realised local Jews were speaking a language similar to Spanish. This (re)encounter paved the way for the re-Hispanicisation of Ladino (Yebra López 2021e). In parallel, since 1860, the *Alliance Israélite Universelle* had a profound Westernising effect among Sephardim in the Ottoman Empire and Morocco. Their schooling in French and/or Spanish meant at best the Westernisation of Ladino and at worst, its intergenerational loss.

The Creation of the Middle East (1910s–40s)

The modern boundaries of the Middle East emerged from World War I. In 1916 the French and the British signed the Sykes-Picot agreement, which effectively divided the Middle East into difference spheres of influence for their respective countries. It was then superseded by a mandate system of French and British control approved by the League of Nations. In particular, and as fictionalised in *The Beauty Queen of Jerusalem* (2021) (see Chapter 5), the Mandate for Palestine put the territories of Palestine and Transjordan under British control after they were conceded by the Ottoman Empire in 1918. The preamble and several articles addressed the issue of a national home for the Jewish people in Palestine. Shortly after the Holocaust had decimated the Jewish population in Europe, including Sephardim (in cities like Thessaloniki, over 90% of Jews were killed), the State of Israel was founded (1948), following the 1947–49 Palestinian War. Sephardic Jews could now claim a land, albeit one shared with other Jews and where modern Hebrew was gradually implemented at the expense of Yiddish and Ladino, turning the latter into minoritised languages of the country.

Decolonisation of Asia and Africa (1945–60s)

Between 1945 and 1960, more than 30 new states in Asia and Africa obtained independence from their European colonial rulers. This process redefined the geopolitical landscape, showing that Westernisation could (and should) be reverted. Instead, it emphasised the principles of self-governance, decolonisation, and national self-determination, for which the adoption of (a) new national language(s) is critical. Although it does not have official status in any country, Ladino has been acknowledged as a minoritised language in Israel, Bosnia and Herzegovina, France, and Turkey (Cruz Çilli 2021).

In sum, whether we talk about Spain, Portugal, France, Bosnia, Turkey, Israel, or the United States, to name the main countries featuring Ladino speakers, historically the coexistence of Sephardim with their host society has resulted in colonisation, discrimination, poverty, genocide, ethnic strife, and/or stigma, to which one needs to add, of course, the gradual decline of Ladino in favour of national languages (be it Castilian/Spanish, Portuguese, Serbian/Bosnian, Turkish, Hebrew, or English). It is this historical record that justifies (and arguably, makes necessary) the voluntary creation of a network state where Sephardim and their allies can preserve their language and community of speakers as less an outlandish philosophical exercise than the most logical solution to an ethnolinguistic problem that remains unsolved after centuries of different nation-state-language setups.

In turn, this process participates in the simultaneous development of further network states as part of "the gradual fragmentation of nation-states by experimental, more efficient, and more accepted models of governance – as measured by the very citizens of these future republics" (Alejandro 2021). This is particularly true of diasporic communities, where as acknowledged by Srinivasan and further instantiated by the Panarmenian Network State (see above), geodesic proximity trumps geographical proximity.

> When the network identity is more salient than the neighbor relationship, it challenges the very premise of the Westphalian state, which is that (a) people who live geographically near each other share values and (b) therefore laws

> should be based on geographic boundaries. The alternative is that only people who are geodesically near each other in the social network share values, and therefore the laws that govern them should be based on network boundaries.
> (2022, 52)

Moreover, in his book Srinivasan explicitly alludes to social networks revolving around the Jewish diaspora. He describes them as a combination between the Leviathans of God and Network, (as opposed to the State),[19] as in the case of the pre-Israel diaspora (or the current Sephardic one, in our case), or else a mixture of God, Network and the State, as in the post-Israel Jewish diaspora (in the case at hand, could a Sephardic-only diaspora claim a State on its own?)

> When you have three Leviathans (God, State, Network) that keep struggling with each other, they won't remain pure forms. You'll see people remix them together to create new kinds of social orders, new hybrids, new syntheses in the Hegelian sense (…) For example
> – God/Network: this might be something like the Mormons, or the Jewish diaspora before Israel, or any religious diaspora connected by some kind of communications network. It's a community of shared values connected by a communications network without a formal state.
> – God/State/Network: this is something like the Jewish diaspora after Israel. Our One Commandment model also draws on this, as a startup society can be based on a traditional religion or on a moral imperative that's on par with many religious practices, like veganism.
> (2022, 59)

Our discussion so far raises a two-fold critical question: what would a SNS look like, and how could Web 3.0 technology optimise it? Let us elucidate it step by step:

Step 1: The Sephardic Startup Society

At the very beginning, one or more members of the current Ladino-speaking global community, particularly a subset of well-respected activists with true and trusted leadership skills, of which at the very least one should have some sort of technological expertise vision for the stages to come, would launch a Sephardic startup society, i.e., an online community. To that purpose, the leaders would write a manifesto premised upon a particular moral innovation and approve it by consensus. This 'One Commandment' could read something like this: "preserving Ladino is good for its community of speakers (Sephardim and their allies) and the world at large." This would make the new online community a 1-network, i.e., a social network whose coherence is predicated on the collective adoption of a moral innovation that effectively turns the community into a missionary society (rather than a mercenary one), strengthening an already pre-existing national consciousness. Additionally, preserving Ladino would be the collective purpose upon which to make contingent the ability of this online community to become a network union.

The leaders of this new digital community would then start an educational and recruitment campaign whereby they would educate potential followers as to where they are all going, how and why (think of modern-day Herzls), specify their desired etiquette, and request an expression of interest from anybody willing to join the community. These actions would effectively set in motion an opt-in process (that is, every member needs to apply to join), characterised by selective admission and revocable account privileges (in case of undesirable behaviour). This campaign could have a shot at succeeding if carried out via a simple platform following a one-to-many mode of interaction, such as a closed Telegram group used to disseminate the manifesto, explaining its concepts as well as posting updates, events, videos, invitations, etc.

When and if that campaign has led to the recruitment of a critical mass, the next stage would be to take the collective purpose of the digital community (i.e., the preservation of Ladino for its speakers and the world at large) and break it down into actionable goals, such as creating a unified digital archive of Ladino by the end of 2030, or making every Ladino app open access by 2027. A list of goals would be created and approved by consensus by members of the community. Then the accomplishment of these goals would be measured through team dashboards. When and if the global digital community proves successful at accomplishing the goals in question, it would effectively become a network union.

Step 2: The Sephardic Network Union

The organisation of periodic offline activities (e.g., excursions to Sephardic landmarks, academic conferences in Ladino-speaking areas) where members of this digital community can meet and bond (which already exists as part of current Web 2.0 platforms such as *Ladinokomunita*) would be highly instrumental to consolidating a high-trust society based on high in-person levels of civility among community members.

Accomplishing this high level of trust would pave the way for the next step, which would be the adoption of a native digital currency using encryption algorithms (let us call it the *e-sefardito*, or the *e-groshiko* – see above), which would in turn be used to manage every bureaucratic process (smart contracts, so-called 'digital assets,'[20] public national statistics, Web 3.0 citizen logins, property registries, birth and marriage certificates) across the boundaries of different nation-states. Moreover, citizen logins, which could take place through blockchain credentials, such as our ENS, would grant members of the Sephardic network union access to the so-called 'open metaverse' administered by that startup society.

Given that the above step is unprecedented, premised on the implementation of the Metaverse/Web 3.0 technology, and conducive to a form of (digital) citizenship independent from legacy nation-states (thus rendering obsolete so-called Sephardic 'laws of return' from legacy states such as the Spanish or the Portuguese), the adoption of a native digital currency by global community of Ladino speakers would represent a critical leap forward. As such, it would require the previous consolidation of a high level of trust and a comprehensive educational and recruitment campaign. Conversely, unless this step is made, the potential of the SNS will be reduced to a mere aggregation of Ladino-speaking platforms from the Web 1.0-to-2.0 environment.

The next move would be to crowdfund physical real estate (office space, homes, shops, perhaps even traditional Sephardic spaces, such as synagogues) across the globe, rather than just in contiguous territories. The clustering of these crowd-funded physical territories via the Internet would effectively turn the Sephardic network union into a network archipelago, thus spearheading a unique process of reverse diaspora.

Step 3: The Sephardic Network Archipelago

The Sephardic network archipelago would then set up laws reflective of the nation, including a voting system and election method conducive to the formation of a consensual government (whose degree of consensus could and would be measured via specific methods, such as on-chain evidence of a contract), as well as the right to leave should the agreement no longer be congenial. At this point, the original leaders of the Sephardic startup society could be replaced by new system administrators, depending on the results of the elections. Whether novel or not, by virtue of a social smart contract, these administrators would have limited privileges over the digital life of the Sephardic network archipelago members in exchange for admission to the startup society. Once again, this step would be unprecedented within the global Ladino-speaking community, effectively introducing two disruptive innovations, namely: removing the governance of Ladino speakers from the hands of legacy nation-states (e.g., Israel, Spain, Portugal), and transforming government into a digital one for the first time in Sephardic history.

At this point, blockchain credentials, such as their ENS, would allow Sephardic network archipelago members to log in to both the so-called 'open metaverse' administered by that startup society and the offline territory owned by the network archipelago. Or, conversely, to have their deposits frozen and their ENS locked out of all physical access for a time period as a punishment for misbehaviour in the digital (and eventually, physical) sphere constituted exclusively by those who have opted in by signing a social smart contract with their ENS names.

At this stage, the virtual capital of the potential SNS would have already evolved from the initial closed Telegram group (or equivalent) that catalysed Sepharad as a startup society to a private network of the open metaverse. This would probably imply a VR-*cum*-AR environment allowing members of the Sephardic Network Archipelago to see offline reality digitally as well as to perceive digital reality in the offline world. Combined VR and AR technology could virtually reconstruct no longer existing places that are dear to the Sephardic imagery (e.g., synagogues), dramatically increasing their members' sense of aliveness and national consciousness, which in turn would decisively contribute to their own well-being. As discussed by Ghil'ad Zuckermann in *Revivalistics* (2020), there is a robust positive correlation between cultural preservation and well-being: "(…) language revival has an empowering effect on the community wellbeing and mental health of the people involved in such projects. Participants develop a better appreciation of and sense of connection with their cultural heritage" (267).

The penultimate step would be the consolidation of a distributed, on-chain census proving a large population, income, and real estate footprint, as well as its subsequent incorporation into an all-encompassing site allowing others to track these statistics in real time. Last but not least, this publicly verifiable census would be submitted to legacy nation-states for diplomatic recognition. Of paramount importance for the legitimisation of the incipient SNS would be the diplomatic recognition of legacy nation-states to which the history of Sephardim is intractably linked, including Spain, Portugal, Greece, Turkey, France, Israel, and the United States. When and if diplomatic recognition of the Sephardic network archipelago reaches a critical mass of legacy nation-states, the SNS would be officially born.

Step 4: The Sephardic Network State

Unlike in the case of the Sephardic meta-intergalactic star of the Metaverse, to the extent that a SNS would also feature its own form of citizenship, governance, and reverse diaspora via mixed reality, as far as I am concerned, one would be completely justified in conceptualising it as the inaugural milestone of Sepharad 5 understood as a qualitatively different new stage in the (online) articulation of the Sephardic diaspora in general and the evolution of Ladino as a cyber-(post)vernacular in particular.

Drawing upon Yiddish and Hebrew Programs to Assimilate Ladino Speakers into Web 3.0

The hypothetical mass adoption of Web 3.0 technological developments such as the Metaverse and the SNS will very likely require a great deal of gerontechnological accommodation, which in turn will be contingent on reversed intergenerational transmission (i.e., from the younger to the older generation). In this sense, young Ladino speakers and activists could model their educational efforts after a number of programs used to advance Yiddish and Hebrew where younger speakers instruct older ones, focusing their attention on what is the Metaverse/network state, and how it can be used for the purpose of keeping Ladino alive.

First, Yiddish activists have successfully implemented the Master-Apprentice Language Learning Program (Hinton 2002). This initiative is typically conducted through summer programs, does not require instructors to have extensive linguistic training (which, in our case, would fit the instructors' young age), features mini-immersion settings (which the Metaverse could help catalyse), and has been proved to be particularly effective when teaching adults (which again, would suit the old age of Ladino students) (Meissner 2016).

Second, the Ulpan system has been productive to teach Hebrew to new immigrants to Israel ever since the foundation of the State (Ministry of Aliyah and Integration 2021).[21] Ladino activists could draw upon this model to inspire more proficient users (on average, the younger generation) to assist less proficient ones (on average, elderly adults) in their assimilation into the Metaverse and/or the SNS. This initiative would further reduce an already narrowing digital gap whose mitigation is critical to the intergenerational transmission of Ladino (Yebra López 2021c, 106 and ff.).

Conclusion

In this chapter I have discussed the extent to which the current transition to the Web 3.0, understood as a new version of the Internet characterised by decentralisation and the use of blockchain, may or may not crystallise into a new stage in the (online) articulation of the Sephardic diaspora in general and the evolution of Ladino as a cyber-(post)vernacular in particular, which I have dubbed 'Sepharad 5.'

First, I have concluded that as shown by the gradual tokenisation of cultural heritage and language preservation through projects such as B.U.I.L.D., OBTranslate and Global Heritage Fund, blockchain technology features remarkable potential for a more decentralised, transparent, updatable, and permanent storage of cultural heritage (including endangered languages such as Ladino). This promise includes the ability to provide assurance about historical data and attract new investment through cryptocurrency. On the one hand, in the case of Ladino, implementation of blockchain technology is still in its infancy and will require a great deal of intergenerational transmission from a minority of younger speakers to a majority of elderly ones. On the other hand, we are already witnessing the first steps in this direction through the recent launching of crypto currency as payment rail and the development and popularisation on Web 2.0 Ladino-speaking platforms featuring machine learning applications of AI.

Second, I have discussed the Metaverse as a particularly appealing use case of the Web 3.0 technology concerning the preservation of Ladino and its community of speakers, both because of its disruptive potential (including its immersive aspect) and the vast amount of investment it has been able to attract to date. Drawing upon Ball's understanding of it (2022), I have characterised the Metaverse as an interoperable network of virtual worlds within which Sepharad would be a specific subset, i.e., a meta-intergalactic star. In particular, Sepharad would be a collection of Ladino-speaking virtual platforms cutting across those already hosted and/or owned by GAMAM, but also featuring emergent properties such as interoperability, real-time rendering, and an enhanced individual sense of presence, and perhaps even a different model of governance (namely, a decentralised, autonomous one). After supplementing my analysis by walking the reader through a thought experiment consisting of 24 hours in Sepharad using metaversal devices and apps that are already available in the market, I have concluded that on the one hand, a metaversal Sepharad could exacerbate the challenges already undergone by the global online Ladino-speaking community (algorithms of oppression, virtual isolation, cultural appropriation). On the other hand, though, it is far more likely to empower Ladino speakers and their allies by granting them more autonomy as users and developers, increasing national consciousness, and bringing them together in a more immersive fashion. Notwithstanding the above, I have also observed that none of these characteristics and innovations would amount to a qualitative leap in the (online) articulation of the Sephardic diaspora in general and the evolution of Ladino as a cyber-(post)vernacular in particular, only to a significant innovation within Sepharad 4 which one could consequently dub 'Sepharad 4.5.'

Third, I have discussed the hypothetical creation of Sepharad as a network state (SNS) comprising (yet going significantly beyond) the (open) metaverse. Drawing upon Srinivasan's work, I have observed that network states constitute a subset of Web 3.0 communities that manage to decentralise the functions of the nation-state (economics, through cryptocurrencies; law, through smart contracts; governance through DAOs; physical territories and immigration, through blockchain cities) to implement a moral imperative related to social justice. I have further argued that network states are instrumental for the preservation of Ladino and its community of speakers because the nation-state experiment has consistently failed Sephardim for over 500 years, falling ever short of delivering a land Sephardim can claim as their own and where Ladino can be the national language, instead subjecting Ladino speakers and their language to various degrees of colonisation, discrimination, poverty, genocide, ethnic strife, and/or stigma. In light of this humiliating record, creating, developing, and implementing a SNS is not only an appealing possibility, but a pressing necessity.

Then I have discussed what the SNS would require and look like, including its inception as a startup society, the subsequent adoption of its own native digital currency, new forms of governance and citizenship, and the acquisition of real estate, effectively leading to a partial form of reverse diaspora via mixed reality, and eventually, obtaining diplomatic recognition by legacy nation-states emblematic of the Sephardic diaspora. Lastly, I have concluded that all the above aspects would justify speaking of the SNS as a qualitative leap in the (online) articulation of the Sephardic diaspora in general and the evolution of Ladino as a cyber-(post)vernacular in particular, which consequently we would be fully justified to call 'Sepharad 5.'

Ultimately, though, neither the Metaverse nor the network state will arrive overnight or feature an obvious start date (let alone their respective Sephardic versions). Rather, like many other previous technological revolutions, including the Internet itself, they have been long predicted, even though they lack(ed) concrete instantiation, and will exist long before the circumstances are ripe for them to experience mass adoption, perhaps somewhen around 2030, depending on various factors such as the rate of technological advancement, government regulations, and the level of acceptance and understanding among the general public. In this sense, I have stressed the importance for the younger generation of Ladino activists to draw upon the successes of the Ulpan program, which has reclaimed Hebrew and the Master-Apprentice program, which has reinvigorated Yiddisha. They should educate the older generation of Ladino speakers on the use of Web 3.0 developments (particularly the Metaverse and the SNS) to further the prospects of Ladino while continuing to reduce the digital gap.

Moreover, even if none of the maximalist aspirations discussed above apropos a new iteration of Sepharad 4 as Sepharad 4.5 (within the Metaverse) and Sepharad 5 (as a network state), respectively, were to materialise, we are still (very) likely to continue to witness the current servicing of Web 2.0 communities with Web 3.0 products. Sepharad 4 should be no exception to this trend, from the creation of virtual worlds reproducing past Sephardic landmarks (or their fictionalisation) to the launching of NFTs for Ladino speakers that grant recipients access to and ownership of a specific percentage of the platform and/or citizenship within it, and content creators direct control over their content and unmediated access to their audience.

In the meantime, and as of 2024, I have noted that the partial innovations and developments that are most likely to emerge and expand as part of the Web 3.0 as relates to Sepharad 4 are plentiful.

First, machine learning applications of AI. Existing examples include the Yiddish course on Duolingo (whose AI system, known as 'Birdbrain,' tracks users, making individualised prediction about their learning journey) (see Chapter 3), *Ambezandomos Muestra Lingua* (a Ladino course I created in 2018 for AI-assisted language-learning app Memrise, which deploys a SRS algorithm), and LadinoType (Berman 2006), which was relaunched in 2022 as a smart transliteration engine.

Second, the use of crypto currency as payment rail. This service already exists on *Ladino 21*, where students can pay in bitcoin and Ether, in addition to any traditional fiat currency.

Third, the deployment of Oculus Quest or equivalent products for an enhanced experience of Ladino-speaking content stored in Web 2.0 platforms. This would be something similar to the thought experiment described in the section apropos Sepharad in the Metaverse, minus interoperability.

Lastly, a more holistic development would consist in the updatable storage of Sepharad 4 on the blockchain as a distributed ledger containing the cultural heritage of Sephardim, including their language. As per Srinivasan's own admission, this form of public record would be disruptively innovative:

> in theory you could eventually download the public blockchain of a network state to replay the entire cryptographically verified history of a community. That's the future of public records, a concept that is to the paper-based system of the legacy state what paper records were to oral records.
>
> (2022, 38)

Unlike what the above quote seems to suggest, though, it is worth noting that Sepharad 4 would not need to evolve into an SNS (Sepharad 5) for the storage and download of that public record to take place.

At any rate, I have stressed that any of the hypothetical developments described in this chapter apropos the development of Web 3.0 platforms to assist the digital revitalisation of Ladino, would require a significant pedagogical effort apropos the technicalities of it from the younger generation (a minority among Ladino speakers) to the older one (an authoritative majority). On the other hand, such improvement is likely to arrive (at least partially) in the short term, as the Ladino-speaking communities of the Web 2.0 become less siloed and their participants become more aware of the need to collaborate to preserve Ladino in particular and the Sephardic cultural heritage at large. To say it with Srinivasan, "With the internet [i.e., the Web 3.0, as opposed to the 2.0], we can digitally sew these disjoint enclaves together into a new kind of polity (…)" (2022, 18).

Notes

1 In this sense, Daniel Gross has gone as far as remarking that "2020 will be seen by future historians as the year when the internet age truly began" (Srinivasan 2022, 171).

2 The replacement of markets with these privately owned platforms that offer "free" services where users (that is, their data) are the product in addition to major content providers, has led some authors to speak of a new economic mode known as 'techno-feudalism' (Varoufakis 2021; Žižek 2022): "When, due to the crucial role of the 'general intellect' (social knowledge and cooperation) in the creation of wealth, forms of wealth are more and more out of all proportion to the direct labor time spent on their production, the result is not, as Marx expected, the self-dissolution of capitalism, but the gradual transformation of the profit generated by the exploitation of labor into rent appropriated by the privatization of the 'general intellect' and other commons. Let us take the case of Bill Gates: how did he become one of the richest men in the world? Because Microsoft imposed itself as an almost universal standard (almost) monopolising the field a kind of direct embodiment of the 'general intellect.' Things are similar with Jeff Bezos and Amazon, with Apple, Facebook, etc, etc. – in all these cases, commons themselves – the platforms (spaces of our social exchange and interaction) – are privatized, which puts us, their users, into the position of serfs paying a rent to the owner of a common as our feudal master" (Žižek 2022, 20–1).

3 For a more detailed breakdown of the technical aspects of blockchain technology, see Lewis (2018).

4 More on Bitcoin in Champagne (2014).

5 Shortly after the emergence of Bitcoin, two of its early users, Vitalik Buterin and Gavin Wood, began to develop a new blockchain by the name of 'Ethereum.' Like Bitcoin, Ethereum is a decentralised mining network that pays those operating it through its own cryptocurrency (Ether, in this case). Unlike Bitcoin, Ethereum is also a programming language (Solidity) that allows developers to create their own decentralised, permissionless, and trustless apps (dapps), through which they can also issue their own cryptocurrency-like tokens to contributors. For an in-depth analysis of blockchain from a financial perspective, see Tapscott and Tapscott (2016) and Burniske and Tatar (2017).

6 For a discussion of the 'Talknological Revolution,' see Zuckermann (2020); see also

7 As explained in previous chapters, this shift from language(s) (as an *in vitro* object) to languaging (the '-ing' prefix making reference to the use of language as a social and dynamic activity) goes against the traditional (and colonial) understanding of languages as reified, self-contained, autonomous entities that can then be dissected by armchair linguists, and it is at the heart of Revivalistics as a grassroots endeavour (Zuckermann 2020, 207–8; see also Introduction and Chapter 2).

8 For a similar experiment, see Stern (2021). For a more protracted experiment (100 days in the Metaverse), see Trahan (2022).

9 From 'gerontechnology,' which is a professional field combining the study of all aspects of aging (gerontology) and that of technology. It revolves around creating technological solutions to facilitate the participation of older adults with varying degrees of health, comfort, and safety issues (International Society for Gerontechnology 2023). Given that

the vast majority of Ladino speakers are 60+ years old, this field is particularly important in the case of Sephardim and Ladino. For a guide to the Metaverse for older adults, see Eisenberg (2022).

10 See Stern (2021).

11 Stern (2021).

12 Meta Quest blog 2021.

13 Immigration of Jews to Israel (see Chapter 2).

14 As well shall see below, whenever Balaji Srinivasan refers to the Metaverse (2022), he does not envisage it as run by corporations (as it is the case of the Web 2.0 as ruled by GAMAM). Hence his use of the adjective 'open' in his recurring collocation 'open metaverse' (in lower case in this chapter, to reflect Srinivasan's use of it).

15 Srinivasan's understanding of the Metaverse differs from Ball's in at least two important regards. Whereas according to Ball, the Metaverse need not be premised on Web 3.0 (which as discussed in the previous section, is not to say it will not, that there is not a strong correlation between them, or that their interaction might not be mutually beneficial), Srinivasan makes the latter a *conditio sine qua non* of the former: "Access to a network state's virtual capital, like everything else in a network state, is gated by Web 3.0 login limited to citizens" (227). Similarly, while Ball stresses that the Metaverse need not rely on either VR or AR (which again, need not and does not rule out the possibility that the Metaverse be strongly correlated to either), Srinivasan insists that the (open) metaverse necessitates from a VR environment projected into the physical world via AR: "people (…) digitally assemble in one place. That (…) will eventually be (…) the open metaverse. That means a virtual reality (VR) environment with parts that can be seamlessly projected into the physical world with augmented reality (AR) glasses" (227).

16 This encompasses forced displacement, thus including a subset of North Moroccan Sephardim known as *megorashim*, who arrived as a consequence of the anti-Jewish persecutions of 1287, 1391, and the expulsions of 1492.

17 Safety Wings is a Y Combinator company that seeks to build a country on the Internet, beginning with a global social safety net made of insurance products.

18 For a discussion of misconceptions and assumptions apropos *shtetelekh*, see Estraikh (2017). On the centrality of Yiddish as the *shtetl*'s vernacular, see Shandler (2014). Lastly, for an exploration of the *shtetl*'s golden age (1790s–1840s), see Petrovsky-Shtern (2014).

19 All three concepts are capitalised consistently by Srinivasan to emphasise their importance as master signifiers, i.e., a pivotal or central signifier that holds a significant symbolic function within a given socio-political or cultural context (see Butler 2004). Henceforth, I will only capitalise them when referring to this conceptualisation by Srinivasan.

20 For a discussion of the propagandistic shortcomings behind this collocation, see Yebra López (2024b).

21 See Dolève-Gandelman (1989) for a specific case study (Ehiopian Jews) and a discussion of the educational principles that undergird Ulpan *vis-à-vis* other language schools.

Conclusion

Main Findings and Future Avenues for Research

Main Findings

The Consolidation of Sepharad 4 and Its Benefits for Ladino Revitalisation

As a diasporic language whose last thousands of speakers remain scattered across the globe (51,000 – Ethnologue 2024), largely isolated from each other, with limited mobility due to their overall advanced age, and a notable degree of linguistic attrition, Ladino has found in online revitalisation a genuine, cost-effective lifesaver and paradigm changer. The Internet has brought together the worldwide community of Ladino speakers into Sepharad 4, enhancing intergenerational transmission, ameliorating the digital gap, and expanding the use of Ladino into new and contemporary domains, thus contributing to its positive transvaluation.

It is my sincere hope that the analysis and discussion in this volume will inspire further online and self-reflective revitalisation efforts among the readership, whether it is by creating new platforms and/or contributing to existing ones.

Additionally, I have demonstrated in this volume that the most popular and successful online Ladino-speaking platforms (i.e., Digital Home-Lands – Held 2010; Yebra López 2021c), notably *Ladinokomunita*, *Los Ladinadores*, *Enkontros de Alhad*, and the Ladino courses at the Oxford School of Rare Jewish Languages, are all premised on the ability to build and strengthen a community of Ladino speakers by taking advantage of the interactive, participative, multimodal (linguistic, visual, aural, gestural, and spatial)[1] multisemiotic (vernacular/postvernacular)[2] and engaging affordances of the Internet, which following the 'Ladino Zoom Boom,' has become the default option for interacting in this language. Likewise, the most promising Web 3.0 platforms (Metaverse, network state) are predicated on their ability to represent the next evolution of online communication, taking the interactive affordances of the Web 2.0 to unprecedented levels by providing immersive experiences that blend the virtual and physical worlds, including the ability to embark on an eventual process of reverse diaspora (Srinivasan 2022), thus bringing the evolution of Sepharad (and Ladino) in full circle (Sepharad 5) (Chapter 6).

Moreover, I have also proved that the burgeoning online revitalisation of Ladino has had additional positive repercussions for the purposes of documenting

DOI: 10.4324/9781003473664-11

and teaching this language. On the one hand, open-access digital archives have allowed Ladino activists to showcase how (and *that*) the language is spoken in the 21st century, storing large amounts of data from across the globe (Chapter 2). On the other hand, online educational initiatives such as the Sephardic Digital Academy and the Ladino courses at the Oxford School of Rare Jewish Languages have displayed an unrivalled capacity to maximise enrolment and worldwide reach, establishing the Internet as the default option for Ladino teaching and learning on a global scale, plus paving the way for the emergence and growth of an international community of Ladino scholars with the ability to read and write in its Hebrew scripts (Rashi, Solitreo) (Chapter 4).

Furthermore, my adoption of a methodological framework revolving around Revivalistics (see Introduction) has proved fruitful in several, interconnected respects.

First, it has encouraged me to make my discussion more self-reflective by taking the transdisciplinarity of this field of inquiry to its logical conclusion, i.e., using it to complement Revivalistics while also problematising its blind spots (e.g., through the ethnography of digital archives – Chapter 2; via translanguaging – Chapters 3–5).

Second, it has inspired me to shed light on the importance of conceptualising Ladino in anti-prescriptivist terms capable of highlighting and preserving its sociolectal, geolectal, genderlectal and even idiolectal capaciousness (Chapter 1).

Third, it has directed my analytical attention to community engagement over Ladino reification, allowing us to avoid the pitfalls of language objectification and armchair linguistics (Chapter 2).

Fourth, Revivalistics has urged us to provincialise prescriptivism, interrogating recurring and widespread practices of authentication, standardisation and gatekeeping related to Ladino (Chapters 1 and 3; see also below).

Fifth, it has drawn our attention even more to the pivotal centrality of Ladino to the Sephardic nation, encouraging us to continue to explore the importance of language ethnicisation (Linke 2004; Eisenlohr 2006) when it comes to conjuring up a sense of belongingness (Yebra López 2021c) (Chapters 1–6), which in turn and in further alignment with Revivalistics, serves to enhance the cultural autonomy and well-being of the Ladino-speaking global community (Chapter 6). In this sense, the deployment of Revivalistics has hopefully increased our awareness of the fact that contributing to the online revitalisation of Ladino is the right thing to do, and serves to right the wrongs of the past.

Sixth, engaging with Revivalistics has allowed us to better understand the magnitude of Ladino's 'Talknological Revolution' (i.e., the combination of digital media and social media leading to 'big data' – see Introduction), as well as the role played in it by each of the main Ladino-speaking online platforms discussed in this volume, particularly as regards the turning point represented by the 'Ladino Zoom Boom' (Chapter 4).

Seventh, this methodological lens has facilitated the conceptualisation of the transvaluation of Ladino within Sepharad 4 (see also Eisenlohr 2004) as a case of axiological reversal predicated on amelioration whereby Ladino is increasingly perceived as belonging to our contemporary world.

Finally, my intellectual dialogue with Revivalistics has reminded us that it is key to offer comparative insights into revivalist movements worldwide and without delay.

Concerning this last aspect, I very much hope that the present volume will serve as a useful blueprint and inspire further scholars and activists to apply my critical and online approach to Revivalistics to the revival of other rare Jewish languages (including Aramaic, Judeo-Arabic, Judeo-Greek, Judeo-Italian, Judeo Neo-Aramaic, Judeo-Persian, Judeo-Tat, Judeo-Turkish, Karaim) and, ultimately, endangered languages on a global scale.

In this sense, my own contrastive analysis *vis-à-vis* similar and additional initiatives to reinvigorate Yiddish (and to a lesser extent, also projects developed between the late 19th century and the early 20th century towards the reclamation of Hebrew) has yielded a number of useful insights.

In Chapter 1, concerning email lists and online forums, the comparison with Yiddish counterparts has allowed me to understand that while standardisation is both necessary and useful for the purpose of reviving an endangered language, this process does not need to be explicit. It has also helped me comprehend that (non) nativespeakerism is recurring in Ladino-speaking platforms because it serves to expel and/or downplay the legitimacy of non-L1 speakers, their very presence being often read as a challenge to the idealisation of Ladino by L1 and heritage speakers as featuring a supposed Golden age where the language was "authentically" and exclusively spoken by "*ladinoavlantes*" [literally 'Ladino speakers,' but often used by L1 Ladino speakers to refer exclusively to "native speakers"].

In Chapter 2, my comparative analysis with YouTube-hosted Yiddish digital archives has inspired me to urge further Ladino activists to strive towards the creation and curation of archives of superior longevity and depth, more inclusive of non-binary and LGBTQIA+ voices and narratives, able to visibilise the importance of (vernacular) written literature, and capable of exploiting the popularising potential of postvernacular use cases for preservation and/or disruptive purposes.

In Chapter 3, my discussion of Duolingo's course of Yiddish for English speakers has allowed me to understand that emphasising diversity over (implicit) standardisation might not always offer the best reviving results (particularly when the performative aspect of the language in question overshadows its reflective element).

In Chapter 4, my analysis of the influence of Zoom in Ladino and Yiddish, respectively, has helped me appreciate the uniqueness of the former, both concerning its revolutionary impact within Sepharad 4 and its exceptional steadfastness in post-pandemic times. Moreover, these elements conclusively disprove the idea that speaking Ladino is the exclusive prerogative of elderly speakers, while also showing the active and relevant role played by this language in new domains as well as in the lives of younger speakers, ultimately bringing it slightly closer to the status of Yiddish as a "definitively endangered" language, rather than a "severely endangered" one (UNESCO 2003, 8).

In Chapter 5, my contrastive analysis between Ladino-speaking and Yiddish-speaking Netflix series, respectively, has shown that *Unorthodox* (Schrader 2020) provides a very useful blueprint after which to model upcoming Ladino content on Netflix (and, by extension, Video On Demand/streaming services in general). In particular, I have underscored the series' superior methodological repertoire, including the wide recruitments of local speakers as actors and/or consultants and the pervasiveness of the language in question (inclusive of careful dubbing and subtitling[3]), which ultimately crystallises into a robust process of language ethnicisation conducive to diasporic intimacy (Boym 1998) and citizenship (Weheliye 2005, 145–97).

In Chapter 6, concerning 3.0, I have noted that to continue ameliorating the digital and intergenerational gaps (see Yebra López 2021c), Ladino speakers and activists could emulate educational initiatives used to promote Yiddish and Hebrew where younger individuals instruct older ones, particularly on utilising the Metaverse and the Sephardic network state (SNS) to preserve Ladino. For instance, Yiddish activists have effectively used the Master-Apprentice Language Learning Program (Hinton 2002), which features summer editions, does not require extensive linguistic training (which is suitable for young instructors), and employs mini-immersion settings (which the Metaverse could facilitate). This method has proven effective for adult learners (Meissner 2016), aligning well with the older age of Ladino students. Additionally, the Ulpan system has successfully taught Hebrew to new immigrants to Israel since its inception (Ministry of Aliyah and Integration 2021). Ladino activists could adapt this model to have younger, more proficient users assist older, less proficient ones in integrating into the Metaverse and SNS.

Ameliorating Ladino Online Revitalisation and Addressing Language Ideologies

My discussion in this volume has also imparted sobering lessons apropos the shortcomings of the Internet as well as negative language attitudes and ideologies. We should seek to mitigate both if we are to further the online revitalisation of Ladino in the 21st century in a manner which is both productive and socially just.

Concerning Internet limitations, first I have noticed that a major issue of the Web 2.0 revitalisation of Ladino is that the bulk of current virtual Ladino-speaking communities, including some of the most successful Digital Home-Lands, such as *Ladino 21*'s digital archive (YouTube, owned by Google), *Los Ladinadores* (Facebook, whose parent company is Meta), and *Estamoz whatsapeando* (WhatsApp, acquired by what is now Meta), are partially or entirely hosted (in a sense, owned) by Google, Amazon, Meta, Apple, or Microsoft (GAMAM). The substitution of traditional markets with these type of privately owned platforms that provide "free" services (where users, through their data, become the product alongside major content providers) has prompted some scholars to call this new economic system 'techno-feudalism' (Varoufakis 2021; Žižek 2022).

Moreover, I have also noted, in dialogue with Safiya Noble's concept of the 'algorithms of oppression' (2018), that these and other Web 2.0 companies often incur algorithmic bias against Ladino, which reproduces the social inequalities behind traditional discrimination against this linguistic variety and results in its online ideological erasure (Gal and Irvine 1995, 974). The best way to remedy this problem is to raise awareness about Ladino's existence and nature as a legitimate linguistic variety, both offline and online, while at the same time petitioning GAMAM and further companies for the inclusion of Ladino, from Google Translate to Duolingo, passing through the languages allowed by Wix for the creation of websites. For instance, as observed in Chapter 2, since June 10, 2021, YouTube includes Ladino in its language list, which means that content creators who wish to upload a video on YouTube and add subtitles, can now choose 'Ladino' as the language (though automatic subtitling in this language is not an option yet).

While we wait for Web 3.0's promising decentralisation to reach critical mass adoption (see Chapter 6), Ladino activists would be wise to try to find hosting alternatives to the GAMAM (e.g., *Ladinokomunita* was hosted by Yahoo Groups and now by Groups.io, both of which are private, independent companies – see Chapter 1) and/or to back up the Ladino-speaking content in question to protect themselves against de-platforming and content loss. For instance, in the case of *Ladino 21*, all our content is privately backed up, and we are actively exploring the possibility of donating a copy to a national library or university archive.

Additionally, as much as many Ladino-speaking online groups and communities have managed to virtually remove all monetary considerations by keeping participation free of charge and/or occasionally relying on donations (e.g., *Ladinokomunita*, *Ladino 21*'s digital archive, *Los Ladinadores*, *Estamoz whatsapeando*, *Enkontros de Alhad*, the Oxford School of Rare Jewish Languages), or else adopting a cost-effective model (e.g., Netflix series), as I have cautioned the reader in Chapter 5, we need to be wary of the potential dangers of passive consumerism as part of the digital capitalism landscape. In particular, I have drawn upon my own original survey to conclude that while Netflix series (and further Ladino content on the Internet, for that matter) have succeeded at raising awareness about this linguistic variety, such enlightened understanding has seldom translated into the recruitment of Ladino students and digital documentarians of the language, let alone the eventual formation of Ladino instructors.

A possible solution to this predicament is to make more explicit the connection between consuming Ladino content, on the one hand, and the possibility of taking advantage of this opportunity to learn, document, and/or teach the language, on the other. This can be achieved, for example, by inserting advertisements or notices promoting these possibilities at the beginning, during, or at the end of the Ladino content. For instance, at the start of each *Ladino 21* video, there is a 15-second clip featuring either myself or Alejandro Acero Ayuda asking viewers whether they would like to learn Ladino, and referring them to the link they need to click on in that case. Additionally, as we have seen apropos Gabor Szabo's WhatsApp group *Echar Lashon* and Alexandra Fellus' Instagram account @ladino.with.lex (see Chapter 3), creating new groups and communities is not only a great opportunity to help others learn something about or in Ladino, but also a way for content creators to practise Ladino consistently.

Lastly, I have noted that while the digital and intergenerational gaps have been steadily reduced for the last few years (Yebra López 2021c), worldwide access across all ages to the affordances of the Web 2.0, let alone to the futuristic possibilities offered by the Web 3.0, will necessitate a significant investment into gerontechnology, whose initiatives will have to be led, for the most part, by the younger generation (see Chapter 6).

Thus, in addition to the Master-Apprentice (Yiddish) and Ulpan (Hebrew) programmes discussed above (see also Chapter 6), it would be highly beneficial to implement intergenerational workshops featuring tailored training sessions (introducing elders to new technologies at a comfortable pace, using simple language and hands-on demonstrations), one-on-one support (pairing each elderly participant with a younger mentor who can provide individual assistance and guidance throughout the learning process), step-by-step guides (developing easy-to-follow printed and digital manuals with clear instructions and visual aids to help elders navigate new tools and platforms), accessible interfaces, practice and repetition, and feedback mechanisms where elders can express difficulties and receive prompt assistance, ensuring their comfort and confidence with the technologies.

On the other hand, and regarding negative language attitudes and ideologies, the increasing cyber-koinesation of Ladino as a post-geographical variety has found mixed reactions among the global community of Ladino speakers, including some couched in exclusionary terms. In fact, the currently hegemonic tendency is to express scepticism towards this emerging lect, instead pushing for the adoption of functional differentiation (Ferguson 1959; Fishman 1967)[4] and the standardisation of Ladino as a cyber-vernacular (in the Latin script, following the *Aki Yerushalayim* orthography),[5] often in conjunction with pernicious language ideologies such as (non)nativespeakerism and language ownership. This is the strategy followed by *Ladinokomunita*, *Los Ladinadores*, uTalk's Ladino course, and *Enkontros de Alhad*, among others. While praising the commendable efforts and success achieved by the managers of the above platforms *enroute* to the online revitalisation of Ladino, I have also problematised their *modus operandi* and conceptualisation from the perspectives of critical linguistics (translanguaging) and Revivalistics (while also nuancing the latter), dismantling (non) nativespeakerism and language ownership.

To begin with, I have demonstrated that authenticity (whether couched in nativeness, heritage, and/or ethnicity terms) does not have an intrinsic, self-evident meaning, but is instead the result of a socially negotiated and defined process of authentication (Creese et al. 2014, 939). Second, even if we were to agree on nativeness, ethnicity, and/or heritage as proofs of legitimacy, only a majority of participants on *Ladinokomunita* consider Ladino their "*lingua maternal*" ["mother tongue"][6] (Brink-Danan 2011, 113), plus the community of Ladino speakers is increasingly diverse (Santacruz 2019).

In spite of this (or precisely because of it), Ladino is constantly performed in idealised fashion, often by resorting to ethnic and linguistic stereotypes conducive to the suppression of an otherwise *de facto* heteroglossic reality (e.g., the binary '*ladinoavlantes*' vs. '*no ladinoavlantes*' – see above – and pejorating the perceived 'mixing' of Ladino dialects – see Chapter 3). Once again, and as observed by Brink-Danan, this manoeuvre is less a solution than a symptom of an underlying anxiety: "by delimiting the possible topics for discussion, as well as the language to be used online, *LK*'s members do boundary work that otherwise would leave blurred edges and an undefined community, or, alternatively, a group of postvernacular Ladino aficionados" (2011, 113).

Additionally, and concerning language ownership, on the one hand, I continue to believe that the possibility of developing Ladino-speaking Digital Home-Lands featuring language ethnicisation and a sense of home, is partially predicated on the ability of Sephardim to make key decisions about a language which has been traditionally associated with them as a marker of identity (Yebra López 2021c, 110). In the absence of this decision-making power, we risk incurring benevolent (neo) colonialism (Spivak 1988; Morton 2003) and even cultural appropriation (Yebra López 2020). On the other hand, I disagree with Zuckermann as to the Revivalistics perspective that there are "native speakers" of Ladino (or any other language, for that matter) and that they are the "custodians" of that language (2020, xxix, 212–3). On the contrary, nobody needs permission from anybody else to speak any linguistic variety, lest we discriminate against a subset of people (Huddart 2014, 6–7) (see Chapter 3).

The reality is that the development of Ladino on the Internet means that people from an increasing variety of backgrounds might (and do) feel compelled to learn this language, thus inevitably diversifying the global roster of Ladino speakers in terms of ethnicity, gender, age, disability, religion or belief, national origin, sexual orientation, family status, and political opinion, to name but a few characteristics whose protection (which is already rightly enshrined in various international human rights standards, national laws, and regulations) is non-negotiable, if we are to promote fairness, equality, and dignity for all Ladino speakers, ensuring that they are not treated unfairly or unjustly based on inherent or personal attributes.

Overall, the ability of Sephardic Ladino speakers to make key decisions related to how they would like to produce, store, and share their online interaction, including choices on key aspects pertaining to Ladino (e.g., glottonym, scripts, spelling, lexical choices), all of which contribute to the enhanced cultural autonomy and well-being of community members, does not (and cannot) entail the stigmatisation and/or delegitimsation of non-L1 speakers by L1 speakers (however ego-invested the latter might be in an idealised notion of Ladino and/or their own role in its preservation). Nor can it lead to shaming the (unselective) activation of the repertoires of non-L1 speakers around Ladino understood as the partial overlap of idiolects shared by people of Sephardic culture (Yebra López 2023b; see also Chapter 1). Additionally, we ought to bear in mind that vulnerable communities, such as the global Ladino-speaking one, can and do benefit from allyship, which, at its best, genuinely amplifies the voices of language activists from the community and contributes to the sustainability and revitalisation of their endangered linguistic heritage (see Introduction).

In this sense, I must stress that in recent years, I have observed a more tolerant attitude by L1 speakers on Digital Home-Lands such as *Ladinokomunita* and *Los*

Ladinadores whereby perceived 'mistakes' are not so much deemed necessarily 'incorrect' but rather, framed in terms of not having been heard at home by the L1 speaker in question. This attitude shift represents a step in the right direction, as it does away with the incorrect and intolerant assumption that what L1 speakers heard at home during their childhood should be the only and last word on how Ladino is to be used online in the second decade of the 21st century.

On the other hand, *contra* Zuckermann's enthusiastic celebration of language hybridisation and diversity, it is hard to ignore that the sustained popularity and success enjoyed by Digital Home-Lands such as *Ladinokomunita*, *Los Ladinadores*, and *Enkontros de Alhad* is at least partially contingent precisely upon cyber-standardisation and functional differentiation (rather than being hindered by them). In turn, this realisation forces us to nuance the wholesale endorsement of anti-prescriptivism à la Revivalistics. Moreover, as I have shown in this volume, removing explicit prescriptivism does not result in the disappearance of implicit forms of prescriptivism as pertains to Ladino's glottonym, script, spelling, and related lexical choices, as well as concerning specific cultural aspects and the selection of Ladino-speaking participants.

Consequently, a compromise seems to be required between standardisation and hybridity to revitalise Ladino (online) while at the same time ensuring effective communication. As far as I am concerned and in alignment with Revivalistics, the task of specifying the nature of that balance rests on the shoulders of the global Ladino-speaking community (rather than academic specialists in Ladino, notwithstanding the existence of a minor overlap between these two groups).

Since the vast majority of Ladino speakers already call the language 'Ladino' and use the Istanbul geolect as written in the Latin script, it seems to me that revitalising Ladino in this format would make the most sense for the foreseeable future. However, this point should not prevent us from acknowledging that such policy implies sacrificing a great deal of glottonymous, geolectal, sociolectal, genderlectal, idiolectal, and script variety. At the same time, and given the historical and intellectual importance of Rashi and Solitreo, for educational purposes, at the very least, the possibility of learning about these lects, spellings, and scripts, particularly how to read and write Ladino in its Hebrew scripts, should continue to exist.

Future Avenues for Research

New research frontiers are heralded by the present volume, which build on its limitations (see Introduction). Or, to put it in Ladino, *kuando una puerta se sera, syen se avren* ['when one door closes, a hundred open'].

First, the fact that, at least in its first edition, this book encompasses solely online Ladino-speaking initiatives established by June 1, 2024, means that there is room left to engage in the critical analysis of online platforms that have either emerged or experienced significant growth after this date. A case in point could be the American Ladino League (2024), a promising 501(c)(3) organisation which supports Ladino speakers and educators in the United States, including free Ladino conversations on Zoom via the initiative 'Ladino Lounge.' Additionally, the *Bivas* ['May You Live'] Ladino Highschool Club of America (2023) caters to Jewish high schoolers in grades 9–12, featuring weekly online meetings to learn Ladino (including in Rashi and Solitreo), Sephardic Trope, and further liturgies and texts of Sephardic heritage, as well as virtual learning sessions with Sephardic scholars from abroad.

Last but not least, the fact that in this volume I have for the most part, restricted my discussion to online initiatives concerning Judezmo (rather than any other Ladino variety such as proto-Ladino, calque, Haketia, Judezmo, Judeo-Spanish – see above), constitutes an open invitation for further scholars to engage in similar academic endeavours concerning the online revitalisation of, e.g., Haketia (where postvernacularity is much more prominent) and Judeo-Spanish (e.g., drawing upon the Oxford School of Rare Jewish Languages, *Documenting Judeo-Spanish*, LadinoType and the Sephardic Studies Digital Collection, *inter alia*, as case studies).

The prospects for the revitalisation of Ladino in the 21st century and beyond appear promising, offering hope for its continued existence across future generations. By leveraging online platforms and resources within Sepharad 4, particularly Ladino-speaking Digital Home-Lands, we can ensure that Ladino remains a vibrant and living language. It is my sincere hope that for as long as we remain committed to this cause and remember the importance of preserving this linguistic heritage, Ladino will thrive for many years to come, and with it, its global community of speakers. *Inshallah*.

Notes

1 Kress (2003); Arola et al. (2014).
2 Shandler (2004, 2005).
3 Here the lack of current Yiddishists wanting to assimilate Yiddish into German has inspired me to problematise the equivalent subtitling practise in *The Beauty Queen of Jerusalem*, which seemingly re-Hispanicises Ladino as a means to preserve it.
4 See Chapters 1 and 4.
5 See Chapter 1.
6 For a critique of the notion of 'mother tongue,' see Chapters 3 and 4.

References

Afropolitan. n.d. "Introducing Afropolitan: A Digital Nation." *Afropolitan*, n.d. https://www.afropolitan.io/.

Ağır, Seven, and Cihan Artunç. 2019. "The Wealth Tax of 1942 and the Disappearance of Non-Muslim Enterprises in Turkey." *The Journal of Economic History* 79 (1): 201–43.

Aguado, Benni. 2017. "Djohá i la supa kayente- Nu York, EE.UU." Ladino 21. Published on October 28, 2017. YouTube video, 2:23. https://www.youtube.com/watch?v=DLG0TKsZLcM.

"*Aki Yerushalayim*: Revista Kulturala Djudeo-Espanyola." (1979) 2021. *Wix*. Accessed January 13, 2023. https://yerushalayimaki.wixsite.com/ladino.

Alejandro, Julio. 2021. "Immigration, Technology, and Civilization Building." *COMPAS (Centre on Migration,* Policy and Society), University of Oxford, October 21, 2021.

Alsop, Thomas. 2023. "VR Headset Unit Sales Worldwide 2019-2024." *Statista*, November 6, 2023. https://www.statista.com/statistics/677096/vr-headsets-worldwide/.

Altaras, Nesi. 2022a. "Ladin°: Sefarad dilinde eşcinsellik ve kuirlik." *Avlaremoz*, February 2, 2022. https://www.avlaremoz.com/2022/02/02/ladin%D9%A5-sefarad-dilinde-escinsellik-ve-kuirlik/.

Altaras, Nesi. 2022b. "Nesi Altaras: Kuantos Avlantes de Ladino Kedan en La Turkiya? // Montreal/Estambol, Kanada/Turkiya." Ladino 21. Published on February 8, 2022. YouTube video, 9:39. https://www.youtube.com/watch?v=xlkwmyc16qk.

Álvarez López, Cristóbal. 2017. "Estudio lingüístico del judeoespañol en la revista 'Aki Yerushalayim.'" PhD dissertation, University of Seville. https://idus.us.es/bitstream/handle/11441/68487/Crist%C3%B3bal%20Jos%C3%A9%20%C3%81lvarez%20L%C3%B3pez%20-%20Tesis%20doctoral.pdf?sequence=1&isAllowed=y.

Aminian Jazi, Iona. 2019. "Ioana Aminian - Commission of Vanishing Languages and Cultural Heritage (VLACH)." Vanishing Languages and Cultural Heritage. Published on June 11, 2019. YouTube video, 1:27. https://www.youtube.com/watch?v=lCbnOOkJhQs.

Anderson, Benedict. 1983. *Imagined Communities: Reflections on the Origin and Spread of Nationalism*. London: Verso.

Aneja, Geeta A. 2016. "(Non)native Speakered: Rethinking (Non)nativeness and Teacher Identity in TESOL Teacher Education." *TESOL Q* 50 (3): 572–96.

Arkontaky, John (ed.), Tommaso Di Bartolo, Cathy Hackl, Dirk Lueth, and Yat Siu. 2022. *Navigating the Metaverse: A Guide to Limitless Possibilities in a Web 3.0 World*. Hoboken: John Wiley & Sons, Inc.

Armistead, Samuel. 1995. "Review of Death of a Language." *Language in Society* 24 (4): 604–7.

Aroeste, Sarah. 2018. "Sarah Aroeste i Carlos Yebra echan lashon en el Greek Jewish Festival- Nu York, EE.UU." Ladino 21. Published on May 7, 2018. YouTube video, 1:51. https://www.youtube.com/watch?v=VErpBfJBxX4.

Arola, Kristin L., Cheryl E. Ball, and Jennifer Sheppard. 2014. *Writer/Designer: A Guide to Making Multimodal Projects*. Bedford/St. Martin's: Macmillan Higher Education.

August-Zarębska, Agnieszka, and Natalia Paprocka. 2021. "Les enjeux de la traduction littéraire en langue périphérique et post-vernaculaire. Le cas du judéo-espagnol." *Romanica Wratislaviensia* 68: 9–26.

Austin, John L. 1962. *How to Do Things with Words*. Oxford: Clarendon Press.

Austin, Peter, and Julia Sallabank, eds. 2011. *The Cambridge Handbook of Endangered Languages*. Cambridge: Cambridge University Press.

Austin, Peter, and Julia Sallabank, eds. 2014. *Endangered Languages: Beliefs and Ideologies in Language Documentation and Revitalization*. Oxford: Oxford University Press.

"Austrian Academy of Sciences Vanishing Languages and Cultural Heritage." n.d. *VLACH*. Accessed April 19, 2024. https://www.oeaw.ac.at/vlach/.

Babbel. 2007. *Babbel Language Learning Platform*. Accessed October 3, 2024. https://www.babbel.com/

Ball, Matthew. 2022. *The Metaverse: And How It Will Revolutionize Almost Everything*. New York: Liveright.

Bangkok Video Productions. n.d. "Dubbed Audio Style Guide - Lip Sync Dubbing." n.d. https://www.bangkokvideoproductions.com/film-services/Post-Production/multilingual-film-dubbing-services/dubbed-audio-style-guide-lip-sync-dubbing.

"Basic Facts about Yiddish." 2014. *YIVO Institute for Jewish Research*. Accessed February 8, 2024. https://www.yivo.org/cimages/basic_facts_about_yiddish_2014.pdf.

Basu, Tanya. 2014. "Oy Vey: Yiddish Has a Problem." *The Atlantic*, September 9, 2024. https://www.theatlantic.com/national/archive/2014/09/yiddish-has-a-problem/379658/.

Baub, Andrea. 2022. "אף פעם לא מאו"חר." *Yiddishspiel*. Accessed May 4, 2024. https://yiddishpiel.co.il/plays/אף-פעם-לא-מאוחר/.

Beede, Penina. 2020. "An Enduring Feature of the Pandemic So Far: Jews are Flocking to Online Classes." *Jewish Telegraphic Agency*, July 22, 2020. https://www.jta.org/2020/07/22/culture/an-enduring-feature-of-the-pandemic-so-far-jews-are-flocking-to-online-classes.

Belk, Zoë, Lily Kahn, and Kriszta Szendrői. 2020. "Complete Loss of Case and Gender within Two Generations: Evidence from Stamford Hill Hasidic Yiddish." *Journal of Comparative Germanic Linguistics* 23: 271–326.

Belk, Zoë, Lily Kahn, Kriszta Szendrői, and Sonya Yampolskaya. 2022. "Innovations in the Contemporary Hasidic Yiddish Pronominal System." In *Contemporary Research in Minoritized and Diaspora Languages of Europe*, edited by Matt Coler and Andrew Nevins, 143–87. Berlin: Language Science Press.

Benchetrit, Elie. 2017. *El mazzal de los pobres*. Madrid: Hebraica Ediciones.

Benedict, Eli. 2021."'האָט אונדזער חסידישער ייִדיש אַ סטאַנדאַרט, צי נישט? [So Is Our Hasidic Yiddish Standardized, or Not?]" *Yiddish Forward*, April 14, 2021. https://forward.com/yiddish/467723/so-is-our-hasidic-yiddish-standardized-or-not/.

Benmayor, Jacky. 2022. "Jacky Benmayor: Komo es vijitar Saloniko en 2022?// Saloniko, Gresya." Ladino 21. Published on August 12, 2022. YouTube video, 19:35. https://www.youtube.com/watch?v=RI-Wm5rH6xE.

Benor, Sarah B. 2002. "Jewish Languages." *Jewish Language Project*. Accessed April 28, 2024. https://www.jewishlanguages.org/.

Benor, Sarah B. 2009. "Do American Jews Speak a 'Jewish Language'? A Model of Jewish Linguistic Distinctiveness." *The Jewish Quarterly Review* 99 (2): 230–69.

Benor, Sarah. 2023. "Jewbellish and YidLife Crisis: Contemporary Engagement with Yiddish." *Paper presented at the YiLaS 3: Yiddish in the 21st Century International Conference*, University College London (UCL), UK, March 2023.

Bentolila, Ya'akov. 2008. "La lengua común (coiné) judeo-española entre el Este y el Oeste." *El Prezente* 2: 159–76.

Benveniste, Liliana. 2021a. "Liliana Benveniste: Komo Se Nasieron Enkontros de Alhad i eSefarad // Buenos Aires, Ardjentina." Ladino 21. Published on August 6, 2021. YouTube video, 11:27. https://www.youtube.com/watch?v=8-_Nr34dzBw.

Benveniste, Liliana. 2021b. "Liliana Benveniste: El Avenir del Ladino komo Lingua Djudia // Buenos Aires, Ardjentina." Ladino 21. Published on August 13, 2021. YouTube video, 10:28. https://www.youtube.com/watch?v=qHGq69KW6iU.

Benveniste, Liliana. 2024. "CCS: CURSO DE LADINO / ONLINE con LILIANA BENVENISTE – NIVELES Y PROGRAMAS 2024 – Inscribite AQUI." *eSefarad: noticias del mundo sefaradí*. Accessed April 28, 2024. https://esefarad.com/ccs-curso-de-ladino/online.

Berman, Brian. (2006) 2022. "Convert Ladino Text to Solitreo and Rashi Scripts." *Ladino-Type*. Accessed May 11, 2024. https://solitreo.com/.

Biale, David, David Assaf, Benjamin Brown, Uriel Gellman, Samuel Heilman, Moshe Rosman, Gadi Sagiv, and Marcin Wodziński.. 2018. *Hasidism: A New History*. Princeton, NJ: Princeton University Press.

Bigscreen. 2023. "Bigscreen: your virtual reality living room." Accessed October 4, 2024. https://www.bigscreenvr.com/software.

Billig, Michael. 1995. *Banal Nationalism*. London: Sage Publication Ltd.

Birnbaum, Salomo. 1979. *Yiddish: A Survey and a Grammar*. Manchester: Manchester University Press.

Biskowitz, Sarah. 2022. "The Golden Peacock and the Green Owl: Analyzing Yiddish Language Learners' Experiences with Duolingo." *In geveb: A Journal of Yiddish Studies*, November 17, 2022. https://ingeveb.org/pedagogy/duolingo.

Blackledge, Adrian. 2000. "Monolingual Ideologies in Multilingual States: Language, Hegemony and Social Justice in Western Liberal Democracies." *Sociolinguistic Studies* 1 (2): 25–45.

Blaine, Louis. 2023. "If You Speak Yiddish, What Is Your Opinion on the Duolingo Yiddish Course? I'm Using It Right Now, and I Think It's Pretty Good, but Do Any Fluent Speakers Think That It's a Bad Tool to Learn?" *Quora*. Accessed March 15, 2024. https://www.quora.com/If-you-speak-Yiddish-what-is-your-opinion-on-the-Duolingo-Yiddish-course-I-m-using-it-right-now-and-I-think-it-s-pretty-good-but-do-any-fluent-speakers-think-that-it-s-a-bad-tool-to-learn/answer/Louis-Blaine.

Bleaman, Isaac L. 2020. "Implicit Standardization in a Minority Language Community: Real-Time Syntactic Change among Hasidic Yiddish Writers." *Frontiers in Artificial Intelligence* 3 (35): 1–20.

Blommaert, Jan, and Jef Verschueren. 1992. "The Role of Language in European Nationalist Ideologies." *Pragmatics* 2 (3): 355–75.

Bonfiglio, Thomas P. 2010. *Mother Tongues and Nations. The Invention of the Native Speaker*. Berlin/Boston: De Gruyter Moutons.

Bortnick, Rachel A. 2004. "The Internet and Judeo-Spanish: Impact and Implications of a Virtual Community." In *Proceedings of the Twelfth British Conference on Judeo-Spanish Studies*, edited by Hilary S. Pomeroy and Michael Alpert, 3–11. Leiden: Brill.

Bortnick, Rachel A. 2018. "Ladinokomunita i la emportansa de Internet." Ladino 21. Published on October 26, 2018. YouTube video, 02: 46. https://www.youtube.com/watch?v=7mz5IA_JMl0.

Bortnick, Rachel A. 2020. "Un 'App' Para Ladino." *El Amaneser* 179: 19.

Boyd, Sydney, K. Abram, and Alejandra Leos. 2024. "Teaching First-Year Writing to the Post-pandemic, AI Generation." *139th MLA Convention.* Session at the Marriott Downtown, Philadelphia, PA, January 5, 2024.

Boym, Svetlana. 1998. "On Diasporic Intimacy: Ilya Kabakov's Installations and Immigrant Homes." *Critical Inquiry* 24 (2): 498–524.

Brink-Danan, Marcy. 2011. "The Meaning of Ladino: The Semiotics of an Online Speech Community." *Language & Communication* 31: 107–18.

Bunis, David. 1981. "A Comparative Linguistic Analysis of Judezmo and Yiddish." *International Journal of the Sociology of Language* 30: 49–70.

Bunis, David. 1999. *Judezmo: An Introduction to the Language of the Ottoman Sephardim.* Jerusalem: Magnes Press.

Bunis, David. 2016. "Twenty-First-Century Talk About Judezmo in the Ladinokomunita Website." In *Languages of Modern Jewish Cultures: Comparative Perspectives*, edited by Joshua L. Miller and Anita Norich, 321–60. Ann Arbor: University of Michigan.

Bunis, David. 2017. "Judezmo (Ladino)." In *Handbook of Jewish Languages*, edited by Lily Kahn and Aaron D. Rubin, 366–451. Leiden/Boston: Brill.

Bunis, David M. 2018. "Judezmo (Ladino/Judeo-Spanish): A Historical and Sociolinguistic Portrait." In *Languages in Jewish Communities, Past and Present*, edited by Benjamin Hary and Sarah Bunin Benor, 185–238. Berlin/Boston: De Gruyter Mouton.

Bunis, David. 2019. "La Ortografia de Aki Yerushalayim: Un pinakolo en la estoria de la romanizasión del djudezmo (djudeo-espanyol)." *Aki Yerushalayim* 101: 8–24. https://yerushalayimaki.wixsite.com/ladino/aki-yerushalayim-no-99-100.

Bunis, David. 2021. "La lingua de los sefaradim en romanizasion." In *Las Ortografias del Ladino*, edited by Ora Schwarzwald, 21–37. Jerusalem: La Akademia Nasionala del Ladino en Israel.

Bürki, Yvette. 2016. "Haketia in Morocco. Or, the Story of the Decline of an Idiom." *International Journal of the Sociology of Language* 239: 121–55.

Bürki, Yvette. 2020. "Das Judenspanische im Internet als Merkmal einer Ausbausprache?" In *Translation und Sprachlicher Pluricentrismus in der Romania 'minor'*, edited by Martina Schrader-Kniffki and Elton Prifti, 271–312. Bern: Peter Lang.

Bürki, Yvette. 2021. "El activismo lingüístico y la lengua sefardí en el siglo XXI." In *Ovras son onores: estudios sefardies en homenaje a Paloma Díaz-Mas*, coordinated by Zeljko Jovanovic and María Sánchez Pérez, 211–32. Bilbao: University of the Basque Country.

Bürki, Yvette. 2024. "Spanish and Judeo-Spanish Today." In *New Perspectives on Judeo-Spanish and the Linguistic History of Sephardic Jews*, edited by Laura Minervini and Frank Savelsberg, 310–36. Leiden: Brill.

Burack, Emily. 2021. "The Funniest Tweets About Duolingo's New Yiddish Course." *heyalma*, April 6, 2021. https://www.heyalma.com/the-funniest-tweets-about-duolingos-new-yiddish-course/.

Burniske, Chris, and Jack Tatar. 2017. *Cryptoassets: The Innovative Investor's Guide to Bitcoin and Beyond.* New York: McGraw-Hill.

Busuu. 2008. *Busuu Language Learning Platform.* Accessed October 3, 2024. https://www.busuu.com/

Butler, Rex. 2004. "Slavoj Zizek: What is a Master-Signifier." *Lacan.com*, n.d. https://www.lacan.com/zizek-signifier.htm.

Calderwood, Eric. 2019. "Spanish in a Global Key." *Journal of Spanish Cultural Studies* 20 (12): 53–65.

Calvet, Jean. 1974. *Linguistique et colonialisme: petit traité de glottophagie.* Paris: Payot.

Carlsson, Nina. 2021. "One Nation, One Language? National minority and Indigenous recognition in the politics of immigrant integration." PhD dissertation, Södertörn University. https://www.diva-portal.org/smash/get/diva2:1510021/FULLTEXT01.pdf.

Carrión, Pablo. 2012. "[Comunidades] Todos somos Ladinokomunita!." *Curso de Ladino Djudeo-Espanyol*, April, 2012. https://kursodeladino.blogspot.com/2012/04/comunidades-ladinokomunita.html.

Caspar, Stephan. 2020. "Virtual Worlds and VR at CMU." *Askwith Kenner Global Languages & Cultures Room*, November 5, 2020. https://kenner.dotsandspaces.uk/blog/uncategorized/virtual-worlds-and-vr-at-cmu/.

Champagne, Phil. 2014. *The Book of Satoshi: The Collected Writings of Bitcoin Creator Satoshi Nakamoto*. Austin, TX: e53.

Charatan, Debrah Lee. 2020. "Resolving Conflict Over Zoom Is Easier Than You Think" Thrive Global. Accessed October 4, 2024. https://community.thriveglobal.com/resolving-conflict-over-zoom-is-easier-than-you-think/#:~:text=It%E2%80%99s%20much%20easier%20to%20ask%20for%20attentive%20listening%20and%20presence.

Chohan, Usman, ed. 2024. *Non-Fungible Tokens (NFTs): Multidisciplinary Perspectives*. London/New York: Routledge.

Chow, Rey. 2014. *Not like a Native Speaker: Languaging as a Postcolonial Practice*. New York: Columbia University Press.

Chun, Jon. "How AI Large Language Models like GPT Are Disrupting, Redefining, and Revitalizing the Academy." In *Ethics and Practice of AIs in the Academy*, presided by Avery Wiscomb. 139th MLA Convention. Session at the Marriott Downtown, Philadelphia, PA, January 4, 2024.

Comben, Christina. 2020. "Extinct or Extant: Can Blockchain Preserve the Heritage of Endangered Populations?" *Magazine by Cointelegraph*, May 5, 2020. https://cointelegraph.com/magazine/blockchain-preserve-heritage-marshall-islands/.

"Contemporary Hasidic Yiddish Joint UCL Hebrew & Jewish Studies-Linguistics AHRC research project." n.d. UCL Hebrew & Jewish Studies. Accessed March 12, 2024. https://www.ucl.ac.uk/hebrew-jewish/research/research-projects/contemporary-hasidic-yiddish.

Coronel-Molina, Serafin, and Teresa McCarty. 2011. "Language Curriculum Design and Evaluation for Endangered Languages." In *The Cambridge Handbook of Endangered Languages*, edited by Peter Austin and Julia Sallabank, 354–70. Cambridge: Cambridge University Press.

Creese, Angela, Adrian Blackledge, and Jaspreet Kaur Takhi. 2014. "The Ideal 'Native Speaker' Teacher: Negotiating Authenticity and Legitimacy in the Language Classroom." *The Modern Language Journal* 98 (4): 937–51.

Cruz Çilli, Kenan. 2021."'Ladino's Renaissance': For This Dying Jewish Language, COVID Has Been an Unlikely Lifesaver." *Haaretz*, April 28, 2024. https://www.haaretz.com/middle-east-news/2021-01-05/ty-article-opinion/.premium/ladinos-renaissance-covid-the-unlikely-lifesaver-for-a-dying-language/0000017f-f461-d47e-a37f-fd7df1120000.

Cuende, Luis. 2018. "Aragon - The Fight for Freedom." Aragon. Published on March 29. YouTube video, 05:50. https://www.youtube.com/watch?v=AqjIWmiAidw.

Darby, Langston, Scott Keeney, and QuHarrison Terry. 2022. *The Metaverse Handbook*. Harlow: Ascent Audio.

Davidoff, Oded, dir. 2021. The Beauty Queen of Jerusalem. Yes.

Del Valle, José. 2007. "La lengua, patria común: la hispanofonía y el nacionalismo panhispánico." In *La lengua, ¿patria común? Ideas e ideologías del español*, edited by José Del Valle, 31–56. Madrid: Iberoamericana/Vervuert.

Del Valle, José. 2009. "Total Spanish: The Politics of a Pan-Hispanic Grammar." *PMLA* 124 (3): 880–6.

Del Valle, José. 2011. "Panhispanismo e hispanofonía: breve historia de dos ideologías siamesas." *Sociolinguistic Studies* 5 (3): 465–84.

Dembowski, Paweł. "Paweł Dembowski - Lenguaje inklusivo...tambyen en Ladino // Wrocław, Polonia." Ladino 21. Published on January 22, 2022. YouTube video, 05:17. https://www.youtube.com/watch?v=m_6n2-ef1rw.

Derrida, Jacques. (1971) 1982. "*Signature, Event, Context.*" In *Margins of Philosophy*, Jacques Derrida (translated by Alan Bass), 307–30. Chicago: University of Chicago Press.

Dolève-Gandelman, Tsili. 1989. "'Ulpan' Is Not 'Berlitz': Adult Education and the Ethiopian Jews in Israel." *Social Science Information* 28 (1): 121–43.

Drops. 2015. *Drops Language Learning Platform.* Accessed October 3, 2024. https://languagedrops.com/

Duolingo. 2011. *Duolingo Language Learning Platform* Accessed October 3, 2024. https://www.duolingo.com/

Duolingo. 2019. "Yiddish Dialects." *Google Forms.* Accessed March 31, 2024. https://docs.google.com/forms/d/e/1FAIpQLScCQOmyI6ksbN9sQM3L77ak6aDSbK_b9wCELgZqjce4TTLkIA/viewform.

Duolingo. n.d. "The World's Best Way to Learn Yiddish." *Duolingo.* Accessed April 13, 2024. www.duolingo.com/enroll/yi/en/Learn-Yiddish.

Dussel, Enrique. 1993. "Europa, modernidad y eurocentrismo" In *La colonialidad del saber: eurocentrismo y ciencias sociales. Perspectivas latinoamericanas*, edited by Edgardo Lander, 24–33. Buenos Aires: CLACSO.

Eisenberg, Richard. 2022. "For Older Adults: A Hitchhiker's Guide to the Metaverse." *Forbes*, April 15, 2022. https://www.forbes.com/sites/nextavenue/2022/04/15/for-older-adults-a-hitchhikers-guide-to-the-metaverse/?sh=757cc3563477.

Eisenlohr, Patrick. 2004. "Language Revitalization and New Technologies: Cultures of Electronic Mediation and the Refiguring of Communities." *Annual Review of Anthropology* 33: 21–45.

Eisenlohr, Patrick. 2006. *Little India: Diaspora, Time, and Ethnolinguistic Belonging in Hindu Mauritius.* Oakland, CA: University of California Press.

"El Amaneser" n.d. *Sephardic Center of Istanbul.* Accessed May 22, 2024. https://istanbulsephardiccenter.com/urun-kategori/el-amaneser-en/?lang=en&v=7516fd43adaa.

Endangered Language Alliance (ELA). 2023. Endangered Language Alliance. Accessed October 3, 2024. https://www.elalliance.org/about/how-we-work/tools.

"Enkontros de Alhad." 2024. *eSefarad: Noticias del mundo sefaradí.* Accessed April 28, 2024. https://esefarad.com/tag/enkontros-de-alhad/.

Epstein, Lita. 2006. *If You Can't Say Anything Nice, Say It in Yiddish: The Book of Yiddish Insults and Curses.* New York: Citadel Press.

Erdemir, Aykan. 2016. "The Turkish Kristallnacht." *Politico Europe*, September 7, 2016. https://www.politico.eu/article/the-turkish-kristallnacht-greece-1955-pogrom-polites-orthodox/.

Eriksen, Thomas Hylland. 2007. "Nationalism and the Internet." *Nations and Nationalism: Journal of the Association for the Study of Ethnicity and Nationalism* 13 (1): 1–17.

eSefarad. 2009. "SEFARADIMUESTRO – Foro en judeo-español." *eSefarad: noticias del mundo sefaradí*, March 8, 2009. https://esefarad.com/sefaradimuestro-foro-en-judeo-espanol/.

eSefarad CCSefarad. 2020. "Unidos por el ladino 1- Esta montanya d'enfrente." eSefarad CCSefarad. Published on April 25, 2020. YouTube video, 2:12. https://www.youtube.com/watch?v=iC_MnKRt1TE.

"eSefarad: Noticias del Mundo Sefaradí." n.d. *eSefarad: noticias del mundo sefaradí*. Accessed April 19, 2024. https://esefarad.com.

Eskenazi, Jojo. 2019. "Which One Is Our Language? - Judeo-Spanish Collection." Vanishing Languages and Cultural Heritage. Published on September 24, 2019. YouTube video, 15:54. https://www.youtube.com/watch?v=YZ7GziwQFbw.

Estraikh, Gennady. 2017. *The Shtetl: Image Reality*. London/New York: Routledge.

Evans, Leighton, Jordan Frith, and Michael Saker. 2022. *From Microverse to Metaverse: Modelling the Future through Today's Virtual Worlds*. Bingley: Emerald.

"Fact Check. - Mission Forward" 2023. *Fact Check. - Mission Forward*, April 19, 2023. https://www.missionforward.us/finding-the-words/fact-check#:~:text=%E2%80%9CIf%20you%20talk%20to%20a,widely%20shared%20of%20Mandela%27s%20quotes.

Fader, Ayala. 2020. *Hidden Heretics: Jewish Doubt in the Digital Age*. Princeton, NJ: Princeton University Press.

Farooq, Umar. 2021. "Netflix 'The Club' Connects Mainstream Turkey to Jewish Heritage." *AlJazeera*, November 19, 2021. https://www.aljazeera.com/news/2021/11/19/netflix-the-club-connects-mainstream-turkey-to-jewish-heritage#:~:text=One%20of%20the%20most%2Dwatched,and%20inside%20churches%20and%20synagogues.

Feld, Steven, and Keith H. Basso. 1996. *Senses of Place*. Santa Fe, NM: School of American Research.

Feldman, Deborah. 2012. *Unorthodox: The Scandalous Rejection of My Hasidic Roots*. London: Bravo Ltd.

Ferguson, Charles. 1959. "Diglossia." *Word, Journal of the International Linguistic Association* 15: 325–40.

Fernández de Arroyabe Olaortu, Ainhoa, Iñaki Lazkano-Arillaga, and Leyre Eguskiza-Sesumaga. 2018. "Digital Natives: Online Audiovisual Content Consumption, Creation and Dissemination." *Comunicar* 57: 61–9.

Finlay, Susannah. 2021. "Yiddish for the 21st Century." *Vashti*, May 19, 2021. https://vashtimedia.com/2021/05/19/issues/the-jewish-left/yiddish-for-the-21st-century/.

Fishman, Joshua A. 1967. "Bilingualism with and without Diglossia: Diglossia with and without Bilingualism." *Journal of Social Issues* 23 (2): 29–38.

Fishman, Joshua A. 1991. *Reversing Language Shift: Theoretical and Empirical Foundations of Assistance to Threatened Languages*. Bristol: Multilingual Matters.

Flores, Nelson. 2013. "Silencing the Subaltern: Nation-State/Colonial Governmentality and Bilingual Education in the United States." *Critical Inquiry in Language Studies* 10 (4): 263–87.

FluentU. 2011. *FluentU Language Learning Platform*. Accessed October 3, 2024. https://www.fluentu.com/

"Forging a Future for Languages." n.d. *Endangered Language Alliance*. Accessed April 19, 2024. https://www.elalliance.org/.

Fox, Jon E., and Cynthia Miller-Idriss. 2019. "From Everyday Nationhood to Everyday Nationalism." *CRCC 'MigNation' seminar series (CRCC-LUNN seminar series)*, May 8, 2019.

Frost, Alanna, Brandy Bagar-Fraley, Katherine Elkins, Ruth Li, Daniel Pintos. 2024. "AI and What It Means to Create: A Cross-Disciplinary Conversation." *139th MLA Convention*. Session at the Pennsylvania Convention Center, Philadelphia, PA, January 5, 2024.

Gal, Susan, and Judith T. Irvine. 1995. "The Boundaries of Languages and Disciplines: How Ideologies Construct Difference." *Social Research* 62 (4): 967–1001.

García, Ofelia. 2009. *Bilingual Education in the 21st Century: A Global Perspective*. Malden, MA/Oxford: Basil/Blackwell.

García, Ofelia. 2013. "El papel del translenguar en la enseñanza del español en los Estados Unidos." In *El español en los Estados Unidos: e pluribus unum? enfoque multidisciplinar*, coordinated by Domnita Dumitrescu and Gerardo Piña Rosales, 353–74. New York: Academia Norteamericana de la Lengua Española. https://ofeliagarciadotorg.files.wordpress.com/2014/03/el-papel-del-translenguar.pdf.

García, Ofelia, and Li Wei. 2014. *Translanguaging: Language, Bilingualism and Education*. Basingstoke/New York: Palgrave Macmillan.

Geertz, Clifford. 1973. *The Interpretation of Cultures: Selected Essays by Clifford Geertz*. New York: Basic Books.

Global Heritage Fund. 2018. "Can Blockchain Save Cultural Heritage" October 2, 2018. https://www.wmf.org/blog/celebrating-our-new-affiliation-global-heritage-fund/2018/10/02/can-blockchain-save-cultural-heritage#:~:text=Blockchain%20may%20not%20be%20a%20perfect%20solution%20for%20saving%20endangered

Gobbo, Federico. 2017. "Beyond the Nation-State? The Ideology of the Esperanto Movement between Neutralism and Multilingualism." *Social Inclusion* 5 (4): 38–47.

Gramling, David. 2016. *The Invention of Monolingualism*. New York: Bloomsbury Publishing.

Gusoff, Adrienne. 2012. *Dirty Yiddish*. Berkeley, CA: Ulysses Press.

Güven, Dilek. 2011. "Riots against the Non-Muslims of Turkey: 6/7 September 1955 in the Context of Demographic Engineering." *European Journal of Turkish Studies* 12: 1–18.

Haelion, Moshe. 2021. "Moshe Haelion: Ekspulsyon de Salonik i Kampos de Konsentrasyon // Tel Aviv, Israel." Ladino 21. Published on November 12, 2021. YouTube video, 08:58. https://www.youtube.com/watch?v=s34vFIVa4tA.

Halphie, Michael. 2020. "'Ladino Forever': Reflanes en muestra lingua // Estambol, Turkiya." Ladino 21. Published on October 30, 2020. YouTube video, 07:32. https://www.youtube.com/watch?v=mH_Sv2k5gEc.

Harris, Tracy. 1994. *Death of a Language: The History of Judeo-Spanish*. Newark, NJ: University of Delaware Press.

Harris, Tracy. 2011. "The State of Ladino Today." *European Judaism: A Journal for the New Europe* 44 (1): 51–61.

Hassán, Jacob M. (1968) 1971. "Problemas de transcripción del judeoespañol." In Rosetti, Alexandru and Sandra Reinheimer-Ripeanu, eds. *Actele celui de- al XII Congreso International de Lingüistica si Filologie Romanica, II*, 1235–63. Bucarest: Editura Academiei Republicii Socialistre Romania.

Hassán, Jacob M. 1978. "Transcripción normalizada de textos judeoespañoles." *Estudios Sefardies* 0 (1): 147–50.

Hassán, Jacob. 1995. "El español sefardí (judeo-español, ladino)." In *La lengua española hoy*, coordinated by Manuel Seco and Gregorio Salvador, 117–40. Madrid: Fundación Juan March.

Heath, Alex. 2021. "Facebook is Planning to Rebrand the Company with a New Name." *The Verge*, October 19, 2021. https://www.theverge.com/2021/10/19/22735612/facebook-change-company-name-metaverse.

Held, Michal. 2010. "The People Who Almost Forgot: Judeo-Spanish Web-Based Interactions as a Digital Home-Land." *El Prezente* 4: 83–101.

Heller, Monica, and Marilyn Martin-Jones, eds. 2007. *Bilingualism: A Social Approach*. New York: Palgrave Macmillan.

HelloTalk. 2013. Accessed October 3, 2024. https://www.hellotalk.com/

Hernández González, Carmen. 2001. "Un viaje por Sefarad: la fortuna del judeoespañol." In *El español en el mundo*, Instituto Cervantes/Plaza & Janés/Círculo de Lectores.

Hinton, Leanne. 2002. *How to Keep Your Language Alive: A Commonsense Approach to One-on-One Language Learning*. Berkeley: Heyday.

Hinton, Leanne, Leena Huss, and Gerald Roche, eds. 2018. *The Routledge Handbook of Language Revitalization*. Abingdon: Routledge.

Holliday, Adrian. 2018. "Native-speakerism." In *TESOL Encyclopaedia of English Language Teaching*, edited by John I. Liontas, 1–7. Hoboken: John Wileys & Sons, Inc.

Huddart, David. 2014. "Introduction" In *Involuntary Associations: Postcolonial Studies and World Englishes*. Liverpool University Press. https://doi.org/10.5949/liverpool/9781781380253.003.0001.

Hwang, Janice. 2021. "Ethan Marcus, 25, Revolutionizing Sephardic Education." *Jewish Telegraphic Agency*, April 28, 2024. https://www.jta.org/2021/07/12/ny/ethan-marcus-25-revolutionizing-sephardic-education.

IMDb. 2016. "Dead Tongues." *IMDb*. n.d. https://www.imdb.com/title/tt7317254/.

International Society for Gerontechnology. 2024. "Empowering Aging with Gerontechnology." *International Society for Gerontechnology*, n.d. https://www.gerontechnology.org/.

Irvine, Judith T. 2008. "Subjected Words: African Linguistics and the Colonial Encounter." *Language & Communication* 28 (4): 323–43.

Irvine, Judith T., and Susan Gal. 2000. "Language Ideology and Linguistic Differentiation." In *Regimes of Language*, edited by Paul V. Kroskrity, 35–83. Santa Fe: School of American Research Press.

Isaacs, Miriam. 1999. "Haredi, Haymish and Frim: Yiddish Vitality and Language Choice in a Transnational, Multilingual Community." *International Journal of the Sociology of Language* 138: 9–30.

Jacobs, Paula. 2021. "The New Sephardic Generation." *Tablet*, June 1, 2021. https://www.tabletmag.com/sections/community/articles/new-sephardic-generation.

"Jewbellish." n.d. *Jewbellish*. Accessed April 19, 2024. https://jewbellish.com/.

Jewish Language Project. 2022. "Name Changing for Healing," *Facebook*, September 1, 2022. https://www.facebook.com/jewishlanguages/photos/pb.100060053229578.-2207520000/624138269148169/?type=3.

Jones, Taylor. 2021. "Duolingo Yiddish: A Guide for the Perplexed." *Language Jones*, April 22, 2021. https://www.languagejones.com/blog-1/2021/4/22/duolingo-yiddish-a-guide-for-the-perplexed.

Jørgensen, Jens N., Martha S. Karrebæk, Lian M. Madsen, Janus S. Møller. 2011. "Polylanguaging in Superdiversity." *Diversities* 13 (2): 24–37.

Jur Team. 2022. "Network States Are Not DAOs." *Jur*, November 27, 2022. https://jur.io/blog/network-states-are-not-daos/#:~:text=The%20crypto%20phenomenon%20is%20based,DAOs%20or%20asset%2Ddriven%20logic.

Kahn, Lily, and Riitta Valijärvi, eds. forthcoming. *Challenging the Binary: Non-Binary, Genderqueer, and Gender-Neutral Language*. Berlin: De Gruyter.

Kalinka, Irina 2023. "The Metaverse Is a Lie: Dreams of Escape in Facebook's Connect 2021 Announcement Video." In *California in Science Fiction*, presided by Frances Tran. 138th MLA Convention. Session at the Moscone Center, San Francisco, CA, January 6, 2023.

Karabelnicoff, Shaked. 2022. "The True Story Behind 'Beauty Queen of Jerusalem'." *Jewish Unpacked*, June 1, 2022. https://jewishunpacked.com/the-true-story-behind-beauty-queen-of-jerusalem/?gad_source=1&gclid=Cj0KCQjwudexBhDKARIsAI-GWYW0cy-i5R6lTLerIq1EGtKgeAiXauDY8lomOw-1mAaFydQ8oHrstWeYaAsq3EALw_wcB.

Kave Shtiebel. 2012. Accessed October 3, 2024. https://www.kaveshtiebel.com/.

Khalil, Joe, and Mohamed Zayani. 2021. "De-territorialized Digital Capitalism and the Predicament of the Nation-state: Netflix in Arabia." *Media, Culture & Society* 43 (2): 201–18.

Kirschen, Bryan, n.d. "Documenting Judeo-Spanish in Solitreo." *Documenting Judeo-Spanish*. Accessed May 23, 2024. www.documentingjudeospanish.com.

Kirschen, Bryan. 2024. "Ladino Linguist: Begin or Continue your Ladino Language Today." *Ladino Linguist*. Accessed April 28, 2024. https://ladinolinguist.com/.

Kirschen, Bryan, and Susanna Zaraysky, dirs. 2015. *Saved by* Language. n.p.

Klein, David I. 2021. "Netflix's 'The Club' Offers a Rare Portrait of Turkish Jews, Shattering Historical Taboos in the Process." *Forward*, November 17, 2021. https://www.aljazeera.com/news/2021/11/19/netflix-the-club-connects-mainstream-turkey-to-jewish-heritage#:~:text=Released%20earlier%20this%20month%2C%20The,nationalist%20fervour%20gripping%20the%20country.

Kohenak, Jake. 2020. "Jake Kohanek [sic] – Ladino." Endangered Language Alliance. Published on June 17, 2020. YouTube video, 5:48. https://www.youtube.com/watch?v=5l_yGVgUzZw.

Kohn, Marek. 2019. "One Nation, One Language." In Kohn, Marek, ed. *Four Words for Friend: Why Using More Than One Language Matters Now More Than Ever*, 151–87. New Haven: New Yale University Press.

Kooperativa "Konsilyo de Lingua Neutrala". "Por ke los pronombres son emportantes?" *Pronouns.page*. 2023. Accessed February 12, 2024. https://lad.pronouns.page/.

Kress, Gunther. 2003. *Literacy in the New Media Age*. London/New York: Routledge.

Kushner, Aviya. 2020. "Why Zoom means boom time for Ladino." *Forward*, May 1, 2020. https://forward.com/culture/445344/why-zoom-means-boom-time-for-ladino/#:~:text=By%20Aviya%20Kushner%20May%201,%202020.%20A%20remarkable%20class%20in.

Kutzik, Jordan. 2019. "Yiddish Duolingo Dialect Question a Subject of Great Interest." *Forward*, November 21, 2019. https://forward.com/forverts-in-english/435240/yiddish-duolingo-dialect-question-a-subject-of-great-interest/

Kutzik, Jordan. 2021. "I Took Duolingo's New Yiddish Course for a Test Drive. Here's What I Found." *Forward*, April 5, 2021. https://forward.com/culture/467106/i-took-duolingos-new-yiddish-course-for-a-test-drive-heres-what-i-found/.

Kuznitz, Cecile. 2014. *YIVO and the Making of Modern Jewish Culture*. New York: Cambridge University Press.

"*La Autoridad Nasionala del Ladino.* **הרשות הלאומית לתרבות הלאדינו**." n.d. *La Autoridad Nasionala del Ladino. הרשות הלאומית לתרבות הלאדינו*. Accessed April 19, 2024. https://autoridadnasionala.wixsite.com/autoridadnasionala/.

"Ladino." 2024. *Ethnologue*. Accessed May 30, 2024. https://www.ethnologue.com/language/lad/.

"Ladino 21 Community Interest Company." n.d. *Ladino 21*. Accessed May 23, 2024. www.ladino21.org.

Ladino Culture Forum. 2002. *Ladino Language Forum*. Tapuz

"Ladinokomunita main@Ladinokomunita.groups.io." 1999. *Groups.io*. Accessed April 9, 2024. https://ladinokomunita.groups.io.

Lambright, Anne M., and Stephan Caspar. 2023. "Immersive Technologies for Arts and Culture." In *Language and Literature Program Innovation Room*, presided by Lydia Tang. 138th MLA Convention. Session at the Marriott Marquis, San Francisco, CA, January 6, 2023.

"League for Yiddish ייִדיש ליגע." n.d. *Yidish Lige/League for Yiddish*. Accessed April 19, 2024. https://leagueforyiddish.org/afnshvel.html.

Leitch, Thomas, Sunggyung Jo, John Murray, Nagmeh Rezaie, Anastasia Salter, and Tanja Grubnic 2023. "Adaptation and the Metaverse." *138th MLA Convention*. Session at the Moscone Center, San Francisco, CA, January 6, 2023.

Lewis, Antony. 2018. *The Basics of Bitcoins and Blockchains*. Coral Gables: Mango.

Lewis, Gwyn, Bryn Jones, and Colin Baker. 2012. "Translanguaging: Origins and Development from School to Street and Beyond." *Educational Research and Evaluation: An International Journal on Theory and Practice* 18 (7): 641–54.

Linke, Uli. 2004. "Ethnolinguistic Racism: The Predicaments of Sovereignty and Nationhood under Global Capitalism." *Anthropological Theory* 4 (2): 205–28.

Linn, Mary. 2014. "Living Archives: A Community-Based Language Archive Model." In *Language Documentation and Description 12: Special Issue on Language Documentation and Archiving*, edited by David Nathan and Peter K. Austin, 53–67. London: SOAS.

Lippi-Green, Rosina. 1994. "Accent, Standard Language Ideology, and Discriminatory Pretext in the Courts." *Language in Society* 23 (2): 163–98.

Los Ladinadores. 2021. Los Ladinadores. Accessed October 3, 2024. https://www.facebook.com/groups/ladinadores/

Los Ladinadores. 2023. Los Ladinadores. Accessed October 3, 2024. https://www.facebook.com/groups/ladinadores/permalink/3348732758759276/?mibextid=rS40aB7S9Ucbxw6v

Los Serenos Sefarad. 2015. "'La Vida Do Por El Raki' - Los Serenos Sefarad - Djudeo Espanyol Hip-Hop." Los Serenos Sefarad Sephardic Hip-Hop. Published on November 9, 2015. YouTube video, 4:55. https://www.youtube.com/watch?v=4Znd8wAVVqY.

Makoni, Sinfree, and Alistair Pennycook, eds. 2007. *Disinventing and Reconstituting Languages*. Bristol: Multilingual Matters.

Makoni, Sinfree, and Alistair Pennycook. 2012. "From Monological Multilingualism to Multilingual Francas." In *The Routledge Handbook of Multilingualism*, edited by Marilyn Martin-Jones, Adrian Blackledge, and Angela Creese, 439–53. London/New York: Routledge.

Martínez, Ramón Antonio, Michiko Hikida and Leah Durán. 2015. "Unpacking Ideologies of Linguistic Purism: How Dual Language Teachers Make Sense of Everyday Translanguaging", *International Multilingual Research Journal,* 9(1): 26-42. DOI: 10.1080/19313152.2014.977712.

Meissner, Dirk. 2016. "Adults Shamed for Speaking Indigenous Languages Hold Key to Revival." *CBC News*, October 30, 2016. https://www.cbc.ca/news/canada/british-columbia/indiginous-languages-bc-1.3828536.

Memrise. 2010. *Memrise Language Learning Platform*. Accessed October 3, 2024. https://www.memrise.com/

Mendele. 1991. Google Sites. Accessed October 3, 2024. https://sites.google.com/site/mendeledervaylik/vegnundz

Meta Quest blog. 2021. "Introducing 'Horizon Workrooms': Remote Collaboration Reimagined." *Meta*, August 19, 2021. https://www.meta.com/en-gb/blog/quest/workrooms/.

Mezistrano, Makena. 2022. "Crowdsourced Photos Capture Purim Costumes Inspired by Ottoman Fashion." *Stroum Center for Jewish Studies*, March 17, 2022. https://jewishstudies.washington.edu/sephardic-studies/crowdsourced-photos-capture-purim-costumes-inspired-by-ottoman-fashion/.

Mihelj, Sabina, and César Jiménez-Martínez. "Digital Nationalism: Understanding the Role of Digital Media in the Rise of 'New' Nationalism." *Nations and Nationalism* 27: 331–46.

Minervini, Laura. 2006. "El desarrollo histórico del judeoespañol." *Revista Internacional de Lingüística Iberoamericana* 4 (2) (8): 13–34.

Minervini, Laura. 2013. "Los estudios del español sefardí (judeoespañol, ladino). Aportaciones, métodos y problemas actuales." *Estudis Romànics* 35: 323–34.

Ministry of Aliyah and Integration. 2021. "Ulpan – Learning the Hebrew Language." *Ministry of Aliyah and Integration*, July 26, 2021. https://www.gov.il/en/pages/ulpan_main.

Morton, Stephen. 2003. *Gayatri Chakravorty Spivak*. London/New York: Routledge.

Musnik, Sara Y. "The Ladino Language, Casually Spoken | Sara Speaking Ladino | Wikitongues." Wikitongues. Published on March 11, 2021. YouTube video, 6:16. https://www.youtube.com/watch?v=E3qV-_Ba4PU.

Nakamoto, Satoshi. 2008. "Bitcoin: A Peer-to-Peer Electronic Cash System." *The United States Sentencing Commission (2018 National Seminar)*. Accessed May 11, 2024. https://www.ussc.gov/sites/default/files/pdf/training/annual-national-training-seminar/2018/Emerging_Tech_Bitcoin_Crypto.pdf.

Nathan, David, and Peter K. Austin. 2014. *Language Documentation and Description 12: Special Issue on Language Documentation and Archiving*, 53–67. London: SOAS.

National Science Foundation. 2015. "Award Abstract # 1500753. Software for Enriching Endangered Language-Annotated Databases with Crowd-Sourced Linguistic and Cultural Input." *National Science Foundation*. Accessed April 16, 2024. https://www.nsf.gov/awardsearch/showAward?AWD_ID=1500753.

Netflix. 2023. "*Inclusion & Diversity*." *Netflix*, May 5, 2024. https://jobs.netflix.com/inclusion.

Nieto, Miguel Ángel, dir. 2003. *El Último Sefardí*. Alea Docs & Films.

Noble, Safiya. 2018. *Algorithms of Oppression: How Search Engines Reinforce Racism*. New York: New York University Press.

OBTranslate. n.d. "MT/AI Assistance for Languages." OBTranslate. Accessed May 11, 2024. https://www.obtranslate.org/.

Olko, Justyna, and Julia Sallabank, eds. 2021. *Revitalizing Endangered Languages: A Practical Guide*. Cambridge: Cambridge University Press.

Oren, Michael. 2021. "The Beauty Queen of Jerusalem" *Tablet*, August 5, 2021. https://www.tabletmag.com/sections/arts-letters/articles/the-beauty-queen-jerusalem.

O'Shannessy, Carmel. 2011. "Language Contact and Change in Endangered Languages." In *The Cambridge Handbook of Endangered Languages*, edited by Peter Austin and Julia Sallabank, 78–99. Cambridge: Cambridge University Press.

Otheguy, Ricardo, Ofelia García, and Wallis Reid. 2015. "Clarifying Translanguaging and Deconstructing Named Languages: A Perspective from Linguistics." *Applied Linguistics Review* 6 (3): 281–307.

"Oxford School of Rare Jewish Languages." n.d. Oxford Centre for Hebrew & Jewish Studies. Accessed May 25, 2024. https://www.ochjs.ac.uk/language-classes/oxford-school-of-rare-jewish-languages/.

Panarmenian Network State. n.d. "Uniting Armenians and the World for Global Renaissance and Harmonious Future." *Armenian Network State*, n.d. https://networkstate.io/.

Papo, Eliezer. 2020a. "Eliezer Papo mos konta sovre la LADINO APP - Ladino21 // Londra, Inglaterra." Ladino 21. Published on January 13, 2020. YouTube video, 04:56. https://www.youtube.com/watch?v=J77smoo_PRw.

Papo, Eliezer. 2020b. "Kualo es el Ladino? Eliezer Papo i Alice Corr para Ladino 21 // Londra, Inglaterra." Ladino 21. Published on February 7, 2020. YouTube video, 8:40. https://www.youtube.com/watch?v=Fsb7xqSXGrU.

Papo, Eliezer. 2021. "ENKONTROS DE ALHAD: 'EL DJUDEO-ESPANYOL, kuanto djudio, kuanto espanyol' con E.Papo y C.Yebra." eSefarad CCSefarad. Published on Dec 4, 2022. YouTube video, 1:15:08. https://www.youtube.com/watch?v=oRHAbXv5cU8.

Papo, Eliezer. 2022. "Kakografia, Cacademia i la letra 'Ka.'" *El Amaneser* 163 (September): 4.

Pellin, Mendy, Menachem Weinstein, and Yossi Sofer. "Talk Yiddish to Me (Nisht-Dirty Parody)." JEWBELLish. Published on April 11, 2014. YouTube video, 2:18. https://www.youtube.com/watch?v=sX2rm-jLLFY.

Pentas NFT Marketplace. "Tokenisation of Heritage & Culture, It's What Pentas Is All About." *Medium*, August 8, 2021. https://blog.pentas.io/tokenisation-of-heritage-culture-its-what-pentas-is-all-about-f9151a797a72.

Petrovsky-Shtern, Yohanan. 2014. *The Golden Age Shtetl: A New History of Jewish Life in East Europe*. Princeton, NJ: Princeton University Press.

Pimsleur. 2010. *Pimsleur Language Learning Platform*. Accessed October 3, 2024. https://www.pimsleur.com/

Pitel, Laura. 2022. "Netflix Strikes an Uneasy Compromise in Erdogan's Turkey." *Financial Times*, February 23, 2022. https://www.ft.com/content/d1c90aaa-f437-42fc-8f63-617aafcff44b.

Plumia. n.d. "Unlocking the Future of Global Mobility." *Plumia*, n.d. https://plumia.org/.

Pons, Neda. 2018. "La ideología del purismo lingüístico en la comunidad virtual 'Ladinokomunita.' *Beoiberística Revista de Estudios Ibéricos Latinoamericanos y Comparativos* 2 (1): 251–85.

Pressman, Hannah. 2013. "Speaking Jewish: Thoughts on Ladino, Judezmo, & Identity." *Stroum Center for Jewish Studies*, October 16, 2013. https://jewishstudies.washington.edu/sephardic-studies/speaking-jewish-ladino-judezmo-identity/.

Quintana, Aldina. 2010. "El judeoespañol, una lengua pluricéntrica al margen del español." In *Los sefardíes ante los retos del mundo contemporáneo: identidad y mentalidades*, edited by Paloma Díaz-Mas and María Sánchez Pérez, 33–54. Madrid: Consejo Superior de Investigaciones Científicas.

Refael, Shmuel. 2008. *Un grito en el silencio: la poesía sobre el Holocausto en lengua sefardí: estudio y antología*. Barcelona: Tirocinio.

Refael, Shmuel. 2012. "The Geography of the Memory: The Representation of the Pre-Holocaust Salonican Jewish Community in Post-Holocaust Sephardic Poetry." *eHumanista* 20: 321–333.

Refael, Shmuel. 2018. "Tribuna del Hispanismo Judeoespañol." Instituto Cervantes. Published on June 21, 2018. YouTube video, 1:35:31. https://www.youtube.com/watch?v=csYMSmdvKbg.

Reinhardt, Jonathon, and Steve Thorneteve. 2020. "Digital Games as Language-Learning Environments." In *Handbook of Game-Based Learning*, edited by Jan Plass, Richard Mayer, and Bruce Homer, 409–35. Cambridge, MA: MIT Press.

Romero, Rey. 2017. "*En tierras virtualas*: Sociolinguistic Implications for Judeo-Spanish as a Cybervernacular." In *Sepharad as Imagined Community*, edited by Mahir Şaul and José Ignacio Hualde, 275–90. New York/Bern/Frankfurt/Berlin/Brussels/Vienna/Oxford/Warsaw: Peter Lang.

Rosetta Stone. 2009. *Rosetta Stone Language Learning Platform*. Accessed October 3, 2024. https://www.rosettastone.com/

Rouy, Laurent, dir. 2021. *Last Words*. Trans Euro Media Doo.

Saada, Hila. 2021. "מלכת היופי של ירושלים - קראתי ספר מפגש4." Salti Institute - מכון סלטי לחקר הלאדינו. Published on April 5, 2021. YouTube video, 1:29:36. https://www.youtube.com/watch?v=-l0RA-_Xz88.

Salmon, Simone. "United by Ladino in Times of the Coronavirus." Paper presented at the 2021 MLA Annual Convention, Washington, DC, January 2021. Accessed April 19, 2024. https://mla.confex.com/mla/2021/meetingapp.cgi/Session/10824.

Santacruz, Daniel. 2019. "Ladinokomunita: 20 Years Old and Still Going Strong." KolSefardim*: News and Features about the Sephardic World*, December 8, 2019. https://www.kolsefardim.net/post/ladinokomunita-20-years-old-and-still-going-strong.

Şarhon, Karen. n.d. "Judeo-Spanish Classes." *Sephardic Center of Istanbul*. Accessed April 28, 2024. https://sefarad.com.tr/en/judeo-spanish-classes/.

"Saved by the Digital: Ladino Communities of the 21st Century." 2019. *Language Acts and Worldmaking*. n.d. Accessed April 14, 2024. https://languageacts.org/events/saved-by-the-digital-ladino-communities-of-the-21st-century/.

Savoldelli, Sofia, and Giselle Spiteri Miggiani. 2023. "The Rendering of Multilingual Occurrences in Netflix's Italian Dub Streams: Evolving Trends and Norms on Streaming Platforms." *Languages* 8 (2): 1–23.

Schrader, Maria, dir. 2020. *Unorthodox*. Studio Airlift/Real Film Berlin Gmbh.

Schwarzwald, Ora. 2019. "Judeo-Spanish throughout the Sephardic Diaspora." In *Languages in Jewish Communities, Past and Present*, edited by Sarah Benor and Benjamin Hary, 145–84. Berlin/Boston: De Gruyter.

Schwarzwald, Ora C. n.d. "Judeo-Spanish/Judezmo/Ladino." *Jewish Languages*, February 20, 2023. https://www.jewishlanguages.org/judeo-spanish-judezmo-ladino.

Sefaradimuestro. 2008. Google Groups. Accessed January 13, 2023. https://groups.google.com/g/sefaradimuestro

"Sephardic Digital Academy." n.d. The Sephardic Jewish Brotherhood of America: La Ermandad Sefaradi. Accessed April 28, 2024. https://www.sephardicbrotherhood.com/sephardicdigitalacademy.

Sephiha, Haïm V. 1977. "Archaïsmes Lexicaux Du Ladino (judéoespagnol Calque)." *Cehm Cahiers De Linguistique Hispanique Médiévale* 2 (1): 253–61.

Shandler, Jeffrey. 2004. "Postvernacular Yiddish: Language as a Performance Art." *TDR / The Drama Review* 48 (1): 19–43.

Shandler, Jeffrey. 2005. *Adventures in Yiddishland: Postvernacular Language and Culture*. Berkeley/Los Angeles/London: University of California Press.

Shandler, Jeffrey. 2014. *Shtetl: A Vernacular Intellectual History*. New Brunswick: Rutgers University Press.

Silverstein, Michael. 1979. "Language Structure and Linguistic Ideology." In *The Elements: A Parasession on Linguistic Units and Levels*, edited by Paul R. Clyne, William F. Hanks, and Carol L. Hofbauer, 193–247. Chicago: Chicago Linguistic Society.

Sisso Raz, Alicia. 2019. "'Don Quijote' meldado por Alicia Sisso Raz - Voces de Haketia - para Ladino21 // Tetuan, Moroko." Ladino 21. Published on November 23, 2019. YouTube video, 29:09. https://www.youtube.com/watch?v=-KdCsyzOsRc.

Skutnabb-Kangas, Tove, and Robert Phillipson. 1995. "Linguicide and Linguicism." In *Papers in European Language Policy*, edited by Tove Skutnabb-Kangas and Robert Phillipson, 83–91. Roskilde: Roskilde University Centre.

Šmid, Katja. 2002. "Los problemas del estudio de la lengua sefardí." *Verba Hispanica* 10 (1): 113–24.

Spivak, Gayatri Chakravorty. 1988. "Can the Subaltern Speak?" In *Marxism and the Interpretation of Culture*, edited by Cary Nelson and Lawrence Grossberg, 271–313. Champaign: University of Illinois Press.

Srinivasan, Balaji. n.d. "The Network State Dashboard." *The Network State*. Accessed May 11, 2024. https://thenetworkstate.com/dashboard.

Srinivasan Balaji. 2021. "*How to Start a New Country.*" *Balajis.com*, April 9, 2021. https://balajis.com/p/how-to-start-a-new-country.

Srinivasan, Balaji. 2022. *The Network State: How to Start and New Country*. n.p. https://thenetworkstate.com/.

Stephenson, Neal. 1992. *Snow Crash*. New York: Random House.

Stern, Joanna. 2021. "Trapped in the Metaverse: Here's What 24 Hours in VR Feels Like | WSJ." Wall Street Journal. Published on November 12, 2021. YouTube video, 07:33. https://www.youtube.com/watch?v=rtLTZUaMSDQ.

Stoler, Ann Laura. 2008. *Along the Archival Grain: Epistemic Anxieties and Colonial Common Sense*. Princeton: Princeton University Press.

Stroud, Christopher. 2018. "Linguistic Citizenship." In *The Multilingual Citizen: Towards a Politics of Language for Agency and Change*, edited by Lisa Lim, Christopher Stroud, and Linel Wee, 17–39. Bristol: Multilingual Matters.

Stroum Center for Jewish Studies. 2022. "Perspectives on Cosmopolitan Istanbul in the Hit Netflix Series, 'The Club.' Stroum Jewish Studies. Published on April 13, 2022. YouTube video, 1:24:42. https://www.youtube.com/watch?v=OJ2_TfxyqS8.

Sultana, Kishwar. 2022. Learn Yiddish for Beginners. Accessed October 3, 2024. https://apps.apple.com/us/app/learn-yiddish-for-beginners/id1614218623#:~:text=%E2%80%A2%20Over%20100%20different%20beginner%20and%20intermediate%20lessons%20covering%20Yiddish.

Szulmajster-Celnikier, Anne, and Marie-Christine Varol. 1994. "Yidich et judéo-espagnol: dynamique comparée de deux langues de diaspora." *Plurilinguismes* 7: 93–132.

Tanasescu, Raluca, and Chris Tanasescu. 2024. "#GrahPoem: Analytical-Creative AI for Minority Languages and Community-Involving Performance." In *AI Poetics across Languages and Cultures*. 139th MLA Convention. Session at the Marriott Downtown, Philadelphia, PA, January 5, 2024.

Tandem. 2015. *Tandem Language Learning Platform*. Accessed October 3, 2024. https://tandem.net/

Tapscott, Don, and Alex Tapscott. 2016. *Blockchain Revolution: How the Technology behind Bitcoin Is Changing Money, Business, and the World*. New York: Penguin.

"The Sephardic Studies Digital Collection." n.d. University Libraries (University of Washington). Accessed May 23, 2024. https://content.lib.washington.edu/sephardicweb/index.html.

The Video Consortium. n.d. "Colleen Cassingham Producer, Multitude Films." *The Video Consortium*. https://videoconsortium.org/es/members/colleen-cassingham.

"The Wired Interview: Facebook's Mark Zuckerberg." *The Wired*, June 29, 2009. https://www.wired.com/2009/06/mark-zuckerberg-speaks/.

Tirosh-Becker, Ofra, and Sarah B. Benor. 2024. "Journal of Jewish Languages." *Brill*. Accessed April 28, 2024. https://brill.com/view/journals/jjl/jjl-overview.xml.

Trahan, Ryan. 2022. "I Spent 100 Days in the Metaverse." Ryan Trahan. Published on February 18, 2022. YouTube video, 16:49. https://www.youtube.com/watch?v=mufeRQYgqZc.

Trivasse, Madeleine. 2022. "Oxford School of Rare Jewish Languages: Impact Report 2021–22." *Oxford Centre of Hebrew and Jewish Studies*. Accessed April 28, 2024. https://www.ochjs.ac.uk/wp-content/uploads/2022/09/OSRJL-Impact-Report-2021-22-COMPRESSED.pdf.

Trivasse, Madeleine. 2023. "Oxford School of Rare Jewish Languages: Impact Report 2022–23." *Oxford Centre of Hebrew and Jewish Studies*. Accessed April 28, 2024.

https://www.ochjs.ac.uk/wp-content/uploads/2023/09/COMPRESSED-OSRJL-Impact-Report-2022-23.pdf.

Tutunović, Drita, and Ivana Vučina Simović. 2022. "Ken guadrara la lingua en tu famiya? // Belogrado, Serbia." Ladino 21. Published on November 4, 2022. YouTube video, 17:38. https://www.youtube.com/watch?v=HsglNYOXUGA.

UNESCO Ad Hoc Expert Group on Endangered Languages. 2003. *Language Vitality and Endangerment.* UNESCO. https://ich.unesco.org/doc/src/00120-EN.pdf.

uTalk. 2016. *uTalk Language Learning Platform.* Accessed October 3, 2024. https://utalk.com/

uTalk. 2019a. "International Effort to Save and Endangered Jewish Language." (Press Release).

uTalk. 2019b. "uTalk's Ladino Journey." *uTalk Blog*, December 11, 2019. https://utalk.com/news/utalks-ladino-journey/.

Van Rijmenam, Mark. 2022. *Step into the Metaverse.* Hoboken, NJ: John Wiley & Sons, Inc.

Varol, Marie-Christine. (1998) 2008. *Manual of Judeo-Spanish Language and Culture.* College Park: University Press of Maryland.

Varoufakis, Yanis. 2021. "Techno-Feudalism Is Taking Over." *Project Syndicate*, June 28, 2021. https://www.project-syndicate.org/commentary/techno-feudalism-replacing-market-capitalism-by-yanis-varoufakis-2021-06.

Ventura, Marcelo C. 2023. "Marcelo C. Ventura: El Dialekto Izmirli i la Filosofia Sefaradi// Buenos Aires, Ardjentina." Ladino 21. Published on February, 2023. YouTube video, 19:41. https://www.youtube.com/watch?v=aJcS7TIo4KA.

Verdi, Giuseppe. (1853) 1988. *La Traviata.* Chicago: Home Vision.

Viveiros de Castro, Eduardo. 2008. *Metafísicas Canibais.* São Paulo: Cosac Naify.

VLACH. 2016. OEAW. Accessed October 3, 2024. https://www.oeaw.ac.at/vlach/mission/#:~:text=The%20commission%E2%80%99s%20members,%20project%20leaders%20and%20scientific%20staff%20strive%20to.

Walsh, Olivia. 2021. "Introduction: In the Shadow of the Standard. Standard Language Ideology and Attitudes towards 'Non-Standard' Varieties and Usages." *Journal of Multilingual and Multicultural Development* 42 (9): 773–82.

"Wander on Meta Quest." n.d. Meta, n.d. https://www.meta.com/en-gb/experiences/wander/2078376005587859/.

Warshavsky, Hanna. 2013. "Ladino - Dulse de Bimbrio – לאדינו". Autoridad Nasionala del Ladino i su Kultura הרשות הלאומית לתרבות הלאדינו. Published on June 18, 2013. YouTube video, 55:06. https://www.youtube.com/watch?v=dzbeL0X1kpU.

Weheliye, Alexander G. 2005. *Phonographies: Grooves in Sonic Afro-Modernity.* Durham/London: Duke University Press.

Wei, Li. 2018. "Translanguaging as a Practical Theory of Language." *Applied Linguistics* 39 (1): 9–30.

Weinreich, Max. 1937. "Le yiddish comme objet de linguistique générale." Paper presented at the 4th International Congress of Linguistics, Copenhagen, August 27, 1936. Vilnius: YIVO.

Weinreich, Max. 1953. "Yiddishkayt and Yiddish: On the Impact of Religion on Language of the Ashkenazic Jewry." In *Mordecai M. Kaplan: Jubilee Volume on the Occasion of His Seventieth Birthday*, edited by Moshe Davis, 481–514. New York: Jewish Theological Seminary.

Weinreich, Max. 1959. "History of Yiddish language: The Problems of Their Implications." *Proceedings of the American Philosophical Society* 103 (4): 563–70.

Weinreich, Uriel. 1967. *Languages in Contact, Findings and Problems*. The Hague: Mouton and Co.

Weinreich, Max. (1973) 2008. "Yiddish in the Framework of Other Jewish Languages." In *History of the Yiddish Language*, edited by Paul Glasser (translated by Shlomo Noble), 124–74. New Haven/London: Yale University Press.

Weiss, Shayna. 2016. "Shtisel's Ghosts: The Politics of Yiddish in Israeli Popular Culture." *In geveb: A Journal of Yiddish Studies*, March 6, 2016. https://ingeveb.org/blog/shtisel-s-ghosts-the-politics-of-yiddish-in-israeli-popular-culture.

"Welcome to Bivas.org!" 2023. *Bivas.org: Ladino High School Club of America*. Accessed May 29, 2024. https://www.bivas.org/.

"Welcome/Bienvenidos to the American Ladino League." 2024. *American Ladino League*. Accessed May 29, 2024. https://americanladinoleague.org/.

Well, Tom B. 2018. *Your Next Government? From the Nation-State to Stateless Nations*. Cambridge: Cambridge University Press.

Wex, Michael. 2005. *Born to Kvetch: Yiddish Language and Culture in All Its Moods*. New York: St. Martin's Press.

Wexler, Paul. 1981. "Jewish Interlinguistics: Fact and Conceptual Framework." *Language* 57: 99–149.

Wikitongues. "Episode 2: The Tapestry of America | John Kazaklis." *Medium*, May 25, 2020. https://medium.com/wikitongues/episode-2-tapestry-of-america-e6c3ce10c99f.

Wittgenstein, Ludwig. (1953) 2009. *Philosophical Investigations*. Malden: John Wiley.

World Economic Forum. 2020. "Crypto, What Is It Good For? An Overview of Cryptocurrency Use Cases." World Economic Forum, December, 2020. https://www3.weforum.org/docs/WEF_Cryptocurrency_Uses_Cases_2020.pdf.

"Workers Circle" n.d. *The Workers Circle: Jewish Culture for a Just World*. Accessed May 21, 2024. https://www.circle.org/.

Wu, Tim. 2017. *The Attention Merchants: How Our Time and Attention Are Gathered and Sold*. London: Atlantic Books.

Yaffe, Simon. 2019. "New App Launched in Bid to Save Ladino" *Jewish Telegraph*. December 13, 2019.

Yampolskaya, Sonya, Lily Kahn, and Kriszta Szendrői. forthcoming. "The History of the Yiddish Writing System." In *Handbook of Germanic Writing Systems*, edited by Dimitrios Meletis, Martin Evertz-Rittich, and Rebecca Treiman. Berlin: De Gruyter.

Yebra López, Carlos. 2014. *Shoá y ética ciudadana: la figura del "bystander" en el cine como herramienta pedagógica*. Valencia/Jerusalem: Olé Libros/Yad Vashem.

Yebra López, Carlos. 2018. "Ambezandomos Muestra Lingua." *Memrise*. Accessed May 11, 2024. https://community-courses.memrise.com/community/course/757096/ambezandomos-muestra-lingua/.

Yebra López, Carlos. 2019. "LADINO APP - uTalk para Ladino21- Londra, Inglaterra." Ladino 21. Published on December 11, 2019. YouTube video, 07:35. https://www.youtube.com/watch?v=jdqUBFTU5aY.

Yebra López, Carlos. 2020. "Is Speaking 'Foreign' Languages 'Cultural Appropriation'?" Published on October 6, 2020. YouTube video, 3:00. https://www.youtube.com/watch?v=nxIZ1cLgaWs.

Yebra López, Carlos. 2021a. "Why Flags DO NOT and SHOULD NOT Represent Languages." The Hyperpolyglot Activist. Published on January 5, 2021. YouTube video, 08:00. https://www.youtube.com/watch?v=Umc1xke9MgE.

Yebra López, Carlos. 2021b. "The 'Native Speaker' Myth." The Hyperpolyglot Activist. Published on January 25, 2021. YouTube video, 09:25. https://www.youtube.com/watch?v=aGJkmICo_t0.

Yebra López, Carlos. 2021c. "The Digital (De)Territorialization of Ladino in the Twenty-First Century." *WORD, Journal of the International Linguistic Association* 67: 94–116.

Yebra López, Carlos. 2021d. "Decolonising the MFL Curriculum: Step 1." The Hyperpolyglot Activist. Published on July 11, 2021. YouTube video, 14:00. https://www.youtube.com/watch?v=4qp1BZq14v8.

Yebra López, Carlos. 2021e. "Medievalist Passports: Contested Rights of Return for the Descendants of Medieval Iberian Jews and Muslims." In *Al-Andalus in Motion: Travelling Concepts and Cross-Cultural Contexts*, edited by Rachel Scott, Abdoolkarim Vakil, and Julian Weiss, 227–51. London: Boydell & Brewer.

Yebra López, Carlos. 2021f. "There's No Mother Tongue. Here's Why." The Hyperpolyglot Activist. Published on July 30, 2021. YouTube video, 22:07. https://www.youtube.com/watch?v=8Nm1H37qDYs.

Yebra López, Carlos, and Julio Alejandro. 2021. "Can Blockchain Save Endangered Languages? (ft. by Julio Alejandro)." The Hyperpolyglot Activist. Published on November 25, 2021. YouTube video, 35:17. https://www.youtube.com/watch?v=HsO1_KzXwNQ.

Yebra López, Carlos. 2022a. "Why Nobody Speaks Any Language." The Hyperpolyglot Activist. Published on May 22, 2022. YouTube video, 05:30. https://www.youtube.com/watch?v=5QPRT4k3zig.

Yebra López, Carlos. 2022b. "Decolonizing Spanish: Ladino and Chavacano as Sites of Global Hispanophonia." *TRANSMODERNITY: Journal of Peripheral Cultural Production of the Luso-Hispanic World* 9 (8): 69–92.

Yebra López, Carlos. 2023a. "Ladino on Netflix." *Google Forms*. https://docs.google.com/forms/d/1FRUZrjfgck9CHCphUkYydA9VUk5URG_sMY2XtxxB2Q4/.

Yebra López, Carlos. 2023b. "Specters of Judeo-Spanish: The Case for Judeo-Spanish as a Partial Overlap of Idiolects Shared by People of Sephardi Culture." *Journal of Jewish Languages* 11: 82–114.

Yebra López, Carlos. 2024a. "Terminolojía LGBTQIA+ en Ladino." *Aki Yerushalayim* 111: 36–44. https://25637f6e-7c1f-4643-b151-9b5ce9be74b2.filesusr.com/ugd/e6c4a6_eb3697c40ae44d47a95992f1280f9b0f.pdf.

Yebra López, Carlos. 2024b. "The Fetishizing Language Behind the NFT Craze: A Semiotic-cum-semantic Critique." In *Non-Fungible Tokens (NFTs): Multidisciplinary Perspectives*, edited by Usman Chohan, 125–38. London/New York: Routledge.

"Yiddish Book Center Celebrating Yiddish Language & Culture." n.d. The Yiddish Book Center. Accessed April 19, 2024. https://www.yiddishbookcenter.org/.

Yildiz, Yasemin. 2012. *Beyond the Mother Tongue: The Postmonolingual Condition*. New York: Fordham University Press.

Yishai-Levi, Sarit. 2015. *The Beauty Queen of Jerusalem: A Novel*. New York: Thomas Dunne.

Yüce, Seren, and Zeynep Günay Tan, dirs. 2021. *Kulüp (The Club)*. O3 Medya. Zingman, Alon, dir. 2018. *Shtisel*. Yes.

Žižek, Slavoj. 2022. *Surplus Enjoyment*. London/New York: Bloomsbury Academic.

Zuckermann, Ghil'ad. 2020. *Revivalistics: From the Genesis of Israeli to Language Reclamation in Australia and Beyond*. Oxford: Oxford University Press.

Index

For Product Safety Concerns and Information please contact our EU representative GPSR@taylorandfrancis.com Taylor & Francis Verlag GmbH, Kaufingerstraße 24, 80331 München, Germany

Printed and bound by CPI Group (UK) Ltd, Croydon, CR0 4YY

18/12/2024

01808233-0004